Date due: 10/25

Multicultural Education

A Caring-Centered, Reflective Approach

Valerie Ooka Pang

San Diego State University

Boston   Burr Ridge, IL   Dubuque, IA   Madison, WI   New York   San Francisco
St. Louis   Bangkok   Bogotá   Caracas   Lisbon   London   Madrid
Mexico City   Milan   New Delhi   Seoul   Singapore   Sydney   Taipei   Toronto

McGraw-Hill Higher Education

*A Division of The **McGraw-Hill** Companies*

MULTICULTURAL EDUCATION: A CARING-CENTERED, REFLECTIVE APPROACH

Published by McGraw-Hill, an imprint of The McGraw-Hill Companies, Inc., 1221 Avenue of the Americas, New York, NY 10020. Copyright © 2001 by The McGraw-Hill Companies, Inc. All rights reserved. No part of this publication may be reproduced or distributed in any form or by any means, or stored in a database or retrieval system, without the prior written consent of The McGraw-Hill Companies, Inc., including, but not limited to, in any network or other electronic storage or transmission, or broadcast for distance learning.

Some ancillaries, including electronic and print components, may not be available to customers outside the United States.

This book is printed on acid-free paper.

1 2 3 4 5 6 7 8 9 0 DOC/DOC 0 9 8 7 6 5 4 3 2 1 0

ISBN 0–07–236953–1

Vice president and editor-in-chief: *Thalia Dorwick*
Editorial director: *Jane E. Vaicunas*
Sponsoring editor: *Beth Kaufman*
Developmental editor: *Teresa Wise*
Marketing manager: *Daniel M. Loch*
Senior project manager: *Marilyn M. Sulzer*
Production supervisor: *Sandy Ludovissy*
Coordinator of freelance design: *Michelle D. Whitaker*
Cover designer: *Nathan Bahls*
Cover image: *©Peter Cade/Tony Stone Images*
Senior photo research coordinator: *Carrie K. Burger*
Senior supplement coordinator: *Audrey A. Reiter*
Compositor: *Carlisle Communications, Ltd.*
Typeface: *10/12 Times Roman*
Printer: *R. R. Donnelley & Sons Company/Crawfordsville, IN*

The credits section for this book begins on page 284 and is considered an extension of the copyright page.

Library of Congress Cataloging-in-Publication Data

Pang, Valerie Ooka, 1950–   .
    Multicultural education : a caring-centered, reflective approach / Valerie Ooka Pang.—1st ed.
      p.   cm.
    Includes bibliographical references and index.
    ISBN 0–07–236953–1
  1. Multicultural education—United States. 2. Curriculum planning—United States. 3.
  Prejudices—Study and teaching—United States. I. Title.

LC1099.3 .P35   2001
370.117—dc21   00–036433
                                       CIP

www.mhhe.com

*Dedicated to
Gerry, Jenn, Matt, Ariana, Cameron,
Mirei, Connor, Nicole, Sophie, Cheryl,
Debbie, Karen, Kathy, Naomi, and Trish.*

*Special Dedication to Carl Masami Ooka
and Marie Horiuchi Ooka*

Brief Contents

Contents

About the Author

Valerie Ooka Pang is a professor in the School of Teacher Education at San Diego State University. She was a first and second grade teacher in rural and urban schools.

This is her second book. Dr. Pang was senior editor on a text called *Struggling To Be Heard: The Unmet Needs of Asian Pacific American Children* published by State University of New York Press. It is the only multidisciplinary text on Asian Pacific American children and was awarded honorable mention by the Gustavus Myers Center for the Study of Bigotry and Human Rights at Boston University.

Due to her work in multicultural education, social studies education, and teacher education, Dr. Pang has been a consultant for corporations like Sesame Street, Fox Children's Network, Family Communications (producer of Mr. Roger's Neighborhood), McGraw-Hill, and Scott Foresman.

Dr. Pang has published in a variety of journals including *Harvard Educational Review, The Kappan, Educational Forum, Theory and Research in Social Education, Social Education, Equity and Excellence,* and *Multicultural Education.*

She was a Senior Fellow at the Annenberg Institute for School Reform at Brown University. She was honored with the 1997 Distinguished Scholar Award from the American Educational Research Association's (AERA) Standing Committee on the Role and Status of Minorities in Education. Dr. Pang has also received the Outstanding Teaching Award in the Liberal Studies Program at San Diego State University.

Her own children are pursuing careers in immunology and engineering.

Foreword

Over eighty years ago, H. G. Wells noted:

> Human history becomes more and more a race between education and catastrophe.

The race is swifter in the twenty-first century. Ever-increasing speed of communication, trade, and transportation has made global existence and cooperation a requirement, not merely a possibility.

Few issues are more complex and explosive than the interactions among multiple cultures and subcultures that define our twenty-first century. We know more about more people in more places at more times than ever before. This is a challenge to contemporary humankind because civilization is enhanced or threatened by cultural interactions. Obviously, these interactions involve all of us because we are all members of some culture and we share in that culture's traditions and ongoing changes. We have met culture, and it is us, to modify an old POGO statement from a comic strip by Walt Kelly. In our multicultural world, a caring-centered, and reflective education offers hope for progress in that race with catastrophe; this book provides assistance in that direction.

The civilizing impulse, an expanding and encompassing movement toward human freedom, justice, equality, and democracy, is a major dimension of human history. It is always in process, a work under construction. The continual renewal and development of the civilizing impulse occurs through education. Your work as a teacher will be to offer liberation from ignorance, oppression, prejudice, and bias. Such an education incorporates a strong sense of caring about students and society, and involves critical and reflective thinking on the part of teachers and students. This is the kind of multicultural education that Val Pang describes in this book. It is consistent with what H. G. Wells had in mind as the positive force opposing catastrophe. This education recognizes differences among peoples and individuals, but celebrates those differences. It does not use such differences to segregate, denigrate, or discriminate. Tolerance and intolerance are both products of education.

In a rapidly changing multicultural world, catastrophe lurks in the fears, superstitions, ignorance, and prejudices that one group has about others. Unfounded fears and prejudices are inculcated, a form of miseducation; children are not born with them. Doctrinaire miseducation includes a puffing up of the traditions and history of one society, along with the denigration and stereotyping of other societies that are perceived as potential enemies or competitors. This miseducation has been used to inflame passions in support of slavery, war, holocaust, ethnic cleansing, and terrorism. The Nazi reformation of German education programs included book burning; censorship; political domination of curriculum, teachers, and teaching methods; and the rewriting of cultural history. It is a particularly stark and troubling example of indoctrination parading as education. Human history is filled with examples of the human capacity for inhumanity, cruelty, war, oppression, and genocide—usually the result of ignorance, prejudice, bias, fears, and excessive or absolutistic pride in clan, religion, nation, or peoples (ethnic pride).

Most nations engage in forms of nationalistic education that are inaccurate, self-serving, and prejudicial against others, though clearly not as extreme or dangerous as the Nazis. Lands of the globe are currently populated by mixes of cultures, often with potentially catastrophic results. Events in the Middle East, Africa, Ireland, Kosovo, and East Timor illustrate this point. Nations like the United States, a polyglot of cultures, are more the rule than the exception—and we in the United States have had our share of racism, discrimination, prejudice, and bigotry. The United States, for all its ideals of multicultural equality and justice, has itself suffered a bleak history of extensive racial, religious, gender, and national-origin discrimination in society and in its schools. The United States has also had shining examples of mutual support, delight, and celebration of its intercultural heritage, and widely recognized long-term efforts to correct the mistakes of cultural bias in its history. The catastrophe side of human history is always looming; reflective and caring education offers relief.

A sound approach to multicultural education must honestly address the unfortunate history of human inhumanity committed in the name of cultural separation—the wars, slavery, racism, genocide and oppression that have accompanied excessive cultural pride—in addition to dealing with the increasing positive efforts to expand and enhance civilization. Civilization will not be improved by trying to hide the human and cultural defects that have been fostered by cultural propaganda from self-serving agencies or organizations.

High-quality multicultural education provides inspiration for social progress by involving students in critical examination of the causes and results of unfounded fears and prejudices. It also develops a thoughtful and reasoned pride in the multicultural movement toward civilizing the globe. This is reflective teaching and learning. Broad international agreements and actions based on fundamental human and social values have expanded significantly over the past century. This global movement toward cultural tolerance and shared interests is often overshadowed by news of the violence of warfare between factions in various cultures, but civilizing of the globe continues. Caring-centered and reflective multicultural education, as Val Pang promotes in this text, does not overlook or sterilize the many evils that people and cultures do to each other, but offers a better vision of what a more civilized world of multiple cultures could be.

Despite its promise and potential, multicultural education is a major battleground of the "culture wars" continuing from the past decade. At stake in this war are such things as affirmative action, civil rights legislation, English-only laws, immigration policies, police profiling, standardized testing and school accountability, college admissions, campus speech codes, and what is taught in the schools. Each of these topics incites strong opinions in discussions along the battle lines of the culture wars.

One position holds that emphasizing differences among cultures harms the web of core social values that hold American society together. They argue that rather than parade as Irish- or African- or Asian-Americans, we should parade as Americans. On the other side is the argument that these core social values are a myth, a self-serving facade to help those already in power to retain privilege and prejudice. This side holds that monocultural education hides and distorts underlying discrimination and intolerance that more fundamentally harm the social fiber. To use the words on our coins, "e pluribus unum" (from many, one), one side wants to increase the focus on the unum while the other wants a concentration on the pluribus. This is one of the major intellectual battles of the twentieth and now twenty-first century, and it has myriad repercussions in everyday life. Multicultural education is one of the most important sites of the culture wars because the sides recognize the power of education in the development of individual and social values.

Clearly, Val Pang views multicultural education as valuable and necessary, and she wants to help develop teachers who can do it well. For this book, she draws from the contemporary literature on the subject, as well as significant work on the ideas of caring and reflective teaching that have emerged in the philosophic literature about high-quality schooling. This is a good match: a curricular concept that addresses profound current human issues and an instructional program that emphasizes human understanding and reflective thought.

Multicultural education, with caring and reflective teachers, should be a term that merely describes what happens in good schools with good teachers and good programs. Val Pang's personal, professional, and scholarly experiences help to enliven and enlighten an important effort to bring cultural understanding, appreciation, and celebration into schools, through caring and reflective teachers. Teaching attracts those who want to engage in the battle for civilizing our world, holding off catastrophe in the race Wells so eloquently defined. A measure of idealism and human service among young people can be found among students preparing to go into teaching; multicultural education in a caring-centered and reflective school offers hope. There are many good reasons to pursue this course for education; improving civilization is one of the most important.

Jack L. Nelson
Professor Emeritus, Rutgers University

Preface

S chools can be places of great hope, mediocrity, or severe oppression. Teachers are the key element in schools. Can teachers create and sustain an atmosphere of hope and community where students actively learn and work toward social justice? In what ways can they build compassion and equity into their classrooms?

My goal in this book is to encourage the readers to explore and think about how they can make changes in their own teaching, changes that are based on strong pedagogy, a clear understanding of schools as social systems, and the importance of compassion in that endeavor. The book is also written to encourage teachers to build a community of care, because through collaborative effort they can make structural changes in their schools.

People utilize a variety of filters when looking at issues. For example Martin Luther King, Jr.'s, orientation was heavily based on civil rights and his religious beliefs. The primary lens I used in writing this book is caring, a moral commitment to care for and teach students. In my work with children, I have found that most seek and respond to human connection and care. Older students also value trusting relationships with teachers who believe in them. The relationships teachers and students create are critical in the learning process because these relationships not only form the context but also motivation for growth.

Additional lenses that form my belief system include culture, community, and social justice. Culture is critical because each student develops within a complex cultural context. In addition, learning occurs within a social environment where there are continual interactions with others. These interactions can serve to extend or clarify a person's thinking. This learning occurs best within a strong community where caring and social justice serve as integral values. When students and teachers feel personal connections with each other, they develop a unity of struggle to create a more loving and equitable community (Gibson 1999).

The Organization of the Book

The prologue provides the reader with an overview about the personal impact Multicultural Education has on my development as a teacher and as a person. Though I have much more to comprehend, I have become a more effective professional because of what I have learned from students and my struggle with implementing equity, culture, and compassion into the classroom.

The book is then divided into four sections focusing on the following questions:

Part One: Why is culture important?
Part Two: What is Multicultural Education? What is caring-centered
    Multicultural Education?
Part Three: What does prejudice look like in individuals, schools, and society?
    What can be done to eliminate discrimination?
Part Four: How can a caring and culturally relevant curriculum be created?

Each part consists of several chapters that present relevant information and raise important issues. In addition, at the conclusion of each chapter I have included questions for teacher reflection. These questions encourage thoughtful consideration of complex issues. The questions often are designed to direct the reader to synthesize and analyze the information presented and apply the content to his/her teaching.

The book begins with two chapters about culture to initiate thinking about the complex and comprehensive nature of culture. People's worldviews evolve from the values, behaviors, beliefs, history, and many other aspects of their culture(s). Often culture and its components are invisible to one who lives within its daily workings and are difficult to perceive. As Jack Nelson (2000) shared with me, "Cultures define us and we define culture. We come to know and absorb our own culture's values and behaviors, and we recognize differences from others through education. It is the multi part of multicultural that makes multicultural education so important." In order for teachers to better understand and encourage many of their students, it is important for educators to have a knowledge of the power of culture and how it is created, transmitted, and sustained. The first two chapters are general discussions of various aspects of culture.

In Part two, the chapters describe and define the framework for Caring-Centered Multicultural Education. This framework is not only dedicated to good teaching, but it is also committed to an educational philosophy that utilizes the Ethic of Care at its foundation. The framework calls for change on an individual, school, and societal level. It is critical for us to address issues of prejudice, discrimination, and oppression in our schools and in other societal institutions in order to build communities where compassion and collaboration guide our actions.

Part three focuses on individual and institutional social oppression. One of the most difficult challenges that many of us face is to confront our own racism, biases, and participation in institutional oppression. It is usually easier to identify one's own biased remarks toward others through the use of language like "those people," than to identify accepted school practices that harm students. It may be difficult to see how some practices are damaging to students because these practices have been seen as legitimate and rational for many years. For example, Gibson (1998) provides data that demonstrate how standards are "veiled literacy tests" because from standards come tests. The tests that measure student knowledge of standards then become even more powerful than the standards because the understanding of students will be seen as measured by these tests. Secondly, students who have similar middle class and ethnic backgrounds as the individuals who wrote the standards are more likely to do well on the standardized examinations. The standards and their tests are extremely influential, though like the *National History Standards* (National Center for History in Schools 1994), represent a "common legacy" that are nationalistic and elitist in its orientation (Gibson 1998).

This section also discusses how people and children develop prejudice and bias towards others. Research is presented to describe how prejudice and social oppression can impact the development of one's racial identity and sense of affiliations. Chapter 8 provides examples of prejudice and discrimination in schools. There is also a culture of power; a hegemonic culture that attempts to choke off divergent ethnic cultures of students or conveys negative messages about various social differences due to gender, racial differences, class, religious beliefs, and sexual orientation.

Part four is devoted to discussing culturally relevant teaching. How can teachers create a curriculum that reflects and resonates with their students who may come from

a multitude of ethnic and cultural communities? How can relevance and meaning become the core of the teacher's pedagogy? There are research projects that carefully describe how ethnic, family, and neighborhood contexts can be integrated into the teaching strategies utilized and curriculum content presented in schools.

Finally, chapter 11 and the epilogue focus on personal reflection. Reflection refers to the importance of teachers continually contemplating about and reevaluating their teaching. These efforts toward change will produce new levels of learning in students and overall reform in school policies and structures.

The appendix at the end of the book recommends additional teacher resources and children's literature for use in the classroom for that purpose.

The value of this text is what the reader does after thinking about the issues raised in the book. I hope that teachers continue to seek more effective ways to reach all their students.

This book is one of hope, the hope that teachers along with their students and parents will work together to form bonds of trust that lead to the creation of exceptional schools. Bonds of humanity and caring propelled the civil rights movement in the 1960s. Today they can propel us toward definitive actions that will address the damaging social practices of inequities due to race, class, ethnicity, gender and other differences in schools and society.

References

Gibson, Rich. 1998. "History on trial in the heart of darkness." *Theory and Research in Social Education 26*(4): 549–564.

Gibson, Rich. 1999. "Pay no attention to that man behind the curtain." *Theory and Research in Social Education 27*(4): 541–601.

National Center for History in the Schools. 1994. *National standards for world history: Exploring paths to the present.* Los Angeles, Calif.: Author.

Nelson, Jack. 2000. Private interview. San Diego. March 17.

Acknowledgments

Many people have shared their insights with me. Some read over initial drafts of chapters. Others provided suggestions and new ideas. I am very grateful to many people who have supported my work for many years. I would like to thank the following people: Geneva Gay, Jack and Gwen Nelson, Jenn, Matt, and Gerry Pang, Candee Chaplin, Stan Sue, Lilly Cheng, Jessica Gordon Nembhard, Ray Valle, Pat Larke, David Strom, Mary McCabe, Carl Grant, Rafaela Santa Cruz, Wayne Ross, Jackie Jordan Irvine, Cynthia Park, MyLuong Tran, Jill Kerper Mora, Kathy Ooka, Libby Gil, Rich Gibson, Lois Wetzel, Karen Swisher, Valerie Grayson, Rick Stewart, Jackie Brunner, Muriel Green, Ron Torretto, Jackie Irvine, Juan Rivera, Jamie Lujan, Russell Young, Lucille Hee, Andrea Saltzman, Anna Perliss, James Wood, Léo Bennett-Cauchon, Gene Sommers, Neil Kooiman, Maria Marshall, Suzanne Negoro, Lisa Dillman, Renee de la Torre, Heidi Mellander, Cameron Erwood, Matthew Heibel, Connor Howard, Nicole Marie Howard, Anthony Evans, Michael Small, Christina Lovaas, Jennifer Adams, Jennifer Covell, Leslie Warren, Ronie Daniels, Jennifer Stahl, Arturo Salazar, Krystal Rodriguez, Hindeliza Flores, and Margie Gallego.

There are also many others who have shared their thoughts and beliefs. I appreciate the contributions of my students, colleagues, and teachers who have inspired me. In addition, I would like to thank Beth Kaufman, senior editor at McGraw-Hill, who I am extremely indebted to for nourishing the completion of this book. Also this book would not be finished without the extensive assistance and advice of Terri Wise and Marilyn Sulzer.

Finally, I would like to acknowledge the help of the following individuals who have reviewed the manuscript throughout its creation.

Scott Arnett, *Morningside College*
Joan Bissell, *University of California–Irvine*
Janice W. Clemmer, *Brigham Young University*
Frank Guldbrandsen, *University of Minnesota*
Jackie Irvine, *Emory University*
Anthony Koyzis, *University of Wisconsin–Oshkosh*
Susan Mills, *University of Central Florida*
Jack Nelson, *Rutgers University*
Jeannie Oakes, *University of California–Los Angeles*
E. Wayne Ross, *State University of New York, Binghamton*
Cynthia Anast Seguin, *Emporia State University*
Carlos Vallejo, *Arizona State University*

Prologue

Dear Reader,

Multicultural Education can take you on an exciting new voyage of discovery in which you may develop new ways of seeing others, get to know yourself better, and learn how to more fully build upon what children know and bring with them to school. I believe caring is at the heart of being a teacher and caring teachers are powerful influences in the lives of young people. As teachers, we can be strong advocates for all children and guide them toward excellence and self-direction.

How Did I Become Interested in Multicultural Education?

My interest in Multicultural Education began many years ago when I was a 20-year-old and I started teaching at the only neighborhood Black elementary school in a large urban district. It was March and I had just received my bachelor's degree in education from a small private university. I felt I was ready to tackle the problems of the world. My first teaching assignment was in a school of 300 children; 93 percent of the students were Black, 3 percent were Asian and Native American, and 4 percent of the youngsters were White. All my students were either on reduced or free lunch.

Of the fourteen teachers at the school, only three had more than six years of teaching experience. Most of us were new or had been teaching for less than three years. There was an underlying atmosphere of frustration and hopelessness in the school, especially in the upper grades.

Most of the staff didn't think that I, a relatively quiet, young, and short Asian American woman (barely five feet tall), would make it at this tough, neighborhood school. The week after I took the job, the principal mentioned to me, "We had a knifing in the parking lot last year, so be sure to lock your car." I was definitely a greenhorn, who would learn much from the school and parents in the neighborhood in the next year and a half.

Right away, I realized that I knew little about the lives of the children in my first grade class. Though my apartment was only five miles from the school, it was as if I lived in another city. The good news was that I finished out the year and taught another full year at this school. The bad news was that I wasn't as well prepared as I should have been. Fortunately, the students were patient and forgiving toward me and all of my mistakes. In those sixteen months, I learned more from the children than they learned from me.

Though I wanted to assist children in becoming the best they could be, I was unprepared to teach in a school where the life experiences of children were different from my own. For example, the district had chosen reading materials that weren't suited for most of the children in my class. Many of the children spoke Black English, but the district mandated the use of a highly phonetic commercial reading series for the primary grades. The basal reader was built upon the phonemes and semantic structure of standard

English. The methods used at that time were mechanical and did not encourage students to make their own meaning out of the text. The stories in the texts were about a boy named Sam and had little to do with the lives of my students. The reading selections used word families, but the stories did not make much sense.

Upon reflection, I realized that I was teaching students how to decode without teaching them comprehension skills. I was also asking the children to learn a new dialect of English while simultaneously trying to teach them to read standard English. The problems were my approach and the textbooks, not the kids. I had never thought about *myself* as being culturally disadvantaged. At that time, it was common practice to label low-income, culturally diverse children as culturally disadvantaged. Now I believe the schools were culturally disadvantaged institutions because many of us did not understand the life experiences or background of our students. Children are children. They come to school with a rich knowledge of their cultures and neighborhoods. They have hard-working parents. I didn't understand or value the students' shared life experiences and I didn't know how to make school meaningful for them.

After teaching for several months I realized I had little knowledge about my students or the community. I began to search out various African American community groups and read about African American and American Indian history. I also knew it was important for me to earn the respect of parents and the students. I hadn't grown up in the school neighborhood, and the parents didn't know if they could trust me. So I visited many students at home and regularly called parents in order to get to know them. Out of twenty children in my classroom, I had three American Indian students, one European American child, and sixteen African American youngsters. All of the children spoke Black English and were bright and eager to learn. I began to understand that I held misconceptions about the community and didn't know what the critical issues were in the neighborhood. Through home visits and phone calls, I developed relationships with parents in the school community. They slowly began to trust me because I cared and was honest. I made mistakes, but the parents were very open-hearted because they understood I was a new teacher. In fact, they were extremely accessible. Jimmy's mom told me to call her in the morning because she worked in the late afternoon. I called Lisa's mother at work at the telephone company in the evening to give her an update on Lisa's reading progress. Cecilia's grandma came in regularly to read to small groups of children in the classroom.

I wish I had been a more effective teacher. I didn't know where to begin. What did I need to learn? What changes did I need to make to be a better teacher? This is how my interest in Multicultural Education began.

Years Later as a University Instructor

Many years later my commitment to Multicultural Education was dramatically affirmed. I was teaching at a university in the same large urban city where I landed my first job as a first grade teacher. I often took teachers on field trips. On one trip, we went to a public high school, one of only two public institutions in the nation devoted to the schooling of American Indian students. As the vice principal led my class through the buildings, I noticed a female student, obviously pregnant, walking toward us. There was something familiar in her eyes.

As she passed by, I realized the student was Rosemary. I remembered her as a scrawny little 6-year-old in my first grade class fourteen years ago. I asked the counselor about her. Rosemary was 20 years old and trying to earn her high school diploma. She had a toddler who attended the high school daycare and another child on the way. I remembered her as a spunky, curious, loving 6-year-old, and though I didn't know what happened during the past fourteen years, I could see that life had not been easy on her. The energy in her eyes was no longer there. The counselor was concerned because he didn't think that Rosemary would finish her high school degree before her twenty-first birthday. The funding for her education would cease on that day.

I kept asking myself, "What happened to Rosemary? She was excited about learning in first grade. Did I fail Rosemary? Did schools fail Rosemary? Did society fail Rosemary? Did her parents fail Rosemary? Did she fail herself?"

Seeing Rosemary reminded me how important our job is. Rosemary was one child who had fallen through the cracks. I felt as if we as a community had lost the precious gift of Rosemary's dreams and enthusiasm that I saw fourteen years earlier.

Who Will Benefit from Reading This Book?

I have written this book primarily for teachers, though the ideas and resources can be adapted for use by counselors, administrators, and community people. Because European Americans make up about 86 percent of the teaching force, many of my comments will be directed to this audience.[1] However, the messages in the book can benefit most educators.

This book is written in a conversational and narrative style because I want to create a dialogue with the practicing teacher. I would like you to feel as if we are conversing and raising various issues together in this book. In addition, I try to paint pictures of various situations in the classroom using many different examples of what teachers are doing. Teaching is about people and their interactions. The book reflects this philosophy.

Children are life's most precious gifts. They give us magical moments of hope, joy, and excitement. In an environment of mutual respect, we can build an atmosphere of trust and care with our students as a community of learners. I have learned from students, parents, colleagues, friends, and my own children over the years and know that learning is a life-long process of growth.

I hope this book will help you to examine biases, reflect more fully on the importance of culture, and encourage you to try new methods that will make schooling increasingly meaningful to students.

The journey toward caring, equity, and diversity is an exciting struggle. We can learn more when we work with each other in an atmosphere of caring. Though there may be challenging spots along the way, I hope you will join me through the book. As Robert Fulghum has written, "No matter how old you are—when you go out into the world, it is best to hold hands and stick together."[2]

Take care,
Val

---

[1]Perrone, Vito. 1998. *The Teacher with a Heart.* New York: Teachers College Press, p. 35.
[2]Fulghum, Robert. 1988. *All I Really Need to Know I Learned in Kindergarten.* New York: Ivy Books, p. 6.

DENNIS THE MENACE

"WHATEVER HIS TEACHER'S SALARY IS, IT'S NOT NEARLY HIGH ENOUGH."

The Dennis the Menace cartoon reinforces the importance of teaching as a career. Teachers have a critical role in the social, emotional, and intellectual development of their students.

Part One

Culture: A Powerful Force

Chapter 1

Why Is Culture Important? The Power of Culture

Chapter 2

How Does Culture Impact Schooling?

Chapter 1

Why Is Culture Important?
The Power of Culture

In the past decade there has been a flood of books written about multicultural education. Some cover the history of various groups and discuss the importance of social justice. In other texts, teachers are directed to integrate art techniques or customs from various ethnic communities. Additional books present social categories like race, class, gender, sexual orientation, religion, disability, and ethnicity as separate categories. However, few multicultural education books describe the elements of culture and how they can impact the learning and teaching process. One of the key differences of this text is its attention to culture and its use of Vygotsky's sociocultural learning theory (Cole 1996).

Children come to school with different cultural backgrounds. Their backgrounds are a complex mixture of many cultural subgroups. In fact, Gibson (2000) believes that subgroup cultures are a far more accurate description of a person/group than a larger generalization like the term, African American culture. He gives the example that there are African American industrial working class, African American labor union, African American Southern land owner, and bourgeois African American cultures. Though members of each of these groups may hold, as a collective, common elements of language, music, signs, and some understandings, their cultures are primarily taken from contexts that are shaped by specific social class and labor values. In addition, children may be shaped by a multitude of other social forces like neighborhood, gender, and ethnic cultures. For example, a child may be Mexican American female from a middle-class rural community in California's Imperial county whose parents are Presbyterian. Or a child may be Swedish male from a working-class family who lives in St. Paul, Minnesota and within a large Hmong neighborhood.

This book also differs from others because it comes from the ethic of care, a philosophical framework defined by Noddings (1984; 1992). The framework places at the core of teaching an ethical commitment to others and recommends that trusting relationships be at the center of quality instruction and community building. This framework is coupled with an education for democracy orientation that is student-centered, examines the integration of race, class and gender in schools, and addresses glaring inequities

3

in schools and society (Dewey 1916; Freire 1970; Darder 1991; Gibson 1999). The three theoretical philosophies, the ethic of care, education for democracy, and sociocultural context of learning build a cohesive foundation for Caring-Centered Multicultural Education. Each component holds the strands of mutual respect for oneself and others, the learner at the center of instruction, the learner who makes meaning of her learning, and the importance of creating a just and compassionate society.

The book is organized into four sections. The next two chapters will present a general discussion of culture. Chapters three and four describe the framework for the book. Chapters five through seven discuss prejudice and discrimination in individuals, institutions, and society. Chapters eight through ten focus on culturally relevant teaching, both strategies and content. Finally chapter eleven and the prologue offers a review of the text and offers ideas about successful students and teachers.

The population of the United States is rapidly changing. In fact, a recent *Newsweek* magazine cover story article called this phenomenon, "the browning of America." In about 50 years, the member's of the President's Initiative on Race described the following changes in our demographics (Spring 2000: 113): By 2005, Latinos will be the largest ethnic "minority" group in the country; and as of 1997, almost two-thirds of Asian Pacific Americans were immigrants as was 38 percent of Latinos, while only 8 percent of European Americans, 6 percent of American Indians and African Americans were foreign-born. In addition, by 2020, demographers predict that over half of the U.S. school population will be made up of non-European ethnic groups and that in the western portion of our country no one single racial group will make up a majority (Sadker and Sadker 2000, 92).

The purpose of this chapter is to assist you in reflecting on how culture shapes who you are and also who your students are. Culture is a large part of how we identify and understand our lives. Culture is a collective experience and reflects ways in which people meet their needs (Valle 1997). However, students and teachers may come from different cultural orientations. In a community centered on caring for others, people want to understand life from other perspectives because relationships of trust are built on dialogue. Sometimes conflicts between people from different cultural orientations may arise, however, those disagreements can be eliminated or reduced when people learn about each other.

What Is Culture?

People are expressions of culture (Bruner 1990). They are expressions of several cultures that arise from different groupings such as ethnicity, language, social economic status, neighborhood, generation, and religion. Whether they were brought up in a family which is Somali, Swedish, Mexican, Cambodian, Navajo, Hawaiian, Puerto Rican, Irish, or several ethnic communities, people are cultural beings. A common misconception people hold is that others may have the same world views. Since the United States is a nation of many peoples, there are many cultural views represented in the United States.

Culture is all that is created by people; this represents behaviors, values, attitudes, customs, viewpoints, history, and many other aspects (Valle 1997). It is always changing because people change, however culture also shapes the way you see and interpret the world. It is almost like a pair of glasses through which you see the world. As a baby

perspective

you learned language, the meaning of words, and how to use language from the adults in your environment as you came into contact with them. Language shapes the way we categorize and see the world. For example, in the cold lands of Canada and Alaska, there are Innuit communities who have over two hundred words to describe snow (Christiansen 1997). Languages construct the way people categorize and perceive the many different types of snow. For example, snow can be hard, soft, wet, powdery, or icy. In southern California where I live, snow is not an important part of the environment. We don't need multiple words to describe snow because it never snows in San Diego.

Let's look at cultural values. When I was little, my mother would tell me that when someone offered me a cookie or dessert, I should "enryo." If I were to translate it, that means I was supposed to "hold back" and not take anything. Actually the term, "enryo" means much more than that. My mom was saying, "I want you to act 'properly' and that means you must be reserved." She also gave me the message indirectly that it isn't proper to act greedy and so don't take the cookie. In this way my mother was teaching me an important norm and expectation of the Japanese American community.

Culture is like the air; it is always there but people who live in and follow its ways may have difficulty seeing it. One of the best descriptions about how culture is taught from a multitude of sources comes from the novel, *Ishmael,* by Daniel Quinn (1990). As an ecologist, Quinn has created a powerful novel about cultural perspective. His story is about a teacher and a student. Interestingly, the teacher, Ishmael, is a gorilla and the student is a human. Quinn describes how their different cultural perspectives and backgrounds gave both Ishmael and his student contrasting views about why the world was created. The male student thought the world was created for humans. Ishmael asked the man how he learned that belief. The man wasn't sure. The following is what Ishmael tells his pupil about culture:

> "Mother Culture, whose voice has been in your ear since the day of your birth, has given you an explanation of how things came *to be this way.* You know it well; everyone in your culture knows it well. But this explanation wasn't given to you all at once. No one ever sat you down and said, 'Here is how things came to be this way, beginning ten or fifteen billion years ago right up to the present.' Rather, you assembled this explanation like a mosaic: from a million bits of information presented to you in various ways by others who share that explanation. You assembled it from the table talk of your parents, from cartoons you watched on television, from Sunday School lessons, from your textbooks and teachers, from news broadcasts, from movies, novels, sermons, plays, newspapers, and all the rest" (Quinn 1990, 40).

We are products of what Ishmael would call a "cultural prison" because the culture that surrounds us teaches us how to look at and respond to our life experiences. He attempted to teach his student how to transcend that cultural prison and to view life from the perspective of other living beings.

People transmit culture from one generation to the next (Brislin 1993); it is dynamic and ever changing. As I wrote in the Prologue, since Multicultural Education focuses on teaching the whole student, it is critical that teachers understand the cultures children bring to the classroom because that knowledge can help teachers to create a more affirming place of learning. What is culture? Often culture is formally defined as a social system of rules, language, customs, rituals, arts, government, expectations,

norms, values, and ideals that people share. In actuality it is much more because it includes behaviors, assumptions, ways of doing things, ways of seeing things, methods of
learning, methods of interacting, and how people relate to others.

Culture shapes much of who we are and what we think. The answers to the following questions may help you to more fully understand cultural knowledge.

Who are we? How do we define ourselves?
What is expected of us? What is our purpose?
How are we motivated?
How do we relate to each other?
What are our ideals?
How do we behave?
How do we teach our children?
How do we care for ourselves? For others?

What has helped me to better understand culture's impact on education is to look at culture from someone else's viewpoint. Gregory Cajete, a Tewa from New Mexico, wrote
in his book, *Look to the Mountain:*

> "When teachers examine culture, they need to look at the affective elements—the
> subjective experience and observations, the communal relationships, the artistic and
> mythical dimensions, the ritual and ceremony, the sacred ecology, the psychological
> and spiritual orientations—that have characterized and formed Indigenous education
> since time immortal" (Cajete, 1994 20).

Cajete reminds us that culture is a large holistic sense of who one is, what one believes, and how one acts. It includes meanings, values, actions, and decision-making
shared by and within a social group. As a child we eat culture, we live culture, we breathe
it, we see it at work every day and we don't even realize it. We learn to understand even
subtle nuances of culture. I went to a photography exhibit and admired the work of Carl
Mydans who was a *Life* magazine photojournalist. One of the most famous pieces of his
work was the photo of General MacArthur during World War II landing on Luzon in the
Philippines as he is walking in the water onto shore. The photo sends messages of
strength and determination needed to win the war. It was his confident stride and look
on his face which, in part, conveyed that strength. As a photographer, Mydans was a
careful observer of people. He said, "I am fascinated by human behavior. By the time I
used a camera seriously, I had become an obsessive people-watcher, observing manner-
isms and body postures, the slants and curves of mouths, the falseness of smiles, the di-
rectness or evasion of eyes. When I learned to understand these signals and interpret
them, I had found a source of stories as wide and varied and as captivating as the human
race" (Mydans 1997). What guided Mydans in his work was that he was a careful student of culture.

Turning to your classroom, what do you know about the culture or cultures your
students bring to school? What you know about your students' cultures may be more
about the explicit culture. The explicit culture is expressions of culture which an outsider
may see (Valle 1997). An outsider mostly sees the tangible or outward symbols of culture, like food, ceremonies, music, dance, dress, history, and nonverbal behaviors. What
do you know about the implicit culture or the hidden culture of your students? This includes the underlying meanings and beliefs of a culture, which can be seen in gender role

orientations, philosophy, religion, interactional patterns, and cultural values. Unfortunately, when teachers primarily present elements of the explicit culture, then children begin to see those tangible articles as culture.

Help children to understand that

> Tacos and frybread are *not* cultures.
> Origami, paper folding, is *not* culture.
> Kwanza is *not* culture.

Rather

> Tacos and frybread are specific elements within various cultures.
> Origami is a specific art form within a culture.
> Kwanza is a specific celebration within a culture.

Later in the chapter, information about how to guide students in learning the underlying significance and meaning of expressions of culture will be discussed. For example, why is Kwanza important to the lives of some people? What is the history of origami? What values does origami have within its original cultural context?

How Do Children Learn Culture?

Children learn culture from their families. Families are holders and transmitters of culture (Bruner 1990). That is why getting to know parents and the family can be critical in understanding students. Let's look at how culture can be conveyed in the family.

Let me share a story about a friend of mine. When Gerry was 10 years old, he went to his grandmother's eightieth birthday party in Hawaii. The family had the party at a Chinese restaurant. Everyone was smiling and talking. Gerry sat at a round table with nine other people. He sat next to his Auntie Sara. This was a big birthday celebration and so the family wanted to honor their grandmother with a nine-course dinner.

Many years ago, Gerry's grandmother traveled to Hawaii from Canton, China, by ship when she was only 15 years old. She was betrothed to his grandfather, who at that time was about 25 years old. The couple eventually had eight children. His grandfather died when Gerry was 4 years old and left his grandmother as matriarch of the family.

In honor of the grandmother, the family had golden peach pins for everyone. Peaches symbolize long life and so every family member was given not only pins, but also vases with peaches painted on the front panel.

As each course was brought out to the table and served, Gerry became more full. He wanted to rest his stomach, so he stuck his chopsticks into his bowl of rice. The chopsticks stuck straight up. His Auntie Sara placed her hand on his shoulder and whispered, "Gerry, don't do that because it means death."

Gerry quickly took the chopsticks from his bowl of rice and placed them on his white dinner plate; his face was slightly red because he was embarrassed. He knew children were not supposed to do anything to bring disgrace to their family. Just like in school, children were supposed to act properly.

One of the nine courses was a noodle dish. Noodles are served at birthday parties in many Chinese and Chinese American families because noodles are long and therefore represent long life. When the large blue platter of noodles was pushed before Gerry on the table's lazy susan, he took the large spoon and began to put noodles on his plate.

However, some noodles were falling off the serving plate so he cut them with the spoon. His Auntie Sara frowned and leaned down toward Gerry gently whispering in his ear. This time she said, "Gerry, don't cut your noodles or you will be cutting the life of your grandmother short."

The young man quickly scooped the noodles onto his plate and pushed the lazy susan toward the next diner.

In the course of the meal, each person was also given a small packet of dried coconut and fruit that had a sugar coating. The sweetness of the dessert represented more sweetness in life for his grandmother.

Gerry learned much about the importance of long life and symbols of longevity within a cultural family context. He understood more clearly not only the explicit aspects of culture, but he also knew that he had to obey elder members of his family like his Auntie. The education of children is often given not only by parents, but also grandparents, aunts, uncles, and other important family friends. It wasn't only that it took a village to educate a child, but also that he, as a child, had to treat all elders in the village with respect.

Gerry, like most children, learned values and beliefs besides other cultural elements like traditions and customs through social interactions with family members. The example demonstrated that Gerry grew up in a supportive, extended family context. His learning came not only from direct statements from his auntie, but also from other elements like tone of voice and nonverbal behaviors of other family members. The birthday party was a powerful cultural context for learning. Gerry learned in more detail which behaviors were expected and accepted, while learning cultural values that emphasized longevity, respect for grandparents, and the importance of obedience.

Culture Shapes Our World View

Culture shapes how we see the world and interpret the world. Sometimes children come to school with different perceptions and values because they have diverse cultural orientations. Children of color may experience cultural clashes when what they are taught at home is in conflict with what they are learning at school.

In order for teachers to better understand the difference people have in their worldviews, I ask my students, who are teachers, to volunteer time with a community that is culturally different from their own. This has been an excellent opportunity for teachers to unpack the surface aspects of culture and to understand more about their values; this can happen when people develop personal relationships with others from other cultures. For example, a teacher volunteered at a local YMCA in an African American and Latino low-income neighborhood. She chose this site because she realized that she had little knowledge of the life of a student from another neighborhood, a neighborhood which was not only African American, but what she perceived as violent. She described herself as a "23-year-old White, blond, green-eyed woman from a conservative white city doing volunteer work in the community of City Central. What a mismatch!"

Her first instinct when she got out of her car at the YMCA was, "Oh my gosh what am I doing in this part of the city!" She wrote in her paper, "I wanted to get back in my car and find another place to go, a place without so many problems. Looking around all that I saw was a rundown YMCA in a horrible area of town with police raiding a house across the street. I won't be able to relate to these kids."

She stayed at the YMCA and learned that life looked differently through someone else's cultural glasses. She wrote, "The children are surrounded daily by a world that is uncaring and unkind. Their parents care, but they were busy supporting their family." During one of their games with preschool children, she learned a valuable lesson about how her world view was different from some of the young people in the neighborhood.

In a game called "Guess that Sound," she played a variety of sounds and the children had to guess them. The children were having lots of fun until she played the sound of a siren. When the children heard the siren about four of them began to cry and others screamed, "It's the police! Hide! Hide!" She was flabbergasted to learn that three- and four-year-olds believed that the police were not there to protect them. Some of the children were scared of the police in that neighborhood. She did not make any judgments about their views, but she realized that not all the children thought in the same way she did. She began to understand how the issues of race and class were intimately linked and did impact children and how they grew up, saw the world, and responded to others.

You Are a Cultural Being

Just as your students are cultural beings, you, the teacher are also a cultural being. Your worldview and perspectives shape the way you teach, what you teach, how you interact, and what you value and expect in the classroom. The classroom is a highly contextualized environment that may reflect your cultural orientation. Ask yourself the following questions:

1. What do you expect from your students?
2. How culturally based are those expectations?
3. For example, do you expect all children to participate in class discussions?
4. Have you taught the skills children may need to talk in class if their culture is primarily one where they have little opportunity to practice "public" talking or sharing?
5. What types of activities do you use in your classroom most often? Lecturing, small group projects, individualized instruction, demonstration, private practice of skills, socratic discussions, worksheets, etc.? Though there is controversy about different ethnic groups having preferred learning styles, you can still ask yourself if you use a variety of learning activities to meet the different learning styles of your students.
6. What motivates you? Are you motivated by what your friends and family think of you? Maybe you are most motivated by what you think of yourself? How about the child who may be motivated to make his parents happy or proud? How about if a child is more motivated because he wants to be a good role model for his siblings? This is a critical aspect of teaching and learning.
7. How do you interpret certain tasks? For example, do you believe that flashcards are an efficient way to learn some information? Do you explain that view to your students? What if your students think using flashcards is boring and they don't understand why the multiplication tables or Spanish vocabulary needs to be learned?
8. What if you believed that it was critical to develop cooperative skills in your students because we live in a democracy, but a parent thought the other kids in the group were holding back her child because not all the other students were on task?

9. Do you believe it is important for students to give answers in class so that you can assess their learning? That seems reasonable to me too. I am a teacher and do this all the time, but what if you had a child who had been taught to practice in private before sharing in class? You might need to talk with the child individually in order to assess her competence. These are examples of culturally based viewpoints.

Many of us have grown up in the American culture. The next section describes some elements of this culture.

What Is U.S. American Culture?

I believe there is something which could be called U.S. American culture. (The term *U.S. American* is used throughout this book, because the concept of American is not only used in the United States. For example, people in South and Latin America also use the term *American.*) This culture is, for the most part, U.S. American middle-class Caucasian culture (Brislin 1993), though it does include elements from other ethnic groups. In the U.S. American culture, holidays like the Fourth of July, Thanksgiving, Easter, and Christmas are observed; however not everyone personally celebrates those days, and some U.S. Americans may celebrate other holidays like Rosh Hashanah and Kwanza. Our nation has a strong Judeo-Christian orientation, so many of the holidays come from that tradition. Looking at our daily lives, there are aspects of U.S. American culture that we may take for granted. For example, we may be accustomed to having the newspaper published every day, national news on television every night, and professional sporting events every season of the year, from football in the fall, basketball in the winter, to baseball in the spring and summer.

What is another aspect of U.S. American culture? Let's look at how we are governed. We are a democratic republic and have different organizations like the state government and federal government to carry out our rules and values. There are institutions like the Office of the President, the Congress, and the Supreme Court who often symbolize who we are as a nation. On a local level, the court system, the police, and the governor's and mayor's offices also are important elements of what we know as the U.S. American culture.

Another aspect of what I will loosely call U.S. American culture is economic status. Many people in this country who are wealthy also have more political, economic, and social power than those who have less financial resources. Lately, there have been many discussions about campaign contributions to political parties and whether that is a way individuals can "buy" influence from our lawmakers. As a nation founded upon capitalism, how much money a person has is often seen as an important measure of her status in society. Bill Gates has been on the cover of many of our nation's magazines like *Time* and *Newsweek* not only because he built Microsoft, but because he is the richest ($90 billion at this time) person in the United States.

Unfortunately, U.S. American culture is also laced with racism, sexism, and classism. When women were not allowed to vote or people of color could not testify in court or have their freedom, these beliefs were held for many years, not only by citizens but also by lawmakers. These values guided the way people made decisions and acted. Though our belief system as a nation has moved away from those limiting ideas, people disagree as to how to create a just and fair society. For example, in the 1970s and the 1980s, affirmative action programs were instituted and praised as encouraging integration and providing more equal opportunities to those from underrepresented groups who had been treated unfairly due to race, class, or gender. Today, there is much conflict over affirmative action and many of those programs have been eliminated. People in the United States may believe it is important to support equality for all, yet how to accomplish this goal is not clear.

Schools are a large part of that culture. We teach U.S. American culture throughout the years children attend schools. Let me share an example. Young children are often taught nursery rhymes. In fact, some teachers are mandated by their districts to teach specific nursery rhymes. One of them is "Peter, Peter Pumpkin Eater." When my friend's son, John, was in kindergarten, he had to learn this rhyme. The teacher first introduced the poem to the whole class and then later she had different learning centers and "Peter, Peter Pumpkin Eater" was one of them. At the center, John cut two identical pumpkin shapes out of orange paper to act as the front and back covers. He then stapled the stems together and pasted a copy of the rhyme inside, making a book. Then the teacher told all the students to cut out a magazine picture of a woman and glue it inside the pumpkin on the other side of the rhyme. John was so proud of his pumpkin, he brought it home and showed his mother, his face beaming. "Look, Mom. I did a good job of cutting and pasting," he said. John had cut out a picture of a woman in a bathing suit and pasted it inside his pumpkin. His mother was mortified. How could *her* son place such a gender-biased picture of a woman inside his pumpkin. Of course his answer was, "Mom, why don't you like my pumpkin. It is just a picture of a lady." John was only five years old and he was learning social messages about women from curriculum in the school culture.

Though censorship is a difficult issue in schools, the poem "Peter, Peter, Pumpkin Eater" seemed to be giving out distinct values about women and men. First, the husband couldn't keep his wife so he had to put her in the pumpkin. Does that mean he was not a loving person and so she wanted to run away? Also, why would a woman need to be put in a pumpkin shell? Couldn't she take care of herself? There are other meanings which could be consciously or unconsciously interpreted from the rhyme too. The poem gives out negative messages about both women and men. In addition, it had a strong gender role message. Unfortunately, neither John's teacher nor her kindergartners talked about gender roles; rather the children were intently involved in cutting, pasting, and coloring.

Older students also learn about U.S. American culture in schools. In high school, the "smarter" young people are placed in Advanced Placement classes and others are placed in regular classes. Advance Placement classes are college-level courses taught in high school. How do we measure who is smart? This is a cultural question. As I sat at my daughter's high school graduation I noticed several students who were great at auto mechanics and could fix any car were not given much recognition, but students who scored in the top 1 percent of the PSAT (Preliminary Scholastic Achievement Test) received a special National Merit award and were recognized in front of all the parents. Who do we value more, the young person who scores well on the national test or the youth who has the talent and knowledge to fix one of the most used machines in our society today? Maybe we should honor both students for their diverse accomplishments and abilities. Yet, what message does our culture and schools give out about who is more valued?

In more general terms, our culture is also heavily influenced by our history; a history which focuses upon the revolution of the thirteen colonies from Britain. Our children learn that the colonies fought for freedom and democracy. Children learn about historical events like the Boston Tea Party, the Battle of Bunker Hill, and Paul Revere's ride as examples of bravery and strong beliefs in independence and fairness. Children may have learned that people such as Benjamin Franklin, George Washington, and Thomas Jefferson founded our country with courage and great leadership. Many textbooks gloss over the fact that George Washington and Thomas Jefferson both owned slaves. Why? Because the mythology being taught about our nation is that the United States stands for democracy, freedom, and equality.

Our mythology also contains a strong theme of hero-making (Loewen 1995). We have many stories about famous people like Betsy Ross and Woodrow Wilson. However, few students know that Ross never had anything to do with the making of the first flag and Wilson was extremely racist (Loewen 1995). Why aren't students taught accurate information? As Loewen wisely explains, we, like many other nations, teach ideals. Through our national mythology, which includes heroes, we teach our students the values of courage, independence, and hard work. In addition, because underrepresented groups have often pointed out the paradox between reality and our ideals, schools have been reluctant to provide a comprehensive view of history by including the perspectives of African Americans, Latinos, or Native Americans who may challenge and question our national mythology. Like most countries, history is usually written from the perspective of the victors or those in powerful positions. In chapters 9 and 10, I discuss how I believe our curriculum, an important part of our school culture, gives influential messages to our students about race, class, and gender.

The mythology transmits the message that society is working for the best interest of all citizens and this myth is conveyed over and over through the media, newspapers, schools, businesses, and government (Sherman and Wood 1989). One of the most powerful ideological myths of U.S. American culture is that "your dreams will come true if you work hard." Does it matter if people are rich or poor, Black or White, female or male (Sherman and Wood, 1989)? The mythology of our culture glosses over the inequities in our country.

How would you define U.S. American culture? What do you think or do in your life which you could say is part of American culture? What are some of the ideals of U.S. American culture? What are some of the important social institutions in U.S. American culture? A great deal of U.S. American culture, which I am involved in, has to do with my children. Our daughter is in college now, which is an important U.S. American institution, but when she was little I took her to ballet lessons, guitar lessons, and Girl Scout meetings, and when she was older she was involved in cross-country running and the high school newspaper. We took our son to soccer practice, tennis lessons, and to the movies. All these activities are what I would term elements of U.S. American culture.

Culture: Deep and Surface Levels

Culture has both surface and deep elements. Many of the things I mentioned in the previous section on U.S. American culture were surface elements like holidays, soccer games, and famous Americans. However, I also pointed to values like freedom, equality, and democracy, which are a part of the deep structure of culture.

Let's look at examples of explicit expressions of U.S. American culture: Symbols such as the U.S. flag, the scroll to represent the U.S. Constitution, dollar sign meaning money ($), and the White House; institutions such as schools, universities, police departments, fire departments, and hospitals; and businesses such as McDonald's, Sears, Microsoft, Kleenex, Purex, and Kellogg.

What are some of the underlying values which the symbols represent? The dollar sign ($) not only represents money, but that we are a capitalist nation. A major aspect of capitalism is the belief in individualism and that being an entrepreneur is an acceptable and valued career. The U.S. Constitution represents the belief that we are a nation committed to the values of freedom, justice, and equality, and that those values are at the foundation of who we are as a society. To some the U.S. flag means the United States, and to others it represents the United States as a nation, which fights for freedom not only in this country but throughout the world. Many of our cultural expressions have two levels of meaning, the surface and hidden. These two levels of culture create an extremely complex system of symbols, behaviors, and values. Culture is an extremely important aspect of our lives.

The implicit cultural aspects of a person are often difficult to see. However, it is easier for others to recognize the explicit or surface elements of culture, like the type of clothing a person wears or the language an individual speaks. It is much more difficult to learn about the implicit cultural components, like what motivates a child or what her values are, however this is important information for a teacher to utilize.

Multiple Layers of Culture

Brislin (1993) sees culture as being widely shared by people and transmitted from one generation to the next over time. He believes culture is not often discussed because there is a mutual acceptance of it. This makes the concept of culture difficult to explain. Valle (1997) provides a multidimensional model to explain culture. Culture is defined by Valle (1997) as having three layers:

language, symbols, and artifacts;
customs, practices, and interactional patterns; and
shared values, norms, beliefs, and expectations.

Culture is made up of many elements and together they make an integrated whole. Separating culture into distinct elements tends to fragment it. However, I believe the following typology helps teachers to understand how many different elements contribute to culture. When looking at culture through Valle's three layers, it is easier for teachers to see that culture represents a complex system of thinking, behaving, and valuing.

Breaking down the three layers further, I find it helpful to think of them in the following way:

Language, Symbols, and Artifacts (means of communication)—language, dialects preferred, proverbs, signs, jokes, stories, myths, analogies, folklore, art forms, heroes, dances, rituals, children's games, currency, holidays, history (family, national, and global)

Customs, Practices, and Interactional Patterns (means of interaction)— verbal (tone of voice, phrases used) and nonverbal (eye contact, proximity of stance, gestures) communication patterns, family behaviors, governmental and social institutions, conversational styles (formal-business, casual, ritualized), friendship patterns, community roles, gender roles

Shared Values, Beliefs, Norms, and Expectations (values driving people,
  groups)—attitudes, religious and spiritual beliefs, fears, laws, standards,
  levels of political participation

Valle believes these three layers of culture shape a collective social environment. The
most difficult aspects of a culture to understand are the underlying values. The comic
above shows the culture of kindergarten on the first day of school. One level of culture
consists of the clothing and backpacks students are wearing and carrying. On the next
level, many parents take or walk their children to school. Some even believe it is an important historical event in their child's life, so they take photos. Underlying these two
levels are values. Children around the age of five are expected to go to school and this is
a strong belief held by our society.

Unpacking Layers of Culture

There are many aspects of culture that may be invisible. In Caring-Centered Multicultural Education, teachers know that culture is an important aspect of children's lives.
They try to "unpack" the layers of culture and identify what children respond to and understand in human relationships. Remember Gerry's experience at his grandmother's
birthday party. Gerry was learning the meanings behind many symbols in his family culture. He gained a better understanding of what behaviors were expected of him and why.
His Auntie Sara helped him to "unpack" what was going on and what was expected of
him in the cultural context of his family. She explained what to do and the reasons why.

Culture is an extremely complicated concept and depends on many variables. A
cultural concept can differ depending upon the context. So, though the following is a list
of specific aspects of culture, the context they appear in is also important to understanding culture. What have you noticed and what have you not even thought about?

Communication

When do you use formal language patterns? When do you use slang? Do you use
  words that have different meanings from what your students understand?

What analogies do you use in your teaching?

What jokes do you tell?

What is your interactional style (aggressive, formal, warm, quiet, talkative)?

History

What is your family history?

What family stories do you like to tell?

Where in this country or in what other country did your ancestors first live? What kind of careers are important in your family?

Who are your role models and why?

Gender Roles

What do you believe the role of women is in society?

What role do you believe men should have in society?

Who has the most power at your work? Who has the least? Is it gender related?

Who was the disciplinarian in your family?

Traditions

Were there certain holidays that your family celebrated?

How did your family prepare for the beginning of the school year?

Value Orientations

What kind of behavior do you expect out of your students? When they do not behave in the manner that you expected, who do you believe is at fault?

How important are letter grades to you?

How important are national standards to you? To the faculty at your school?

What do you believe the role of parents should be in student achievement?

Though I have asked about various aspects of culture, they do not occur in isolation. Cultural elements are used in a social context and many are used in coordination with other aspects. Culture represents the components and interactions of people.

A teacher named Lucille told me this story about one of her students. She was explaining that there was a cultural generation gap between herself and a youngster named Jacob. In class, she said in an enthusiastic voice, "Yahoo, that is a great job, Jacob!"

Jacob gave her a puzzled look. He said, "Mrs. Wong, Yahoo is a search engine. What are you talking about?!"

Mrs. Wong laughed and laughed.

Jacob then went on to explain, "Yoohoo is also a chocolate milk drink. I don't know what you mean."

After Mrs. Wong saw that there was a real conflict, she said, "We hold different meanings of the same word. I think Yahoo means hurray. I guess we are learning new vocabulary together."

Then Jacob smiled, "I'll think of some more examples that you won't know tomorrow."

Mrs. Wong gave him a big smile.

In my experience, teachers vary in their knowledge of children's culture and children also come to school with different levels of cultural knowledge. Children may also be the product of multiple cultures. The next section gives examples of how culture

shapes the way we think through the images created and folk sayings used within a community. These images and beliefs shape the way people look at life. Teachers can begin to utilize these culturally familiar models if they are aware of or understand them.

Connections Between Deep and Surface Elements of Culture

Valle uses his model of the layers of culture to show that we often only see the explicit elements of culture; the aspects we can readily see are things like food, paintings, and clothing. However, what is really much more difficult to see is the implicit culture. Valle reminded me, "Kids don't come with a list that says these are my values. Teachers are going to have to watch kids. They will learn by talking with young people. It will take a while before teachers may develop a real understanding of the values of their students." This is an awesome task. Table 1.1 presents several examples about how tangible elements may represent much deeper, implicit cultural values. Teachers must be cultural translators or mediators, people who understand the implicit culture, in order to make schooling most meaningful and effective. They must understand underlying values and beliefs that may motivate or give a sense of purpose to students.

Let's take one of the examples from the table. *Origami* is often used by teachers to teach about Japanese American or Japanese culture. Most times teachers teach students how to make a crane or ball. What do you think students are learning about the culture of the Japanese? They may see that *origami* is clever. Students may also sharpen their spatial relationship skills. However, what underlying values of the culture are communicated?

When our daughter was only 5 years old, we went to a wedding of one of my friends. A beautiful exhibit of a thousand cranes hung above the head table at the

T A B L E   1 . 1

Cultural Elements: Examples of Surface and Deep Culture

	Language, Symbols, and Artifacts	Customs, Practices, and Interactional Patterns	Shared Values, Beliefs, Norms, and Expectations
Example 1	First Amendment	**a.** Stand up and speak out about one's views **b.** Organize group and community meetings **c.** Worship as one chooses	**a.** Value an individual's or group's right to speak out, assemble, and worship **b.** Safeguard the right of an individual or group to speak out, assemble, or worship
Example 2	Malcolm X	**a.** Spoke to many people in community **b.** Taught about the importance of freedom, education, and justice **c.** Built community organizations	**a.** Valued equality **b.** Valued freedom **c.** Valued education **d.** Believed in social change **e.** Believed in community unity **f.** Held Muslim religious beliefs **g.** Believed in African American self-determination
Example 3	Eighteen-year-old male in a Cuban American family gives opinion during a family dinner	**a.** Parents and grandparents encouraged children to express themselves **b.** Son (and grandson) spoke respectfully to family members **c.** Son waited his turn to talk in the conversation	**a.** Family believed in respectful and loving family relationships **b.** Family valued a strong cultural community **c.** Family wanted son to develop confidently and competently **d.** Son lived at home until after college because he chose to be close to his family

(Continued)

TABLE 1.1 (Continued)

Cultural Elements: Examples of Surface and Deep Culture

	Language, Symbols, and Artifacts	Customs, Practices, and Interactional Patterns	Shared Values, Beliefs, Norms, and Expectations
Example 4	*Origami*—Japanese paper-folding crane	**a.** Child watches another child or adult fold paper. **b.** Child folds paper one section at a time modeling the "teacher" **c.** "Teacher" waits patiently and shows folds several times, if needed **d.** Child and teacher treat each other with respect	**a.** Develops a sense of patience **b.** Reinforces a sense of community **c.** Teaches respect for the teacher or for someone with a skill **d.** Cranes represent good luck and long life in Japanese culture **e.** Reflects value of simplicity and beauty
Example 5	The Wampanoags and Thanksgiving	**a.** Wampanoags lived in the area now known as Massachusetts for many years **b.** Massasoit, leader of the Wampanoags, welcomed Pilgrims and invited them to settle in Plymouth **c.** Wampanoags invited the Pilgrims to join them in their celebration **d.** Pilgrims and other Europeans brought new diseases like cholera, typhus, tuberculosis, small pox, bubonic plague, and diphtheria to Native Americans who had no immunity (Loewen 1995) **e.** Wampanoags and Pilgrims helped each other and built strong community relationships (Loewen 1995)	**a.** Wampanoags like many Native Americans gave thanks yearly for the fall harvest **b.** Wampanoags cared for other humans and for the land **c.** Though few Wampanoags live today, Thanksgiving represents to many of them a sad chapter in their history because most Wampanoags were killed within fifty years of the settlement of the Pilgrims because of disease or wars (Loewen 1995)

reception. Our daughter enjoyed the many strands of beautiful colored *origami* cranes. She went up to the head table and asked the bride why she had so many of them at her wedding. The bride told her that the thousand cranes symbolized good luck. In addition, since cranes live a long time, the cranes represented a long and wonderful marriage.

Our daughter became very interested in making cranes that day. I took a napkin from the table and taught her how to make a crane. The first crane she and I made together was from a cloth napkin! It took a little time. Our daughter folded the napkin carefully by observing what I did. Since that was the limit to my expertise in *origami,* she bought several short how-to books and taught herself to create beautiful flowers, geometric paper boxes, and many sided-hanging balls by following the pictures. When her brother was small, he often watched her fold paper into birds, elephants, and flowers. It was too difficult for him and he did not have the patience to learn until he was about 8 years old. Then, he asked his sister to sit down with him and teach him the crane. From then on, he became very interested in *origami.* They began making things together and sharing their paper. They would carry small sheets about 3 inches square in their pockets in the car and make things during the drives to the doctor or supermarket. One of their favorite activities was to go to Chinatown in Seattle and buy new origami paper at Uwajimaya's, a Japanese food and variety store. Uwajimaya's carried many different colors of paper; some were gold, silver, or traditional Japanese patterns.

To my children, *origami* represents not only an ancient Japanese art form, but also family and a special brother-sister bond. It also exemplifies a personal art form. It takes much patience and accuracy to create a successful piece. Today both of our children still share ideas with each other and make various shaped boxes, kangaroos, and five-pointed stars.

Historically, *origami* is an art form that is over a thousand years old. *Ori* means folded and *kami* refers to paper in the Japanese language. So when the two parts are put together, the word is *origami.* The art form was an activity of the Imperial Court.

Origami, as Valle explains, represents not only the tangible product, but also interactional cultural patterns and underlying values. To provide students with a more complete understanding of culture, teachers must share with them not only the how-to sequence of folding, but explain how it is an art form that reinforces the importance of observation skills, working with others, and patience, and it represents simple beauty. Using a single piece of paper, a person can create a myriad of objects and artistic expressions. There were various levels of cultural significance.

Read through the other examples in Table 1.1 and notice the connections between the tangible outward behaviors and symbols, the interactions between people, and the underlying values that the implicit culture refers to within the specific cultural context.

What does this have to do with teaching?

Oftentimes you as a teacher might have to act as a cultural translator or mediator, who understands the layers of culture (Bustamante-Jones 1998). Cleary and Peacock (1998) give numerous illustrations of how majority and Native American cultures may hold different expectations. For example, many Native American young people grow up in families where children are expected to listen rather than speak. Young people learn to watch others before they do something that might make them look like a fool. Children are also advised not to show off. So some students have difficulty participating in class and may choose to withdraw instead of showing up for school, knowing that they must speak out or act aggressively. Other times, Native American youngsters may choose not to participate because they do not trust or feel comfortable with teachers. Some teachers may feel this lack of participation shows disinterest in learning, though this is not accurate. Cleary and Peacock (1998) also note that if the young adult chooses to participate, he may have to take on a different cultural role. This role may be uncomfortable because the student must discard cultural behaviors and beliefs. For example, the student might need to learn how to interrupt in order to be heard in a socratic social studies discussion. This can be extremely uncomfortable for someone who was taught that this behavior is disrespectful. However, in many discussions, if a person does not interrupt, she/he may not have the opportunity to participate and be heard. And school culture rewards aggressive verbal behavior. The school represents the powerful culture of mainstream society. It also has deep cultural values.

Throughout the text, more examples of how school culture may conflict with family, ethnic, and class cultures will be presented.

How Can We Find Cultural Keys to Help Us Reach Others?

Why is it important for teachers and others to consider culture in their work? Sometimes teachers may have a difficult time reaching or understanding students. There are many reasons why students do not respond to materials found in their textbooks and other materials. Maybe students do not have much of a reference point. For example, if the story is about life on the farm, but a student has never been to the country, she/he may need a cultural bridge to help her/him to understand the context. Sometimes materials that are more meaningful to students are also more motivating. If a Filipino American student discovers that yo-yos were made popular by a business person named Pedro Flores, she/he may become more interested in reading the materials if they knew that the word *yo-yo* means "come back" in Tagalog. More about Flores can be found in chapter 10.

Let me share a wonderful example of how researchers used their knowledge of culture to reach a large number of people (Smith 1999). In Mexico malnutrition is a grave problem because people live in deep poverty. People cannot afford to eat much protein or fresh vegetables. Children do not have normal energy and are underweight because their bodies do not have a healthy diet. They also get sick more often, which impacts their ability to learn.

Health researchers from Mexico's Health Ministry and National Nutrition Institute, and agencies like the United Nations Children's Fund found an element of culture to aid in their fight against malnutrition (Smith 1999). They searched for a cultural element in the diet of the people. The key was the tortilla! The tortilla is a corn-based food that has been a traditional staple for thousands of years in what we now know as Mexico.

Since researchers found that most families received more than two-thirds of their nutrition from tortillas, they realized that tortillas could be used as a vehicle to enrich the diet of many families. Officials asked the major cornmeal manufacturers to add six vitamins and numerous minerals to cornmeal that they sold. The addition was not that costly. This change has had a major positive impact on the health of many Mexicans, children and adults.

Researchers are also studying ways in which protein can be added to the tortillas. They would like to fortify tortillas with protein-rich soy. Health officials say that the addition of soy will help increase the height, birth weight, physical and mental ability of children (Smith 1999). Because researchers knew the population and understood their cultural lifestyles, it was possible for them to find something that was common in the lives of many Mexicans. The tortilla is becoming an important nutritional tool because of the combination of scientific research and culture. Think carefully about the lives of your students and how what they know and value can be integrated into your curriculum.

How Culture Can Be Distorted in Schools

When a teacher uses separate elements of culture in isolation like a holiday to teach about a culture, then the teacher is dividing culture into small pieces and fragmenting it from its important underlying values and interactional patterns. That is why I caution teachers about using food fairs as an activity to teach the culture of other ethnic groups, because foods are only one aspect of a culture. Isolated and noncontextualized information about food by itself may serve to stereotype. If students learn only a small fragment about a group of people, this information may create overgeneralized images about individuals from a group based upon superficial knowledge.

Students may not understand that the food eaten may be an example of how people responded to their environment. Many years ago in what is now Guatemala, the Mayans developed a culture where maize was a key element. In fact, the people honored a goddess of maize called Centeotl (Cornelius 1999). People had a special ceremony to give thanks for the corn and were careful to make sure to harvest all the corn so as not to waste any of the precious life that was shared with them. Social studies textbooks may indicate that corn was important, but they may not explain how the culture of several ethnic communities centered around corn. Their food was highly correlated to strong philosophical and religious beliefs about the origin of corn (Cornelius 1999).

There are also other implicit cultural values that may come from family experiences. For 15-year-old Gabriella, corn tortillas her mom makes are her favorite food. When she comes home from school and sees her mother making tortillas, Gabriella smiles. She and her brothers help mix and roll out the dough. Her mom places the flattened dough on the grill. The house is filled with the wonderful smell of tortillas. Gabriella knows that corn is an important part of her family's diet, but to her, making tortillas reminds her of good dinners with her family. Her teachers usually did not emphasize the community and family aspects of food. So the symbol might have been corn tortillas, but it also refers to the value of the family and her mom choosing to make it because everyone likes them so much. In addition, many people may not understand how corn is an important part of the Guatemalan culture because not only does corn continue to feed families, but in doing so it ensures that families survive (Cornelius 1999).

When people enjoy food from another ethnic group, dress in traditional clothing of another community, and sing songs in another language, they may still have little knowledge of another culture's viewpoints about gender roles, the meaning of life, what is the best way to raise children, and many other important issues. The students may feel an aesthetic connection with the music or dance that they are participating in; however, most times it takes a knowledgeable teacher to explain the underlying interpretations and meanings of the cultural elements to students so they can understand the historical, social, and belief systems that they represent. External manifestations can provide stepping stones for further comprehension and investigation into another culture, but they usually cannot represent the "culture" as understood by insiders.

When deciding upon presenting cultural information, use the examples in Table 1.1 to help you clearly identify the implicit values that you are presenting about a cultural group in your classroom lessons. The table demonstrates how a more holistic view of culture can be presented. How would you feel if a teacher in Russia taught his students that U.S. American culture dealt with eating hot dogs, going to baseball games, and wearing Levis? What would you want Russian teachers to teach about Americans (U.S. citizens)? Teachers in my classes have said they would want Russian educators to focus upon our commitment to equity, justice, and freedom, and how we have heroes, local and national, who have worked to bring the dream of equality to all Americans. Teachers could also explain how although those are our ideals, we have many families living in poverty and that we are struggling as a nation to do something about the gap between our ideals and realities of society.

Teaching culture is most difficult in a classroom where most of the children are from mainstream culture. It is often difficult for students to see that they have a culture. It can be puzzling for them to identify elements of culture because they have been taught this is what to do, how to express themselves, and how to act. It is usually easier to teach about culture when you have several different cultures in the classroom. Often cultural conflicts or issues will naturally arise; then the teacher can discuss culture as an integrated part of the curriculum.

In some of our classrooms, children bring twenty different languages and cultures to school. It is easier to bring in foods from many cultures rather than beliefs and values because presenting underlying values of a group takes a deep understanding of that culture. It is a great challenge to act as a cultural mediator, especially if students come from quite different cultural groups like Somali or Hmong, where value orientations are extremely different from the U.S. majority culture and whose countries may be historical enemies. If you are a European American, you probably will be more like the child who is an immigrant from an English-speaking province of Canada not only because of the language, but also because of the religious and political similarities of Canada and the United States. If you have little cultural knowledge of some of the students in your classes, find social workers, school liaisons, or community counselors who are willing to speak with you or members of your faculty to help initiate the process of understanding some of the cultural conflicts children face in school. You may also find cultural conflicts with children who were born in the United States, when the students come from strongly traditional Mexican American, African American, Native American, or Chinese American families. Again, cultural mediators can help you identify roots of the conflicts.

The Cultural Identity Continuum: Traditional, Bicultural, and Assimilationist

Have you ever seen people from the same cultural group disagreeing about a cultural issue? Let's say that a predominately Mexican American community is going to be cut in two by a new freeway. On one side of debate, people are concerned about ruining the community, but because a priest of the local Catholic church assured them that the city was hearing their concerns they decided not to openly fight the city. This part of the community chose several male members to work with city transportation officials. Those who decided to work with the governmental officials held more traditional values about

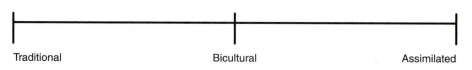

| Traditional | Bicultural | Assimilated |

FIGURE 1.1 *Cultural Identity Continuum*

authority in working with religious leaders and trusting elected officials. However, another group of people from the same community is extremely unhappy. They write letters to the newspaper and to city officials demanding a meeting. They operate from a more bicultural perspective. Those who use more mainstream techniques like picketing, holding news conferences, and testifying at city council meetings may be part of a bicultural group. They are able to function in both the ethnic community and mainstream society. When the two factions come together in a community meeting, the traditionalists and biculturalists cannot agree on a collaborative strategy.

The two groups fall on different places on the cultural identification continuum. Please see Figure 1.1. Those who are traditional follow the ways, beliefs, and patterns of the cultural group much of the time and continue to speak the native language. The bicultural members retain cultural values, customs, and ways of seeing life, yet they may have adopted practices and beliefs of the host culture. There is a third group. This segment of the community is made up of individuals who have assimilated into society and do not identify with being a member of the ethnic group. They are more highly associated with mainstream society and may take on a mainstream view that the new freeway benefits many other people, so it doesn't matter if the neighborhood is cut in half. Though cultural identity and cultural patterns are more complicated than a linear model, the model does provide an understanding of how individuals within the same community may adopt different levels of cultural assimilation (Valle 1997).

One of the key aspects of culture is language. Many traditionalists in a culture can speak the native language of the group. "Language, both spoken and written, embodies the ties that people have with one another, their culture, and their own thinking" (McNamee 1990, 288). Language is the vehicle of culture and shapes the way people receive information, think, and process information. It transfers much of the images, beliefs, assumptions, norms, and cognitive concepts of a cultural group. Today there is much discussion about language instruction. Following is a discussion of bilingualism and the importance of language instruction.

Bilingualism and Multilingualism

The United States is not only a culturally diverse nation, it is also a multilingual society. The issue of bilingualism is an important one. In the United States approximately one-third of all students come to school with a language other than English (Ovando and Collier 1998, 7). Unfortunately in many schools, students are encouraged to learn English, and other languages are regarded as secondary to English. Every student needs to learn English, but I also believe it is important for teachers to value the languages children bring to school because their language is like a cultural blanket. Students have grown up with the language and language is the most important means of communicating. It is through language that children relate to family, community members, and other important individuals. Language is also a large part of who students are and how they define themselves.

According to Bruner (1977), children learn language through their interactions with adults. Much of what youngsters learn deals with social context. The adults in their lives provide various patterns of expression, a scaffolding of interactions (Minami and Ovando 1995). For example, a mother might say to her daughter, "Can you say Mommy? Say Mommy." Then the child responds. The mother has used a simplified form of language. This form may be considered good, while in another community like the Kaluli of Papua New Guinea, youngsters are expected to speak as an adult (Minami and Ovando 1995) and so are not encouraged to speak in "baby talk." Children from various communities learn social rules. In addition, young people learn grammar, vocabulary, emotional emphasis, and meanings placed on words through their interactions with adults. When teachers understand the cultural and linguistic context that students bring to school, educators can provide more examples and links from the home to school knowledge. Native language can be effectively used to learn English. So no matter if students speak Farsi, Hindi, Somali, or Russian, a native language can act as a linguistic bridge in learning English.

Bilingualism and multilingualism should be encouraged in schools, especially with our shrinking world and the need for workers to be able to communicate with others from many other countries. A bilingual person will be able to utilize two different languages. There are also individuals who can speak and write in several languages. They are more prepared to participate in a global community because of their linguistic abilities. These days many of our problems are not local or even national, they include other nations. These issues may involve our environmental, political, and economic survival. We live in a world where a car may be assembled in Mexico, but the parts come from the United States, Korea, and Germany. The car is a global product. We live in a time where nations from around the world are part of a global system of economics. When the mark is down in Europe, people in Japan are impacted too. When the dollar is strong, then we are not able to sell as many of our goods to other countries because they cost more. This all ties into our international relationships with other countries. In addition, with the creation of nuclear weapons, countries can target distant countries. However, the nuclear fallout would impact everyone who lives on the planet. Therefore, cross-national communications is extremely critical today.

Valuing Native Languages

We have a history of teaching academic subjects in languages other than English. Ovando and Collier (1985) describe how bilingual instruction in the 1800s could be found in many schools around the country. They wrote, "During the second half of the nineteenth century, bilingual or non-English-language instruction was provided in some form in some public schools as follows: German in Pennsylvania, Maryland, Ohio, Indiana, Illinois, Missouri, Nebraska, Colorado, Oregon; Swedish, Norwegian, and Danish in Wisconsin, Illinois, Minnesota, Iowa, North and South Dakota, Nebraska, Washington; Dutch in Michigan; Polish and Italian in Wisconsin; Czech in Texas; French in Louisiana; and Spanish in the Southwest (Ovando and Collier 1985, 24). When nationalism became much more of an is-

sue and the importance of cultural assimilation dominated the nation, society began to see the importance of schools acting as places of "Americanizing" students, especially new immigrants, into the (U.S.) American way (Ovando and Collier 1985). This signaled a new direction away from encouraging and maintaining home languages.

Today, there is a definite bias in many schools about language. Why do schools offer foreign language classes for students in German, Russian, Italian, and French, but do not encourage students who bring Vietnamese or Spanish into the school community to use it? In Chapter 6, Hindeliza Flores, an elementary teacher today, describes how she and others were forbidden to speak Spanish in school. In fact, her teacher would not use the name her parents had given her. The teacher gave her a different name because she said she couldn't remember Hindeliza's name. Ms. Flores felt humiliated since so many aspects of who she was were taken away from her. The teachers in her school gave her negative messages about her family and culture by how they tried to eliminate her home language. This was extremely harmful to her developing cultural and linguistic identity. It wasn't until she was an adult that Hindeliza chose to be called by her given name.

Many schools emphasize the teaching of languages from European countries, but do not offer languages like Japanese, Arabic, Tagalog, and Mandarin. Yet, our continued success as an economic and political power rests on our ability to communicate with dignitaries and individuals from other countries. The need for multilingual citizens in the United States has become an important priority in businesses and corporations because not only will multilingual individuals be able to communicate to people across the globe, but they will also understand cultural motivations and ways of living in various markets. The comic above shows that Hector and Jeremy both understand the importance of knowing languages other than English, but that it also takes work to develop those skills.

Summary

Remember Ishmael? As the teacher who was a gorilla, Ishmael strongly suggests that we break out of our own cultural prisons in order to see other possibilities about life. What does this mean in schools? Teachers will be able to make more meaningful connections with students when they are able to see life from their viewpoints. As a cultural mediator, someone who understands the deep and surface layer of culture, teachers can create

E. Bsul

bridges between their family and/or cultural perspectives to what they are learning in schools. Students will benefit from maintaining their home cultures so they can continue to communicate with those in their families and ethnic communities, but they also can learn multiple worldviews of people from other cultural groups. This will assist them in developing respectful and caring relationships with many others.

This chapter also emphasized that culture is made up of multiple layers. As defined by Valle (1998), the three layers are language, symbols, and artifacts; customs, practices, and interactional patterns; and shared values, norms, beliefs, and expectations. It is important for teachers to understand the culture of children from a holistic orientation. In addition, one of the most important components of culture is language. Language shapes our identity, how we process information, how we interpret experiences, and how we relate to others. It is the vehicle of culture.

The United States is a multilingual and multicultural society. It is imperative that teachers understand not only the importance and power of culture, but also how to make schooling meaningful to all their students, including those who come to school with a native language other than English.

Teacher Reflections

Your journalizing will move to another aspect of Multicultural Education, which is culture. It can be extremely helpful if you could articulate clearly your own culture. The following questions are designed to assist you in thinking about your own cultural background. Please write your answers in your journal.

1. What is your culture?
   Where were you born? Where did you grow up?
   Who are your parents and siblings?
   What is your home language? Other languages you learned?
   What holidays do you celebrate?
   What is most important to you? Your career? Financial security? Friends?
   What are the values by which you try to live your life? What values do you teach your children?
   How would you define yourself?
   Do you have a religious preference? If so, what is it and what principles do you adhere to in your life?
   What are the institutions or clubs in which you hold memberships?
   What is your ethnic background? (You may be a descendant of several ethnic communities.)
   How would you describe your ethnicity?
   What is your gender? How has that impacted your growing up?
   Who are your heroes? Why did you choose them?
2. Have you seen cultural conflicts between people in your lives? Between your students in the classroom? Among your peers? With supervisors? What do they look like? Describe the situations and how you could act as a cultural mediator.
3. List some ways that you could begin to learn about a child's culture without asking the child to become the expert. Students enjoy being the expert about some aspects of their lives such as teaching you phrases like "good morning" in Tagalog or Spanish; however, a teacher can overwhelm a student by asking too many questions if the

student is not prepared to volunteer that much information about herself, her family, or her culture.

4. Case study: a teacher naturally integrating culture into the curriculum. Do you know a teacher who naturally integrates culture into the classroom without stereotyping? Describe that person to us. What does she/he do that is different from other teachers? How does the teacher infuse culture effectively and meaningfully into the curriculum?

References

Brislin, Richard. 1993. *Understanding culture's influence on behavior.* New York: Harcourt Brace College Publishers.

Bruner, Jerome. 1990. Acts of Meaning. Cambridge, MA: Harvard University Press.

Bustamante-Jones, Evangelina. 1998. *Mexican American teachers as cultural mediators: Literacy and literacy contexts through bicultural strengths.* Claremont Graduate University and San Diego State University.

Christiansen, Linda. 1997. Reading, writing, and outrage. Keynote address, National Association of Multicultural Education. October, Albuquerque, N. Mex.

Cleary, Linda Miller, and Thomas D. Peacock. 1997. Collected wisdom: American Indian Education, Boston, MA: Allyn and Bacon.

Cole, Michael. 1996. *Cultural psychology: A once and future discipline.* Cambridge, Mass: Belknap Press of Harvard University.

Cornelius, Carol. 1999. *Iroquois corn: In a culture-based curriculum.* Albany, N.Y.: SUNY Press.

Cummins, Jim. 1989. *Empowering minority students.* Sacramento, Calif.: California Association for Bilingual Education.

Heath, Shirley Brice. 1983. Way with words: Language, life, and work in communities and classrooms. Cambridge, MA: Cambridge University Press.

Loewen, James. 1995. *Lies my teacher told me.* New York: Simon & Schuster.

McNamee, Gillian. 1990. Learning in an inner-city setting: A longitudinal study of community change. In Luis Moll's, Ed., *Vygotsky and education: Instructional implications and applications of sociohistorical psychology.* New York: Cambridge University Press.

Minami, M., and Ovando, C. 1995. Language issues in multicultural contexts. In J. A. Banks and C. M. Banks, eds., *Handbook of research on multicultural education.* New York: Macmillan.

Moran, C. E., and K. Hakuta. 1995. Bilingual education: Broadening research perspectives. In J. A. Banks and C. M. Banks, eds., *Handbook of research on multicultural education.* New York: Macmillan.

Mydans, Carl. 1997. Carl Mydans. Flyer on Carl Mydans exhibition. The Studio Gallery of Old Town, 2501 San Diego Avenue, San Diego, Calif. 92110, October.

Noddings, Nel. 1984. *Caring: A feminine approach to ethics and moral development.* Berkeley, Calif.: University of California Press.

Noddings, Nel. 1992. *The challenge to care in schools: An alternative approach to education.* N.Y.: Teachers College Press.

Ovando, Carlos, and Virginia Collier. 1985. *Bilingual and ESL classrooms.* New York: McGraw-Hill Book Company.

Quinn, Daniel. 1992. *Ishmael.* New York: Bantam/Turner Books.

Sadker, Myra Pollack, and David Miller Sadker. 2000. *Teachers, schools, society.* 5th ed. Boston, Mass.: McGraw-Hill Publishers.

Sherman, Howard, and James L. Wood. 1989. *Sociology: Traditional and radical perspectives.* New York: Harper and Row.

Smith, James F. 1999. The lowly tortilla gets a boost. *Los Angeles Times,* 4 August, A1, A6.

Spring, Joel. 2000. *American Education.* 9th ed. Boston, Mass.: McGraw-Hill Publishers.

Valle, Ramon. 1997. *Ethnic diversity and multiculturalism: Crisis or challenge.* New York: American Heritage Custom Publishing.

Wang, L. 1976. Lau v. Nichols: History of a struggle for equal and quality education. In E. Gee, Ed., *Counterpoint.* Los Angeles: Regents of the University of California and the UCLA Asian American Studies Center.

Chapter 2

How Does Culture Impact Schooling?

*C*ulture impacts our schools. It influences the kind of buildings we construct for elementary and secondary schools. It shapes how students are assigned to different classes. Even teacher training comes out of a long tradition that emphasizes the basics seen as reading, writing, mathematics, and now the addition of technology. Unfortunately, since culture is like the air we breathe, we don't readily see how it impacts our lives in numerous ways. In schools, ethnic cultures of people from underrepresented groups are often ignored. The next section will discuss why that poses a problem.

Why Is Culture Often Ignored in Schools?

Ethnic culture is usually seen as a marginal aspect of schools by many educators because they do not believe it impacts learning. I spoke with a friend of mine who is an effective principal. His school won an award from the district for bringing up test scores. He told me about how his one large elementary school was divided into three small schools that shared the same campus. Class size had been reduced. The curriculum was clearly articulated between the primary school and the intermediate school. However, when I asked my friend if they considered culture in the curriculum, there was a long pause and then he said, "No, we don't do much with culture." As a person of color, I thought he might have developed a cultural thread within the school, especially since he learned English as the language of school and at home he spoke Spanish.

I believe he didn't really think much about the impact of the ethnic culture of the students. He felt the school structure that was already imposed with resource teachers in place, carefully outlined curriculum guidelines, small classes, parent training, and school policies that emphasize small schools were the most important aspects of creating an effective school. Ethnic culture was not one of them. As I talked with him, the principal explained that he believed students who spoke Spanish, Vietnamese, Russian, Somali, and Lao would quickly adapt to the expectations of the school and in doing so would make the cultural shift to English and mainstream ways. He wasn't really concerned about how the assimilation process might affect student self-image or relationships with non English speaking parents. To him, academic achievement was most important. He believed it was critical to bring up student standardized test scores. It never occurred to him what students might be giving up in the process of replacing home culture with school culture. Other teachers believe students will need to give up some aspects of culture, if students want and expect to do well in school. However the educators do not understand how the assimilation process can impact student self-identity negatively or cause students to give up home languages, behaviors, and community affiliations. Though I asked him about Multicultural Education, he said his staff didn't think it was relevant to the education of his students, because they didn't believe in holding international potlucks and the parents weren't really that interested in participating in the school.

A common misconception about Multicultural Education is that it is mainly the presentation of cultural fairs. The principal and his staff didn't realize Multicultural Education is about school reform; this includes curriculum, teaching practices, and materials that are relevant and meaningful to students. In this way Multicultural Education is a paradigm shift from a teacher-centered to a student-centered orientation.

In addition, many of the teachers at this school believed what they taught was culturally neutral. They never had the opportunity to examine how schools teach a strong mainstream culture and that many students must shift to new assumptions, beliefs, and values in order to do well in school. *it's not so much about telling students that having the highest grades is the most important, but finding out what they find important in their culture and showing them how to utilize basic subjects in that importance.*

❧ Schools Are Cultural Institutions

Culture is often ignored in schools because school personnel do not understand how schools themselves are cultural institutions. As stated in the last section, many teachers believe schools are neutral places; schools are culture free. These teachers have never questioned the structure or practices of schools. The message is that schools present life the way it should be. Yet schools are vehicles of culture that often foster maintenance of the status quo.

Schools have a culture. They hold the three layers of culture (Valle 1997) discussed in Chapter 1. Schools have symbols, rules, policies, practices, assumptions, and norms. For example, schools measure how much students have learned through performance on standardized tests. The underlying value conveyed is performance on these tests accurately describe a student's "fixed" level of knowledge. These tests are then used to "fairly" group students according to ability (Gibson 1999), though no measure is culture-free. Intertwined in this concept of testing is the value of meritocracy; those who are most gifted will do best on achievement tests (Darder 1991). However, there is much evidence to show these tests may have strong cultural biases (Darder 1991, Gibson 1999). Generally those who do well are from middle and mainstream communities, and students who are at the lower levels of achievement are from communities of color.

Schools have routines and structure too. In the morning at elementary schools, lunches are ordered. At the beginning of every high school period, attendance is taken. Most schools also have particular periods. These periods are usually set blocks of time. High school students change classes between these periods and children in elementary school go to recess based on the school-designed schedule. There is usually one teacher and many children in a class, and each class is often housed in its own room. All these elements are part of the school culture.

What would happen if students questioned various aspects of schools, from the curriculum to classroom management techniques? It would probably be a different place. Schools would vary from community to community. To some extent this can be seen with the charter movement. However, many charter schools are not really that different from most schools, except they may focus upon certain themes like technology, the performance arts, or math and science curriculum. There are Afro-centric oriented schools and dual-immersion programs for children to learn Spanish, which utilize culture as a major vehicle for education. These kinds of schools are limited in number.

School culture is not often understood by some teachers or parents. Since schooling is a common experience most of us have, we do not see it as a vehicle for the transmission of cultural values. As students we may not have seen how schools taught us certain values and beliefs. For example, much research has shown that teacher talk dominates about 95 percent of the conversation in the classroom. Teachers not only talk more often than children, they talk most of the time. In some way, this reinforces the belief that children are to be seen and not heard. Though teachers in some schools are encouraging students to be responsible for their own learning and to choose the activities they become involved in, for the most part, this is the exception in schools. If you were to visit many high schools across the country, you would probably see most students sitting in rows of about five or six students and facing the front of the classroom. The teacher's desk is located somewhere near the front or back of the classroom. All students face the teacher and this gives the assumption that the teacher is the giver of knowledge. Few people question this arrangement and what the physical layout of the classroom says about how learning occurs. Many schools are based on a teacher-centered paradigm to learning.

The most powerful reason why culture is ignored in schools is that most teachers cannot see the elements of culture in their own lives. Teachers may not understand that culture is always operating. Some cannot identify aspects of their culture. They don't see themselves as cultural beings. Many teachers believe they are individuals, not cultural beings. This is almost like a feeling that when a person comes from the majority, they are culturally neutral. As the book *Ishmael* described, culture is almost like air—we don't see it, but we breathe it in every moment of our lives. The next section examines how various cultural tools shape how we conceptualize and learn.

Cultural Tools: Analogies, Proverbs, Similes, and Metaphors

Let's turn to how cultural tools can help teachers make instruction more meaningful. Have you ever attended an interesting lecture about a theory of teaching? As you are listening, do you find yourself thinking, "That's a great idea, but how would I use this method with Maria or Brian?" This is why giving examples in which you can understand how the theory works in practice is critical to your understanding and using the principles the speaker shares. Cultural examples and comparisons can assist people in developing new understandings of how things work in another context. In the following comic strip the mother explains how long it will take them to get to their destination by using

the analogy of time as related to a television program. The mother linked the children's knowledge of television with their trip in the car.

As a teacher you might be looking for images or explanations that make sense within your classroom. There are cultural anthropologists, linguistics, educators, and psychologists like Holland and Quinn (1987) who believe that examples are elements of cultural models. Cultural models are composed of shared cultural knowledge, folk theories, and folk wisdom. Those shared values can be found in proverbs, myths, metaphors, and stories of a group. They represent fundamental themes and values in a culture.

Cultures differ from society to society. In order to understand how cultures differ it is important for teachers to understand the meaning system of a group (Holland and Quinn 1987, 3). Metaphors, similes, analogies, and proverbs are elements of that cultural meaning system. The meaning system not only includes cultural knowledge but also socially acceptable goals and motivations.

Cultural models are cognitive schemas that are shared by a group of people (D'Andrade 1987, 112). These schemas can act as tools of conformity where people learn what is desired, but these schemas can also act as bridges that teachers can use to deepen student understandings of new concepts and ideas. Using cultural tools like metaphors and analogies from the lives of students, teachers may be able to tap into existing networks of cultural knowledge, ways to solve problems, and value orientations. I believe we, as teachers, consciously need to use cultural analogies, metaphors, similes, and sayings in our teaching. Cultural models are important resources that many teachers do not utilize in their instruction to more effectively teach new content. Cultural tools can assist children to make connections, reason, and develop mental models about their world. Teachers can learn cultural models by studying the cultural knowledge, linguistic patterns, cultural behaviors, discourse patterns, and cultural assumptions of the students' communities.

Cultural models can make learning more meaningful because they tap into what children already know about the world and act as important scaffolding. This process adds to children's cognitive mapping of images and conceptual understandings of the world. Relationships become more clear to students because they may see new connections between what is being taught and what they already understand. This section of the text is written to help teachers to better understand how they can use analogies, similes, metaphors, and proverbs in their teaching to make cultural connections and provide clearer meaning to new concepts, ideas, and information. It is best to use a comprehensive cultural context when using metaphors, similes, and other examples. They were developed by a society to explain or problem solve. They represent how people reason (Quinn and Holland 1987).

Here are definitions showing the differences between analogies, similes, metaphors, and proverbs:

Analogies provide an inference about how identified objects or concepts are similar. Culturally familiar analogies can provide a bridge between one cultural context to another (Au 1990; Baker 1998; Collins and Gentner 1987; Moll 1990). Analogies present mental models of how the world works using what an individual already knows (Collins and Gentner 1987). By using existing information, people can develop new understandings about relationships and comparisons through analogical mappings (Collins and Gentner 1987).

Metaphors are words or phrases that imply a comparison; they suggest a new comparison for an object or concept. Cultural metaphors are comparisons that link one cultural context to another.

Similes show a comparison between two distinct things using the words 'like' or 'as'.

Proverbs are common sayings usually providing a belief about life.

The Use of Cultural Tools

This part of the chapter presents various similes, metaphors, and proverbs from U.S. majority culture and other cultures. I want you to think about how your own experience is shaped by these models in your own life. You may not have had the opportunity to think about how culture is part of your everyday life in figures of speech that you use automatically. Knowledge in a culture is organized, and culture gives understanding to people's experiences and beliefs (Holland and Quinn 1987).

I hope that after you have looked at these examples, you consider using cultural tools that are relevant and familiar to your students, especially those students who are from communities different from your own. Since young people learn more effectively when the materials and instructional activities make sense and are related to what they already know (Smith 1979; Moll 1990), it is important for teachers to bring in culturally familiar analogies, metaphors, similes, examples, proverbs, and sayings to make connections with them. In fact, D'Andrade (1987) found that by using concrete examples in a reasoning task, the performance of students improved. The heart of learning, according to Tobin (1991) is to negotiate meaning, that is, compare what is known to new experiences and to resolve inconsistency between what is known and what is new knowledge. Using these cultural elements can help students access their schema more quickly and aid in creating deeper understandings.

In order for teachers to tap into the cultural understandings of their students, they will need to know and have shared life experiences with their students. Cultures vary in how language and orientation of a group has shaped cultural images, whether about anger, marriage, proverbs, or other aspects of life (Holland and Quinn 1987).

Many phrases and images come from our physical world and are culturally bound. They not only bring to the mind various images from the shared cultural experience, but the images reinforce cultural values and reasoning. For example, here are some common

U.S. proverbs, which you may have heard, that express ways in which a person looks at or solves a problem (White 1987):

Every cloud has a silver lining.
The grass is always greener on the other side.
Don't make a mountain out of a mole hill.
Where there is a will there is a way.
God helps those who help themselves.
Rome wasn't built in a day.
The squeaky wheel gets the grease.
You can't have your cake and eat it too.
There's no use crying over spilt milk.

These proverbs are culturally based viewpoints. Some of the sayings have strong pictorial images using concepts like cake, milk, and grass; these images are common in U.S. culture. Proverbs are helpful to people because they appeal to a person's reasoning and are based on accepted cultural values (White 1987). The sayings represent cultural folk wisdom used to help people deal with everyday life experiences. Several of these proverbs advise people to work hard and to keep persevering. Other sayings remind people that there may not be a problem, rather it is the way a person looks at an issue. The wisdom of the other proverbs says to be patient or not to worry about things from the past.

We also use many similes and metaphors in our lives. The following is a small sampling:

Similes
run like the wind
smooth as silk
strong as a bear
cold as ice
flies like an eagle
sweet as a rose

Metaphors
Time is money.
Love is blind.
Honesty is the best policy.
Life is a journey.

Similes, metaphors, and proverbs give glimpses into how a culture uses images to create values and beliefs. In the United States, similes and metaphors are often part of everyday life. There are many people who grow roses or who enjoy them. The eagle and bear come from the history of the United States. Bears and eagles were part of the frontier environment and their images are often used to present the idea of strength and courage.

Let's look at proverbs and similes from other cultural viewpoints. The examples show important differences in how similar values are expressed. Read through the examples and see if you can understand their implicit meanings.

China: Similes (Cheng 1998)

as red as fire
as black as lacquer
as smooth as a mirror
as soft as cotton

China: Proverbs

If you lose one sheep, it is not too late to mend the fence. (Don't worry about one
    problem because it is possible to make sure that it doesn't happen again.)
A piece of rotten wood cannot be carved. (A person with a rotten heart, cannot be
    changed.)
A piece of jade needs to be polished to look beautiful. (One must struggle in life in
    order to acquire wisdom.)
You can draw the picture of a tiger, but you cannot draw his bones. (You can know a
    person's face, but you cannot know what's in her/his heart.)

Mexico: Similes (Mora 1998)

Son muy cuates. (They are such good friends as to be like twins.)
Te queda como anillo al dedo. (It fits you like a ring on a finger.)
Es más feo que pegarle a Dios. (It's uglier an act than hitting God.)
Echar la casa por la ventana. (A party or a gift that is so great, it's like throwing the
    house out the window.)

Mexico: Proverbs

Dime con quien andas, y te diré quien eres. (Tell me who you go around with, and
    I'll tell you who you are. Or you are known by the company you keep.)
Aunque la mona se vista de seda, mona se queda. (Although the monkey dresses up
    in silk, she is still just a monkey. You can't make a silk purse out of a sow's ear.)
No hay mal que dure cien años, ni enfermo que lo aguante. (There is no illness that
    lasts 100 years, nor a sick man that could last through them; or somewhat like,
    "This too shall pass.")
Al nopal lo van a ver sólo cuando tiene tunas. (No one goes to the cactus plant until
    it has prickly pears; sort of like, no one cares about you until you're rich and
    famous.)

Additional Proverbs from Mexico (Park 1998)

Cada cabeza es un mundo. (Each head is a world: Everyone has a world of experience
    within his/her mind and memory which bespeaks of a separate reality.)
La experiencia es madre de ciencia. (Experience is the mother of skill, or one learns
    from experience. Similar to English metaphor: Necessity is the mother of
    invention.)
Camarron que duerme, se lo lleva el corriente. (Animals are used in an Aesop's tale
    saying: The shrimp who sleeps will be carried away by the current, or he who
    snoozes loses.)

Puerto Rico: (Park Proverbs 1998)

No sea una mosquita muerta. (Don't be a dead fly, means: either don't be a tattletale
or don't be socially isolated.)

Vietnam: Similes (Tran 1998)

fresh as a flower
fast like lightning
black like ink (like a very dark night)
pretty as a fairy
aggressive and mean like a tiger
ugly like a ghost

Vietnam: Proverbs

You want a fairy and an elephant. (You can't have your cake and eat it too.)
Don't open your shirt for people to see your back. (Don't say bad things about
someone from your own family.)

Discussion of Cultural Tools

The metaphors, similes, and proverbs listed in the previous section are examples of cultural images and beliefs found in the lives of people in various cultural contexts. Let's
take the image of the tiger. The tiger is a symbol found in various Asian images and sayings. For example, my colleague from Taiwan shared the proverb, "You can draw the picture of a tiger, but you cannot draw his bones." This saying refers to the importance of
knowing what is in a person's heart, not only her/his physical appearance. My colleague
from Vietnam also shared an image of the tiger. In her simile, she noted that a person
might be as "aggressive and mean as a tiger." Tigers are important in the Chinese and
Vietnamese cultures. They represent strength, intelligence, and courage. Some characteristics of the tiger can be compared to the image of the brown bear in the United States.
The bear is often used in the United States to symbolize courage and natural strength.

Moving to one of the proverbs from Vietnam, a similar value can be found in the
majority U.S. culture. In the United States, some people are said to "want their cake and
eat it too." Cake is a pleasurable and important food for some people, so they want to
have and eat it too. To provide the same message in Vietnam, it is said that people want
both the elephant and the fairy. The elephant represents supreme power and the fairy represents beauty. People often want to be both powerful and attractive. However, it isn't always possible to have both at the same time.

In the section of proverbs and metaphors from Mexico, the images of the cactus
and monkey are used. Both objects are part of the folk culture of Mexico. Just like the
use of jade, cotton, and lacquer in cultural images from Taiwan, people grow up with
culturally based images and values. The proverbs from Mexico, Latin America, Vietnam,
and Taiwan show how personal integrity is an important aspect of the cultural folk wisdom of many societies. People are encouraged to develop strong character by working
hard and gaining wisdom from experience.

In the United States, African Americans have created important proverbs that are used
not only in everyday communication, but also in the lyrics of songs (Smitherman 1977).

Geneva Smitherman has written an excellent book about Black Vernacular called *Talkin and Testifyin.* She discusses how proverbs can be found in the titles of songs such as Aretha Franklin's "Still Water Runs Deep" and Undisputed Truth's "Smiling Faces Sometimes Tell Lies" (Smitherman 1977, 95). Proverbs are also important components used in child rearing in the African American community and represent African cultural-linguistic patterns that were adapted in the New World. Smitherman shared some common proverbs:

"If I'm lying, I'm flying. (Proving truth: I must not be lying, if I were, I'd be flying.)"
"A hard head make a soft behind. (Being stubborn, refusing to listen can make you
        pay a stiff price.)"
"Pretty is as pretty does. (You are known by your actions.)"
"What goes around comes around. (You reap what you sow.)"
        (Smitherman 1977, 245–246).

Think of other cultural analogies and sayings. In exploring these images, you can learn more about the shared life experiences of people from other cultures.

℘ Culturally Familiar Analogies in the Classroom

I had the opportunity to study several African American and European American teachers. They let me sit in on their classes. I was particularly interested in how the teachers naturally integrated phrases, metaphors, examples, and images into their teaching. I focused on culturally relevant analogies that made connections to the students in the classroom. The following are examples found in elementary and secondary classrooms.

First Grade: Using a Cultural Analogy

The teacher is standing at the front of the class by the chalk board. The children are sitting on a large rug. They have their reading textbooks open to a story they were introduced to the day before.

Teacher:	What are some of the ways we read?
Rayleen:	Echo reading.
Teacher:	That's when we repeat after someone else.
Teacher:	What's another type of reading?
Scott:	Silent reading.
Teacher:	How do we read silently?
Maria:	We read quietly.
Teacher:	Our lips are sealed and our eyes are reading. Your lips are closed. Your eyes are moving. This is silent reading.
Teacher:	What's another type of reading?
Paul:	**Choral reading.**
Teacher:	Clarise, do you remember what choral reading is? That's when we all do what?
Clarise:	(She looks up at the teacher and doesn't answer.)
Teacher:	Let's give her some wait time.
Clarise:	I don't know.
Teacher:	You do know. Just like when **we sing together in the choir at church,** we read together. That's why it is called choral reading.

This was an effective analogy that the teacher integrated naturally into her reading lesson. The children knew exactly what she was talking about. Many of her students attended the same church she did and they listened to the choir every Sunday. This was not a forced analogy. The example was not part of the formal curriculum. Yet, because the teacher knew her students, she easily used schema that the children already had developed to reinforce new concepts in her instruction in reading!

First Grade: Using Similes and Role Models

After lunch, children go to sit on the classroom rug at the front of the room for a story.

Example 1:

One of the girls is moving toward the rug and this is what the teacher says:

Teacher: (Teacher is smiling. Her eyes are sparkling and she is laughing warmly as she speaks.)

Becky is still dancing like she's on "Soul Train."

Becky smiles and gives the teacher a hug. The other children dance toward the rug too.

Example 2:

One of the other children is humming as she finds a spot on the rug.

Teacher: (The teacher is watching Ana and smiling at her.)

Ana sings like Diana Ross.

Ana: (Has a very wide smile across her face. She hugs the teacher and finds a seat.)

Third Grade: Sharing a Family Experience and Using a Geographical Area

This example was shared during a language arts lesson. The students had discussed Birmingham as an important place in the history of the Civil Rights Movement earlier in the year.

Teacher: I want you to think about a time when you were honored or a time when you really appreciated something. (Teacher writes *honored* and *appreciated* on the chalkboard.)

Teacher: I remember when I was young. I went on a vacation to visit my aunt in **Birmingham, Alabama.** My family spent a long time there. My brothers and sisters were really anxious to get back home.

When I got off the plane, I really appreciated being back home in San Diego.

Third Grade: Using a Cultural Simile

After a story about a couple named Trudy and Ruby in their reading textbook, the teacher brings up a familiar analogy.

Teacher:	What did Trudy mean when she asked Ruby, "Is it time to go?"
Student:	It's time to go to the mountain to die there.
Teacher:	I think she meant it's time to sell the store now and retire and buy that house in the mountains and live the rest of their days in peace and tranquillity. Now, they're making a new life again. **Life is like a circle,** they're starting over.

The following is an example of how cultural images and tools were used in a high school English class.

High School English: A Raisin in the Sun

Teacher:	Why did Lorraine Hansberry name her play, *A Raisin in the Sun?*
Linda:	I think it comes from a poem by Langston Hughes called "Harlem," where he wrote about dreams being deferred and drying up like raisins in the sun. She is referring to how African Americans have been poorly treated.
Teacher:	Why do you think Hansberry picked the image of a raisin?
Akio:	Because it is the only part of Hughes's poem that could be both a negative and a positive. It could be negative in that it is rotting and drying up in the sun or it could be sweeter because as a raisin it might be more powerful.
Teacher:	What is the main message of the play?
Linda:	When society kills your dream, it breaks you. Walter found what was important to him. It was his family and so no matter what happened in life, his family would always be there for him and he would be there for them. His dream was to be someone, to be successful. His epiphany was that he didn't need to own a liquor store. His dream turned from owning a business to being a real part of the family.
Matt:	Walter didn't want to be subservient any more. He was festering. He knew that people didn't treat him equally. Walter felt he had a dead end job. But even through all of that, he was proud of himself and didn't need the dream. He had grown past it.

These are examples of how teachers used culturally familiar tools in the classroom, which enhanced connections children made from their lives to new information. Another excellent way to integrate culture is to use examples from the neighborhood or community near the school. Knowing the community is part of building shared life experiences with your students. Do you know where your children go to the grocery store? Do you know what your students do for fun? Do you know what careers their parents, other family members, or close friends have? These are all aspects of life that can be carefully woven into the classroom. The following is a discussion of how teachers can bring culturally relevant content into a variety of subject areas by utilizing children's knowledge of the community.

Community Resources: Using Culturally Relevant Experience and Role Models

There are activities where teachers use the information and experiences of children to teach new concepts. In this way learning becomes connected to their own lives. School learning and a child's life are intertwined. Then children see more meaning in what they are learning and how learning at school is connected to their lives at home.

Teachers may take students on a community walk. Through this activity, children may be encouraged to share information they know about their neighborhood in their learning at school. Here are some samples:

For Math (Chizhik 1998)

Children may be studying various shapes and they are asked to identify and classify them.

Windows in the school (rectangles)
Sidewalk pieces (squares)
Red Button on the traffic pole (circle)
Brown bread at the bakery (circle and cylinder)
The steeple on the church tower (triangles)

For Reading and Language Arts

a. Children may be asked to bring in **newspapers** from the community. The newspapers may be sponsored by the local African American, Chinese American, or Cuban communities. They may also be newsletters from neighborhood **churches, temples,** or **synagogues.** These newspapers and newsletters may have ads from **local businesses** like:

Howard's Dress Shop
Sally's Books: An African American Bookstore
Safeway
The Cleanest Vacuum Cleaners
The Midcity Piano Tuner
The New Orleans Police Station
The César Chavez Library

High-frequency and new vocabulary words from the neighborhood can be highlighted showing children that learning occurs all the time. In addition, children can be asked to write poems, stories, and narratives about their experiences in the neighborhood.

b. Integrating social studies and language arts is a natural link. Children have been asked to identify their **landmarks** in the neighborhood (Bustamante-Jones 1998) and to use creative images in their essays. My colleagues Evangelina Bustamante-Jones, Estella Chizhik, and I talked in depth about different landmarks in the community. We picked places like the police station, the elementary school, and a church, but we noted that children chose much more personal aspects of the neighborhood. They usually had some type of emotional attachment to a landmark. Here is a sample of the landmarks children picked:

1. My Favorite Place in the Neighborhood

I look for money wherever I go. I find pennies on the sidewalk. I find more money
   under bus benches on my way home from school.
After saving up 25 cents, I put all my money in a plastic bag and stuff it in my
   pocket. I run out the door and down the street to my favorite store in the
   neighborhood.
As I walk to the store, I smell sweet things. I can't wait to get there. At the store, I
   see so many cookies, sweet buns, and little pies.
I have a hard time deciding what I will buy. Usually I buy a ginger brown pig cookie.
   It lasts a long time.
Where do I like to go? It is Maria's Bakery.

2. My Landmark in the Neighborhood

John and I played basketball every day after school. We went to the park and checked
   out basketball number 10.
I could bank it off the backboard.
John could throw it high into the air and it would fall right down into the net.
I remember we were the best team in the neighborhood.

These learning activities can also move students to consider social issues.

For Social Studies—Community Heroes

One of the most important aspects of social studies is to encourage students not only to
learn the history of their community, but about community leaders who have contributed
to the well-being of the neighborhood. Community leaders can be studied; in many communities it is possible not only to interview, but also to invite them to school. These individuals are people children know in the neighborhood, making history and the study
of communities relevant. These role models can talk about issues that the students and
parents are dealing with as citizens.

A local high school social studies classroom invited Dorothy Smith. Dr. Smith was
a former chair of the San Diego School Board. She had lived all her life in the city and
worked hard to make schools a better place for all students. As an African American parent, she knew the importance of preparing all children for the possibility of college. It
was through her leadership that a core curriculum policy was adopted in the district. Dr.
Smith was invited into the classroom to talk about her work as a professor and why the
core curriculum issue was important.

All students in the class developed interview questions. Then each student had different responsibilities. A group of students videotaped her discussion with the students
so her interview could be shown to other classes. Another group of students took notes
and wrote an article for the school newspaper about the importance of a core curriculum
so that high expectations and high levels of instruction were provided for all students.
Dr. Smith was not only a professional role model, but she was also a community role
model. She talked about growing up in San Diego and how she went from teaching high
school to being president of the school board. In addition, Dr. Smith shared with the students how she was searching her family roots. She told the students how important it is
to be proud of who one is. Dr. Smith shared her journey to a plantation in the South

where members of her family had lived as slaves. She talked about meeting the great grandson of the plantation's master and how they were making connections with each other.

Dr. Smith is a community hero. Children can identify with her because she is from the neighborhood. In addition, her personal story and her professional life helped students make connections with historical events in history dealing with issues of civil rights, slavery, equal education, and self-esteem. She also brought up many issues: How rigorous should the high school curriculum be for every student? What does it mean to be an African American? What is equal educational opportunity in schools today? How can I make a contribution to my neighborhood?

Community heroes not only provide children with important role models and connections to the neighborhood they know, but they also bring the importance of the neighborhood to learning. Dr. Smith represents and affirms the value of the local community. She is part of a cultural context that children have understanding and knowledge of through their own experiences in the community. The next section of this chapter talks more specifically about the importance of cultural context in everyday life.

❧ Cultural Context and Everyday Learning

Though it is easier to list various components of culture, it is often more difficult to describe the domains or the cultural context of learning. Many activities we are engaged in occur within the cultural context. Barbara Rogoff has studied everyday thinking and wrote, "Central to everyday contexts in which cognitive activity occurs is interaction with other people and use of socially provided tools and schemas for solving problems. Cognitive activity is socially defined, interpreted, and supported . . . For example, people seldom commit a list of shopping items to memory in preparation for a trip to the grocery store. Rather, they make use of aids such as written lists of items, they ask other people to remind them of what to purchase, or they use the grocer's arrangement of items to jog their memory as they peruse the aisles for the needed items." (Rogoff 1984, 4).

In this example, Rogoff explained, using Vygotsky's theory, how the shopper operates within a sociocultural historical context where there are specific tools and practices. Maybe the shopper is using the tools of writing things down and a calculator to decide if he/she can afford the items. In addition, the practices that are familiar help the person solve the problem; how grocery items are arranged on the shelves and various words/phrases found in the supermarket may aid one's memory. As a child, the shopper may have been taught how to shop for groceries within a cultural context using tools and skills of that culture. It was through social interactions with others like clerks, parents, and friends that the child learned to use various tools in the supermarket.

Scribner and Cole: Paying a Debt and Literacy Development

Children learn a great deal of context-specific knowledge before coming to school. Their everyday thinking has been shaped by the specific goals of the community. There are daily functions that must be accomplished and children respond to those family and community needs. Young people may be charged with doing the dishes, taking out the garbage, or sweeping the floor. Within those contexts may be specific symbols, practices, skills, and tools used to teach how to function and address the goals of family and community members.

For example, Scribner and Cole studied literacy of the Vai people in West Africa (Scribner and Cole 1981). The researchers wanted to understand the role of literacy, the use of knowledge and written language, within their specific cultural context. They found that different cognitive skills were developed from literacy used in the schools and literacy in everyday life. Many Vai who were literate had specific writing skills such as writing a letter, because in their lives, letters were written to secure payment for a debt (Scribner 1984). In this way, people used the written language to reach a specific goal; literacy had a particular function within the culture. The prior knowledge of the literate Vai was within the context of letter writing. They did not show any exceptional skill in repeating a story or remembering a list of words. However, Scribner observed that students who learned the Vai indigenous script did so more effectively by utilizing a system of learning a chain of three words at a time. Several chains would then be learned and put together. This informal observation led to Scribner and Cole's understanding of how literacy skills are shaped by the everyday needs and activities of a community or cultural group. Before this study, they had believed literacy was a set of fixed universals. After this study, they theorized that literacy represented a variety of skills and differed within various cultural contexts.

The previous example shows how a child may have certain literacy skills because they have been reinforced throughout their lives, but they may not have other skills. The children in families from the Vai community could learn strings of words quickly and efficiently because this was a commonly used method in their society. However, the Vai did not do well at repeating a story told to them or in learning a list of unrelated words. For the people in this community, work, literacy, and the written word were primarily seen in relationship to writing business letters. The purpose of their learning was clear. The context was an important aspect of shaping the way they learned.

Saxe: Economic Survival and Math Skill Development

Another example of how culture impacts cognition, comes from the work of Geoffery Saxe. As an educational psychologist, Saxe studied the way children who never went to school developed mathematical skills (1988a, 1988b). The children were 10- to 12-year-old candy vendors on the streets of Brazil. Because of the high inflation rate in the country, the value of money was continually changing. The children had to mentally convert money all the time in order to sell their candy on the streets. Saxe found that these children, who would be considered by U.S. standards illiterate and unschooled, were able to compute complex math problems more accurately than students who were formally educated.

The children who worked in the streets and sold candy regrouped large bills and added 500 + 500 and 200 + 200 + 100 in sets. The children did not need to use pencil and paper to compute these problems correctly. During the study, Brazil's inflation rate was 250 percent; children had to be able to manipulate large numbers when selling their candy and adjusting for continual changes in the inflation rate. Saxe's study found that children developed complex mathematical problem-solving strategies based on the currency system. The children had a specific goal; their goal was to sell candy and make money. The cultural context created a goal. The children were able to develop their own mathematical procedures to solve their problems and they had specific skills. As Scribner has pointed out, there are skills that are school oriented and there are skills that address the functions of a specific community. Though all learning is not culturally familiar, teachers need to understand that some children have learned much within a cultural context that may differ from majority culture. Teachers may be able to better reach children when using the culturally familiar content and contexts, which act as bridges to school knowledge and skills.

℘ Culturally Responsive Education

Research on the impact of culture has become an essential aspect of "good teaching." Educators like Geneva Gay, Jacqueline Jordan Irvine, Kenji Ima, Kathryn Au, Donna Dyle, Don Nakanishi, Karen Swisher, Joyce King, Lisa Delpit, Asa Hilliard III, Luis Moll, Janice Hale-Benson, Sonia Nieto, Michele Foster, Valerie Ooka Pang, Lilly Cheng, and Gloria Ladson-Billings have created a knowledge base of information that is extremely helpful to teachers of African American, Asian Pacific American, Latino, and Native American students. They believe educators can and must be **culturally responsive and relevant** teachers. I have listed many scholars who I believe can help you to better understand the needs of children from diverse groups. A trip to the library can be an exciting journey of new insights and effective strategies. Use these names to guide you.

Let me share with you an insight of Gilbert and Gay (1985). They explain why teachers need to be aware of culture and give an example of how it impacts the learning of African American children:

> "The means appropriate for teaching poor urban black students differ from those appropriate for teaching other students because teaching and learning are sociocultural processes that take place within given social systems. When different social systems interact, the normative rules of procedure often conflict. This is the case when the school culture comes up against the urban black culture. Many of the instructional procedures used by schools stem from a set of cultural values, orientations, and perceptions that differ radically from poor black students." (Gilbert and Gay 1985, 134)

Who are culturally responsive or culturally relevant teachers? These terms refer to educators whose manner and ways of teaching are meaningful to the children they teach. Jacqueline Jordan Irvine and James Fraser (1998) outline ways some African American teachers are culturally responsive to African American students. They suggest that teachers provide a high cultural context in their teaching. They do not suggest using isolated fragmented parts of culture. The list provides a quick overview of how teachers can utilize culture so their teaching becomes more comprehensible and relevant to students. Teachers should:

1. use rhythmic language and a call and response style of communication;
2. be highly emotional and animated in their teaching;
3. use creative analogies;
4. engage in nonverbal gestures and other body movement;
5. use aphorisms naturally in class;
6. encourage spontaneous and lively discussions;

7. integrate students' everyday personal and historical experiences into the curriculum to link past knowledge with new concepts;

8. develop strong interpersonal relationships with students using slang, jokes, or cultural phrases; and

9. teach with authority demanding respect from their students and demanding success from their students.

Teachers who understand various components of hidden and explicit culture are more likely to make connections with students. They often use all of these components naturally as part of the cultural wisdom they have acquired and developed in their teaching.

As discussed in Chapter 1, many teachers tend to integrate isolated aspects of culture into their instruction. For example, teachers may believe that integrating particular events from African American or Iroquois **history** into the curriculum is enough. Other teachers may believe culturally relevant teaching implies the reading of multicultural **children's books.** Individually these are cultural components, but when they are included in the curriculum without a context, the elements cannot provide a comprehensive worldview of a group. It is like reading one page out of a book; you don't really know what the entire book is about. You may have some sense about the book, but it is only a limited understanding. I believe culturally relevant and responsive teaching is a holistic way of integrating culture in the daily curriculum. It is natural and comprehensive. Let me give you an example of a teacher who uses cultural elements in her classroom.

I have had the opportunity to observe and talk with Sarah Gray, a first grade teacher in San Diego. Like many other teachers, she is a warm, caring person who knows her content well. Unlike many teachers, she understands the importance of culture in the classroom too.

I observed Ms. Gray teaching the basic skills like reading, writing, math, social studies, and science. During many language arts lessons, Ms. Gray writes the vocabulary on the board and explains to her students the meaning of the words before they read them in their textbooks. She models lesson activities on the board providing students with examples before asking them to do their seat work. She continually encourages her students, letting them know how successful they will be and how intelligent they are.

Her class is primarily African American. There is also a Latina, three Filipino American males, a Caucasian female, and a Caucasian male in the class of twenty-one first graders.

Part of her success as a teacher is Ms. Gray's ability to use culture in her classroom; there's almost a rhythm of teaching that occurs between Ms. Gray and her students. Geneva Gay would describe Ms. Gray and her children as being expressive in their behavior. The teacher is demonstrative in communicating with children. During a lesson, she may use many different facial expressions and clasp her hands in her lap and say, "Oooooh," in a tone so that a child knows that she doesn't approve. Her stiff stance coupled with a displeased tone is almost like she is saying, "Don't go there!" Her inflections and nonverbal behavior get the attention of her students right away and they know what she expects of them.

Ms. Gray is extremely animated. She often emphasizes words that are important. Sometimes she elongates a word and sort of sings not just says "comfortable," but C-o-m-m-f-o-r-r-t-a-b-l-e. In this way, her students know that it is an important vocabulary word or the right answer.

In addition, Ms. Gray is also very physically caring. I have observed lessons where several students got up from the rug and gave her a hug at many different times, even when she was teaching. It didn't disrupt the lesson; in fact it added to the lesson. A student would come up and hug her. Ms. Gray would then give the child a hug and go right on explaining the vocabulary or phonics lesson. It was as if they were responding to her teaching not in a verbal way, but a physical way. She allowed some movement in the classroom, but the movement was not distracting. It was almost as if the children and the teacher were part of a wonderful dance. She was able to make every child feel as if they were important at the same time. It is a remarkable ability of a seasoned and experienced teacher.

She often refers to herself as "Miss Gray" and she uses the same respectful title for her students, sometimes calling someone Mr. Matthew or Miss Penny. The students are very comfortable with her, know the rules, and are responsible for themselves.

From watching Ms. Gray, I learned how she naturally integrates culture into elements like classroom climate, classroom curriculum, classroom motivational style, and classroom management.

Summary

Culture is often ignored in schools because teachers do not understand that schools reflect specific cultural values or that they personally are expressions of culture. It is also difficult for teachers to understand the cultures their students bring to school.

This chapter was written to help you to better understand how culture can be integrated naturally into the classroom environment. Think of the cultural sayings, metaphors, or similes that you use all the time. Maybe it is as simple as a remark like, "Time flies."

The impact of underlying cultural models is still being investigated by cognitive psychologists, linguists, and anthropologists. They have only scratched the surface of the complex nature of folk theories and cultural models. The works of Dorothy Quinn, Naomi Holland, Barbara Rogoff, Luis Moll, Kathryn Au, Michael Cole, and Geoffrey White can help teachers to better understand how visual images and language schemas students bring to school are rich networks of information. There are still many more questions about cultural models that need to be researched.

After reading this chapter, you will see how you bring your culture into your classroom as the teacher and that you might want to use more concrete and visual examples from the lives of your children. Many teachers do not have similar shared life experiences with their children because they live in neighborhoods far from the school in which they teach. In addition students and teachers may have grown up in different cultures. It is important for teachers to shop at neighborhood stores, read community newspapers, and to get to know community leaders of the school area. In that way, you will be more in tune with the rhythm of life and culture of your students. Bring examples from the children's lives into your teaching. Though textbook teacher editions are excellent resources for providing you with information about learning objectives and content that needs to be taught, only *you* can bring local meaning to generic and general content.

Most textbooks are developed to be used nationally and so they do not provide local information or examples. It is up to you to enhance the instruction given in the teacher guide. Teacher guides are only that—guides, not "bibles." Teacher guides, if followed too closely, can inhibit the creativity and stifle the infusion of culturally relevant teaching.

As the teacher, you are the critical element of the instruction. Before teaching the lesson, think of additional examples you could use which are not found in the teacher manuals. This way you can give students more relevant examples, which also may spark more cognitive connections in their minds. Have fun. It can be great fun to come up with innovative analogies to insert into the lesson—analogies not in the teacher's guide. I notice when teachers bring in information about their students or the neighborhood, the eyes of their students seem to brighten. Not only do they often see more connections with the information in textbooks, but they are surprised you remembered what they told you or know about the community and feel more affirmed. Using culturally familiar teaching can help you reach those children who may now feel somewhat isolated from learning and can also serve to enhance the effective teaching you are already doing with other students!

Teacher Reflections

1. Read pages 38–42. How would you begin to identify cultural information that naturally exists in your classroom? Your classroom is probably full of many cultures. Watch and see what you find. For example, what languages do children use with each other? Are there phrases they use often? What kind of information do students share about their lives, community, and values?

2. Go to your language arts or social studies teacher's guide. Read through the next lesson you are planning to teach. Write down new similes, metaphors, or examples that bring in information about your students, the neighborhood, or community groups and provide additional examples of the information or principles you will be teaching. Today you might be able to think of only one new example, but tomorrow you might use two. It can become a habit; bringing relevant analogies to your teaching will make lessons more interesting for your students, but also for you. Write them in your journal.

3. Listen to your students as they interact. What examples do they use in their own discussions? Are any of them culturally based? Write them in your journal and keep track of them. You might be able to naturally infuse those examples, or others like them, in your teaching.

References

Au, Kathryn. 1990. Changes in a teacher's view of interactive comprehension instruction. In Moll, L., ed., *Vygotsky and education.* New York: Cambridge University Press.

Baker, Keith. 1998. Magic bullets, slate, and Stradivarius: Analogies, research, and policy making. *Phi Delta Kappan,* January, Vol. 79(5): 402–405.

Bustamante-Jones, Evangelina. 1998. *Mexican American teachers as cultural mediators: Literacy and literacy contexts through bicultural strengths.* Claremont, CA and San Diego, CA. Claremont Graduate University and San Diego State University.

Cheng, L. 1998. Private communications.

Chizhik, E. 1998. Private communications.

Cole, Michael, L. Hood, and R. P. McDermott. 1978. Ecological niche picking: Ecological invalidity as an axiom of experimental cognitive psychology. San Diego University of California, San Diego, and the Rockefeller University.

Collins, Allan, and Dedre Gentner. 1987. How people construct mental models.. In Dorothy Holland and Naomi Quinn, eds., *Cultural models in language and thought.* New York: Cambridge University Press.

D'Andrade, Roy. 1987. Folk models of the mind. In Holland and Quinn, eds., *Cultural models in language and thought.* New York: Cambridge University Press.

Darder, Antonia. 1991. *Culture and power in the classroom.* N.Y.: Bergin and Garvey.

Delpit, Lisa. 1995. *Other people's children.* New York: New Press.

Gibson, Rich. 1999. Paulo Freire and pedagogy for social justice. *Theory and Research in Social Education 27* (2): 129–159.

Gilbert, Shirley, and Geneva Gay. 1985. Improving the success in school of poor black children. *Phi Delta Kappan, 66:* 133–137.

Hanesbery, Lorraine. 1994. *A raisin in the sun: The unfilmed original screenplay.* New York: Signet Publishers.

Holland, Dorothy, and Naomi Quinn. 1987. *Cultural models in language and thought.* New York: Cambridge University Press.

Hughes, Langston.

Irvine, Jacqueline Jordan, and James Fraser. 1998. 'Warm demanders': Do national certification standards leave room for the culturally responsive pedagogy of African-American teachers? *Education Week,* May 13: 56, 42.

Ladson-Billings, Gloria. 1994. *Dreamkeepers.* San Francisco, Calif: Jossey-Bass.

Moll, Luis. 1990. Vygotsky and education. NY: Cambridge University Press.

Mora, Jill Kerper. 1998. Private communications.

Pang, Valerie Ooka, and Li-rong Lilly Cheng. 1998. *Struggling to be heard: The unmet needs of Asian Pacific American children.* Albany, N.Y.: SUNY Press.

Park, Cynthia D. 1998. Private communications.

Quinn, Naomi, and Dorothy Holland. 1987. Culture and cognition. In Holland and Quinn, eds., *Cultural models in language and thought.* New York: Cambridge University Press.

Rogoff, Barbara. 1984. Introduction. In Rogoff, Barbara, and Lave, Jean, eds., *Everyday cognition: Its development in social context.* Cambridge, Mass.: Harvard University Press.

Saxe, Geoffery. 1988a. Candy selling and math learning. *Educational Researcher, 17* (6): 14–21.

Saxe, Geoffery. 1988b. The mathematics of street vendors. *Child Development, 59:* 1415–1425.

Scribner, Sylvia. 1984. Studying working intelligence. In Rogoff and Lave, eds., *Everyday cognition: Its development in social context.* Cambridge, MA: Harvard University Press.

Scribner, Sylvia and Michael Cole. 1981. *The psychology of literacy.* Cambridge, MA: Harvard University Press.

Smith, Frank. 1979. *Reading without nonsense.* New York: Teachers College Press.

Smitherman, Geneva. 1977. *Talkin and testifyin.* Detroit, Mich.: Wayne State University Press.

Tobin, K. G. 1991. Constructivist perspective on teacher learning. Paper presented at the Eleventh Biennial Conference on Chemical Education. Atlanta, Georgia.

Tran, MyLuong. 1998. Private communications.

Tran, Thong. 1969. Vietnamese Culture—A 1970's perspective, Issue #17, Vietnam Bulletin, November, 1969.
www.destinationvietnam.com/aboutvn/culture/tranthong/tranthong17.Htm

Valle, Ray. 1997. Ethnic diversity and multiculturalism: Crisis or challenge. NY: American Heritage Custom Printing.

White, Geoffrey M. 1987. Proverbs and cultural models: An American psychology of problem solving. In Holland and Quinn, eds., *Cultural models in language and thought.* New York: Cambridge University Press.

Part Two

Multicultural Education: Framework and Concepts

Chapter 3

What Is Caring-Centered Multicultural Education?

One of my favorite educators is Herbert Kohl. Kohl is real; he knows kids. He has been teaching for numerous years and has inspired many of us. In his book, *"I Won't Learn From You,"* Kohl tells the story of when he was a kid and followed an old man in the neighborhood. Kohl was fascinated with the tattered and proud man who bought rags every week. One day, Kohl asked the man, "What are you selling?" The man turned to him with a twinkle in his eye and said, "Hope, I am selling hope."

Since this event, Kohl calls himself a hopemonger. This book is about hope too, a hope in teachers and in students. The trusting relationships of care among teachers and students can create the foundation for a strong democracy. This chapter describes how the integration of the ethic of care, sociocultural theory of learning, and education for democracy form the framework for an orientation called Caring-Centered Multicultural Education. In order to share my beliefs, this next chapter is devoted to answering the questions, "What is caring-centered Multicultural Education? What are the main principles of this framework?

❧ Moving from Multicultures to Caring-Centered Multicultural Education

Have you ever held a belief about something and then found out you were mistaken? Many years ago, I thought Multicultural Education was about presenting cultural information in schools. Just like the children in the following comic strip I had a limited understanding of culture and cultural differences.

When I read the following comic, I chuckled to myself. Don't children come up with the most creative ways of looking at life? In the lesson, the teacher carefully describes how Canada is a multicultural nation with people from many different ethnic

groups. When she asks her students about how they were the same, April comes up with an important insight. They all have belly buttons. April sees a physical sameness. She and all her classmates check out April's hypothesis; they each find their belly buttons.

As the teacher in the comic explained, the concept of multiculturalism is a complex one. What April didn't see was their cultural sameness because it is more difficult to see beneath the surface.

I find the same situation when I ask teachers about Multicultural Education. The following are examples of what they've said:

"It's about sharing culture. We, as teachers, should get kids to appreciate each other's culture."

"It's about prejudice."

"It's about good teaching."

"Multicultural Education focuses mainly on kids who aren't doing well, and in many cases the kids may be African American, Cambodian, Mexican American, or from other groups of color."

"Isn't culture an important aspect of Multicultural Education?"

Teachers have many ideas about Multicultural Education because it is a complex field of study. How would you answer the questions, "What is Multicultural Education?" "What do you think the goals of Multicultural Education should be?"

In my teaching, I find that Multicultural Education is one of the most misused and misunderstood terms in education. Many teachers come into class thinking it is cross-cultural sharing of foods and traditions; however those aspects make up only a small part of Multicultural Education. Other educators believe Multicultural

Education is primarily about eliminating prejudice in students and school personnel. Some believe Multicultural Education is about using culture as a vehicle for instruction. However for this book, Multicultural Education is seen as a field in education. The field calls for total school reform, where the achievement of children from low-income and/or underrepresented ethnic communities equals that of their majority middle-class peers.[1] See Table 3.1.

❧ What Are Some Misconceptions About Multicultural Education?

As I explained above, when I talk with educators about Multicultural Education, I find people hold a variety of misconceptions about the field. Teachers may not have had opportunities to take a class or read materials about the discipline. Some misconceptions show that people do not have a clear understanding of the goals and principles of Multicultural Education. Other misconceptions demonstrate that individuals are reluctant to examining their personal and professional values and actions for bias (with regard to areas such as culture, language, ethnicity, class, gender, disability, sexual orientation, religion, and age). Also some individuals are unwilling to change because change takes effort. Oftentimes this change requires people to give up long-held beliefs and views. Read through the chart on the next page. Do you hold any of the misconceptions listed? How did you learn these misconceptions? Are you willing to rethink through beliefs that may act as a barrier to understanding the principles of Multicultural Education?

There are other misconceptions that people hold about the field. Those discussed previously are some of the more common myths that serve as barriers to understanding what Multicultural Education is really about.

❧ Caring-Centered Multicultural Education

As the preceding section discusses, teachers must examine their misconceptions about the field because Multicultural Education is far more than an acknowledgment of cultures and cultural differences. As a discipline in education with a strong philosophical framework, it sends out a message of self and community empowerment. The philosophy celebrates the importance of education. How does Caring-Centered Multicultural Education differ from a general view of the field?

A caring-centered approach to Multicultural Education is built upon the importance of building trusting relationships and understanding the sociocultural context of learning. It is a people-centered and a culture-centered framework in education. One of the key principles of the field is its holistic perspective. Not only is teaching seen within

---

[1]Multicultural Education is an academic discipline that holds a range of views from total school reform to curriculum infusion to societal change. For more information about the views of others in the field, I suggest reading the following authors: Banks 1981; Bennett 1995; Cajete 1994; Gay 1994; Gollnick and Chin 1990; Moll 1990; Nieto 1992; Pang 1994; Sleeter 1995; Sleeter and Grant 1987; Yeo 1997.

TABLE 3.1

Misconceptions about Multicultural Education	Underlying Beliefs of Multicultural Education
Multicultural Education emphasizes separatism and causes divisiveness.	Multicultural Education builds upon our values of equity and diversity. "Unity amidst diversity" "*E pluribus Unum*"
Multicultural Education seeks to replace U.S. culture with the cultures of ethnic groups.	People from many communities including African Americans, Asian Pacific Americans, Latinos, and Native Americans are a part of, have, and continue to contribute to the development and success of this nation.
Multicultural Education is only for schools with high numbers of ethnic "minority" students or schools with racial tension.	Multicultural Education is for and about everyone because equity and diversity are important national beliefs. In fact, even groups that appear to be monocultural are diverse in regard to aspects like class, gender, and language.
Multicultural Education seeks to replace current school curriculum with Afrocentric curriculum or curriculum that opposes the dominant society.	Multicultural Education seeks total school reform so that all aspects of schools will reflect our national diversity. Schools will be effective with all students. Curriculum content can be taken from the students' lived experiences, which come from many cultural communities.
Multicultural Education encourages lower standards for students from underrepresented groups.	Multicultural Education seeks to eliminate the achievement gap between majority students and those from underrepresented communities by making schools more effective. Standards will be raised in the process. Equity and excellence are interwoven.
Multicultural Education is about food fairs, ethnic costumes, and cultural traditions.	Multicultural Education is a field in education that calls for total school reform and is built on the importance of culture (which includes language), caring, and social justice.

the development of the whole person, but also teaching is seen as a comprehensive process. Teaching is an art; it is not made up of many isolated skills. Rather, teaching is a complex combination of skills, knowledge, and beliefs that work in correlation to create an environment that encourages maximum growth in the student and the teacher. The underlying premise is that conditions of caring, community, and culture in classrooms produce higher levels of achievement that lead to greater social efficacy. This more effective learning community empowers and prepares all students to work toward social, political, and economic justice.

The Ethic of Caring

The caring-centered philosophical framework builds on the work of Carl Rogers and Jerome Freiberg (1994). They believed that the development of strong caring relationships was key to a foundation for humanistic schools. Elements that they identified were teacher empathy, positive school climate, and trusting relationships; they believed these characteristics fostered effective learning environments where students developed high self-esteem, confidence, and commitment to personal growth. In addition, other scholars have presented caring as a fundamental human capacity that translates into a coherent pattern of interpersonal behaviors rather than a romantic notion or sentimentality (Chaskin and Runer 1995; Gilligan 1982; Ianni 1996; Noddings 1984; 1992). Care represents an educational orientation that stresses the creation of trusting relationships as the foundation for building an effective academic and social climate for schooling (Chaskin and Rauner 1995; Eaker-Rich and Van Galen 1996; Erickson 1993).

One of the most important contributors to the work on the ethic of care is Nel Noddings (1984, 1992). Noddings believes education is based on a moral purpose and should produce individuals who are ethical (Noddings 1992). She writes, "We should educate all our children not only for competence but also for caring. Our aim should be to encourage the growth of competent, caring, loving, and lovable people." (Noddings 1992, xiv). When teachers operate from the ethic of care, they consciously make a moral commitment to care for and teach students and to develop reciprocal relationships with them. These teachers create schools that are centers of care.

In these schools, students, teachers, and parents form a community where relationships are at the heart of school, and where the curriculum and policies focus on compassion, respect, and community building. Students are also encouraged to care for ideas, plants, nonhuman animals, distant others, and the self. In this way the ethic of care is a holistic orientation toward education with themes of care woven throughout the curriculum. It is not only about teaching knowledge; the perspective focuses on the whole student within an empowering and compassionate environment. Teachers consider the development of the whole person, whether it is a math class, English class, or government class. Since this book is based on the importance of action, I use the term ethic of *caring* rather than ethic of care.

Noddings sees the ethic of caring as an alternative approach to education. She raises the critical questions, "If we were to start from scratch and founded schools on care, what would they look like?" and "What kind of schools do you want for your children?" Noddings reminds us that probably schools would be very different if we could build them from the beginning. The way that we might structure our schools would, in part, depend on our definition of caring.

One of the most powerful definitions that I have found about caring was written by Noblit, Rogers, and McCadden (1995). They defined caring as a value that may not be visible in an educational environment, however this value guides the interactions and organization of schools and classrooms. They wrote:

"Morally and culturally, caring is a belief about how we should view and interact with others. In this way, caring is essential to education and may guide the ways we instruct and discipline students, set policy, and organize the school day. . . Caring in our schools lies hidden beneath the technical and instrumental ways of viewing culture and schooling . . . [Though] more technical aspects of teaching dominate our thinking . . . Caring gives priority to relationships." (Noblit, Rogers, and McCadden 1995, 680–681)

The next section moves to the second important component of the caring-centered framework, education for democracy justice.

Education for Democracy

Another important component is education for democracy (Dewey 1916, 1938; Noddings 1995; Freire 1970; Gay 1994). I believe this philosophical orientation emphasizes the importance of developing individuals who will actively challenge inequities in our democracy to create a better society. Education for democracy is student-centered and facilitates higher order thinking analysis skills in students so they will examine racial inequities, class struggles, and gender discrimination (Dewey 1916; Freire 1970; Darder 1991; Gibson 1999).

Schools should be places of activity where people work on common problems and establish rules collaboratively (Noddings 1995). Education for democracy focuses on teaching students how to analyze power relationships, build collaborative communities, and encourages social communication skills. In this way schools will be places where students are actively involved in the process of democracy. "Dewey did not look at democracy merely as a system of government in which everyone votes and majority prevails. For Dewey, democracy was a mode of associated living, and decisions were made by a shared process of inquiry . . . Democracy . . . is not a state; it is more a process, and its rules must be under continual scrutiny, revision, and creation" (Noddings 1995, 35). At the base of education for democracy is the value of social justice.

One of our country's strongest values is justice. Social justice as a part of education for democracy works in tandem with the ethic of caring because both orientations hold the values of mutual respect and community at the center. What is social justice? It can be viewed in many ways, however I see it as a value where individuals look to the common good. This common good is defined by discussions people have with each other and through reflection on the needs of our members from different groups (Bellah, Madsen, Sullivan, Swidler, and Tipton 1985). It is not easy to define common good. What is common? Toward what good are we referring? In order to discuss this in depth, it would be a book itself. However, for this framework, social justice refers to the values of fairness and equality. From the work of Bellah and his colleagues, they found in their interviews of U.S. Americans across the country that justice is often seen "as a matter of equal opportunities for every individual to pursue . . . Equal opportunities are guaranteed by fair laws and political procedures . . . applied in the same way to everyone." (Bellah et al. 1985, 26) Coupled with this view is the importance of equity. Gordon (1999) calls for schools to provide for both equal access and for equity, which he says refers to addressing specific needs of students from nonmajority communities in order for them to reach the same levels of achievement as other students.

Our national value of social justice has given rise to the call for civil rights, which has led to the call for equal education of all students. Therefore, social justice directs us as a society to do all we can to effectively teach students. Unfortunately, research has shown that students from underrepresented groups do not have the same opportunities or outcomes in our schools (Banks 1995; Bennett 1995; Cajete 1994; Gay 1996; Irvine 1990; Moll 1990; Oakes 1985; Ovando and Collier 2000; Pang and Cheng 1998). This issue led to the development of the field of Multicultural Education (Banks 1995). Since teachers who care are concerned when their students aren't successful, they work tirelessly to restructure schools. In fact, many teachers believe the extensive work they do with students is part of their social activism. At the heart of the caring-centered framework is caring within a social justice context.

Cultural Deficit, Cultural Difference, and Cultural Congruence Perspectives

The third aspect of the framework deals with how teachers look at the learning abilities of students, especially the impact of their cultural background. One of the most damaging views is the cultural deficit perspective. In this orientation, students from underrepresented groups are seen as coming from culturally deficit communities. When students of color do not do well on standardized tests or in mainstream classrooms, some teachers label the culture of students' families as being "disadvantaged." The blame for student failure is placed on children and their families and cultures. Some teachers blame students because they come to school speaking another language like Spanish or Cantonese. Other teachers complain that the culture children bring to school did not value education; it is as if school personnel held little responsibility for the low grades and low standardized tests scores of students of color or students from lower-income communities.

In contrast, other educators believe students may come from ethnic communities that have knowledge and values that differ from mainstream society. Those with a cultural difference perspective believe the worldviews of some students may clash with school culture. For instance, when Hmong refugees came to the United States from Laos during the Vietnam War, many had a preliterate tradition. Most did not have any formal schooling. So when young Hmong students went to school, they did not know what to expect nor did they know what was expected of them. There were many cultural clashes. Hmong young people were expected to know how to sew, grow crops, and take care of their families. They did not know about school bells or homework. Parents were reticent to participate in school programs because they did not understand their purposes. Also parents believed they did not have the professional training needed to help their children. They respected teachers and relied on them to do the best for their children. This did not mean that the Hmong parents were ignorant. Rather, they brought different skills to this country. For example, Hmong families brought a strong sense of community. In fact, children are taught collective responsibility; the needs of the family are more important than the needs of individual members.

King (1994) believes that the cultural difference theory still calls for the resocialization of students of color, especially African American youth, to mainstream culture because school personnel have not changed their value orientation. The knowledge and processes currently used still emulate mainstream society. King carefully explains that since mainstream society (including social institutions like schools) has continually oppressed African Americans, schools must be transformed from organizations of oppression to institutions of liberation. The entire system of education should be reorganized so that it challenges the status quo and calls for emancipation of the mind of all students. The inclusion of African American cultural knowledge would give all students a sense of presence of the African American community.

In collaboration with King, Au and Kawakami (1994) agree that schools should strive to be culturally congruent, however their view is less political in orientation. Though they do not believe schools must imitate the home setting of students, they do feel that schools must integrate knowledge and practices from students' home cultures. Au and Kawakami (1994) give the example of using communication styles in the classroom that may be more familiar to students. Their research has focused on young people in Hawaii. Many Hawaiian students were quiet and did not participate in discussions. However when the teachers saw the children in other contexts, they were playful, laughing, and spontaneous. Why weren't they talking in class?

Au and Mason (1981) realized that there were probably more than one reason that students were not naturally participating. Since they believed that learning occurred in socially constructed activities as Vygotsky posed, they looked at how social context impacted the reading process and researched the Hawaiian cultural practice called *talk story* (Au 1980). As part of the reading comprehension instruction, they found one of the teachers used a more culturally congruent practice allowing for spontaneous responses. This teacher did not use the mainstream practice of calling on each student as a way of being fair. Au and Mason realized that student responses were more on task and logical when the teacher used the *talk story* format of discussion. Why did this happen? When students worked collaboratively, they built on each other's responses. The social and cultural context of learning encouraged them to work together. So in this instance the social interaction practice that the teacher used built on what students already were comfortable with and encouraged them to participate more fully.

It is critical for teachers to have knowledge of students' culture, and I believe Vygotsky's sociocultural theory of knowledge construction explains how culture impacts human development. In the next section, a short discussion of his theoretical ideas will be presented. Think carefully of how you see them work in your own experiences.

Sociocultural Theory of Cognitive Development

Vygotsky saw learning embedded in sociocultural activity (Moll 1990; Cole 1996). How do we learn? We learn within social and cultural contexts as we interact with other people, ideas, and objects in our lives. He saw speech as key to our intellectual growth. Have you watched a baby coo or babble? The baby is developing her language as she interacts with her environment (Elliott, Kratochwill, Littlefield, Cook, and Travers 2000).

Michael Cole, who has studied Vygotsky's work extensively, discusses why language is one of the most important tools we use in learning. He explains that we use cultural "tools" like language and cultural expectations to mold, shape, and filter what we think. Cole believes tools, like language, ideas, customs, behaviors, and practices, act as cultural negotiators for us and shape our learning.

Learning is also historical. There have been many people who have come before us and our cultural knowledge is built upon what they did in their lives and taught us (Cole 1996). Culture is accumulated over time and is handed down from generation to generation over many years, parent to child. Since people change, culture is also changing and continually being reconstructed.

Through the many sociocultural interactions we have, we learn. Sometimes our learning comes from inner reflection and other times it comes from working with people or ideas or objects. Some teachers create powerful communities of learners, where individuals work together giving those who participate more opportunities to learn from each other. The discussions and nonverbal communications that pass between people not only convey ideas and concepts, but also there is a social process. This social process may be formal, casual, or spontaneous; this context also impacts learning. When we bring different cultural experiences and viewpoints to the discussion, we can enhance our own learning and the growth of others. Cole (1996) suggests that cross-cultural teaching is like a bridge. "I would choose a bridging program in which traffic on the bridge moved in both directions . . . the bridge is a medium for two way exchange. . ." (Cole 1998, 3) We live in a diverse society and the diversity of our students can enrich our schools. When there is reciprocal sharing of perspectives, information, ideas, and practices, learning will be expanded.

Let me give an example. When a fourth-generation Japanese American tenth grader shared her family tree project, the other students learned about how the young girl's grandmother had been placed in a concentration camp in Idaho. Her peers were surprised to learn that the U.S. government took their own citizens who were of Japanese ancestry away from their homes to desolate camps in desert areas in states such as Idaho, Wyoming, and California. The student's grandmother had never been to Japan and was born in the state of Washington. The classmates of the young girl had the opportunity to learn in a personal way how history involves people they knew. The granddaughter provided a bridge for other students to better understand the experience of the Japanese American community. This discussion added to the social cultural knowledge of the classroom. In addition, sharing was beneficial to the Japanese American student, because the class asked her grandmother to talk to them. She learned more about what her grandmother went through as a result of her presentation to her classmates.

Vygotsky's sociocultural theory of development recommends that teachers utilize cultural knowledge, carefully developed social interactions, and activities to heighten learning. Research by Cole, Moll, Au, Gonzalez, Brice Heath, Moses, and many others demonstrate that students can learn more effectively using a comprehensive orientation toward curriculum and instruction that simultaneously uses cultural knowledge, cues, social interaction patterns, and cultural models from the lives of students. Later, in chapter 9, I will provide three excellent programs utilizing culturally relevant teaching. They are the Algebra Project, Funds of Knowledge, and Organic Reading and Writing. All three programs use a holistic approach. They have a powerful value orientation upon which the curriculum is built.

It is also not possible to use culturally relevant teaching without addressing the issue of institutional oppression. As King (1994) reminds us, some children come from cultural communities who face continual and historical social oppression. Oppressive practices are also cultural tools that people utilize in their lives. As this book has presented, prejudice, personal and institutional, hampers our ability to reach all students. Stereotypical cultural knowledge that we hold about others must be purged from our minds, but it may take numerous sessions of self-reflection and continual interactions with people who appear to be different from us, to assist us in realizing the fallacies of our beliefs and to find common ground with others. In this way, those who assist us in better understanding our own misconceptions are extending our zone of proximal development. Vygotsky theorized the zone of learning can be increased when teachers use effective strategies and materials to guide student learning beyond what a person could learn on their own. Chapter 9 will discuss this phenomenon more fully.

Caring-Centered Multicultural Education: A Definition

Now that you have read about the ethic of caring, education for democracy, and cultural theories of learning, how would you define Caring-Centered Multicultural Education? Building on the previous discussions, I offer the following definition:

> Multicultural Education is a field in education that calls for total school reform and is based on the belief that education is an intellectual and ethical endeavor. The field seeks to develop happy, creative, ethical, and fulfilled persons who work toward a more compassionate and just society. Multicultural Education, as part of a life-giving process of growth and joy, focuses on teaching the whole student with the goal of academic excellence and developing the potential of each student by integrating three critical belief systems: the ethic of caring, education for democracy, and the sociocultural context of human growth and development.

What does this mean in the life of a student? Let me ask you, who was your favorite teacher? What did the teacher do? How did the teacher treat you?

When I ask these questions of teachers in my classes, they say:

"She was a teacher who believed in me even when I didn't believe in myself."

"He understood my fears and helped me to see that I could do the math problems and that it wasn't my X chromosomes that held me back."

"She knew there was a lot of racism in the school from all the kids, Black, Asian, Latino, White. She wouldn't let other teachers shove it under the rug, but she also wouldn't let us use it as an excuse not to be the best we could be. She pushed us hard to do our work."

"I came from a poor part of town. I thought my teacher wouldn't like me because of that, but instead he wanted me to write about my life, like the problems I was having paying the rent and finding a job after school. I knew he cared."

These comments show that their favorite teachers believed in them and showed they cared. There was a shared relationship of trust between teachers and their students. Teachers expected them to do their work and supported them. Their favorite teachers accepted them for whoever they were and valued the contributions each student brought to the classroom. When students strongly identified with a culture or a language other than English, teachers saw these elements as enriching and celebrated them. Through an atmosphere of respect, caring, and community, teachers and students developed bonds of trust, and they also shared values of fairness and equality. Students and teachers knew that people were prejudiced and they dealt with discrimination and biased attitudes as part of their writing assignments and class discussions. Life was part of the learning process. These teachers considered the needs of the whole student.

What else can teachers do to create strong relationships with students? They can develop bonds of connection and communication. Teachers may not only listen carefully to their students, but they may also see themselves as members of the community. For example, teachers may buy their groceries at the local supermarket. They may also go to the neighborhood church. Sometimes teachers attend local community festivals. They may also hold parenting classes in Spanish or Vietnamese. Educators who develop lasting bonds also get to know parents and view parents as critical partners. Parents and teachers may both run a "Saturday school" where students may be part of math, science, or literacy clubs.

I believe what sets exceptional teachers apart from others is that these "star teachers" (Martin Haberman's (1995) term for exceptional urban teachers) understand their students. They know that their most effective teaching will occur when they build relationships of trust with their students, and keep trying until they find instructional strategies that work so their students achieve academic excellence. Both teachers and students are responsible that learning occurs; learning is a reciprocal responsibility. Teachers never give up on their students or themselves (Haberman 1995) and students also believe in and have faith in their teachers.

The teachers described above have made a moral commitment to care. I imagine the following self talk:

"I'm going to make a difference in the lives of my students."
"I believe in every child, no matter what their color is or how much money their
    families have."
"I know there are many inequities in school and society, but those obstacles will not
    keep me from finding ways to reach my students."

Teachers who make that important difference in schools have made a conscious choice to provide the most effective and motivating learning environment they possibly can.

STAR TEACHERS MAKE A MORAL COMMITMENT TO CARE.

This commitment is not an easy choice. Jonathan Kozol, in his book, *Savage Inequalities,* writes about the terrible conditions some students and teachers endure in schools. These schools are primarily found in inner cities. The bathrooms don't work, the ceilings are falling down, and it is so cold in the winter that students and teachers can see their own breath. Educators fought to make changes in schools so that children have textbooks; they painted the classroom walls, and they prevented drug dealers from hanging around schools. They are star teachers.

As star teachers, they not only care for students, but they are aware of the life experiences of their students, including cultural background, language needs, economic hardships, personal struggles, and community issues. These teachers see inequities in schools and society that hamper the education of students, however these inequities are not used as excuses for not learning. Rather, teachers work to rid their classrooms and schools of the ugliness brought about by racism, sexism, classism, and homophobia. They listen to their students and integrate the students' own lives—knowledge, experience, and culture—into the curriculum. They also respect their students and believe they can learn; teachers present students with challenges and hold high expectations in the learning process. Students are given opportunities to learn and, in this way, they understand that learning is a reciprocal responsibility.

Teachers know that students can learn and hold high expectations for them. Students are not enabled, rather they are supported and held accountable for their own learning (Pidgeon 1998). Learning is a two-way responsibility. Teachers must care enough to provide effective, interesting, and well developed learning experiences, and reciprocally students must study and work hard in order to become successful in their learning. Teachers know that they cannot take away the struggle that comes when learning is difficult; however, star teachers assist their students as they work through these hard times. They do not give up on their students. These teachers offer support by using strategies such as offering extra tutoring times after school or providing additional study materials.

Star teachers find ways to reach students so that they are successful in school. For example, a teacher may demonstrate a chemical process using three different modes of learning to ensure that students who do not do well with a self-inquiry method will understand the operation: first, the teacher uses a large colorful poster that explains the chemical process; second, the teacher shows students on computers a three-dimensional visualization of the molecules for those students who need spatial pictures; and third, the teacher conducts the experiment and explains the process as she demonstrates it. Then students conduct the experiment themselves. Some students are able to extrapolate the scientific principles of an experiment using the scientific method and with minimal direction. Other students may need different organizers in order to understand what is occurring. When teachers provide numerous ways to view the chemical process through drawings, computer-generated models, and teacher demonstrations/explanations, students can develop a clearer understanding of the chemical principles being taught.

This book is founded upon a model that centers on the ethic of caring, education for democracy with a strong social justice core, and the sociocultural context of human development and learning. As Figure 3.1 shows, all three elements are key building blocks. The ethic of caring forms the base for Caring-Centered Multicultural Education and interwoven with education for democracy and the sociocultural context of human development and learning, form the foundation for the framework.

Caring-Centered Multicultural Education is based upon three important beliefs:

• Many of us care about children.
• Every child possesses an innate desire to learn.
• Education should reflect a life-giving pedagogy. (Rivera and Poplin 1995)

Schooling is not only a life-giving process of growth, but it builds upon children's innate wonder of the world. They are excited learners who achieve and find joy in learning. Like the chick in the comic on page 63, schooling breaks out of a rigid and monocultural shell and becomes a positive life force where teachers and students care for each other and work toward a just and caring society.

In the context of this book, the chick also represents the transformation of a child when she/he learns. When a child learns, she is not a passive being, but becomes an empowered being in a democracy who thinks, questions, and creates. The chick can also symbolize us as teachers. We become transformed when we make a paradigm shift from a teacher-centered, monocultural classroom toward a student and caring-centered orientation about teaching. We understand that teaching is about breathing life into our classrooms and learning is an exciting process of personal and communal growth.

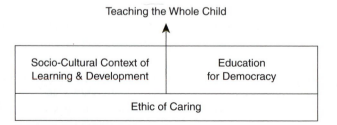

Figure 3.1   *Framework for Caring-Centered Multicultural Education*

ᘛ *Social Justice and the Ethic of Caring*

In the past ten years, there has been a much-heated debate about Multicultural Education, most of which has been political. The conservative camp claims that Multicultural Education is divisive and un-American, while liberals claim that Multicultural Education can ensure equality in our schools. Unfortunately, the discussion often has been diverted from the needs of our students and into the realm of political debate. This clouds the field's most important goal of all students achieving academic excellence. Our main focus must be to close the achievement gap between children from low-income and/or culturally diverse communities and their majority peers.

Caring and social justice in a democracy are intimately connected. When we care, we act. Our laws, policies, politics, and methods for achieving social justice flow directly from what we care about and are committed to in society. Bell hooks reminds us, "The civil rights movement was such a wonderful movement for social justice because the heart of it was love-loving everyone." (hooks 2000, 36). Caring is more fundamental than justice, fairness, and equity. When we care about another person, we will find ways to treat that person justly, fairly, and equitably. But the reverse is not always the case, one can value justice, fairness, and equity, without truly caring or doing things to make life better for others.

Let's look at laws and schooling. Laws do not explain how to accomplish directives in education. For example, using Supreme Court decisions like *Brown v. Board of Education* or *Lau v. Nichols* and civil rights legislation as the foundational principles for an educational field is misguided and leads the field to an educational dead end. Why? Congress and judges recognize that their job is to make and interpret laws rather than to teach educators how to bring compassion, equity, trust, and effective teaching methods to the classroom (Valle 1997).

Policies and the law are representative of our core values; they are merely the context and tools for expressing and manifesting our values and goals from which we work to show caring and to improve society. I have seen that policies and the law can, by themselves, have only a limited influence on learning. Laws and policies do not change the real core of schools, people do. Caring is that important link between fair laws and effective policies within education.

CARING IS A FUNDAMENTAL HUMAN CAPACITY

Caring is a powerful force behind true political and legal reform, both from the right and the left. The ethic of caring is the essential foundation for Multicultural Education, and a central element of our commitment to students; this commitment motivates people to rid

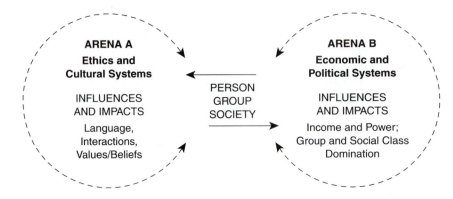

Figure 3.2 *Arenas of Multicultural Interaction and Impact*

schools of prejudice and discrimination. Caring also inspires us from a personal level to incorporate in our daily outward actions culturally relevant practices that make schools more meaningful, effective, and equitable. Caring teachers are willing to tackle painful inequities in schools and take hard looks at our own beliefs because we have made an ethical commitment to our children to make schools more relevant and effective for all kids. Unfortunately, schools are too often a reflection of a society where people are oppressed because of their race, class, gender, sexual orientation, language, and other differences.

Ray Valle (1997) has created a figure that explains there are two major arenas in society that should be considered: political and cultural. His first arena is made up of economic and political systems and includes social class, income levels, social status, and political status. His second arena is made up of ethnic and cultural systems. From one generation to the next the values, language, attitudes, and beliefs of cultural groups are transmitted to their members. The interaction of both arenas, culture/ethnic systems and economic/political systems impacts the way individuals and groups respond to each other. Figure 3.2 may help you to better understand that both dimensions are important in understanding how different social forces impact what people think, do, and value.

Fundamental Beliefs of Caring-Centered Multicultural Education

I have discussed the importance of caring in depth. What does caring mean in the classroom and in school? The following are underlying beliefs about caring in teaching and learning (Pang and Rivera 1998):

- Relationships are reciprocal and built on trust.
- Trusting relationships form the basis and context for teaching and learning.
- Teachers and students feel an interconnection with each other. Each is concerned with the well-being of the other and within this context a community of learners is created.
- Intellectual development is seen through diverse lenses and stimulated through diverse methods.

- Culture is an intimate aspect of how many students identify themselves, define themselves, value, behave, and are motivated; their sense of being may be culturally rooted.
- Caring for others can lead to social justice. We want fairness for those we care for on a personal level. We still believe in social justice for those with whom we do not have a personal relationship, because we care for the humanity of the individual and larger community.
- Caring students develop a capacity to feel, see, or view the world from someone else's perspective, which promotes problem-solving and academic skill development from a community orientation.
- The teacher feels a part of the community and shares life experiences by participating in the community where she/he teaches.
- The teacher along with students create a democratic classroom.

As a core element of Multicultural Education, caring is not only a value that motivates, but also acts as a compass that guides our way. In this analogy the compass directs us through politics, law, the economy, our society, toward a humane, democratic community. No matter whether one is a Marxist, conservative, critical pedagogist, conservative, feminist, constructivist, progressive, perennialist, multiculturalist, or one of many other professional orientations in the field of education, caring should always be a critical component for good teaching. A strong, healthy ability to care will motivate and guide teachers to be open and flexible so they can be more effective, rather than become set in a particular political ideology or teaching method.

Table 3.1 presents beliefs and practices of four different types of teachers. All four teachers could be found in the same school. They do not represent personality types, rather they exemplify different educational philosophies. I believe the first two teachers, the assimilationist and human relations educators, represent the status quo in education. The other teachers, the social action and caring-centered educators, both believe in Multicultural Education and understand the importance of culture. They share many values, but also have different perceptions. Please read through Table 3.1 and think about their diverse orientations.

T A B L E   3 . 2

Comparing Four Teachers
The Assimilationist, the Human Relations, the Social Action Multiculturalist, and the Caring-Centered Multiculturalist

Assimilationist Teacher	Human Relations Teacher	Social Action Multiculturalist Teacher	Caring-Centered Multiculturalist Teacher
Overall Societal Goal	**Overall Societal Goal**	**Overall Societal Goal**	**Overall Societal Goal**
Overall societal goal is to teach the basic knowledge and skills of reading, writing, mathematics, and technology, which students will need in order to become responsible citizens and fit into the mainstream.	Overall societal goal is to teach the basic skills and knowledge of reading, writing, mathematics, and technology and to promote social harmony, unity, and tolerance so students become responsible citizens in society.	Overall societal goal is for all peoples and cultures to experience equality and justice and therefore a lack of oppression. Goal of schooling is to prepare all students to make changes in our society so that it is a socially just community.	Overall societal goal is to value and build a multicultural society based on compassion, justice, and freedom. Goal of schooling is to develop compassionate and fulfilled individuals who achieve their full potential within a community of learners who work together to create a more just society.
Assimilationist	**Human Relations**	**Social Action**	**Caring-Centered**
What Is Excellence?	**What Is Excellence?**	**What Is Excellence?**	**What Is Excellence?**
Excellence means all students are to learn the canon of knowledge as set forth by a monocultural and Western tradition. The curriculum is subject-centered and focuses on a liberal arts education. There is a body of knowledge that all students should master. The teacher	Excellence means all students are to learn the canon of knowledge as set forth by a monocultural and Western tradition. The curriculum is subject-centered and focuses on a liberal arts education. There is a body of knowledge that all students should master. The teacher is	Excellence is interconnected to equity. Equity means freedom from bias and favoritism. Question status quo measures of excellence. If students do not have equal access and outcomes in schools, then excellence cannot occur. Schooling is seen through an equity/political and	Excellence and caring are integrally related. Caring forms the foundation for creating an atmosphere of excellence. Caring means an ethical commitment to the well-being and success of each student. Caring focuses on reciprocal relationships and the building of community. Schooling is

TABLE 3.2

is the authority in the classroom and directs the learning in the classroom. Students are taught to conform to the values of society. The classroom is teacher-centered and teacher talk dominates classroom activities.

the authority in the classroom and directs the learning in the classroom. Students are taught to conform to the values of society. Limited schoolwide programs focus on diversity and racism. Posters may include, "Unity amidst diversity." The self-esteem and self-identification of students is seen as important.

fairness lens. It is a rights-centered view of education. Emphasis is placed on educational equality, equal rights, and changing the social structure. Teacher discusses classroom relationships in terms of rights and responsibilities of citizens/children in the classroom of each other. It is the duty of students as members of a democracy and as citizens to be respectful to each other in the classroom. Posters in the room may include, "Dignity is not negotiable" and "You have the right to ask for help. You have the responsibility to assist."

seen through a caring/ethics lens. Emphasis is placed on building trusting relationships in the classroom between the teacher and students and each other within the context of cultural diversity. As part of relationship building, teachers and students care for each other and are responsible to each other. Students and teachers listen to each other without judgment and provide constructive assistance. Students celebrate each other and who they are. Teacher talks about the importance of civil and human rights within the context of caring and human interconnections. The teacher cares and so respects and supports the rights of others. Posters in the room may include, "Smiles are contagious" and "Pull together."

(*continued*)

TABLE 3.2 (CONTINUED)

Assimilationist	Human Relations	Social Action	Caring-Centered
Key Beliefs	**Key Beliefs**	**Key Beliefs**	**Key Beliefs**
Excellence is promoted by having high standards and a belief in meritocracy. Competition and high achievement is encouraged. The focus is the cognitive development of students. Questions students address may be as follows: How can students better prepare for their tests? How can students be encouraged to become more disciplined?	Cross-racial relationships are valued. Students are encouraged to work together cooperatively in groups to overcome personal social bias due to group membership. Questions students address may be as follows: How can we make our schools a place where everyone feels accepted and belonging? How can we be peacemakers? How can we support each other?	Equity and social activism are promoted in part through actively practicing democracy in the classroom and school, helping students learn how to analyze inequalities in their own lives, training students to develop and use social action skills, and helping students learn to form coalitions to eliminate oppression. Questions students address may be as follows: Who makes the decision? Who has the power? How can the status quo be changed? Whose perspective is being taught?	Caring is expressed in part through getting to know about students' lives both in school and outside of school, talking with children, listening to them, meeting their parents and families, developing trusting relationships with students, sharing power in the classroom, and building a community. Social justice is taught through lens of caring. Respect is one of the key values in the classroom and lack of fairness can be one of the most negative influences in a school. Questions students address may be as follows: What does prejudice look like in a school? What does caring look like in a democracy? How can we develop empathy with others? What does caring look like in different cultures? How are caring and social justice related?

T A B L E   3 . 2

Assimilationist Curriculum	Human Relations Curriculum	Social Action Curriculum	Caring-Centered Curriculum
The curriculum is organized around traditional Western knowledge. Students are seen as sponges that soak up the knowledge teachers teach. Intellectual development involves a focus on "basic" subjects like mathematics, science, English composition and literature, reading, and writing.	The curriculum is organized around traditional Western knowledge. Students are seen as sponges to draw in the knowledge teachers teach. Intellectual development focuses on "basic" subjects like mathematics, science, English composition and literature, reading, and writing. There is a limited emphasis placed on social bias and the societal walls that it creates. Includes schoolwide programs focusing on tolerance and respect of cultural diversity.	The curriculum is organized around current social issues involving oppressed and underrepresented groups, reflects the experiences and perspectives of many different cultural groups and voices, uses the context of students' life experiences to analyze oppression, and teaches critical thinking and social action skills. Social justice issues primarily center on bias due to racism, ethnocentrism, gender and cultural bias, classism, homophobia, language discrimination, and religion.	The curriculum incorporates a wide variety of content and the emphasis is consistent with an overarching theme of respect, honor, compassion, and justice for all people. Teacher naturally integrates students' life experiences and social issues impacting their lives into teaching. Culture is a key element of the curriculum. Teacher provides feedback for each child in content areas and as a caring teacher is sensitive to the need of some students for the teacher to approach the student when student is having problems so student can maintain peer group respect. The teacher knows how peer, ethnicity, and neighborhood culture can be integrated into the curriculum.

(continued)

TABLE 3.2 (CONTINUED)

Assimilationist	Human Relations	Social Action	Caring-Centered
Fundamental	**Fundamental**	**Fundamental**	**Fundamental**
Direction For Curriculum	**Direction for Curriculum**	**Direction for Curriculum**	**Direction for Curriculum**
Fundamentally believes that there is universal and permanent knowledge that should be imparted to students. The curriculum of schools focuses on transferring basic knowledge to children and the development of a rational mind.	Fundamentally believes that there is universal and permanent knowledge that should be imparted to students. The curriculum of schools focuses on transferring basic knowledge to children and the development of a rational mind. There is some focus on coalition building between racial groups to overcome social isolation.	Fundamentally believes that people will never be able to change until societal institutions change, so directs limited educational resources toward equipping students to become citizens who actively work to challenge and change oppressive aspects of social structures so they are more equal, democratic, and just. Much emphasis is placed on discussion of power relationships.	Fundamentally believes that individuals and the society in which they live create a family of learners. Believes it is critical for students to feel part of and contribute to making social institutions and individuals within society compassionate and just. Cultural knowledge is naturally integrated into the curriculum.

Assimilationist	Human Relations	Social Action	Caring-Centered
Discipline	**Discipline**	**Discipline**	**Discipline**
Teachers and administrators handle discipline. Rules for behavior come from the teacher or school rather than students.	Though most discipline is handled by teachers and administrators, schools may have peer mediators available for students to talk with about altercations and other academic/social relationship issues.	Handles classroom discipline by involving students in democratic decision-making. Teacher teaches responsibilities and duties of citizens and allows students to practice these skills in the classroom. For example, procedures for such things as when and how students leave the room for bathroom breaks are determined by majority vote.	Handles classroom discipline by assessing the unique needs of the students in the classroom. Teacher shares control of the classroom with students. Teacher is in control by not being controlling. Teacher teaches students how to care for themselves so they do not need to be managed. She also believes in building democratic skills in students,

TABLE 3.2

but first works to develop in children an empathy for others and respect for themselves. Much discipline is handled one-on-one and not in front of the class because teacher respects the emotional needs of students and does not embarrass or challenge students before others.

Assimilationist	Human Relations	Social Action	Caring-Centered
Staffing Patterns	**Staffing Patterns**	**Staffing Patterns**	**Staffing Patterns**
Staffing patterns reflect the majority population. Little emphasis is placed on diverse role models.	Staffing patterns reflect the majority population; however, there is a limited sensitivity to the need for cultural role models for all students.	Prefers to work in a school in which staffing patterns include diverse racial, gender, and persons with disabilities in traditional/nontraditional roles.	Prefers to work in a school in which staffing patterns address the needs of all students, and believes in balance of intellectual diversity as well as cultural diversity on the faculty.
Assimilationist	Human Relations	Social Action	Caring-Centered
Instructional Strategies	**Instructional Strategies**	**Instructional Strategies**	**Instructional Strategies**
Most learning is in lecture style. Much of the homework is done individually. Standardized testing is extremely important because performance indicates knowledge learned and ability to think.	Most learning is in lecture style. Much of the homework is done individually. Standardized testing is extremely important because performance indicates knowledge learned and ability to think.	Uses cooperative learning for much of the classroom work and avoids testing and group procedures that would result in some students being seen as failures. Students are often involved in community service projects.	Uses a variety of learning and assessment techniques with sensitivity to the personal and academic needs of each of the students. This may include demonstration, roleplaying, field work, and community service.

(*continued*)

TABLE 3.2 (CONTINUED)

Assimilationist	Human Relations	Social Action	Caring-Centered
Critical Obstacle	**Critical Obstacle**	**Critical Obstacle**	**Critical Obstacle**
Sees the biggest obstacle to student success as a lack of student discipline or lack of positive influences in child's background.	Sees the biggest obstacle to student success is existence of stereotypes and individual prejudice.	Sees the biggest enemy to student success as institutional and social oppression.	Sees the biggest enemies to student success as 1) lack of personalized caring attention and 2) lack of inclusion of effective strategies that are sensitive to cultural differences.

❧ Analyzing Critical Differences Between Four Teachers

I chose four different types of teachers to show the differences between two teachers who have little knowledge of Multicultural Education and the issues of equity and culture and two teachers who have more knowledge of the field.

Here is a description of four female teachers, notice the differences.

The Assimilationist Teacher

The assimilationist teacher supports the status quo of schools. Her teaching style is more directed and teacher-centered. She has students sitting in rows facing the front of the classroom. There is student work on the bulletin boards. The teacher usually stands at the front of the room lecturing or directing the learning. As the authority of the classroom, she has a set schedule in her class and has certain periods for each subject that she teaches. Much of the curriculum she uses comes directly from her teacher manuals and textbook guides. Her viewpoints for the most part reflect a monocultural, Western tradition. There is a strong sense of teacher control in this classroom.

The teacher-centered orientation can also be seen in the words the teacher uses to call on her students. When students come to her class and she doesn't know how to pronounce names, she chooses substitutions (Perrone 1998). For example, a young man named Jésus was called Jessie. Another child, whose name was Vito, became Victor and Yin Mui became Nancy (Perrone 1998, 13).

An example of the knowledge taught can be seen in her social studies curriculum. She follows her social studies textbook closely. It discusses the development of the United States from the East to the West. Much of the text focuses on the creation of the thirteen colonies and the activities of the Pilgrims and other Anglo settlers to the East

Coast from the colonist point of view. The majority of history is taught from a European American point of view; for example, the history of indigenous peoples is covered when they come into contact with Europeans. Little is mentioned about the indigenous people who lived in areas renamed as colonies. The students do not study other people who lived in other parts of North America, such as Mexico. Famous men like George Washington, Thomas Jefferson, Benjamin Franklin, and Alexander Hamilton are highlighted. Limited reference to Harriet Tubman and Susan B. Anthony may also be included. For the most part, students read biographies on "founding fathers" and present reports to their peers. A few female students ask her after class about including information about women, so the teacher asks them to research the topic. They do not follow through and little is said about women.

During a staff development session on cultural diversity in schools, the teacher feels defensive and responds with hostility to a conversation about the need for bilingual teachers. She quickly points out that it isn't her fault that children from underrepresented families are not learning as successfully as others. "I don't think people realize how many dysfunctional students come to school here. I can't be expected to solve all their problems," she says loudly from her chair in the back of the room. It is her belief that it is important for students from diverse communities to learn how to fit in and become "American."

The school is located in a diverse neighborhood. There are students whose ancestors were from Nigeria, Russia, Somalia, Poland, China, Ireland, Germany, Mexico, and Sweden. When someone asks the teacher about the importance of culture, she says, "I see students. I treat everyone the same." She believes she is color blind. The teacher has a seating chart and students sit integrated in class. However, at lunch time, it is obvious that white students sit on one side of the cafeteria, while students from underrepresented groups sit on the other. Sometimes there are conflicts between different ethnic and cultural groups in the cafeteria, but like other school personnel, the teacher does nothing in her classes to address the underlying racial tensions. She is concerned not with building a sense of community, but maintaining order and control. She believe this orientation gives her more opportunities to teach reading, writing, and mathematics so students will successfully fit into U.S. society.

The teacher believes she does the best she can, but complains daily about the high numbers of students, 35, in each of her middle school classes. She doesn't feel she can do much to help each student and so she feels it is best to use direct instruction. She gives them seat work to complete individually and does not believe cooperative learning is possible because of her large numbers of students; the noise level will get too loud.

During a faculty meeting, a colleague comments that he sees many students from culturally diverse groups taking classes in remedial English and Math. He asks if this is academic tracking. This teacher replies, "No, it is just where the kids are. They need to work harder. They often don't do their homework. I don't know what else we can do?" She also indicates that she feels picked on during diversity training sessions because she feels she is not racist nor harbors ill feelings toward students from other cultural groups.

It will be difficult for this teacher to understand how her actions could impede the education of students if she does not examine critical underlying conflicts caused by the system, her own viewpoints, and cultural conflicts.

The Human Relations Teacher

The human relations teacher believes it is important that all children treat each other with respect. She explains to her students how the United States is a society comprised of many different cultures that enrich our nation.

She is the faculty counselor to the Human Relations Club at the high school. She is also a member of the Mini-Town staff, a special program on prejudice sponsored by the National Conference of Community and Justice. As a person who believes in equity, she feels it is very important to create cross-cultural bridges between different races and members of ethnic groups. She invites sixty high school student representatives to the Mini-Town four-day retreat to talk about racism, gender bias, classism, and homophobia. In addition, she encourages other student groups to sponsor cultural events during the school noon hour, like special food for Chinese New Year. She also supports their use of different languages to advertise events. The teacher/counselor provides much support to students to create other programs like Peer Mediation in which students help their peers talk about issues dealing with friends, family, and school problems. Some of the problems that arise deal with racism and usually these problems can be solved on an individual basis through one-on-one peer counseling.

As an English teacher, she includes the writings of many different U.S. authors like Amy Tan, Langston Hughes, Sandra Cisneros, and Maya Angelou. She brings in community people to help her students understand the cultural context of several of the writers since most of her students are white. She encourages students to ask questions and to find similarities between different cultural life experiences. Through reading literature and having the opportunity to discuss cultural values, her students understand more clearly the implicit messages of the literature. This also encourages community building among students because many of the themes in literature are universal though they are discussed within various cultural contexts.

Since the teacher believes in diversity, she recommended and was able to get the faculty to agree to offer Mandarin as well as French, Spanish, and German as a foreign language. She supports the Multicultural Education Club, which sponsors the Martin Luther King, Jr. assembly for the school. Often students act out portions of one of Martin Luther King, Jr.'s speeches. In addition, there is a Multicultural Week where students from different cultural groups share traditional dances, music, and speakers. In addition, she is the advisor to the week-long Multicultural Fair where student clubs choose a country, prepare food from that country, and sell the dishes to students during the lunch period. She believes that this activity helps to bring students together on a personal level and integrates cultural diversity. These activities have been highly supported by administrators and teachers in the school.

Like other educators in the school, this teacher believes human relations activities are the key in creating equity in the school because the strategies focus on individual change and bring to the attention of students and other educators fun aspects of culture. Justice is seen as fair and balanced. Students are directed to "care for others" and clarify their values. However, she does not bring up controversial social issues nor asks students to make decisions about them. The teacher does not look at the infrastructure of schools for issues like academic tracking, the sink-or-swim English immersion policy for English learners, majority privilege as it relates to standardized assessment tools, or lack of input from parents of underrepresented groups. The status quo is maintained without working for structural school reform.

The Social Action Teacher

The social action teacher believes strongly in equality in school opportunities and outcomes. The lens through which she sees schooling is political. She believes in educational equality and sees institutional oppression as the most critical obstacle to student success. She tells students at the beginning of the year that they have "the right to be themselves." She teaches in a school where most of the students are Latino, African American, or Vietnamese. When asked if she has a strong commitment to social justice, she said, "Yes, I think social justice is so important that I have my students read biographies of Martin Luther King, Jr. during the month of January. I also have class meetings where children learn how to work with each other. Once during the year, I also have the students, who have earned the privilege, come to my house for an afternoon party." When a controversial issue arises in class, she has the students convene for a community discussion session where everyone in the room can contribute to resolving the problem.

All the walls in her classroom are filled with educational messages and the work of students. It is a classroom where children are busily involved in many projects dealing with social issues. She encourages students to address questions like, "Who has the power? Who makes the decisions? How can the status quo be changed? Whose perspective is being taught?"

Her students choose to learn about U.S. slavery by studying the lives of various abolitionists. They make a videotape presentation for parents and profile important figures like Harriet Tubman, Levi Cofin, John Brown, Frederick Douglass, and Sojourner Truth. Their video shows a courtroom where several people were on trial for helping Black slaves escape to the North during the 1850s. All members of the class participate in the role play.

Many students in her class are involved in the school's student government. Her students campaigned for one of their classmates who was elected president. As president of the student body, the young girl involves many of her classmates in various school projects. For example, they sold grocery store coupons to raise money for new playground equipment. The students learned much about the democratic process. The bulletin board displays the poster: "You have the right to ask for help. You also have the duty to assist." The social action teacher talks much about civil and human rights in her teaching. She wants her students not only to learn about civil rights history, but she also wants them to get involved in the school community to make it a better place for all students. In this way her students will know how democracy works in their city, state, and nation.

This teacher speaks up at faculty meetings regarding the need for the faculty to examine their practices, such as academic tracking. She leads a small group of teachers who continue to raise controversial issues dealing with equity and diversity.

The Caring-Centered Multicultural Teacher

The caring-centered multicultural teacher talked about why she teaches: "I want to make a difference with children. I live close by and am part of the neighborhood community. I know that kids can do well if they are given the chance. This is where I want to be." The teacher is student-centered.

Her high school classroom is filled with the work of her students all over the walls. In addition, she has many posters that focus on the classroom as a family. The posters say things like: "Smiles are contagious," "Pull together," "Learning has no boundaries,"

"We are the future," and "Celebrate your heritage." She believes caring and social justice form the foundation for her belief system.

She is a caring teacher who believes that when her students fail, she fails, and when her students succeed, she succeeds. At the beginning of the year she spends time carefully observing each student and identifying specific skills they need; she can then guide her students to succeed.

She calls parents all the time on the phone, both to remind parents and students about their responsibilities and to congratulate students and their parents on excellent work. She understands that the success of students is dependent not only on her work, but also the support of parents and the students themselves.

Her class climate is one of reciprocal caring and trust; she cares for her students and her students care for her and they also care for each other. It isn't easy to create a cross-cultural and equitable family atmosphere. She says, "It takes a lot of time at the beginning of the year. We have class meetings where we choose the rules together. We talk about what it means to care for each other and what it means to be fair." She also has students sitting with their desks making small groups of four to six students. They often help each other or do group work. She models caring behavior all the time by attending and listening unconditionally to each child as he/she speaks and making sure that all her students have a chance to talk in class. In addition, the teacher has students evaluate her three times a year. She uses her students' comments to help her reflect upon her own practices and where she should make changes. When she wasn't listening to her children, they told her and she became more attentive. Getting feedback from students works well because the teacher has a respectful and trusting relationship with her students.

This teacher proactively works to address the achievement differences and disciplinary problems of students often correlated to factors such as class, gender, ethnicity. For example, in other classrooms, Black students are often sent disproportionately more often to the office for discipline. This teacher prefers to work with parents and students first, before calling in the main office. One of her secrets is that she gives students several options and does not push young people into a corner where they must defy her in order to uphold their personal honor and pride. She understands the cultural and personal dynamics. Because of her respect for students and understanding of peer values, the teacher always disciplines a student one-on-one and not in front of the entire class. Otherwise this again can be seen as a challenge, and students are sensitive to peer beliefs.

Since the teacher believes in providing all students access to higher-level courses, she created a club for students interested in math and science. Many young people attend and the teacher is especially sensitive to inviting women and students from some underrepresented groups who often do not take as many science and math courses as others. Through the activities in the club, the teacher built a social network of support for students who are interested in the sciences. More women and students of color are taking advanced classes because of this club. The members of the group provide each other with tutoring and advice throughout the year.

In her social studies classroom, when she talks about communities in the eleventh grade curriculum, she asks questions like: "What does caring look like in our communities? What does caring look like in different cultures? Are caring and justice related? If so, how?" She gives examples of how her student's parents are volunteering in the school or at church.

One of the biggest differences between this teacher and others is her goal to guide students to become self-directed *and* community oriented. Classroom power is shared between students and teacher. The atmosphere in the classroom is one of mutual respect, between students and students with teachers. In this atmosphere the teacher considers the culture of students and works with them to create an understanding of caring, based on trust, to which they can relate. She knows that their self-esteem may be interwoven with their cultural identity. Her classroom allows students to express their ability to control their learning in their own unique ways, from putting on dramas to creating a song. Her management style is driven by the capacity to care for her students, which transcends race and ethnicity. This leads to collaborative and individual goals of academic achievement. In her classroom the students know that they are at the center of learning.

Since this teacher has developed important connections with the neighborhood, you can see her on Saturdays at the local library checking out books. Sometimes she will be at the Latino bakery buying *pan dulce,* little breads, for her family's Sunday breakfast. This teacher is part of the community.

This teacher, like the social action educator, is an advocate for change. She believes it is critical for schools to have a strong policy of caring and compassion in order to create a socially just learning environment.

STUDENTS KNOW THEY ARE
AT THE CENTER OF LEARNING

This teacher knows the importance of understanding the cultures that students share and uses it as a bridge to supporting children in their learning. She knows that cultural values, language, behavioral codes, and motivational styles may differ in her students. This teacher has a holistic focus where she addresses social problems, focuses on issues of equity and culture, consciously strives to create a compassionate community of learners, understands that schools are social institutions, and addresses individual needs. Her approach is especially important because many high school students "fall through the cracks" of our schools often because of the sheer number of students high school teachers are responsible for in a day.

✍ Comparison of the Four Styles of Teaching

The first two teachers are more assimilationist in their orientation. Students are expected to take on the values and behaviors of the mainstream school culture. This is an accepted belief. Neither teacher incorporates the cultures of their students as a major aspect of their teaching. Assimilationists do not address the imbalance of power in the way schools are structured. If any cultural or equitable activities are presented in schools, they are added to the status quo. It is an additive approach to Multicultural Education. The social action and caring-centered teachers can be transformative in their orientation if teachers actively work to change the way schools are structured and alter the way their own classrooms are organized.

Though both the social action and the caring-centered teachers are dedicated to changing society, the caring-centered multicultural teacher believes caring is at the core of a democratic community. "We care and so we are fair." These teachers understand that consistency and fairness are the cornerstones of an effective classroom. This is evident in the way discipline as well as rewards are carried out in the caring classroom. The teacher is in tune with the need to reprimand students privately and may praise a student privately or publicly depending on what the student prefers. Student behavior may differ when a teacher privately talks with the student, it also shows respect for the student.

The social action and caring-centered teachers have similar value orientations, but they have different value priorities. The social justice teacher uses a political or legal filter as her core orientation. The social action teacher focuses on power relationships and the imbalance of power in U.S. society and how that impacts the employment, housing patterns, and other opportunities of various communities. Though the caring-centered teacher also is concerned about power relationships, this teacher is more likely to address issues of power by teaching students how to direct their own learning, bring in student experiences, and encourage the sharing of diverse viewpoints into the school day. This approach focuses on strengthening trusting relationships within the classroom.

The caring teacher is more apt to bring cultural analogies and other cultural "ways of knowing" to the learning process. To give you a sample of how culture can be infused naturally into the teacher's instruction, remember the story I shared in chapter 2 about how the teacher taught the concept of choral reading? Her first graders did not understand what she meant by the term, so she said to her students, "It's just like we sing together in the choir at church. That's why it's called choral reading. We read together as if we were in a chorus." Many of her students are African American and they attend churches with large choirs. Using this example, the teacher was able to build on the cultural knowledge of her students.

Caring-centered teachers are extremely aware of how culture impacts the hidden or invisible aspects of the classroom (Hilliard 1974). For example Hilliard (1974) sees the influence of culture on the way students and teachers make judgments, label, control space, pay attention, care, isolate, and respond to others. The classroom is a culturally rich environment.

In order to better understand the basis for caring-centered Multicultural Education, the next section lists the core principles.

❧ Principles of Multicultural Education from a Caring Perspective

Caring, education for democracy, and culture are key elements of Multicultural Education. The following principles help to summarize Multicultural Education from this perspective:

1. Multicultural Education, as part of a life-giving pedagogy of human growth, is based on the belief that teachers and students form a family of learners. People care for others, themselves, and the community, as they work together and learn.
2. The roots of a caring-centered multicultural framework rise from the integration of principles from human development, democratic education, and a socio-cultural context of learning.
3. The choice to teach is an ethical one. A moral commitment to care means teachers are committed to finding ways to effectively teach all students and are

especially sensitive to closing the achievement gap between majority children and students from underrepresented cultural groups. Teachers create situations and contexts in which all students are successful.

4. Children are cultural beings; they are born, learn, speak, share, think, and create in complex linguistic and cultural settings. Culture plays important roles in a person's development; it contributes to areas such as identity, motivation, gender roles, and learning modalities. Within this cultural and linguistic environment, teachers support the holistic developmental process including intellectual, emotional, physical, and social growth.

5. A caring relationship is reciprocal based on trust, respect, and honoring of each other among students and teacher. This is expressed in the classroom through using the living experiences of students in the teaching-learning process. When people care, they share their lives and place the interests of others along with their own.

6. Parents and community members are members of a student's social network. Since learning occurs in a sociocultural context, the development of trusting relationships with significant others is critical to effective teaching.

7. Since culture is a key component of learning, culturally relevant teaching is a core principle. Teachers affirm the cultural identities of their students and parents as they skillfully integrate explicit and implicit cultural elements naturally into the classroom and school.

8. Teachers and students look at both personal and institutional oppression. First teachers understand the impact of prejudice and discrimination on the emotional and intellectual development of their students. Second, teachers understand that schools, as social institutions, reinforce, often unconsciously, social oppression brought about by racism, sexism, classism, and other harmful biases. Teachers and students engage in a continual process of examining personal prejudices and addressing discriminatory practices in schools.

9. Teachers and students of all ages learn math, reading, writing, and technology and citizenship skills within the context of actively and compassionately working toward equity and justice in their own classrooms, schools, and communities. They are excited about making a difference in their neighborhoods and communities.

10. Curriculum and instruction are founded on the belief that learning must flow from an attitude of caring and be participatory, hands-on, meaningful, cooperative, and reflective. Students often are more motivated when the curriculum has real-life purposes. Teachers use interdisciplinary curriculum and strategies that recognize intuition, emotional and social intelligences, and the five physical senses.

11. Caring teachers encourage and teach students to democratically take control of their own lives in the classroom while creating a classroom culture in which each student can achieve academic excellence. Teachers have definite expectations for students and encourage them to become self-directed, self-determined, collaborative, and compassionate people.

12. Teachers believe and act on the premise that if students do not learn, then they did not teach. Teachers who care continually seek ways to reach students and help them achieve academic excellence.

Summary

Caring-Centered Multicultural Education differs from other Multicultural Education frameworks because it directs a paradigm shift from a political focus to a caring one, which sees schooling as a life-giving process of learning. Key values are empowerment, compassion, justice, equity, and community. Other orientations are primarily founded upon democratic values. Though I agree that social justice is a key element of Multicultural Education, the commitment to care is most critical and must be interwoven with our democratic values. Caring for others leads to justice and fairness. Simply put, the care we feel for others moves us to develop views and appropriate approaches, such as value orientations and teaching methods that lead to "fairness" or social justice. Caring leads teachers to provide students classrooms that are student-centered. Fairness does not necessarily lead to caring in a classroom.

Caring-Centered Multicultural Education encourages teachers to address student individual needs within community and cultural contexts. The caring paradigm has six major shifts from other views of Multicultural Education:

1. the paradigm places caring for community and self at the foundation for social/economic justice and change;
2. the paradigm moves the focus from the teacher to the learner;
3. the paradigm explains how culture represents different realities—and ways of knowing;
4. the paradigm is founded upon the interconnectedness of the learner and the teacher;
5. learning and teaching are social processes; and
6. teachers and students are both responsible for learning.

A healthy commitment to care rather than a particular political ideology can motivate teachers to create effective learning environments. I believe teachers who care will provide the kind of support that will result in the academic success of all children, especially children from underrepresented communities.

Caring-centered is not a style of teaching or a specific personality type; rather it is a philosophical orientation that focuses on relationship building and the importance of the cultural context. This framework values students and parents and sees learning occurring within a social and cultural context. In this orientation, a teacher has made an ethical commitment to her/himself to create strong lines of communication with her/his students and to affirm the cultural background of students. An assimilationist teacher can be kind to her students, but when the teacher only teaches from a mainstream perspective and encourages students to shed important aspects of themselves like cultural identity, language, and cultural beliefs in order to fit in or become more "American," then students aren't valued. When students aren't valued, then their learning may be more limited because they may not become emotionally vested in the endeavor. When students aren't encouraged to challenge the status quo and address our social problems, they are not being prepared to contribute to our community. When teachers do not model collaboration or respect for different perspectives, then our national diversity isn't being honored.

Today, the dropout rates of many students from underrepresented groups are disturbing and signal a need for change. Perrone (1998) reports that from 35 percent to

55 percent of all African American, Latino, and Native Americans are dropping out of our high schools. This will have dramatic impacts on our economic, social, and political national life. Perrone found that in "interviews with many of these young men and women, they speak of uncaring schools, of seeing little connection between the content of schools and their lives, of settings that are disrespectful of their families, or not having teachers to whom they can relate. (1998, 35). The caring-centered framework seeks to address this disconnection between teachers and students and teachers and parents.

Teacher Reflections:

I suggest that you buy an inexpensive three-ring binder with paper or a spiral notebook to serve as a journal to keep track of your responses to chapter questions and to provide a place for you to write other reflections about topics and issues raised in this text. The questions are designed to assist you in reflecting upon your own perspectives and to identify your underlying values.

1. Which teacher are you most like: assimilationist, human relations, social action, or caring-centered? Why would you place yourself in that orientation?
2. Which teacher would you like to be most like? What characteristics do you think you would like to model in your own teaching? Why are those characteristics important?
3. How are the social action and caring-centered teachers different? Similar?

Sometimes we say we support or believe in certain values, but our actions may not always be in sync with those beliefs. This Calvin and Hobbes comic strip points out the importance of continually reviewing one's actions.

Calvin and Hobbes   by Bill Watterson

References

Au, Kathryn. 1980. Participation structures in a reading lesson with Hawaiian children: Analysis of a culturally appropriate instructional event. *Anthropology and Education Quarterly, 11*(2): 91–115.

Au, Kathryn H., and Alice J. Kawakami, 1994. Cultural congruence in instruction. In Etta R. Hollins, Joyce E. King, and Warren C. Hayman's, ed., *Teaching diverse populations: Formulating a knowledge base.* Albany, N.Y.: SUNY Press.

Au, Kathryn H. and J. M. Mason. 1981. Social organizational factors in learning to read: The balance of rights hypothesis. *Reading Research Quarterly, 17*(1): 115–52.

Banks, James A. 1981. *Multicultural education: Theory and practice.* Boston, Mass.: Allyn and Bacon.

Banks, James A. 1995. Multicultural education: Historical development, dimensions, and practice. In James A. Banks and Cherry McGee Banks, eds., *Handbook of research on multicultural education.* N.Y.: Macmillan.

Bellah, Robert N., Richard Madsen, William Sullivan, and Stephen M. Tipton. 1985. *Habits of the heart: Individualism and commitment in American life.* N.Y.: Harper and Row.

Bennett, Christine. 1995. *Comprehensive multicultural education: Theory and practice.* 3rd ed. Boston, Mass.: Allyn and Bacon.

Cajete, Gregory. 1994. *Look to the mountain.* Skyland, N.C.: Kivaki Press.

Chaskin, R., and Diana M. Rauner. 1995. Youth and caring. *Phi Delta Kappan, 70*(9): 667–674.

Cole, Michael. 1996. *Cultural psychology: A once and future discipline.* Cambridge, Mass.: Belknap Press of Harvard University.

Cole, Michael. 1998. Can cultural psychology help us think about diversity? Presentation delivered at the American Educational Research Association Meetings, San Diego, CA, April 13–18.

Darder, Antonia. 1991. *Culture and power in the classroom.* N.Y.: Bergin and Garvey.

Dewey, John. 1916. *Democracy and education.* N.Y.: Macmillan.

Dewey, John. 1938. *Experience and education.* N.Y.: Collier Books.

Eaker-Rich, D. and Jan Van Galen. 1996. *Caring in an unjust world: Negotiating borders and barriers in schools.* Albany, N.Y.: SUNY Press.

Elliot, Stephen N., Thomas R. Kratochwill, Joan Littlefield Cook, and John F. Travers. 2000. *Educational psychology: Effective teaching, effective learning.* 3rd ed. Boston, MA: McGraw-Hill.

Erickson, Frederick. 1993. Transformation and school success: The politics and culture of educational achievement. In Evelyn Jacob and Cathie Jordan, eds., *Minority education: Anthropological perspectives.*Norwood, NJ: Ablex Publishing Corporation.

Fordham, Signithia & John Ogbu. 1986. Black students' school success: Coping with the 'burden of acting White'. *Urban Review, 18*(3), 176–206.

Freire, Paulo. 1970. *Pedagogy of the oppressed.* N.Y.: Seabury Press.

Gay, Geneva. 1994. *At the essence of learning: Multicultural education.* West Lafayette, IN: Kappa Delta Pi.

Gibson, Rich. 1999. Paulo Freire and pedagogy for social justice. *Theory and Research in Social Education 27*(2): 129–159.

Gordon, Edmund. 1999. *Education and Justice: A view from the back of the bus.* N.Y.: Teachers College Press.

Haberman, Martin. 1995. *Star teachers of children of poverty.* West Lafayette, Ind.: Kappa Delta Pi.

Hilliard, Asa. 1974. Restructuring teacher education for multicultural imperatives. In William A. Hunter, ed., *Multicultural education through competency-based teacher education.* Washington, D.C.: American Association of Colleges for Teacher Education.

hook, bell 2000. How do we build a community of love? *Shambhala Sun, 8*(3): 32–40.

Ianni, F. 1996. The caring community as a context for joining youth needs and program services. *Journal of Negro Education, 65*(1): 71–91.

Irvine, Jacqueline Jordan. 1990. *Black students and school failure: Politics, practices, and prescriptions.* Westport, Conn.: Greenwood Press.

King, Joyce. 1994. The purpose of schooling for African American children; Including cultural knowledge. In Etta R. Hollins, Joyce E. King, and Warren C. Hayman's eds., *Teaching diverse populations: Formulating a knowledge base,* pp. 25–66. Albany, N.Y.; SUNY Press.

Kohl, Herbert. 1994. *"I won't learn from you."* N.Y.: New Press.

Kohn, Alfie. 1991. Caring kids: The role of the schools. *Phi Delta Kappan 72*(7): 496–506.

Kozol, Jonathan. 1991. *Savage inequalities: Children in America's schools*. N.Y.: Harper Perennial.

Moll, Luis. 1990. *Vygotsky and education: Instructional implications and applications of sociohistorical psychology*. New York: Cambridge University Press.

Nieto, Sonia. 1992. *Affirming diversity: The sociopolitical context of multicultural education*. N.Y.: Longman.

Noblit, G., Dwight Rogers, and B. McCadden. 1995. *In the meantime. The possibilities of caring. Phi Delta Kappan, 76*(9): 680–685.

Noddings, Nel. 1984. *Caring: A feminine approach to ethics and moral development*. Berkeley, Calif.: University of California Press.

Noddings, Nel. 1992. *The challenge to care in schools: An alternative approach to education*. N.Y.: Teachers College Press.

Noddings, Nel. 1995. *Philosophy of education*. Boulder, Colo.: Westview Press.

Oakes, Jeannie. 1985. *Keeping track how schools structure inequality*. New Haven, Conn.: Yale University Press.

Ovando, Carlos and Virginia Collier. 1985. *Bilingual and esl classrooms: Teaching in multicultural contexts*. Boston, Mass.: McGraw-Hill.

Ovando, Carlos and Virginia Collier. 1998. 2nd ed. *Bilingual and esl classrooms: Teaching in multicultural contexts*. Boston, Mass.: McGraw-Hill.

Pang, Valerie Ooka. 1994. Why do we need this class?: Multicultural Education. *Phi Delta Kappan, 76*(4): 289–292.

Pang, Valerie Ooka and Li-rong Lilly Cheng. 1998. *Struggling to be heard: The unmet needs of Asian Pacific American children*. Albany N.Y.: SUNY Press.

Pang, Valerie Ooka and John Rivera. 1998. The ethic of caring: The foundation of multicultural education. Unpublished manuscript.

Perrone, Vito. 1998. *Teacher with a heart: Reflections on Leonard Covello and the Community*. N.Y.: Teachers College Press.

Pidgeon, Judith. 1998. Private communication. November 30, San Diego, Calif.

Rivera, John. and Mary Poplin. 1995. Multicultural, critical, feminine, and constructive pedagogies seen through the lives of youth: A call for the revisioning of these and beyond: Toward a pedagogy for the next century. In Christine E. Sleeter, ed., *Multicultural education, critical pedagogy, and the politics of difference*, Albany, N.Y.: SUNY Press.

Rogers, Carl R. and H. Jerome Freiberg. 1994. *Freedom to learn for the 80's*. 3rd ed. N.Y.: Merrill.

Sleeter, C. 1996. *Multicultural education as social activism*. Albany, N.Y.: SUNY Press.

Sleeter, Christine and Carl Grant. 1987. An analysis of multicultural education in the United States. *Harvard Educational Review, 57:* 421–444.

Tharp, Ronald and Ronald Gallimore. 1988. *Rousing minds to life: Teaching, learning, and schooling in social context*. N.Y.: Cambridge University Press.

Valle, Ramon. 1998. Personal interview. San Diego, Calif., January 15.

Valle, Ramon. 1997. *Ethnic diversity and multiculturalism: Crisis or challenge*. New York: American Heritage Custom Publishing.

Chapter 4

How Can We Teach the Whole Student? A Multicultural Model

*A*s an elementary grade teacher, I saw that the emotional, physical, social, and academic well-being of a child were intertwined. If a young female student was hungry, she was less likely to be attentive. If a young man was feeling insecure because someone was calling him names, he couldn't concentrate on writing his essay. If a student in high school was having problems with peers, parents, or a teacher, he might not pay attention in his classes or become defiant. Students are complex whole beings. In Caring-Centered Multicultural Education, teachers focus on the development of the whole student not only academic achievement. As mentioned in Chapter 3, there are three distinct belief systems that act as the building blocks for Caring-Centered Multicultural Education: The ethic of caring, education for democracy, and the sociocultural context of learning and human development. These three elements of caring, culture, and democratic education form an interlocking and integrated system which is oriented toward teaching the whole student.

Though it may be hard to see, the three components hold numerous ingredients that can transform the learning of a child. What is transformation? Have you ever baked a cake or made a tortilla? Let's take the cake for example. After mixing all the ingredients together and baking the cake, it is not possible to see its individual ingredients. However, without the flour or eggs or sugar or milk or chocolate, the object would not be a cake. This is what happens in the process of transformation. There is a metamorphosis; something new is created!

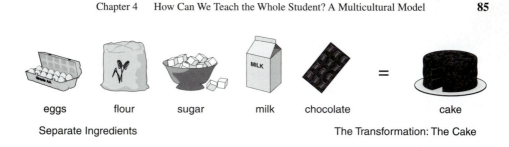

| eggs | flour | sugar | milk | chocolate | = | cake |

Separate Ingredients   The Transformation: The Cake

❧ *Building Block One: The Ethic of Caring*

"To teach involves a giving of self and a receiving of other" (Noddings 1984, 113).

The ethic of caring is the key building block because it represents the moral commitment we make to care for and teach our students. It is a conscious commitment which we, as teachers, make; we are committed to making a difference in the lives of our students. It also directs teachers to view education as a holistic process. It is not only about teaching knowledge. It is about teaching the whole student within an empowering and compassionate environment. Teachers consider the development of the whole person whether they are teaching a math class, English class, or government class.

Chapter 3 carefully describes the ethic of caring. Teachers and students develop strong human bonds with each other. Teachers and students also care for the larger community and for various ideas. Unfortunately, caring and compassion within education are often seen as "touchy feely," holding little academic substance. Gilligan (1982) and Noddings (1984) have studied the importance of relationship building and the need for moral development. What happens when you care for another? You place the interests of another person next to your own; you look at a situation through someone else's eyes.

Noddings (1984) believes there is also an emotional element to caring; one wants to do something to ease the other person's pain or assist them in reaching their dream.

Though some academics in universities often overlook this orientation, as a first grade teacher, I felt this was the most important element of my classroom. I cared for the students. They cared for me and we were a family, a community of learners. Many children are most interested in being accepted and loved. This must occur before they are willing to trust teachers and pour their hearts into the learning process. I believe caring is an integral aspect of the art of teaching. Many teachers are motivated by altruistic values of democracy and justice, and their personal interactions with students is what sustains the students, especially when they find learning difficult or frustrating.

Caring can also mean difficult challenges for teachers. Caring involves the review of our personal racial, social class, and gender biases in our lives and as members of social institutions like schools. This is a challenge because we may need to face aspects of ourselves that are not flattering or positive. How can we truly care for another if our view of the other has been shaped by racist, gender biased, or classist views that we have learned? In addition, in order to care, we must also examine how we, as members of social institutions like schools, may be participating in ways which limit the access of some children to the best education. For example, our daughter was in a school where Sally Ride, the first woman astronaut was visiting. She wanted to have the opportunity to be part of a small group to speak to Ride because of her interest in NASA. Our daughter had attended two local Space Camps and had dreams of becoming an engineer for NASA. Only ten students were allowed to meet Ride. Our daughter was not one of the children chosen. However that wasn't what angered her. Our daughter was disturbed because only three young women were included in the group of ten. As I think back on this issue, I should have encouraged our daughter to speak to the principal about the issue of gender imbalance, especially since the students were meeting the first woman astronaut. Our daughter also felt disappointed that the school staff did not follow through on their convictions about gender equity with this incident. I could have told the principal about our unhappiness with the equity issue, but also about the importance of creating and maintaining a trusting relationship. In not acting, my silence supported the status quo of gender bias. Sometimes it is not what we do that matters most; sometimes it is what we fail to do that is most powerful.

Caring teachers are empowering and not enabling. Caring teachers provide students with constructive and helpful suggestions. In this way, students are encouraged to mature, become more cooperative, and develop their talents and skills. The teacher has high standards of excellence and encourages students to succeed on their own. They do not lower their expectations or do the work for their students. In Harlem at Central Park East Secondary School, students are continually assessed and judged on the habits of their work (Meier 1995). Students must take on increasing responsibility for their learning, communicate effectively with their peers, and maintain deadlines (Meier 1995). Students are encouraged and are mentored to be doers and thinkers.

On the other hand, enabling teachers may not push students to do their work or hold high expectations. Enabling teachers encourage dependency on the part of students by giving students the answer or providing too much help. Empowering and caring teachers understand the importance of providing a safe and positive environment, which encourages students to learn on their own. This means children might fail and learn from their mistakes. Caring teachers provide a learning environment that encourages children to do their best and to strive for excellence. Students know these teachers support them as they struggle through difficult times.

❧ Building Block Two: Education for Democracy

Caring for each other as precious human beings ties in with our nation's values of social justice, democracy, and moral courage. These values affirm the belief in human dignity and our commitment to care for each other. They also tie intimately to our commitment to freedom and equality. I believe people struggle for justice, freedom, and equality because we care for others and hold human life sacred. Democratic education seeks to develop self-directed citizens for a pluralistic world (Dewey 1916).

One of our major objectives as a community must be to challenge an accepted system which has and continues to subordinate people based on race, class, and gender in schools (McLaren 1997). In other words, as educators, we must eliminate inequitable or damaging practices. Practices like academic tracking, lack of a common core curriculum for all students, proportionately more African Americans suspended from school, lower levels of school funding in poor neighborhoods, and overcrowded classrooms in culturally diverse neighborhoods are examples of how we, as a nation, accept inequities in our schools (McLaren 1997; Kozol 1991; Oakes 1982). For example, Deborah Meier, former principal of Central Park East, a high school in Harlem, spoke about this bias:

> "When people think 'those kids' need something special, the reply we offer at CPESS [Central Park East Secondary School] is, Just give them what you have always offered those who have the money to buy the best, which is mostly a matter of respect.
> I think we've created a framework at CPESS for creating such a respectful setting, day by day. We don't create all the conditions that affect our students' lives; we can't stop the world our students live in while we do our work . . . We have no guarantees to offer our kids, their families . . . beyond trying our best to make CPESS a place that at least temporarily makes life seem more interesting and worth the effort . . . This takes time and trust. Trust can't be mandated, but because students and families come to us by choice, at least some modest basis for mutual trust is built in. . . ." (Meier 1995, 49).

As Meier indicated education for democracy will not be created without the underlying values of respect and interconnection. Schools do not seriously address the inequities of race, class, and gender bias. Why? Aronowitz (1997), a sociologist, believes that since the "American" ideology of equal opportunity is so pervasive in the majority culture, most people think that each individual has an equal chance to make it in society. In addition, the United States is an "Open Society" without distinct social class lines; therefore, each person, if she/he works hard enough and long enough has unlimited opportunities in this country. An English teacher tells his class a story about this misconception. His father told him, "When I came to this country from Hong Kong, U.S. Americans told me the U.S. was the 'Land of Opportunity.' They were wrong. It is the land of struggle. And I found out that people don't treat you well. I had a good job as a cook at a large privately-owned hotel, but then a corporation bought the hotel and laid me off. I was their best cook. I cooked French and U.S. American food, but then they hired new immigrants to cook at minimum wage and I was out of a job after 15 years."

We, as educators, must address the issue of social class along with issues of race, ethnicity, culture, and other social groupings because they are all intricately tied together in this nation. As the Chinese immigrant related in his story, his struggles in the United States are primarily those of social class though he did understand there could also be covert racial bias operating. After being let go as a cook, he is now fighting to save a modest deli in an industrial area. He learned that it was not loyalty, length of service, or years of quality, but profit that was the underlying principle of business. The corporation put him out of a job, but also were treating the new cooks unfairly because at minimum wage, they were receiving much less for the work in comparison to others who cooked at other hotels.

Many U.S. citizens also believe that they live in a country ruled by consensus and where cultural assimilation is an accepted aspect of the U.S. culture (Aronowitz 1997; Darder 1991). In order to become a U.S. "American," it is necessary for immigrants or culturally different U.S. Americans in our country to conform to the dominant culture. Though people can air their differences of opinion, the beliefs and ways of the dominant group in society remain dominant and this is reflected in the "canon" taught in U.S. schools. Aronowitz explains, "while Americans may differ with one another concerning economic and social policy and may form distinct political parties, on the whole they agree on the underlying free-market, capitalistic framework of social arrangements. Among other things, this agreement presupposes the historic success of assimilation of immigrant groups into a common ground of values and beliefs (Aronowitz 1997, 191).

What does Aronowitz mean? I believe he is saying that there are conflicts between our value of equality and our economic system of capitalism. You may believe in political equality and that everyone should be treated justly before the law. However, think about how divided we are based on how much money we each have. How are you treated at a department store when you are dressed up? Now imagine yourself going to the store in shorts and a paint-stained t-shirt. Will you be treated differently? Unfortunately, you will probably be treated with more respect dressed professionally rather than casually. Taking that argument further, who will get more political power, someone who works as a food server or someone who is head of a software company? Most likely, the person who is chairperson of a company will probably know others who have political power because they will find themselves at similar meetings.

How can a person with little money and little political influence gain more political clout? The person could join a politically active organization, but it will be difficult as an individual to gain more influence. The system is set up to protect the status quo (Darder 1991). Those in power will continue to hold and increase their power base. Political and economic power are integrally tied. Financially powerful people usually have more access to political power. The conflict between the values of equality and justice and capitalism is one of the most difficult paradoxes for people to see and understand because democracy and capitalism are accepted aspects of the "American" way of life.

The paradox can also be seen in schools. Many people believe that we live in a nation built on the principles of equality and justice and our schools reflect those values. Yet the United States has a long history of underachievement among children of color when compared to their European American peers (Darder 1991). Schooling is the main institutional path children of color and children from low-income families have to climb out of the lower rungs of society. However, schools are also products of that society. For example, parents from more affluent communities may have more clout within the school, than parents with little financial resources.

Since we are a nation that supports social justice, teachers must examine how schools are part of a larger system of privileges. As Peter McLaren (1997) has passionately reminded his readers, our goal is not just to include diverse voices from society and to develop a consensus viewpoint; rather the critical issue is for us to have a "noisy democracy" where people are continually challenging, building, revising and creating a nation where democracy addresses the integral web of race, class, and gender. We live in a society where, as my colleague, David Strom, reminds me, our nation is becoming a democracy. Strom told me, "As a nation we are more of a democracy today than in 1776, but we are still in the process of becoming a democratic nation" (Strom 1999).

In regard to schooling, many scholars have moved from the concept of equality to equity. Edmund Gordon explained the difference clearly, ". . . equality requires sameness, but equity requires that treatments be appropriate and sufficient to the characteristics and needs of those treated" (1999, xiv). Gordon later discussed the New York State Board of Regents's policy statement on education that stated, "Every child in New York State is entitled to the resources necessary to provide the sound, basic education which the state Constitution requires. The requirement is not equality of input, but equity of outcome" (Gordon 1991, 3). These statements celebrate the potential of all students and the importance of school faculty to be sensitive to their diverse needs.

Linda Christiansen:
A Teacher Who Combines Caring and Social Justice

At a conference on Multicultural Education, I attended a speech given by an inspirational teacher, Linda Christiansen. She is a high school teacher from the Portland School District in Oregon. Linda helped me to better understand that in caring, teachers must tackle challenging social questions and review their own views and actions. Christiansen spoke from her heart about teaching English literature in a culturally diverse school with a majority of African American, Asian Pacific American, and Latino students. She believes that critical literacy does not center on language, but it is the teaching of basic skills and teaching about power relationships. Christiansen integrates the importance of both emotional and academic well-being. She provides students with an affirming and caring classroom where they learn to read, to write, to think deeply about social issues, to act upon their convictions, and to trust their own thinking. This is not an easy process for students. The following comic strip shows Jeremy, a high school student, weighing his beliefs and trying to decide what his actions should be. As Christiansen has explained, often students must make difficult decisions.

Christiansen carefully described how schools teach political values, even unconsciously. She said, "Any piece of literature is political, it is part of the social blueprint of our nation. How I correct my students is political. Students must use tools of critical

literacy to expose, toss back, and to remedy inequities. I want children to come away from my class knowing they can make changes in society" (Christiansen 1997).

Christiansen asked the audience difficult questions, which I believe we all must ask ourselves. Though these questions are about language and literacy, they can be applied to other aspects of U.S. culture. Here is a sampling of them:

Whose language has power? Why?
Whose dialect has power? Why?
Whose voice carries more power? Why?
Who benefits from language power?
Who is hurt from language power?
How is language embedded in life? in culture? in power relationships?

When we are committed to caring for all students, we must not only look at our own biases but also the social obstacles that are placed in front of many students of color, students from low-income families, and young women in our society.

Many people believe in social justice in theory or as an abstract thought, but they may not see or feel their human connections with others. I believe that is in part why we have so many children of color not achieving in schools. We, as a nation, feel that nonachieving children, many of whom live in poverty or are from communities of color, are not our responsibility or that there is little we can do. Unfortunately, the result is that our nation has not addressed how our political and economic systems have impacted many young people.

Education for democracy is a major aspect of Caring-Centered Multicultural Education. It calls for effective teaching and the preparation of students to solve our social problems. One of the critical issues in providing equal education is addressing language concerns. Language instruction has been heavily debated. The following section describes why language is a social justice issue and how bilingual education became part of the historical record and a component of many schools in our nation.

A Foundation for Bilingual Education: Latino and Chinese American Activism

Did you know that an important cornerstone in the foundation for bilingual education resulted from the activism of Chinese American and Latino parents? Though many people know the Chinese for the building of the railroads and that many Latinos live in the Southwest, few may realize that members from these two communities have made important contributions to education. This section will discuss several instances where the communities have fought for equality in education because of their strong moral commitment to young people.

In the 1960s, after the large exodus of immigrants from Cuba, Cuban parents in Miami established private schools where Spanish was the primary language of instruction so they could maintain the cultural and linguistic roots in their children (Ovando and Collier 1985). Bilingual classes were instituted due to the efforts of the Cuban community and "the first bilingual program was thus begun at Coral Way Elementary School in Miami" (Ovando and Collier 1985, 26). Other states followed this example. There are several reasons why Cuban Americans were able to implement bilingual instruction. As refugees, they were assisted by the Cuban Refugee Act and it provided special training and resources to new immigrants. Also, many Cubans who migrated were from middle- and upper-middle-class families; they had financial, educational, and social resources which were used to establish schools. Many teachers were part of the immigrant group and could teach in bilingual schools (Ovando and Collier 1985).

Another example of how the local community can impact education occurred in San Francisco in the 1970s. The Chinese American community struggled for many years with the San Francisco Unified School District in order to receive educational services for their children. As part of their moral commitment to education and students, members of the Chinese American community filed a class action suit asking the district to hire bilingual teachers. The teachers would teach students academic content in their primary language so the students could progress academically while they concurrently developed English language skills. Though it took over four years of litigation, the Supreme Court ruled in favor of the parents with the ground-breaking decision of *Lau v. Nichols* in 1974.

How did this momentous educational struggle begin? Kinney Lau and twelve other Cantonese-speaking students along with their parents filed a class action suit on behalf of 1,800 children against Alan Nichols, who was the president of the San Francisco School Board. For many years Chinese American parents had been concerned because they did not feel their children were receiving adequate instruction due to their English language needs.

During the court hearing, the San Francisco Unified School District admitted that many children needed special instruction, but the district argued that it was not legally obligated to provide for those needs (Wang 1976). In *Lau v. Nichols,* the Supreme Court unanimously took the position that in order for children to participate equally in school, their education must be "meaningful" and "comprehensible"; as a result, their civil rights had been violated. To address this problem, bicultural and bilingual programs were needed. The ruling became the backbone for bilingual education programs throughout the nation and supported the right of thousands of children, who spoke languages other than English, to equal access to education.

Other scholars contend that the right to an effective and appropriate education also comes from the Fourteenth Amendment, which calls for equal protection of each person under the law (Baca and Cervantes 1989). The importance of providing equal education to all was established in the 1954 Supreme Court decision of *Brown v. Board of Education of Topeka*, when segregation of Black and White schools was struck down as being "inherently unequal."

Since the decisions are legal ones, there have been many discussions in the years after the rulings debating how bilingual education programs should be implemented. The following is a discussion of one of the most effective models, a developmental bilingual education program.

Bilingual Education Programs

The term *bilingual education* refers to a variety of programs that differ in the use of different degrees of native languages and in the number of years students are participants (Ovando and Collier 1985; Moran and Hakuta 1995). Three of the more common programs are the Transitional Bilingual Education (TBE), Maintenence Bilingual Education (MBE), and Two-Way Immersion.

In the TBE program the goal of teachers is to transition students from their home language to English as soon as possible. Although primary language is used to develop literacy skills which will transfer to English literacy once a certain level of English proficiency is reached, transition programs do not support the continued development of native language skills. In the MBE program, the goal is to support the development of social and academic language in the home/primary language as well as in English. The students become bilingual and biliterate. In a Two-Way Immersion program, students from the majority culture and youngsters from the ethnic community develop competencies in both languages. In this program, mainstream students learn a second language and ethnic students learn English while each community becomes bilingual and biliterate (Moran and Hakuta 1995). This is becoming a popular choice for mainstream students as they look toward learning more about others and developing their language capabilities.

What do many bilingual educators suggest? This is an extremely complicated issue. The research indicates that the longer students remain in transitional bilingual programs, they are more likely to become proficient in English (Moran and Hakuta 1995). Why? When the content of the curriculum is taught in the first or home language of those who are learning English, the students already know the social context, hidden meanings, abstract concepts, and nonverbal communications of the content. Their first language acts as a bridge in learning English because the vocabulary and concepts—especially in subjects like social studies—can be explained more easily and comprehensively in their first language. Since much of the language of mathematics is numbers, more English is utilized in this content area. One of the biggest problems that schools face in implementing solid bilingual programs is that students need approximately five to six years of instruction in both languages before they are truly able to perform at higher levels of academic competence. The bilingual education process takes time and cannot be accomplished in just one or two years. Another obstacle can come from school personnel who do not understand how linguistic bias in schools may be part of institutional racism that exists in society (Cummins 1989).

Reyes agrees with Cummins that institutional bias can hamper the development of quality programs for Spanish-speaking students (Reyes 1992). She studied two bilingual classes of fifty fifth graders. The children were from low- and middle-income families and lived in the Southwest. She monitored the writing progress of the students and in two years there was little progress. Children were making the same grammatical and spelling errors. One of her most troubling findings was that children were not encouraged or allowed to write in Spanish. Their academic writing had to be in English because this was a district-mandated policy. Reyes found this to be a subtle contradiction for a program dedicated to bilingualism and biliteracy. She discovered that when students were allowed to write in their journals in Spanish, they produced richer and more complex pieces. Reyes believed the lack of support for biliteracy hampered the children's development. In addition, she recommended that teachers point out to students the kind of errors they were making in process-oriented approaches like whole language. Teachers were reluctant to correct errors; however, students were not learning what they needed because of the focus on process rather than skill development.

We are a bilingual and multicultural society. It is an advantage to be bilingual and biliterate, whether it provides further employment opportunities, cognitive flexibility, or learning about a new worldview.

Summarizing the importance of building block two, democratic education seeks to prepare students for a complex world where teachers transfer not only important knowledge, but also engage students in opportunities where they develop critical communication skills. In this way students can work with people from diverse cultural, ethnic, and linguistic groups to create strong bonds of community. Communication is at the core of an effective democracy. Within that context students need to examine paradoxes that serve to pull people apart. These paradoxes occur because though as a nation we espouse the values of social justice and equality, in reality social hierarchies abound in our country. These inequities can be seen in many areas of our society including the schools. Dewey proposed that students become active members in our democracy, engage others in continual conversations, and create collaborative efforts that address these inequities.

Building Block Three: Sociocultural Context of Learning and Human Development

Do you remember how you learned what was important or what was expected of you? Your parents were some of your most important teachers. They taught you how they expected you to act and how to talk to and work with others. When you were young, you learned from your parents, siblings, friends, and neighbors. You learned in a family context; it was not in a formal setting like school. In Caring-Centered Multicultural Education, children are believed to learn in a social and cultural context; sometimes others tell children how to act or think, but they also learn from talking, playing, and watching others (Bruner 1990; Moll 1990; Tharp and Gallimore 1988). Learning occurs in a social setting. Children watch other children and adults in their world learning to pay attention to selected cultural stimuli. Other stimuli are perceived as background noise and to be filtered out. Parents and other significant others train children in how to succeed in the community by teaching the cultural worldview. Culture identifies what is important to the community—the values, beliefs, interpretations, skills, and selected ways of solving problems. Adults teach children particular sequencing in the learning process and children, when confronted with new situations, look for that sequence in order to figure out how to solve problems.

Let's look at an example of how children from culturally diverse communities learn what is important to know. Shirley Brice Heath (1983), an educational anthropologist, studied how parents interacted with their children from two communities:

Trackton and Roadville. Though both communities believed in schooling, Heath found basic cultural differences between the two communities.

Cultural Sequencing in Learning: How Babies Are Taught to Respond in Trackton

Trackton is primarily a Black, working-class community with roots in farming. In Trackton, when a newborn is brought home from the hospital, the baby is carried continuously for the first year of life by many different family members. The child is constantly surrounded by verbal and nonverbal communication, though it is usually not directed at the baby. During the first year of life, adults talk about how much the child eats or how they just finished changing the diaper; yet the child is not engaged in a great deal of interaction (Heath 1983). Also during that first year, the child observes how people talk to each other. They observe how people posture, hear how the pace of speaking changes, and how the context of the situation shapes how one responds in a social setting.

This community guides boys, as young as 12 to 14 months old, to begin to participate in public oral communication in the form of teasing, bossing, scolding, and defying. In fact, Heath (1983, 79) writes, "'The measure of a man is his mouth,' so males are prepared early by public language input and modeling for stage performances." Young males learn at an early age how important it is to be verbally competent and also to use the appropriate tone and nonverbal facial expressions. Girls also learn in the same way. They are held constantly, and they observe the talking of adults, but are not encouraged to participate in conversations until 22 months old.

Children learn how to deal with various situations and, when it is appropriate, to use "a particular word, phrase, or set of actions" after being asked, "Now what are you gonna do?" (Heath 1983, 84). For example, adults often tease children, pretending to take away their candy or bottle. Since children do not have physical power, they must learn skills in dealing with others by outwitting, outtalking, or outacting their aggressors (Heath 1983). This is all part of the cultural sequencing children learn from their interactions with adults. Children learn about the type of situations they will need to be able to cope with, they learn acceptable behavior and favorable verbal responses.

What are the cultural cues that children learn in their families? To what type of social situations are children expected to be able to respond? How are they expected to respond? The answers to these questions help teachers understand how adults shape the cultural context of learning.

Cultural Sequencing in Learning: How Babies Are Taught to Respond in Roadville

Roadville is a White, working-class, textile mill community in the Piedmont area of the Carolinas. Many of the families were originally from the Appalachian Mountains and moved to Piedmont in the early 1900s. In this community, the arrival of babies is an important social and familial event.

For the first three months of their lives, babies are placed on feeding and sleeping schedules to encourage them to learn the routine. Relatives and close friends visit the mother and her new baby and offer assistance and advice. Heath (1983) found that new mothers had regular visits from older women with experience with children. These women would talk with the baby, calling her by name and asking her questions using a sing-song intonation. This way both baby and new mother would learn about how they should be behaving and responding to each other.

Mothers are encouraged to respond to their babies, but not to "spoil" them by carrying them all the time. Relatives encourage mothers to let their babies explore, talk baby talk, and make noises. When children begin talking, parents, siblings, and others teach children the names of pets, people, objects, and events. They are taught to "pay attention, listen, and behave" and how to talk appropriately through their communications with adults (Heath 1983, 127).

Comparing Trackton and Roadville: Differences in the Socialization of Children

Heath (1983) found the two communities of Trackton and Roadville to show many differences in their socialization of children. Though it is not possible to describe all of her findings, I will highlight four important variations that Heath discovered. First, children in Roadville are primarily brought up by their own parents, while children in Trackton are tended to by many members of the community including parents, older siblings, children in the neighborhood, relatives, and other adults. Second, verbal interactions and skills are especially coveted in the Trackton community. Children are expected to show their abilities to perform creatively when verbally challenged. They are also taught to be spontaneous and to develop keen role-playing skills. In Roadville, children are expected to develop adult-like speech and engage in adult-like activities such as fishing, cooking, and taking care of younger siblings. For example, parents teach their children to tell stories and to report exact dialogue (Health 1983). Third, both communities have strong oral traditions; however, the way they structure their stories differs. In Roadville, stories are primarily factual, deviate little from actual events, and affirm the values of the community. In Trackton, people creatively describe real-life events and demonstrate their storytelling abilities. Last, the oral tradition is highly valued in the Trackton community. Children are taught and expected to tell stories as young as the age of two. They learn to use gestures and embellish actual events in order to be entertaining. Though children in Roadville are also encouraged to tell stories, they must be told as accurately as possible. Parents also read to their children and ask them questions about the stories. Many of the books contain nursery rhymes or are "simplified" stories from the Bible (Heath 1983).

Trackton and Roadville communities differ in the way they teach and see the use of language. Though the two social groups believe schooling is important, most members do not see how schooling could be linked to the future of their children because many find their occupations through friends, family, or accidentally.

Cultural Values in Conflict

Understanding the sociocultural background of your students can be extremely eye opening. Maybe some of the friction you see in your classroom is not showing a conflict but rather an example of how people express or communicate themselves differently. As

Heath's research has shown, people grow up with different values and ways of interpreting other people's actions. One of the best resources describing how the communication styles of African Americans and European Americans may differ can be found in Kochman's book, *Black and White Styles in Conflict.*

Kochman (1981) provides many situations of how people with different styles misinterpret the actions of others. For example, Kochman describes how Blacks often engage in posturing. This pattern of behavior sends out the message of courage and fearlessness to one's opponent (Kochman 1981). It is a way to settle an argument before physical fighting begins by asserting one's dominance. There is also a sense of drama that plays into this pattern. The posturing behavior often is a sign that the person does not intend to get into a physical fight. Posturing is a talking strategy to resolve a disagreement.

In contrast, Kochman (1981) believes that in the White community verbal threats show that aggressive physical actions will follow. Whites perceive heated verbal exchanges as most likely ending in fighting; verbal fighting will lead to physical fighting. In addition Whites believe that heated discussions are already indications that a fight is in progress.

How will these cultural differences impact the classroom? Kochman illustrates his point by telling a story about a White female teacher who had begun teaching in an Black high school in Louisville (1985, 44). Two Black students were loudly arguing at the beginning of class about who was going to sit in a particular seat. Each looked at the other defiantly and took confrontational stands; however, no physical fighting took place. The teacher sent the students to the principal's office for fighting. After class several Black students asked the teacher why she sent the two students to the office, because they weren't going to do anything. The teacher told them that she disagreed. She said the two students were "fighting" because of their loud arguing. The teacher was sure that the young men were going to throw punches at each other. She wanted to keep the situation from escalating. The students told her the others weren't really "fighting," they were setting up boundaries with their words.

In this situation, it is clear that the teacher and her Black students had different understandings of what was a fight, when it had begun, and if violence was going to arise. The teacher was sure the two students were fighting because of the anger that they expressed. However, the students only saw their behaviors as setting the stage for a possible confrontation, but that words and actions were very different (Kochman 1981). The students and teacher grew up in different cultural contexts where styles of interacting varied. If the teacher had a better understanding of this, she may have been able to diffuse it quickly and quietly. In this case, knowing the cultural values of students in her class would have assisted in her classroom management.

Teaching the Whole Student

People are complex beings, so it is critical for teachers to teach the whole student. Whether you are a secondary or an elementary teacher, you can consider teaching within the context of the whole person. High school teachers have told me that their job is to teach math and not students. I hold a contrasting viewpoint. I believe students are not only beings who soak up information, but they are affective beings who have emotions, values, dreams, and fears. Students do not learn in a vacuum. They learn when they are motivated to learn. They

learn when they eat a nutritional diet. They learn when they feel accepted and not ridiculed in class. They learn when parents and teachers support them. They also learn about society and what society thinks about economics, race, and gender from television, popular music, their friends, the history textbook, and what teachers say to them.

I believe Caring-Centered Multicultural Education affirms those who are already focused on the whole person or assists teachers in transforming classrooms into places of community. A transformation occurs when classrooms become caring and culturally meaningful places where children succeed.

Can you visualize a classroom where Caring-Centered Multicultural Education forms the framework? It is a place where both teachers and students are excited to come every morning. It is a place where students make decisions about topics they can research. It is a place that values them and their cultural heritage. It is a school where people care for each other and work with others to achieve. They want each other to do well in school and support one another. The class becomes a family of learners. Since the pedagogy is student-centered and encourages the development of an empowered, caring, and confident person who works well with others, cultural knowledge and diverse ways of thinking are encouraged and included in the classroom. Meaningful information can be used not only as examples to teach important skills, but it also can provide children with a context with which they understand and learn most efficiently. Children feel most comfortable in an environment where they know and understand the rules, expectations, behaviors, and values. Learning becomes a self-affirming action and is reinforced when teachers create classrooms where children appreciate cultural diversity, respect each other, and value the contributions each person makes to the community. Schooling then becomes a life-giving process of growth. One of the role models my children watched was Mr. Rogers on public television. He is concerned about the growth of the whole person. This is important whether the student is in first or twelfth grade.

Dashelle: Educating the Whole Person

Let's take an example of why it is important for teachers to view the whole student in the learning process. Peggy Orenstein (1994), in her book, *Schoolgirls,* describes a student named Dashelle, an eighth grader. As a seventh grader, teachers labeled her as out of control and threatening. She almost failed seventh grade. One teacher told Orenstein that he hated Dashelle. In eighth grade she became the peacemaker. How did this change come about?

Orenstein asked Dashelle what made her change. This is what Dashelle said:

"I was real bad . . . I thought, 'F school,' you know? I was like other kids. I thought it was nerdy or acting white or something to do good at school. I'd come to class and get kicked out and just sit in the office all day listening to everyone else's business . . . "

She then explained that the night before school started in September, she had ironed her clothes and was ready when her little brother, Demetrius, said to her, "You know . . . I used to look up to you, but *you ain't gonna be nothin'*. You get in trouble at school, you go out every night . . . You still gonna do all that this year?" (Orenstein 1994, 229).

Dashelle told Orenstein that was her wakeup call. She said, "I know I'm not stupid. And all my little brothers and sisters, they probably look up to me like Demetrius. I thought, 'If I go down the bad path, then they might, too.' That would hurt me so much, to see them doing the wrong thing . . . If I do good, they'll see they can do it, too" (1994, 229).

At first the teachers did not believe she had really changed. But at the end of the year, Dashelle graduated from eighth grade with a special award from the school for her leadership and a grade point average of 3.67. At the graduation Dash said, "Look, I made the honor roll in school . . . Everyone is so proud of me, but I'm proud of myself too. Because I couldn't have done it without my brain, I couldn't have done it without me" (1994, 239).

Dashelle listened in social studies, science, English, and her other classes. But most of all she listened to her little brother, Demetrius. Though she learned more that year because she worked hard, Dashelle's story showed how important it is to know the family and understand family relationships in African American communities. What motivated Dashelle was not the school, but the possibility of losing her brother's approval and seeing her siblings make the same mistake. Sibling relationships are extremely important in African American families (McAdoo 1988; Irvine 1991; Ford 1996). The intrinsic motivation of Dashelle's family was the key to her success in school. Dashelle also lived in a tough environment. Reggie Clark, an educational researcher, found that many high-achieving African American girls learn toughness and assertiveness from the neighborhoods in which they live. Some young women who are successful in school are able to transfer that resiliency they learned in the family and neighborhood to academic achievement (Clark 1983). Like Dashelle, there are many students who feel the responsibility to be a positive role model for their siblings. The case study of Dashelle helps to illustrate how important it is for us, as teachers, to know our students.

As a first grade teacher, I was often unaware of the choices some of my African American students were making. Like Dashelle, the students had to deal with the negative perception that if they did well in school, they were selling out and acting White (Fordham and Ogbu 1986). Oftentimes, African American students develop the strategy of dropping out of school or not working in school as a way to combat the frustration and anger they feel about a system which they see is trying to assimilate them and eliminate their culture. As a teacher, I did not understand the resilience it took for Becky, one of my students, to come to school day after day as the best reader in the class. I remember many of the students of color teasing her about her excellent work, but she was always respectful and never boastful toward them. Becky was a loving and shy African

American child and though she was modest, Becky was able to handle those who tried to embarrass her by drawing on her personal strength and family support. Examples like Dashelle and Becky remind me that I teach children, not subject matter. One of the major principles of Caring-Centered Multicultural Education is teaching the whole person. It is an underlying belief that leads to the goals of this framework that incorporate the principles of caring, culture, and social justice.

What Are the Goals of Multicultural Education?

The goals of Multicultural Education deal primarily with children learning skills and knowledge they will need to develop into responsible citizens and people who can think, reason, and communicate. These are the goals that I believe are most important; you may have others that you consider critical. Add those to your journal.

1. **Each child will learn basic skills, be able to think critically, make decisions, learn how to care for herself/himself and others, and participate in making a more just society. Each child will achieve academic excellence.** This is one of the most important goals of Multicultural Education because so many of our children of color or students from low-income families have not found academic success in schools. In fact, for many children school is not about the joy of learning or developing skills, but rather the motivation is high grades and/or competition for prestige. Students, teachers, and parents need to address this underlying value orientation that can take away from authentic and life-long learning.

2. **Each child will have the opportunity to develop her/his interests and/or career aspirations.** In order for a person to develop personal satisfaction in life, she must be encouraged and supported to delve into her career interests. These interests may sustain her financially and help develop in her a sense of accomplishment.

3. **Each child will develop effective interpersonal skills, so she/he can work with culturally diverse people in a respectful and caring manner.** Our world has become extremely complex and it is crucial that people from diverse communities, languages, and value orientations, come together to solve social problems.

4. **Each child will develop a healthy and positive sense of self.** This includes ethnic/cultural identity, gender identity, and sexual orientation. Remember Abraham Maslow's (1970) hierarchy of human needs: physical, safety, belonging, self-esteem, intellectual achievement, and self-actualization. In order for children to become intellectually successful, they must feel accepted and loved by those around them and through this process children develop self-esteem. When children feel accepted and confident they are more likely to be motivated to think and learn new information.

5. **Each child will mature into an independent and rational thinker who has the ability to take on responsibility for her/his own life and contribute to the community.** Each person must be able to take responsibility for her/his own development and well-being.

6. **Each child will develop moral and ethical judgment where she/he has a strong sense of personal integrity and compassion for others.** Each person needs to be an informed citizen who can make difficult decisions about controversial public issues based on a strong sense of morality. Many students struggle with balancing their own needs with the needs of others. This is part of the ethical process people go through in order to develop their own sense of virtue.

    In a democracy, citizens work toward the growth of the entire society through continued dialogue with each other, and this includes the right of those who dissent. It is also important for citizens to fight against the oppression of others, which includes racial discrimination, gender bias, and the exclusion of others based on social class. At times, one of the most challenging aspects of a democracy is to put the well-being of others before one's own. In addition, since our society is made up of many cultural groups, there are many perspectives regarding each issue.

7. **Each child will examine social oppression and social privilege in both her/his personal life and in social institutions, and actively work toward eliminating inequities.** Children and teachers will work together to eliminate social oppression in individuals, institutions, and society. In order for our society to change, all of us, teachers and children, must look at how we add to social oppression and/or benefit from social oppression. It is critical for children to be active learners who have the confidence to develop solutions and then to do something about our social problems.

8. **Teachers will create life-giving classrooms where culture is used to build meaningful learning environments, and compassion and respect form the foundation for classroom interactions.** In order for most children to do well in school, classrooms must be places where they are affirmed rather than ridiculed. For example, my son came home from his first week of eighth grade unhappy. When I asked him what was the matter, he said, "I don't know why I need to know this stuff. It doesn't have to do with anything." It was hard to explain how the Pythagorean theorem was going to help him right away in life.

    The next week my son seemed even more disturbed. "I sure like your teacher," I said. He looked at me funny.

    "What's wrong? The teacher seems like a caring person who knows her subject," I rattled on.

    Though he did not want to talk about the teacher, he finally said, "Mom, the kids don't like being ridiculed in class. When you don't know the answer, the teacher makes fun of you in front of the entire class. It's really embarrassing. Yes, the teacher knows her stuff, but because she ridicules people, we don't learn anything."

    Many times in life, I have been reminded by students about what really counts in schools. My son was trying to tell me that teaching means more than the content. Student-teacher relationships are a critical part of the learning environment. In my son's class, content coupled with compassion would have made a far more effective learning environment.

9. **Each school will be restructured around the principles of democracy and the belief that the United States is a nation of many peoples.** Each school

can utilize democratic values in how they structure school policies and what curriculum is chosen. Children, parents, and community can be contributing members of a school organization. In addition, since the United States is a pluralistic nation, the school calendar, policies, and other aspects can reflect our cultural diversity.

10. **Students, teachers, and parents will work together to eliminate racism, sexism, classism, homophobia, and other types of social oppression in schools and society.**

When I was a first grade teacher it was hard to see past the whirlwind of short legs and wonderful smiles. But now I realize that schools are powerful social systems where relations based on race, class, gender, language, handicapping conditions, and sexual orientation continue to be reinforced. For example, many of my children of color or children from lower-income families were found in the lower reading and math groups. In addition, children called each other negative ethnic terms on the playground. Fortunately, teachers are finding ways to move away from tracking their children, and school personnel have focused on eliminating ethnic jokes or slurs.

In order to examine how well schools mirror our democratic values of equal status, freedom, and justice I began to think about the following questions: How democratic am I? What values am I teaching in how I structure the activities or line up children or choose uniforms? How equitably are my students learning? Are some children involved in their learning more than others? Why? Do I value what the students already know? How do I include the community in our school activities and policies?

As John Dewey, the famous philosopher reminded us, schools are small worlds where democracy can be learned and practiced every day.

All of these listed goals are important and, as teachers, we attempt to pursue them simultaneously. Teaching is an art and not a technical skill and as such there are many things we must do automatically and almost intuitively. This is why I feel it is critical that teachers have clear goals. We have so many decisions to make during the course of a day or week or month of teaching and without a thoughtful understanding of why we teach, we may get bogged down in the quagmire of paperwork and school chaos which has little to do with teaching.

❧ How One School Sends Out Positive Messages

Multicultural Education is about children learning and succeeding in school. As you know it takes a village to raise a child. No matter how effective you are as a teacher, it still takes parents, grandparents, siblings, cousins, friends, ministers, Girl Scout leaders, YMCA leaders, soccer coaches, and others to continually reinforce the lessons children need to learn. At Valencia Park Elementary in San Diego, they post affirmations for each year on the bulletin board, distribute the affirmations to both children and parents, and refer to them continuously throughout the year. Emily Jenkins developed the idea while working as a James Comer School resource teacher. These affirmations help to focus the attention of children, parents, and teachers on positive goals and are part of what Valencia Park Elementary does to "Teach the Whole Child."

Let's take a look at those affirmations:

September	My words of respect show that I care.
October	Only the best is good enough for me.
November	I am an important person in this world.
January	I can dream dreams, and make those dreams come true.
February	Every new day is another opportunity to improve myself.
March	It may be difficult, but it is possible.
April	I care for and help each of my classmates.
May	It is never too late for me to improve.
June	I control the good that happens to me.
July	I can learn from others, and they can learn from me.

What new affirmations would you suggest for coming years? I know that children enjoy creating them too. This could be a whole school project where students suggest possible affirmations and a committee of students writes and chooses them for the new year.

Summary

In this chapter the framework for Multicultural Education is discussed in depth. Caring-Centered Multicultural Education believes in a life-giving process of growth. The three building blocks of this framework are:

The ethic of caring
Education for democracy
The sociocultural context of learning and human development

These building blocks form an integrated philosophy directed at teaching the whole student. Effective teachers look at the holistic needs of children. Caring teachers know that students learn most effectively when they feel accepted for who they are. Culture is a core aspect of how students identify themselves and way children learn new information.

The three building blocks form a united foundation for schooling. This foundation emphasizes the importance of caring for the whole child and reaffirms the moral commitment many teachers have to their students. Though many of my colleagues see Multicultural Education as a historical and political movement against oppression, I believe it is much more. We teach not only because we know that society has not always acted in a moral or humane way toward many groups of people, but because we want to be part of the life-giving process we call learning (Rivera and Poplin 1996).

Teacher Reflections

1. What is Multicultural Education? Thinking about the question, take a moment now and write down what you think it is in your journal and continue to alter it as you read through this book. Keep track of the changes you make. At the end of the text, examine how your views may have evolved as you thought about issues brought up in this book. If you have difficulty writing, use the following sentence starter: I believe Multicultural Education is. . .

TABLE 4.1

Major Goals of Multicultural Education

1. Each child will learn her/his basic skills, be able to think critically, and be an active citizen in society. Each child will achieve academic excellence.
2. Each child will have the opportunity to develop her/his interests and/or career aspirations.
3. Each child will develop effective interpersonal skills, so she/he can work with culturally diverse people in a respectful and affirming manner.
4. Each child will develop a healthy and positive sense of self.
5. Each child will mature into an independent and rational thinker who is responsible for her/his own life.
6. Each child will develop moral and ethical judgment where she/he has a strong sense of personal integrity and compassion for others.
7. Each child will examine social oppression and social privilege in both her/his personal life and in social institutions, and actively work toward eliminating inequities.
8. Teachers will create life-giving classrooms where culture is used to build meaningful learning environments, and compassion and respect form the foundation for classroom interactions.
9. Each school will be restructured around the principles of democracy and the belief that the United States is a nation of many peoples.
10. Students, teachers, and parents work to eliminate racism, sexism, classism, homophobia, and other types of social oppression in schools and society.

---

2. Table 4.1 summarizes the goals I propose for Caring-Centered Multicultural Education. After reading through Table 4.1, answer the following questions in your journal:

   How would you prioritize the goals of Multicultural Education?
   Are there other goals that you would include that I have not included?
   What are they and why do you believe these goals should be added?

3. Table 4.2 provides a summary of how the culturally caring classroom looks in contrast with the status quo classroom. Circle the statements that you agree with in each column. Where do you find more of your circles? Think about what your values are and how those values shape your viewpoints. If you had more circles under the status quo section, examine each of the statements under the culturally caring column and write some questions that you might ask your colleagues or professor during your next class. Can you begin to think about schools from the culturally caring perspective? What is holding you back from agreeing with some of the statements?

   Write how you feel in your journal. If you are frustrated, write why. If you are confused, describe what it is that confuses you. If you agree with many of the culturally caring statements, write why you agree. Share these with a friend or colleague. The dialogue may help you to clarify your thoughts.

TABLE 4.2

The Caring and Culturally Meaningful Classroom

Culturally Caring Classroom	Status Quo
The United States is a color-conscious society. People are treated differently based on their color and race. Merit is a culturally defined concept.	The United States is a color-blind society. People are judged on their personal merit.
Schools are sociocultural institutions of society where racism, sexism, and classism have continued to impact the way children are treated.	Schools have addressed the issue of equal opportunity of education through the implementation of bilingual education, multicultural education, and special education programs.
Equity is a key issue in Multicultural Education. Students must be encouraged to examine social issues for equity. They can take stands on public issues like welfare reform, affirmative action, bilingual education, and employment opportunities.	Diversity has been included in the policies, curriculum, and instructional strategies of schools. Diversity is the key component of multicultural education. For example, children from diverse communities work together in cooperative groups.
Culture is an important aspect of the learning, self-esteem, and communication process.	Good teachers can teach any children. Culture is not a critical aspect of teaching.
Children feel most comfortable with teachers who understand the values, history, behaviors, learning behaviors, expectations, and language they are most familiar with in life. Teachers naturally infuse information about children's lives, whether it deals with food, history, family outings, grandparents, neighborhood or other real-life issues.	Teachers build trusting relationships with their students by caring and providing interesting classrooms.
Decreasing the achievement gap is the most important goal of Multicultural Education. Schools need to change in order to become effective with children who arrive at school with diverse views, ways of learning, and skills. Schools are at risk, not children.	Children come to school from at-risk families and situations, and the source of failure comes from children and their families and culture.
Teachers are partners with parents and children in the learning process. Teachers encourage parents to be active in the classroom and to reinforce learning at home through working with and doing things with their children.	Teachers are the professionals who are best qualified to decide on what works with children.
Children are empowered to think and solve problems and challenge inequities. Teachers are facilitators in that process. Thinking is a critical aspect of their development as caring individuals and citizens of a democracy.	Children are to receive knowledge and learn information from their teachers who are experts.
Teachers who care believe they are called to advocate for their children and involve children in their empowerment.	Advocacy is not part of the job of teachers. Teachers are hired to teach children their basic skills so they can support themselves and be good citizens.

References

Aronowitz, Stanley. 1997. Between nationality and class. *Harvard Educational Review, 67* (2): 188–207.

Baca, Leonard, and Hermes T. Cervantes. 1989. *The bilingual special education interface.* Columbus, Ohio: Merrill Publishing Company.

Banks, James A. 1996. The historical reconstruction of knowledge about race: Implications for transformative teaching. In James A. Banks, Ed., *Multicultural education, transformative knowledge, and action.* New York: Teachers College Press.

Banks, James A. 1996a. The African American roots of multicultural education. In James A. Banks, Ed., *Multicultural education, transformative knowledge, and action.* New York: Teachers College Press.

Bruner, Jerome. 1990. *Acts of meaning.* Cambridge, Mass.: Harvard University Press.

Christiansen, Linda. 1997. Reading, writing, and outrage. Keynote address. National Association for Multicultural Education, November, Albuquerque, New Mexico.

Clark, Reggie. 1983. *Family life and school: Why poor Black children succeed and fail.* Chicago, Ill.: University of Chicago Press.

Cummins, Jim. 1989. *Empowering minority students.* Los Angeles, Calif.: California Association for Bilingual Education.

Darder, Antonia. 1991. *Culture and power in the classroom.* New York: Bergin & Garvey.

Dewey, John. 1916. *Democracy and education.* N.Y.: Macmillan.

Ford, Donna. 1996. *Reversing underachievement among gifted Black students.* N.Y.: Teachers College Press.

Fordham, Signithia, and John Ogbu. 1986. Black students' school success: Coping with the 'burden of acting white'. *Urban Review, 18*(3): 176–206.

Gay, Geneva. 1994. *At the essence of learning: Multicultural education.* West Lafayette, Ind.: Kappa Delta Pi.

Gilligan, Carol. 1982. *In a different voice: Psychological theory and women's development.* Cambridge, Mass.: Harvard University Press.

Gollnick, Donna, and Phil Chinn. 1986. *Multicultural education,* 2nd ed. Columbus, Ohio: Charles E. Merrill.

Gordon, Edmund W. 1991. *A new compact for learning.* Albany, N.Y.: New York State Education Department.

Gordon, Edmund W. 1999. *Education and justice: A view from the back of the bus.* New York: Teachers College Press.

Heath, Shirley Brice. 1983. *Ways with words: Language, life, and work in communities and classrooms.* N.Y.: Cambridge University Press.

Irvine, Jacqueline Jordan. 1991. *Black students and school failure.* N.Y.: Praeger.

Kochman, Thomas. 1981. *Black and white styles in conflict.* Chicago: University of Chicago Press.

Kozol, Jonathan. 1991. *Savage inequalities: Children in America's schools.* New York: Crown Publishers.

Maslow, Abraham. 1970. *Motivation and personality,* 2nd ed. New York: Harper & Row.

McAdoo, H. P. 1988. *Black families,* 2nd ed. Newbury Park, Calif.: Sage.

McLaren, Peter, ed. 1997. *Revolutionary multiculturalism.* Boulder, Colo.: Westview Press.

Meier, Deborah. 1995. *The power of their ideas.* Boston, Mass.: Beacon Press.

Moll, Luis. 1990. *Vygotsky and education: Instructional implications and applications of sociohistorical psychology.* New York: Cambridge University Press.

Moll, Luis, and James B. Greenberg. 1990. Creating zones of possibilities: Combining social contexts for instruction. In Luis Moll's, ed., *Vygotsky and education: Instructional implications and applications of sociohistorical psychology.* New York: Cambridge University Press.

Moran, C. and Kenji Hakuta. 1995. Bilingual education: Broadening research perspectives. In James A. Banks and Cherry McGee Banks, eds., *Handbook of research on multicultural education.* N.Y.: Macmillan.

Noddings, Nel. 1984. *Caring: A feminine approach to ethics and moral education.* Berkeley, Calif.: University of California Press.

Noddings, Nel. 1992. *The challenge to care in schools.* New York: Teachers College Press.

Oakes, Jeannie. 1982. *Keeping track: How schools structure inequality.* New Haven, Conn.: Yale University Press.

Orenstein, Peggy. 1994. *Schoolgirls: Young women, self-esteem, and the confidence gap.* New York: Doubleday Anchor Books.

Ovando, Carlos and Virginia Collier. 1985. *Bilingual and esl classrooms.* N.Y.: McGraw-Hill.

Rivera, Juan, and Mary Poplin. 1996. Multicultural, critical, feminine and constructive pedagogies seen through the lives of youth: A call for the revisioning of these and beyond: Toward a pedagogy for the next century. In Christine Sleeter and Peter McLaren, eds., *Multicultural education, critical pedagogy, and the politics of difference.* New York: State University of New York Press.

Silberman, Charles. 1970. *Crisis in the classroom.* New York: Random House.

Sleeter, Christine, and Carl Grant. 1988. *Making choices for multicultural education.* Columbus, Ohio: Charles E. Merrill.

Strom, David. 1999. Personal communications. January 7. San Diego, California.

Suzuki, Bob. 1984. Curriculum transformation for multicultural education. *Education and Urban Society, 16:* 294–322.

Tharp, Rolland and Ronald Gallimore. 1988. Rousing minds to life: *Teaching, learning, and schooling in social context.* N.Y.: Cambridge University Press.

Wang, L. 1976. Lau V. Nichols: History of a struggle for equal and quality education. In Emma Gee, ed., *Counterpoint.* Los Angeles, Calif.: Regents of the University of California and the UCLA Asian American Studies Center.

Part Three

Confronting Prejudice in Ourselves and Our Schools: Making Changes

Chapter 5

What Are Our Hidden Hurdles?

Chapter 6

How Does It Feel to be Discriminated Against?

Chapter 7

Aren't Maria and Michael Too Young to Be Prejudiced? How Children Learn Prejudice

Chapter 8

How Can I Look Beneath the Surface for Prejudice in Schools?

Chapter 5

What Are Our Hidden Hurdles?

"We have met the enemy and they are us."

–Walt Kelly, Pogo

"Can we talk of integration until there is integration of hearts and minds? Unless you have this, you have only a physical presence, and the walls between us are as high as the mountain range."

–Chief Dan George

*H*idden hurdles exist in all of us. We may have biases about financial status, languages, accents, gender, sexual orientation, disabilities, body shapes, and many other issues. Our beliefs may act as barriers to making connections with other people. Do your beliefs influence the way you interact or see others? As the cartoon character above reminds us, the enemy is not someone else, the enemy is ourselves. Our own biases may act as barriers to our caring for others. Looking at ourselves can be difficult, but it is part of caring for our own development and in creating more authentic and trusting relationships with others.

This chapter examines possible hurdles we may hold about others. One of the key principles of Caring-Centered Multicultural Education is to continually examine oneself for social biases. If, as you begin to "unpack" your own biases, guilt creeps in, move it aside. Guilt is not an effective motivator, rather I believe most of us need a chance to think about our own biases in order to purge them from our minds. Caring teachers work hard at being open-minded and refrain from labeling others. As one teacher said, "labeling is disabling." We are all connected and when one of us succeeds, then we all succeed. The opposite is also true; when a person is treated unfairly, we are all hurt because the act and intention to exclude one person jeopardizes the building of compassion, respect, and equality in our community. The field of Multicultural Education holds the long-term aim of creating a caring society which affirms cultural diversity and emphasizes our common values of democracy, justice, equality, and freedom. As Martin Luther King, Jr., wisely said:

"Injustice anywhere is a threat to justice everywhere. We are caught in an inescapable network of morality, tied in a single garment of destiny. What affects one directly, affects all indirectly."

❧ Hidden Biases

Do you think Multicultural Education is mainly learning about other cultures? Most teachers want me to tell them everything they need to know about African American, Vietnamese, or Hopi culture. In a discussion in one of my classes, I asked teachers, "What do you hope to gain from taking a multicultural education class?"

These are some of the most common responses:

"I hope to gain a better understanding and awareness of other cultures."
"I want to better understand different ethnic groups, because basically, I feel, it's the child who is 'different' who usually has low self-esteem."
"I would like to learn ways to get culturally diverse kids to feel comfortable with each other."
"I hope to learn different strategies for teaching."

Did you have some of the same thoughts? Are you expecting a lot of information about other cultures? In this book, I do provide some information about various cultural groups, but first I think it is necessary for you to begin to examine your personal beliefs and values. Are there any hidden hurdles in you that may prevent you from helping each child do her/his best?

How Have You Learned About Other People?

In your lifetime, you have been influenced by thousands of people. As a child growing up, you had little control over the many messages that you received from friends, parents, sisters, brothers, uncles, aunts, grandparents, and people from your neighborhood. Some of the attitudes, misconceptions, or beliefs that you learned from others may become obstacles to feeling connected with or caring toward others.

Besides people in your family and neighborhood, one of the most influential forces today is the media, especially television. If you were a child who watched a lot of television, by the time you entered school you probably watched as many hours of television as it takes to get a four-year college degree. So the messages you saw on television were continual, verbal, visual, and uncensored. Some of the messages were helpful and others should be deleted from your mind. On the computer, we can easily use the delete key and in less than a second, those thoughts are gone. Unfortunately, it isn't as easy to delete beliefs and attitudes from our brains as it is to erase ideas from a computer.

The Biggest Hurdle

If you are like many teachers, you probably think your most important task in Multicultural Education is to learn more about the cultural customs, holidays, and history of your diverse students. Yes, educators need cultural knowledge. However, I believe the biggest hurdle we will undertake is to challenge and rid ourselves of personal biases and prejudices, and to view others with "new eyes." This can be a *painful and lifelong* process and we need to support each other through this undertaking.

Remember when I asked teachers in my classes what they hoped to learn in a multicultural class, and most wanted cultural knowledge? A few acknowledged the need to look at their own attitudes. Two teachers wrote thoughtful responses about themselves:

"How can I go into a classroom and not just give my narrow-minded, White perspective on subjects?"

"I want to limit my prejudices and biases."

We all have hidden hurdles in our minds. I too have been conditioned by society for many years to see others as either "we" or "they." These hurdles have acted as obstacles to my seeing the ability of some students. It has taken me many years to understand how my own biases have acted as powerful filters which shaped the information I gathered about others every day. I did not want to think that I was a prejudiced person.

You may believe that you are not a prejudiced person because you are fair and have strong morals. I agree. And you probably didn't go into teaching to make money because most people know teachers do not make megabucks. Rather you are committed to making a difference in young people's minds. As a society, we need you. Yet since ethnic and cultural prejudices are often carefully hidden in the "nooks and crannies" of our minds, you may hold some attitudes which may limit ways you view your students. Many teachers arrive at multicultural education classes believing that they do not need any instruction because they are not biased.

> *"INJUSTICE ANYWHERE IS A THREAT*
> *TO JUSTICE EVERYWHERE."*
>
> *Martin Luther King, Jr.*

❧ Eliminating the Roots of Prejudice

Prejudice and bias often have deep roots like weeds. If you cut off the top portion of the weed and leave several tiny roots, there's a possibility that the weed will sprout again. We have all been socialized by society and have heard stereotypical comments or have seen stereotypical images. We took in stereotypical beliefs about others. In our society there are many examples of stereotypes floating around. African American males are often seen as being athletic and therefore must be great basketball players. Children from European American families who have little money are labeled "poor trash" and some people assume they can't read well. Asian Pacific American and Mexican American women are often seen as weak and subservient, rather than competent leaders. Native Americans are stereotyped as people who live on reservations though most Native Americans live in the city. Women are sometimes portrayed as emotional rather than logical, and men are seen as macho instead of gentle. I believe there are few of us who did not learn prejudicial views about others. Most of us continually need to work at eliminating our biases throughout life. Teachers remark that once they begin to see how prejudices are so much a part of life, they cannot go back to "sweeping them under the rug."

Signs of the Hidden Hurdles of Prejudice

On a television news program, reporters sent out two men, one African American and one European American into the community. Both had comparable bachelor's degrees in business. In fact, they were college buddies. First the men went out to buy a car. Though both men showed interest in the same car, the African American man was quoted a price several thousand dollars higher than his White friend. The two were sure that this was just an isolated incident of prejudice, so they found an ad for an apartment and called on its owner. The African American male went first and was told that all the apartments were already rented. Several minutes later, the European American male approached the same apartment manager about an apartment and was shown one. The manager told the European American that an apartment was available and could be rented on the spot. A television camera filmed each incident. The experiences of the two were compared and it was sadly obvious that the Black male faced a great deal of discrimination. The two friends were shocked by their experiences because this was 1990 and over twenty-five years since the Civil Rights Acts of 1964 had been passed.

Why Is It Sometimes Difficult to See Prejudice?

Prejudice may be hard to see unless it is directed *at you*. In the previous example, the European American male was shocked when he viewed the videos showing the high level of prejudice aimed at his friend. The African American male knew that racial discrimination still occurs, but he was surprised at how much he encountered in a short time. The people who would not rent to the African American had no apparent reason to reject him. He had the same qualifications as his friend. They were reacting to his physical and racial differences.

Gordon Allport, a sociologist who has done much research, uses the *New English Dictionary* definition of **prejudice:**

"a feeling, favorable or unfavorable, toward a person or thing, prior to, or not based on, actual experience" (Allport 1954, 7).

Allport believes that most ethnic prejudice is primarily negative. Why? When people use overgeneralizations in looking at others, they do not see the real person. For example, let's say that someone meets you for the first time at a school board meeting. During the course of the meeting, you provide excellent reasons why a new math series should be adopted. You answer questions professionally and effectively. Unfortunately, by the end of the meeting, the person maintains that since you are a female, the person is not sure of your abilities. A prejudiced person will use selective memory in her/his judgment and continue to hold on to overgeneralizations about members of a group. Prejudice acts as a filter that prejudges people.

Our minds automatically use categories to sort the millions of pieces of information that we take in every day. Allport helps us to understand what is really prejudice. Allport believes that you can prejudge a person without being prejudiced when you are open to new information about a group or person. However, ethnic and cultural prejudices are often difficult to get rid of and can contribute to the inequitable treatment of people. Allport defines **ethnic prejudice** as

> "an antipathy based upon a faulty and inflexible generalization. It may be felt or expressed. It may be directed toward a group as a whole, or toward an individual because he is a member of that group." (Allport 1954, 10).

Can Prejudice Be Positive?

The comic brings up the issue of positive stereotypes. Some people have argued that they believe ethnic stereotypes can be positive. Let's talk for a moment about an Asian Pacific American student.

John is a Chinese American student in a fifth grade classroom. The teacher believes he is a bright kid. He works hard and is fairly well behaved in class. The only weakness John seems to have is he doesn't do well in math.

One day the teacher has a chat with John and says, "What's going on with your math? I know that you can do better. Your older sister was a math whiz kid. I think that you aren't working hard enough."

John looks down at the floor and says, "But, teacher, I do work at it. I don't think math likes me."

With a big sigh, John continues, "You sound just like my parents. They tell me I must not be working as hard as my sister."

The teacher doesn't want to believe John because she thinks he is not working hard enough. As the days go by, the teacher watches John work on his math homework. She begins to see that John is on task and struggles with the unit on fractions.

The teacher then asks herself, "Why did I think math should be easy for John? Why did I think that because his sister was good in math, John should also be great at it? Was it because he is Chinese American and I assumed he would be good in math and science? Why didn't I stop and really look at John's strengths and weaknesses?"

In this example, the teacher let her own biases creep into her expectations about this Asian Pacific American student. It limited the way she helped John. Many teachers believe Asian Pacific American students are good in math and that comes from a positive belief system about Asian Pacific Americans. However, there are Asian Pacific American students who are not good at mathematics, but their teachers expect them to excel. Some students, like in any social group, catch on quickly to math concepts, but there are others who may struggle with simple computations. Many Asian Pacific American children are often pushed by parents, teachers, and even themselves toward math, science, and computer careers. Yet they may be more interested in careers in drama, politics, or police enforcement. Sometimes students feel the burden of fitting the stereotype of Asian Pacific Americans (Pang 1995).

You can help all your students by encouraging them to develop their interests and talents in many areas like drama, creative writing, political science, or physical education. Help your students see themselves in many different settings and occupations. After looking at your perceptions of others, you may realize how important it is not only to encourage your students to expand their dreams of who they can be, but you may need to stretch your beliefs about what students from culturally diverse groups can do and accomplish.

Stereotypes: Forms of Bias

Like most people, you probably realize that stereotypes are harmful, but you may find it difficult to catch yourself thinking them. In much of my work, I am in schools supervising student teachers, and I drive on the freeway to see them. I live in San Diego and the freeways are usually busy during the day. One day a driver in a large blue sedan entered the freeway, merged into the slow lane, and then cut over three lanes to the fast lane on the far left. I saw this car moving over without regard for the busy traffic. As the car cut in front of me, I noticed that it was a woman driver. Instantly the thought appeared in my mind, "those terrible women drivers!!" I was shocked by my own bias. I had to tell myself, "Wait a minute. You are a woman and you don't drive like that. In fact, both male and female drivers have cut in front of you on the freeway." In my anger, it was easier for me to fall back into old patterns of thinking. I was labeling all women as bad drivers. Allport would say that I had "a fixed idea." He defines **stereotypes** as:

> "a favorable or unfavorable exaggerated belief associated with a category whose function is to justify our conduct as it relates to the category" (Allport 1954, 187).

A stereotype is like a picture in your mind which has a value judgment attached to it. For example, the woman driver stereotype isn't only that the driver is a woman, but women

are incompetent drivers who can't be expected to drive rationally. Stereotypes are used as a screening measure in accepting or rejecting a person or group. Many stereotypes are based on a fear of the group, a lack of knowledge of the group, differences in beliefs and practices, and/or misconceptions.

Stereotypes are destructive because these overgeneralized images act as filters about others. In the comic above, some people may not recognize Wicky's chosen career as a nurse. The stereotype may seem positive, but it also undermines the position of nurses and shows gender bias. Most of us belong to various groups which may hold stereotypes about other groups. We all need to continue to challenge our perceptions of others throughout life.

☙ New Hurdles: The New Racism and Sexism

Now let's get down to several difficult issues. Maybe you are beginning to settle into your easy chair and feel confident that racism, sexism, classism, and homophobia are not problems in the way you live your life. You believe everyone is equal and you work toward a just society for everyone.

Remember the analogy of the weeds in a garden? Prejudice is like the weeds in our garden. They are there to remind us that the garden needs to be attended to constantly. Like weeds in a garden, new research on prejudice has shown how old-fashioned racism and sexism have sprouted up into modern racism and sexism. Before looking at how prejudice appears today, I would like to share thoughts about the terms *race, ethnicity, personal racism, cultural racism, institutional racism, classism,* and *sexism.*

Race is an extremely complicated and political construct. Omi and Winant view race as a "concept which signifies and symbolizes social conflicts and interests by referring to different type[s] of human bodies" (1994, 55). In traditional sociology, scholars for the most part equated biological characteristics of race with hair texture and color, skin color, head shape, and other body features. Unfortunately, race is often also seen in terms of intelligence. Though people use the term of race all the time, it is not a clearly defined or fixed concept. As a concept which is tied intimately to power and political relationships, Omi and Winant provide an illuminating example of how political the term *race* is in our society.

A Louisiana woman, Susie Guillory Phipps, wanted to change her racial classification from Black to White. She thought of herself as White, but found that records with the Louisiana Bureau of Vital Records listed her as being Black. She sued the agency, but lost. The state contended that since Phipps was a descendant of an eighteenth-century White planter and a Black slave, she had been listed as Black on her birth certificate because of a 1970 state law, which stated that anyone with at least 1/32 "Negro blood" was Black. Why did she lose her case? The court ruled that the state had the right to classify and identify racial identity. During the trial, a Tulane University professor found that most of the Whites in Louisiana were at least 1/20 "Negro" (Omi and Winant 1994, 53–54). Race is often used to place people into a large social category which does not consider individual differences, as in the Phipps example. Race has been used to discriminate against others. Our history has many examples of how race has been used to oppress members of specific groups. African American slaves were prohibited from learning to read during much of the 1800s. In some cases African Americans were killed because of their knowledge of books. Chinese immigrants became the first group to be identified by race and excluded from entrance into the United States with the Chinese Exclusion Act of 1882. Another example is Executive Order 9066, signed in 1942. Through this order, their own government placed 120,000 Japanese Americans in concentration camps during World War II. Racial identification is an extremely political construct in the United States and other countries. It often is about power relationships and oppression.

Ethnicity is a concept which some scholars use to move away from the biological orientation of race to a discussion of domination and power relationships. Like race, ethnicity is also a complex social construct which extends beyond discussions of culture and identity. In this book, ethnicity is seen as a group category that deals with culture, ancestry (Omi and Winant 1994), and sense of oneness (Kleg 1993). Some characteristics often identified with ethnicity are culture, geographical origin, language, religion, shared traditions, common political interests, moral orientation, and sense of kinship. Not all groups emphasize the same characteristics. For example, though African Americans are descendants from many different nations in Africa, because of their common historical experiences of slavery, segregation, discrimination, and victimization, many African Americans have developed a strong ethnic identity (Kleg 1993).

Racism can be both overt and covert, and personal, institutional, and cultural (Bennett 1995). It is the belief that one's race is superior and others are inferior. Nieto (1992) uses the definition of Meyer Weinberg who defines racism as "a system of privilege and penalty" based on the belief that groups of people are inherently inferior. This belief is used to justify the unequal distribution of opportunities, goods, and services. **Personal racism** is the belief that one's race is superior to another.

Cultural racism is the belief that the culture of a group is inferior or that they do not have a culture (Nieto 1992). For example, I have been in classrooms where teachers tell their children that music by Bach is an example of high culture and highly valued; whereas the blues is a form of low culture and not as well developed.

Institutional racism is a system of legalized practices designed to keep the dominant group in power (McIntosh 1992). There are institutional laws, policies, and rules that serve to discriminate against certain groups of people. Underrepresented groups are marginalized by the society, they are placed at the borders of society, and they have little power to make large-scale changes.

Closely related to racism is classism. **Classism** is prejudice or discrimination based on one's financial or economic status. Oftentimes classism and racism are intimately connected. For example, when a Latino or Pacific Islander faces continual societal prejudice, they may find it difficult to find employment or housing. In this way their opportunities to find economic success are limited and they find themselves scrambling to survive economically. Then as they attempt to find additional opportunities, others may discriminate against them not only because of their racial membership, but also because they are from lower-income communities.

Another common form of social discrimination is sexism. **Sexism** "is the belief that females and males have distinctive characteristics and that one gender has the right to more power and resources than the other; it is policies and practices based on those beliefs" (Schniedewind and Davidson 1998, 8). In the following section, I will share with you some new research on how people's perceptions of racism and sexism still exist, but are more hidden than in the past. The work of Swim, Aikin, Hall, and Hunter (1995) found that negative attitudes about women and people of color are more subtle than in the past and there is continual denial that discrimination is a force in society.

WE MUST ELIMINATE PERSONAL, INSTITUTIONAL, AND SOCIAL PREJUDICE.

Before I describe the work of Swim and her colleagues, ask yourselves the following questions. Write down the responses that come to your mind right away. Don't censor your responses. Write them down as quickly as you think of them.

Who would you prefer as a boss, a woman or a man? *don't care*

Who would you prefer to have as your representative in Congress, an African American or European American? *don't care*

Whose responsibility is it to care for the children in a family? *mom & dad*

How do you feel about interracial marriage? If you fell in love with someone from another ethnic group, would you marry that person? How would you feel if your child dated someone from another group? *yes fine*

How would you describe the progress African Americans have made in securing equal rights? *difficult and long*

What were your responses to the questions? Were you surprised by your thoughts?

Swim and her colleagues found that people's views of women and people of color, specifically African Americans, exhibited both old-fashioned racism and sexism, and modern racism and sexism.

✎ Old-Fashioned and Modern Racism and Sexism

In the old-fashioned racism and sexism, the statements used were strong and blatantly prejudicial. For example, statements like the following show powerful biases:

"Women are generally not as smart as men."
"Black people are generally not as smart as Whites."
"It is a bad idea for Blacks and Whites to marry one another."
"It is more important to encourage boys than to encourage girls to participate in athletics."

In order to examine modern racism and sexism, the following were examples of statements used in Swim's and her colleagues' research:

"Discrimination against women is no longer a problem in the United States."
"It is rare to see women treated in a sexist manner on television."
"Blacks have more influence upon school desegregation plans than they ought to have."
"Blacks are getting too demanding in their push for equal rights."

Read through the following tables. Many of these statements place blame on underrepresented people and women for the lack of movement toward equality. The statements were used to distinguish between old-fashioned and modern sexism and racism.

In their findings (see Tables 5.1 and 5.2), Swim and her colleagues found that men held higher levels of old-fashioned and modern sexist beliefs than women. They also found that those who were more individualistic and not egalitarian were more likely to show old-fashioned and modern prejudices. Swim and her colleagues felt that strong individualism and inequitable values correlated with racism and sexism. Individualistic

TABLE 5.1

Reviewing Racism: The Old-Fashioned and the Modern

	Old Beliefs	Modern Beliefs
Racism	Generally speaking, I favor full racial integration.	Discrimination is no longer a problem in the United States.
	I am opposed to open housing.	There is little need for federal programs focusing upon equity.
	Interracial marriage is not a good idea.	People who do not work and who live off welfare are to blame for their own problems.
	The United States Supreme Court should not have outlawed segregation in 1954.	
Resentment Toward African Americans	Blacks are not as smart as Whites.	Discrimination is no longer a problem in the United States.
	Blacks are not to be trusted.	There is little need for federal programs focusing upon equity.
	Blacks do not work hard, so often they are not able to keep a job.	People who do not work and who live off welfare are to blame for their own problems.
	In the United States, blacks have no reason to complain.	The United States is built upon a belief in equity and anyone can make it who works hard.
		Blacks are getting too demanding about equal rights.
		Blacks should not be as influential as they are in the issue of desegregation.
		Blacks have gotten more economically than they merit.
		In the past few years, the news media and the federal government have shown more respect toward blacks than they deserve.

values focus upon individual merit, effort, and achievement. Many people, who support racism and sexism and who believe in individualism, may also think that those who do not do well lack the drive or discipline to work; they believe that the reason for inequalities are deficiencies in women and people of color. However, those who hold egalitarian values believe everyone should have equal access to opportunities. They recognize that in today's society some people have special privileges and entitlements because of their economic, gender, or racial status. Until equal opportunity is a reality, society must develop ways to address these inequalities.

TABLE 5.2

Examining Sexism: The Old-Fashioned and the Modern

	Old Beliefs	Modern Beliefs
Sexism	Women are generally not as smart as men. Women are more emotional and men are more logical. It is easier to work for a male boss than a female boss. Boys should be encouraged more than girls to participate in sports. Women should be the primary caregiver in a family.	Discrimination against women is no longer a problem in the United States. Women are rarely treated in a sexist manner on television. Men and women are treated equally in society. Women have the same opportunities to succeed as men in the United States.
Resentment Toward Women		In the past years, the federal government and the news media have shown more concern about the treatment of women than is warranted by their actual experiences.

Swim's research demonstrated that many Americans do not believe that discrimination is a current problem in the United States. Some people believe that racism and sexism are patterns of the past and that the Civil Rights Movement of the 1960s and subsequent legislation healed our nation. However, evidence points to the contrary. Results of the 1990 Gallup poll found, 54 percent of the female respondents and 43 percent of the male respondents preferred a man as a boss, in comparison to 12 percent of women and 15 percent of men who preferred a woman boss (Swim, Aikin, Hall, and Hunter 1995). Another indication that discrimination is still a social problem is differential salary levels. Catalyst, a research organization, reported that in 1997 women of color made only 57 cents for every dollar a White male earns. Even though women of color make up 10 percent of the workforce in the United States, only 5 percent of the women of color held management positions (Jackson 1997). The opportunities of women from

Asian American, Black, and Latino communities in management were even more limited than White women; White women represent 86 percent of the female managers, Asian Americans represent 2.5 percent, Blacks make up 7 percent, and Latinas make up 5 percent of the management force (Jackson 1997). It is happening today in our nation, right now. This impacts all of us because it limits opportunities of our mothers, sisters, friends, aunts, and grandmothers, and ourselves if we are women. And it also limits the possible impact they could have on organizations. The statistics show how gender and race are intimately tied. The next section discusses Park's theory of race relations.

Park's Theory of Race Relations

As Swim and her colleagues have found, people hold various prejudices about others based on race and gender. Robert Park, a sociologist, believed people become assimilated into the dominant culture; that means to take on the values, behaviors, and belief system of the majority society. The dominant culture gives out specific beliefs about race. Park believed that people see differences, based on physical differences, whether those differences are real or not. For example, in the United States African Americans may be culturally mainstream, but are seen as outsiders because of physical differences. The physical differences may be used to classify African Americans as culturally different. Park's theory of race relations is helpful for teachers to understand because he explains, in part, how powerful the forces of assimilation are in society (Sherman and Wood 1989).

First, Park theorized that when cultural groups come into contact, they may conflict with each other over goods like jobs, housing, or cultural values. For example, when the Irish immigrated to the United States, some Anglo-Saxons became threatened when the Irish moved into the neighborhood. Second, Park believed that as groups lived with each other they learned how to cooperate and then entered a period of accommodation. So the Irish and Anglo-Saxons learned to live more harmoniously. Then the Irish entered into a period of assimilation where they, as the minority community, took on the culture of the dominant group. This happened to many communities like the Irish, Swedish, Japanese, and others.

When people become assimilated in the United States, they adopt values of the dominant society, such as competition, individualism, upward mobility, and an orientation to the nuclear family rather than the extended family (Sherman and Wood 1989). The final stage of Park's theory is amalgamation, where individuals from different groups marry and become more unified. This stage is in contrast to some practices in schools which are designed, consciously or unconsciously, to get rid of cultural traits that differ from the majority culture. For example, if teachers tell children that they must not speak Black English or Vietnamese or Spanish in school because only English is acceptable, then children will tend to assimilate into the dominant culture. In fact, when some people are told they must give up aspects of their culture, they may hold to in-group values even more strongly (Allport 1954).

Park's theory does not take into consideration what Gordon (1964) calls structural assimilation. People may take on the values of the dominant or mainstream culture, but that does not mean the individuals are accepted into all aspects of the group. Though people may have given up their home language and learned English and have mainstream behaviors, they may still be excluded from the more primary relationships found in society's social structure (Sherman and Wood 1989). For example, individuals may or may not be allowed to join specific clubs, live in certain neighborhoods, or attend elite universities. So though people may have been able to culturally assimilate, they have still not been able to be accepted into all realms of society.

Here again, perceived differences are powerful forces in society because people use those differences to exclude, isolate, or segregate others. Whether those differences are seen to be due to physical characteristics, language, dialect, cultural values, gender, political power, and financial resources, they dictate how people treat others and many of those who are from underrepresented groups are excluded from higher-level positions in society. The following section continues the discussion focusing on what happened in Los Angeles during the early 1990s and what happens when people feel continually excluded from participating fully and equally in society.

Does Race, Class, and Gender Matter Today?

Do you remember the 1992 upheaval in Los Angeles? Maybe you viewed it as a race and class riot. Cornel West (1993), a philosopher and theologian, believes strongly that it was not a race riot; rather it was a powerful demonstration of social rage. People are tired of being poor and treated as nonhuman (West 1993). Both liberals and conservatives have placed the blame for the racial, class, and gender problems onto people of color and women; it is our inability as a nation to act with ethics, compassion, and justice which is at the root of many of our social problems. Some people felt a rage much beyond frustration. Though West primarily examines the problems of justice and equity from the perspective of the Black community, he provides a clear picture of how discrimination and prejudice continue to destroy our nation's fulfillment of its promise of a truly just society.

How can we solve such deeply embedded problems? West has hope and believes in our ability to rally as a community. He writes,

> First, we must admit that the most valuable sources for help, hope, and power consist of ourselves and our common history . . . Second we must focus our attention on the public square—the common good that undergirds our national and global destinies. The vitality of any public square ultimately depends on how much we *care* about the quality of our lives together. The neglect of our public infrastructure, for example— our water and sewage systems, bridges, tunnels, highways, subways, and streets— reflects not only our myopic economic policies, which impede productivity, but also the low priority we place on our common life.
>
> The tragic plight of our children clearly reveals our deep disregard for public well-being. About one out of every five children in this country lives in poverty, including one out of every two black children and two out of every five Hispanic children. Most of our children—neglected by overburdened parents and bombarded by the market values of profit-hungry corporations—are ill-equipped to live lives of spiritual and cultural quality. Faced with these facts, how do we expect ever to constitute a vibrant society? (West 1993, 6–7)

West adamantly believes the problems of Blacks and other people of color stem from a social system that has a long history of inequities and cultural stereotypes. Our nation has demanded that people of color fit into the system and act "worthy" of the inclusion, rather than understanding the human connectedness of all people in society. Why does this occur? Does the phrase, "We the People" include all the people? If not, what does the phrase, "We the People" mean in today's nation? Though West is focusing upon the issue of race, his viewpoint could also be used in looking at issues of gender, class, religion, sexual orientation, and other issues dealing with equity.

Summary

This chapter was designed to help you to examine your personal biases. One of the key points in this chapter emphasizes how our individual prejudices are part of a larger social system of racism and sexism that include institutions like schools. We must be attentive in our struggle to eliminate our hidden biases. Getting rid of our stereotypes and prejudices is not easy. Many teachers in my classes have argued that they are not racist. I agree that they are not consciously racist, however they may have a difficult time examining their views. Many are excellent teachers who work extremely hard every day for all kids.

There are various types of prejudice and social oppression. This chapter defines racism, sexism, and classism. Research by Swim and her colleagues found that people had moved from old-fashioned racism and sexism to a more modern version of biases where many feel that discrimination has been eradicated. When people bury their heads in the sand, then they will not feel responsibility to make changes. Unfortunately, there are also some teachers who are unwilling to examine ideas they have about culture and education. For example, I used the text *Other People's Children* by Lisa Delpit with teachers. Many majority teachers have strong feelings about Delpit's chapter on the silenced dialogue. In this chapter, Delpit writes that many teachers of color are not listened to even when giving recommendations about children of color. In this way the dialogue between teachers is silenced. Many majority teachers disagree with Delpit's assertion that teachers of color do not have the opportunity to make their views known in schools. I remember one teacher, Judy, who vehemently said, "I consider myself to be a religious person and I would never not listen to someone else's viewpoint because they were of color. And my best friend at the school, the principal, is African American." Then I asked her if she knew how he felt on this issue of silence. She replied, "I can't speak for him, but I don't think he feels inhibited about what he can say to me. I don't really know though." After reading Delpit's book, Judy realized that she may not really know what others are thinking. She only knew her own perceptions. Judy came to the understanding that she needed to be more willing to seek out and listen to other teachers' viewpoints, especially teachers of color. She planned on having regular dialogues with her principal so she might learn from and see teaching from another person's viewpoint that might contrast with her own. In addition, Judy began to see some of the institutional barriers which teachers of color faced in schools and that if she continued to deny their reality, she wasn't acting out of compassion or in the spirit of inclusion. Judy cared about what happened to her colleagues and students. She was willing to take a painful look at herself because she was concerned that maybe there had been a time when her biases kept her from really listening to the comments of teachers of color. She knew she not only had to listen, but Judy wanted to make changes in how she taught and what she taught.

To do this she needed to build relationships of trust with other colleagues, parents, and students. Judy knew it is hard work to care, but the rewards she would gain as a person and teacher were great.

Most of us have internalized negative views about others and they creep into our lives like weeds. Sometimes we do not know they are part of our garden because they blend so well with other plants.

In the next two chapters, I will look at how children learn prejudice and how we, as teachers, perpetuate racism, sexism, and classism intentionally and unintentionally in schools.

Teacher Reflections

Answer the following questions in your journal.

1. I find dialogue to be the most helpful in carefully thinking through many issues about equity. Find another person with whom to discuss these issues. Do you have a colleague or friend who is willing to talk about issues of equity? If you are unable to do this, dialogue with yourself in a journal. Take time to look at several sides of each issue. Ask yourself these questions:
   - Does racism, sexism, or classism exist today? If so, what do they look like?
   - Is discrimination part of American society? How do I know?
   - Am I biased? What am I doing to eliminate inequities that I see in my personal and professional life?
2. What if you and everyone else in your community held strong prejudices about people from other groups? What would life be like? How would people treat each other?

Here are some of my thoughts:

Prejudice is a powerful social force, and there are many communities around the world who have trouble finding middle ground with others from different ethnic, cultural, and religious groups. Prejudice can be very destructive. Often stereotypical views, which are elements of prejudicial attitudes, are challenged when people get to know each other on a personal and individual basis. It is critical that we develop relationships with people who are different from us because those relationships can enrich our lives and expand our understanding of other realities. Prejudice only serves to build barriers between oneself and others. We often use people who have different ideas from us as scapegoats for our problems.

A world where prejudice is rampant would be a chaotic one. The divisions between people would be like a fifty-foot wall of concrete. People would not have the opportunity to explore new ways of thinking or seeing new parts of the world. In the past, people of color, especially African Americans, were forced to use different drinking fountains, bathrooms, and bus seats from European Americans. We may not have different drinking fountains now, but if we treat others based on stereotypes and group membership, it results in segregation of the nineties.

Though I doubt a world where no one is prejudiced against others will ever come about, I can envision a community where people work together because they realize their destinies are linked together. If we were truly a society where the good of the community was most important, then when one person in the community won, we would all win.

3. Write about a time when you were discriminated against or describe a situation you witnessed when someone was hurt by prejudice. Would you do something differently about it today? If so, what?

Journal writing can assist you in better understanding yourself and can also help you see your growth. In addition, use your journal to write down great ideas like fun instructional strategies that you may see someone try or an insight that you came up with about the impact of culture and the classroom.

4. How would you describe the differences between what Swim and her colleagues considered old-fashioned racism and new racism? Old-fashioned sexism and new sexism?

Write a response in your journal. It is important for all of us to look at the subtle meanings hidden in the messages found under new racism and new sexism. If a person holds the beliefs in tables 5.1 and 5.2, the individual may not be willing to examine how schools have practices which are detrimental to some children more than others.

Further Readings

Allport, Gordon W. 1954. *The nature of prejudice.* Reading, Mass.: Addison-Wesley.
Boyle, T. Coraghessan. 1995. *The tortilla curtain.* New York: Viking Press.

An excellent novel about two liberals who live in California and whose lives become intertwined with a Mexican immigrant couple. The premise of the novel revolves around the couple's values of equity and how difficult it may be to integrate those values in their everyday lives. The couple finds it challenging to understand their social privilege in a world where they feel little connections with others who may be from another community.

Delgado, Richard. 1995. *The Rodrigo chronicles.* New York: New York University Press.

Delgado, a professor of law, is the consummate storyteller. He weaves an engrossing story of how different races challenge each other in life. Delgado has created Rodrigo, an "everyperson," who listens, searches, asks, and tackles complex questions of equality and justice in hopes of making a better nation for all.

I recommend this book highly because it will help you examine your beliefs about issues of equity. Since much of the work of Multicultural Education should begin inside each of us, this book assists us in thinking about our racial fears and the dilemmas of social reform.

References

Bennett, Christine. 1995. *Comprehensive multicultural education: Theory and practice.* Needham Heights, Mass.: Allyn & Bacon.
Delpit, Lisa. 1995. *Other people's children.* N.Y.: New Press.
Gordon, Milton. 1964. *Assimilation into American life: The role of race, religion, and national origin.* New York: Oxford University Press.
Jackson, Maggie. 1997. Slow progress seen for minority women. *San Diego Union-Tribune,* Thursday, October 23, p. C-2.
Kleg, Milton. 1993. *Hate, prejudice, and racism.* Albany, N.Y.: State University of New York Press.
McIntosh, Peggy. 1992. Unpacking the invisible knapsack: White privilege. *Creation Spirituality.* January/February: 33–35, 53.

Nieto, Sonia. 1992. *Affirming diversity: The sociopolitical context of multicultural education.* New York: Longman.

Omi, Michael, and Howard Winant. 1994. 2nd ed. *Racial formation in the United States: From the 1960's to the 1990's.* New York: Routledge.

Pang, Valerie Ooka. 1995. Asian Pacific American students: A diverse and complex population. In James A. Banks and Cherry McGee Banks, eds., *Handbook of research on multicultural education.* N.Y.: Macmillan.

Sherman, Howard J., and James L. Wood. 1989. *Sociology: Traditional and radical perspectives.* N.Y.: Harper and Row.

Swim, J., Kathryn Aikin, Wayne Hall, and Barbara Hunter. 1995. Sexism and racism: Old-fashioned and modern prejudices. *Journal of Personality and Social Psychology,* 68(2):199–214.

West, Cornel. 1993. *Race matters.* Boston, Mass.: Beacon Press.

Chapter 6

How Does It Feel to Be Discriminated Against?

Have you ever been discriminated against? How does it feel? Most of us have felt the hurt, frustration, embarrassment, humiliation, and anger, no matter if we are Irish, Muckleshoot, African American, Filipino American, Cuban American, or Swedish. Discrimination hurts. It doesn't contribute to a compassionate community.

Teachers of all colors in my university classes have written powerful papers about when they have been hurt by prejudicial comments or discriminatory actions. I feel it is important that we understand the pain and destructive nature of discrimination. Before we, as teachers, can truly understand how difficult it is for children to cope with discrimination, we must look at how prejudice hurts people. Prejudice can severely harm the spirit and self-image of any person.

Oftentimes we may not have had opportunities to think about the damage prejudice and discrimination can have on children and adults, and how they limit the possibility of creating caring relationships. I try to link the experiences of teachers in my classes with the experiences of culturally diverse students in their classrooms. When teachers discuss their experiences in small groups, they begin to better understand each other and in their dialogue are actually building bridges with each other. These discussions often help to establish compassion among participants. Sharing experiences with each other provides opportunities to clarify the impact of prejudice and discrimination for all. European American teachers gain a better understanding of how prejudice can be a continual aspect of someone else's life. These discussions also assist teachers from underrepresented groups because they often do not know that European Americans also have been targets of individual prejudice. As the discussions progress, teachers begin to realize the negative impact prejudice can have on the self-esteem and aspirations of their students. There is more understanding of how the commitment to care for children includes knowing how prejudice and discrimination develops and is part of our everyday lives. The bonds of the community are strengthened through this sharing and teachers learn how destructive discrimination can be to anyone.

✑ Teacher Voices

Since this book is for educators, the following are several selections from teachers who have written about the discrimination they felt and the impact the bias had on them.

Hindeliza Flores, Mexican American female

I translated for my mom since I was the oldest of my sisters at that school. We registered my younger brother and my three younger sisters and everything went fine. (The names of my sisters are easy to say and pronounce.) But when it came to filling out my papers the secretary had a hard time. She typed it wrong and I let her know. (By this time I was used to people pronouncing my name wrong, so I'd write it down for everyone.) Anyway, she finally finished and she showed us where our rooms were located. She turned to me and said, "From now on your new name will be Lisa. [Her name is Hindeliza.] Because your name is too hard to say." That's how she introduced me to my new teacher. I used to get in trouble because I wouldn't respond to that name. I wasn't used to it. Also because it wasn't my name. But I eventually got accustomed to it.

For many years I thought of that secretary. She didn't realize what she stole from me. I lost a big part of me when she took my name away. As an 11-year-old child, that was a big part of ME. My name and my language was part of my culture. When that was taken away, I had nothing. I could only be myself at home. Later when other Spanish-speaking children came to the school, we were not allowed to speak Spanish to each other. We were punished for speaking Spanish. Years have passed and I still think about this incident. I wonder if my life would have been different if this hadn't happened. Would I still have wanted to be a bilingual teacher and help other Mexican children?

Suzanne Akemi Negoro, Japanese American female

In my junior high history class, I remember sitting in the rigid single desk, resting my feet on the bookrack of the desk in front of me. I always used to sink low in my seat, and on one particular day I was sinking even lower than normal as our teacher announced that it was Pearl Harbor Day. Usually anything that is given its own day is something that's good; there's Valentine's Day, Martin Luther King, Jr. Day, President's Day, Labor Day, and Independence Day. But Pearl Harbor Day is one of the few dark-designated days, left in the same camp with D-Day. This day not only marks the day that Japan bombed the United States; it also marks that day that my family and other Japanese-Americans officially became suspected traitors. Sitting in my junior high history class, this day also marked me. I can still picture the student in the row next to me, leaning towards me and whispering, "So why'd you bomb us anyway?" Four generations and forty years, and not much had changed.

The biggest problem I had in dealing with this student's comment was my own inability to reconcile my cultural identity, both Japanese and American. I remember words from my childhood: being praised, "You speak so well," "Your English is so good"; being questioned, "What are you anyway?" "No, what are you *really?*"; and being criticized, "You don't speak Japanese? Why not?" "How sad that you've lost your language," "How sad that you've lost your culture." I remember being about three feet tall with the voice of a mouse, trying to talk as loud as possible so that people could hear how well I spoke, i.e., without an accent. I remember my years of adolescent female fun that always ended up matching me with the other Asian boy in my class—and I remember always wanting to be matched with every other boy but him. I wanted to prove to people that I was American, and to me that meant proving that I was White.

I was not, however, simply just trying to prove that I was White. I was simultaneously trying to prove that I was still "Japanese-enough." As a child, the most difficult part was figuring what was enough.

Krystal Rodriguez, Latina

There have been many times in which I have felt discrimination . . . People would verbally tell me such things as, "Are you sure you're in the right place? You look like you don't belong here." But the words and the looks did not hurt as much as my fourth grade teacher did . . .

In the fourth grade, my teacher was Mrs. McGeorge (pseudonym). I will never forget her name. The very first day I started to notice things about her that I never noticed about other teachers. I started to notice that she spoke to the White students with a softer tone and with more passion. She spoke to the rest of us in a voice that was more stern.

The first day she also put the class into reading groups. There were three reading groups: The robins, the blue jays, and the black birds. Everyone wanted to be in the robin group because we all knew that they were the group that could read the best and that the black birds were the "dumb" group. As Mrs. McGeorge was placing people into the groups, I remember thinking that my third grade teacher said I read very well for a third grader so I knew that I was at least going to go into the blue jays. But I was wrong. I was placed into the black birds.

The next day it was reading time so the class had to separate into their reading groups. As I was in my reading group I remember looking around at all three reading groups. That is when I noticed something else. The robins were all White. The blue jays had two minorities and the rest were White. And the black birds were all minorities.

Even though I noticed many things that year, I just thought that that was the way it was supposed to be. I never questioned the teacher or told anyone about the things I noticed . . .

It was time again, in the fifth grade, to get put into our reading groups. Most of the same students that were in my fourth grade class were now in my fifth grade class so the teacher just had us go into the same groups . . . The teacher heard me read. After we were finished the teacher came up to several students in our group, including myself, and told us that she did not know why we were put in the lower group. We read very well. I was then moved up to the robins.

Ronie Daniels, African American female

I am a woman, Black, short in stature, thick in build, with kinky hair. I began my life in a small diverse California city, but as I neared the age of eleven, my family and I migrated to a small town in the Mojave desert . . . There are people of a variety of ethnicities such as Hispanic, African American, and Asian, but they are still in the minority. I attended both private and public schools during my years in the desert and I was often the only or one of the few African Americans in my classes. By this point in my life, race was a well known factor to me and I also knew that I was considered to be a minority . . . I was never taught to be anyone other than myself, which in a large sense is Black.

About two weeks ago, my friend, K, and I were sitting in the living room with a mutual friend. During our conversation, she told me that I was not "Black". I was not majorly affected by it because it came from a friend, but what did she mean by saying that I'm not Black? She told me that I was not really Black. I suppose she meant to say that I was not "ghetto" or like the "other Black" people she sees on campus because I express my Blackness and my culture to her quite often.

How did she discriminate against me if she was not truly harsh? She discriminated against me because she put Blackness in a small little category and she excluded me from it. By doing this she is claiming that I do not know my culture, that I do not accept my culture, or that I have no part of my culture. Could this be true? No. I believe that she made this judgment based on clothing, hairstyles, and other outward appearances. She knows that I grew up with horses and off-road vehicles, which in California is typically termed as White.

Due to the color of my skin I was separated. I had to read the words "GO BACK TO AFRICA NIGGERS" spray painted on the walls of my high school cafeteria one morning. In addition, I had to endure racial jokes at our local public pool, and I had to realize as I grew up that no one looked quite like me in many of my classrooms . . .

As I mentioned before, my home life was very Afro-centric . . . It is sad that I am considered to be non-Black because of my interests and hobbies.

Jennifer Stahl, Irish American female

Instances of discrimination against me occurred when I first began attending preschool. I was an intelligent, motivated, confident red-headed child. I was very compliant with figures of authority, and would do anything to gain their acceptance. I wanted to be a grown up, as I perceived them, as soon as possible. I was absolutely silent during classroom lectures . . . I worked diligently towards perfection and I always raised my hand before talking.

But my attempt at adult perceptions superseded those attempts of my peers. When Rob Gibbs, an obese African American was told by other kids, "Quit drinking so much chocolate in your milk and you won't be so brown and fat," I was quick to tell them that they were being prejudiced and shouldn't judge people by the color of their skin. When they called Carl Feazel "Feazel the weasel" to mock his intelligence, I'd defend him by telling them they should spend the time they spent teasing studying instead, and they wouldn't be so jealous.

Naturally, their antics were directed at me as well. They called me "Horsey-Stahl, Frances the Talking Mule, Mr. Ed, and Chest-NUT" to mock my affinity for horses. Carrot-top came next, naturally followed by the most grotesque of all, "Red on the head like a ____ of a dog." I used to wonder what in the world the other kids' parents were teaching them when mine were telling me to treat everyone with kindness and equality and to right the unjust wrongs around myself.

This wasn't the worst of it. Because my behavior was non-conforming to peer pressure and because of my academic achievement, my instructors always, and I do mean always, stuck me in between three or four of the most disruptive students. They did more than talk without raising their hands. They threatened to poke my eyes out with pencils poised inches from my face if I didn't pass a note for them. They threatened to beat-me-up on the walk home from school if I told on them . . . When I complained to my parents about it they'd visit with my teachers. The teachers would tell them, and in turn, my parents told me the reasons why I was put between them . . . So while everyone on the other side of the room bonded and gained social skills by sharing their favorite colors, drawing pictures for each other, and assisting one-another in their studies, I was overcoming continual verbal and physical abuse and sat surrounded by boys only.

Arturo Salazar, Latino, Mexican

When I was a freshman in high school, I was enrolled in a freshman algebra class with a teacher that regularly called on students for their participation. One day, this teacher called on me for the answer to an extremely easy equation, an equation that had the answer of ten . . . I knew very well the answer was ten but could not get my vocal cords to say it because of my stuttering. Noting that the teacher knew this was an extremely easy equation, he continued to call on me until I was able to give him the answer. In the meantime, he began to laugh in a sarcastic manner, indicating that he thought I was dumb. This implication was evident and increasingly humiliating because the teacher turned to the class and continuously pointed at me, implying that I was dumb for not knowing the answer . . . These types of experiences influenced the level of shyness that I exhibited throughout my preparatory schooling. Stuttering in this forum (my high school algebra class) would have been especially detrimental to my self-concept that was already weak.

Following this class period, I was so humiliated that I never returned to class. I went immediately to my counselor and practically begged him to take me out of that class and to place me with a different teacher. Although I had told the counselor that I stuttered and felt embarrassed when I was not able to answer this question even though I knew the answer very well, he refused to place me with another teacher . . . Feeling uncomfortable with this teacher, I was truant for this class period for the remainder of the semester.

The feeling that I was discriminated against continued into my sophomore year. My counselor decided to place me into remedial English and math courses, even though I consistently scored in the 90th percentile on the yearly Standardized Achievement Tests on all parts. I viewed this as discrimination against people that stuttered, because it was assuming that I was dumb because I had a speech impediment. I complained to my counselor but he did not change my classes.

Teachers from all cultural groups write powerful papers. They demonstrate through different experiences that prejudice can be extremely hurtful. And there are many different reasons why people discriminate against each other. Many of the examples I have included above show how discrimination can be found in a school. I have found that discrimination can be destructive to a 10-year-old fifth grader or a 70-year-old grandfather, because they may question themselves. Thoughts like "What's wrong with me?" and "Why don't people like me?" may surface. Yet discrimination says more about the oppressor than the victim. One of my friends has always reminded me, "When a person points a finger at you, he/she has more fingers pointing back at themselves." People may not realize that discrimination says most about the oppressor and not the victim. In many cases the oppressor wants to maintain a separation or boundary from others based on a belief of superiority (Daniels and Kitano 1970).

✎ Why Do We Discriminate?

Though we may feel the hurt of discrimination, we also may discriminate against another consciously or unintentionally. When a person discriminates against someone, their actions say more about them than those who are poorly treated. Allport has defined **discrimination** as the act which "comes about only when we deny to individuals or groups of people equality of treatment which they may wish" (1954, 50). When this happens, discrimination usually is based upon social categories or groupings and not individual characteristics. For example, there are numerous situations where people are being excluded from living in specific neighborhoods, going to certain schools, or receiving promotions because of categories like race, class, or gender and not due to people's abilities.

We may treat others unfairly for one or more of the following reasons. First, we may have been taught that those from another group are not as capable or as good as those in "our" group. There is an in-group affiliation and sense of belonging. As members of specific in-groups, we may learn that to be part of this group, we are expected to think of other groups unfavorably. People who are members of the out-group are often seen as being less desirable.

When people feel insecure about themselves and who they are, they may want to believe that their way of doing something is the one, right way. Believing that others are not as "smart" or "virtuous" may make one feel "better," but it is often a hollow feeling. You know when you are putting others down without reason.

Another example of discrimination is scapegoating. This involves shifting the blame of a problem to a victim. When we "blame the victim," we shift the fault of a problem to someone else. I have heard comments like, "All those Mexicans are taking our jobs" or "Our economy is so bad here in the United States because those Japanese are flooding the market with cheap cars." Historically there have been numerous examples of scapegoating. Prior and during World War II, the Nazis continually condemned the Jewish community. The Jews were used as the scapegoat for the economic and political problems in Germany. Another group that has been used as a scapegoat in the United States is Native Americans. Many people have grown up believing Native Americans were obstacles to "progress" during the early years of this nation. People do not see that Native Americans were victims of our nation's belief in Manifest Destiny; their land was taken away and their way of life was destroyed as settlers moved Westward. Also Manifest Destiny was a movement that pushed the interests of the elite, especially large land speculators and owners. This was in contrast to common settlers who wanted to coexist with Native Americans.

Blaming the victim is a societal strategy that has been commonly used against people of color, women, poor Americans, and other disenfranchised groups (Ryan 1971). Children who come from poor or low-income families have often been blamed for mediocre achievement in schools. Educators can be heard saying, "Those [poor] parents don't care about their kids. I know they don't care because they never come to parent-teacher conferences. I call parents and they are never home. Heaven knows where they are while their kids are roaming the streets. Those kids come to school speaking Spanish or Black dialect and they don't have any manners. I think it is horrible that we have to put up with these kids." Comments like this show that this teacher has strong underlying prejudicial attitudes against children who do not speak standard English or who may live in a household with little financial resources.

When we "blame the victim," we are engaging in a complex psychological system of beliefs (Ryan 1971). Prejudice represents a complicated social and personal phenomenon because it includes personal and group values. Ryan thinks many prejudiced people hold conflicting beliefs. They may blame others because of group membership, but also want to make a difference in the lives of their students. These teachers know that racism and poverty are barriers in the lives of many students. They also realize that race, class, and gender have been used to discriminate against or exclude African Americans,

Asian Pacific Americans, Native Americans, Latinos, women, and those living in poverty. These liberal teachers may find themselves with a dilemma.

> "In the words of an old Yiddish proverb, they are trying to dance at two weddings. They are old friends of both brides and fond of both kinds of dancing, and they want to accept both invitations. They cannot bring themselves to challenge the system that has been so good to them, but they want so badly to be helpful to the victims of racism and economic injustice" (Ryan 1971, 27).

Ryan discusses how the inclusion of those who have been excluded may threaten our way of thinking. These issues of equity are difficult ethical ones and are not easily solved.

✎ *White Teacher*

Did you know that while increasing numbers of students who attend school are from communities of color and from families with incomes at the poverty level, our teaching force continues to come from White, middle-class communities? By the year 2000, it is projected that 96 percent of all teachers in the United States will be European American and about 40 percent of the student population will come from culturally diverse groups. What does this mean in the classroom? Children and teachers may find that they come to school with different views of life. I suggest that you read the book *White Teacher*, by Vivian Gussin Paley (1979). She describes her own prejudices, biases, and different perceptions of culturally diverse children.

Paley writes her thoughts about race and social class as a kindergarten teacher. In the book, Paley shares her reactions in the classroom toward children of color. She invites us into her mind and heart as she wrestles with her own prejudices. In addition, she lets us see how she began to question those biases and behave in a more equitable and compassionate manner. One of the great lessons in the book is that Paley does not become a martyr or missionary for children of color. Paley understands her role is to teach and guide children toward developing new beliefs about themselves and others. She challenges children to work out their own contradictions, misconceptions, and self-defeating ways. She shows the reader how she learns from her children because she is willing to listen and watch children teach her about her own misconceptions. James Comer and Alvin Poussaint, in the foreword of the book, describe one of Paley's most important insights in that she, as a White teacher, does not slip into the role of "overaccepting do-gooder."

Some important questions you might ask yourself are: Why are you committed to teaching culturally diverse children? Do you feel that you can save them from their "horrible" surroundings? Do you feel that you have the answers? One of the most difficult issues for some teachers to understand is that they are not in schools to "save" students. You can guide and work to support others, but as a teacher, you will not have the answer for all your students.

Yes, many of your children may come from families who live in dire poverty and have difficult home lives. If you begin to think that you know what is best for children and that their parents are the problem, ask yourself what do you really know about their lives. One of the comments that may come from some parents is, "What makes that teacher think she knows better than I do about what is best for my kid?"

Miscommunications often occur when people do not have the same expectations or ways of behaving. This is more likely to happen when teachers and parents do not have open lines of communication. For example, a teacher in an inner-city high school tells his students that every one of them should go to college. The teacher hopes that all of his students develop high-level white-collar skills. He sees that high-paying factory jobs are becoming sparse and that a college degree rather than a high school diploma will become an expected requirement for jobs. A parent who has worked for General Dynamics for many years and who has a high school diploma may want his/her child to go to college, but may not have the finances to send her/him. In fact, the family may be dependent upon the child to find a job right after high school to help support the family. Since this parent has done well without a college degree, he/she may not believe it is an absolute necessity. This parent may comment, "Why do you put these notions into my kid's mind, when he will never be able to afford college? He's got to work now. He can't put it off. We need the money."

Paley's book also helps readers to understand that European American teachers and children of color do have differences. These differences do not have to be obstacles in developing a sense of community. These differences in beliefs also do not mean that one group is better than another, but these differences must be discussed openly. Dialogue can assist people in eliminating misconceptions and help folks come to some common understandings. European American teachers should not be intimidated or scared to talk about ethnic, racial, gender, or social class differences. Children know that we are different in many ways. Paley wrote,

> Each child wants to know immediately if he is a worthy person in your eyes. You cannot pretend, because the child knows all the things about himself that worry him. If you act as if you like him, but ignore the things he is anxious about, it doesn't count. The child is glad you are nice to him, but down deep he figures if you really knew what he was like, you'd hate him (1979, 30).

Paley realized that many of her children were not sure about their racial identity as African Americans and they wanted her to acknowledge their racial difference in a positive manner to help validate their self-esteem. She realized that if she ignored that aspect of her African American students, she was indirectly saying she did not respect an important part of who they were.

In addition, Paley found initially she automatically grouped children by racial similarities. As their teacher, she was not seeing the individuality of each child. But in a balanced perception, Paley also realized that group membership can be an important part of how the child identifies him/herself. If the teacher ignores differences children know they have, children may feel that the differences are something negative, negative enough for the teacher to overlook.

ꙮ Being Part of the Majority

If you feel a little defensive as you read this book, you may say to yourself, "Wait a minute. I'm not one of those bigots. I'm different. I'm not prejudiced." In many years of teaching, I find this to be a common reaction when members of the class discuss issues dealing with racial prejudice. In addition, when teachers read new information about U.S. history that has not been included in most social studies textbooks, teachers feel a range of emotions about race, class, and gender, which will be discussed later in this section.

History provides a lens in which people may interpret and judge present-day experiences. Using Valle's model of culture, discussed in chapter 1, historical experiences and information may represent more than just facts; the history a group has experienced may result in the development of strong values. For example, if a community like the Sioux have historically been pushed from their land, their values about the westward movement may be shaped by their group history. So in order for teachers to begin to understand the viewpoint of another group like Mexican Americans or African Americans, it can be extremely informative to study the history of the group. Teachers in my classes have chosen to read texts like Howard Zinn's book, *A People's History of the United States, Lies My Teacher Told Me* by James Loewen, or Ronald Takaki's *A Different Mirror.* Many teachers are surprised by their lack of understanding of the complexities of many issues in U.S. history. They usually have been given only the perspective of those who are the majority and who also represent the power structure of our country. Most history texts do not raise important perennial issues that continue to arise, which are important for students to grapple with in their social studies classes in order for them to become thoughtful citizens (Loewen 1995). In fact, much history is presented as being truth, though it was shaped within a specific context that included social values of racism, sexism, and classism (Nelson and Pang 2000; Zinn 1990).

Let's look at several examples of how these texts can provide a different perspective on events and people in history. Zinn (1980) discusses Andrew Jackson's land speculation and prejudices toward Native Americans, and how his values shaped much of what he did as president. President Jackson had positional power, and his actions were more destructive than others because he legitimized them using his presidency and the national orientation toward Manifest Destiny. Jackson is often hailed as the great leader; however, as Zinn points out, Jackson even ignored Chief Justice Marshall's ruling in favor of the Cherokees. Jackson did not believe he had to follow the judge's decision. In fact, Loewen quotes Jackson saying, " 'John Marshall has made his decision; now let him enforce it!' " (Loewen 1995, 126).

Loewen (1995), in *Lies My Teacher Told Me,* shares his analysis of twelve textbooks of American history. These books were written for junior and senior high American history courses. Chapter 5 in his book is titled, " 'Gone with the Wind': The Invisibility of Racism in American History Textbooks." Loewen believes that racism is the most important issue of history, and yet he did not find any of the twelve textbooks to connect "history and racism" (1995, 145). He believes that by glossing over or not addressing racism in U.S. society, students do not get the opportunity to look at the beliefs and events that contributed to racism, how racism can be addressed today in order that it will be limited tomorrow.

Living in the Southwest, I have learned a great deal about the history of Mexican Americans. History in this part of the country could be told not from the East to the West, but from the South to the North and then to the East and West. After the Mexican War, the United States, as a victor, took much of what was known as Mexico and later became states like California, New Mexico, Texas, and Arizona. Though the Treaty of Guadalupe Hidalgo of 1848 assured that the Mexican people retained their property and civil rights, this did not happen. Many Mexicans were treated as a conquered people (Knowlton 1972) and became foreigners in their native land (Takaki 1993). There were many instances where land was taken away from Mexican ranchers by U.S. citizens because of changes in the law, taxation, and lack of accurate boundary descriptions (Takaki 1993). Mexicans were often left without their homes.

Do you have a sense of how history can impact the way your students feel about race relations? In many ethnic communities adults pass on from generation to genera-

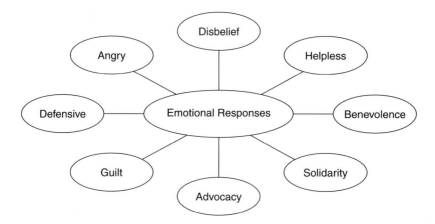

Figure 6.1   *Emotional Responses to Issues of Equity*

tion historical information about the experiences of past family members. These experiences may be the same or conflict with what students are learning in school. If a student's family history includes the taking of the family land after the Treaty of Guadalupe Hidalgo, then this person may view history through a different cultural lens, as Valle (1997) has pointed out.

The books I suggest that teachers read may be difficult for some teachers to contemplate because they provide a different view of inequities in our history and how these inequities are, in some cases, continually perpetuated. The books may help you understand how those in dominant positions shape the teaching of history so that it serves to forward the beliefs of a (U.S.) American ideology of equality within a self-righteous orientation of objectivity and fairness.

Teachers, especially those who are European American, may experience a variety of emotions when reading these books or dealing with issues of equity. They may feel several emotions at once. I find that teachers experience a range of emotions from anger, defensiveness, guilt, disbelief, benevolence, helplessness, solidarity, and advocacy, and sometimes several of these feelings arise simultaneously (Pang and Nieto 1995). I can't say to teachers, "Don't feel that way," because these are honest emotions. Rather, I ask teachers to try to look at experiences and issues from other people's viewpoints and reevaluate their beliefs and attitudes. Where do these feelings come from? How can you work through them and move toward solidarity, advocacy, and social action. See Figure 6.1 for a chart of these feelings.

Emotions are an integral part of prejudice. We may know intellectually that stereotypes are harmful, but our feelings are not as easy to change. These feelings can get in the way of real communication and personal change. I believe lasting change is difficult for everyone and it is only natural to feel somewhat threatened when asked to rethink their views of the world. It takes courage to change and a strong commitment to care for others and for oneself in order to address these complex beliefs. In addition, I believe sometimes people feel uncertain when they are asked to build bridges with new people and examine different ideas. In order to encourage a broader view of U.S. society, I ask teachers to review their knowledge of history.

As already discussed in this chapter, books by Zinn and Loewen provide numerous examples of inequities in U.S. history. For instance, Cherokees were forced from their homes in Georgia to Oklahoma in 1830. When there is discussion of this tragedy, some teachers feel defensiveness arising. I tell them to accept their feelings and then to move beyond those feelings by asking themselves, "What am I doing today to fight for the rights of Native peoples?"

Feeling defensive usually isn't constructive. If you are like I am, when I feel attacked I do not clearly hear the message another person is conveying. Feeling defensive probably won't benefit anyone because it may cause one to shut down. None of us today have anything to do with the forced removal of Cherokees from their land almost two hundred years ago, but I ask myself, "What responsibilities do I have today when similar issues arise?" For example, I believe that if today we stand by and let states take long-standing water rights from various American Indian nations without working toward upholding the contracts they negotiated years ago, then we, as a community, are not committed to social justice for all citizens.

In the next section, I will discuss in more detail feelings which may arise when we think about and discuss issues dealing with race, class, gender, and sexual orientation.

❧ Emotional Responses to Issues

Whether you are a person from an underrepresented community or European American, or female or male, we all have felt varying emotions about these issues. You may have been a victim, perpetrator, observer, or someone who had no knowledge of an event. Yet it is important to understand how your emotions can act as filters to incoming information. As shown in Figure 6.1, I believe people may have a complex set of feelings about an issue. They may feel angry, defensive, and disbelieving all at the same time. Prejudice is difficult to get rid of because it includes not only a set of beliefs about others, but also our emotional reactions, which can include feelings of goodness, morality, and ethics (Brislin 1993, 179–180). Much of our prejudice we have learned through socialization as a child. Parents and other significant adults greatly influenced the shaping of our belief system.

How do you respond when someone asks you to look at a controversial issue? Do you sometimes get very *angry?* What if I begin describing the horrible conditions Africans endured during the middle passage across the Atlantic Ocean and how inhuman some slave owners treated people on plantations? Maybe you might think that my tone or choice of words was directed at you or your ancestors. You may feel anger toward me. You may automatically think or say, "I didn't do anything wrong. Don't point your finger at me. You are picking on me. I had nothing to do with what happened."

Another emotional response you may have to racial and cultural issues is *disbelief.* You may not want to listen to other people's points of view, especially those who criticize the U.S. majority. I have heard people say, "He's giving such a distorted view of history." Yet, it may only be that the person has a different perspective about an event or issue. The feeling of disbelief may come out in another way. After a discussion on diverse learning styles, I have heard teachers say, "There's nothing I can do. Black kids just don't care about learning." Teachers may resist attempts to examine social, economic, and political obstacles that can be based on race, gender, and social class biases.

Teachers may also feel *defensive* and hurt. "Wait a minute, I didn't make the Cherokees move from Georgia to Oklahoma. I didn't put the Japanese in concentration camps. I'm only 22 years old. Besides we don't do this anymore." These comments may reveal an unwillingness to examine issues from the point of view of victims. I try to explain to teachers that though we, individually, may not have actively participated in exclusion, discrimination, or extermination of others, as part of this society we may benefit from the exploitation of others. Most of us live on lands that were once cared for and settled by Native Americans and who were displaced. We expect low prices at the grocery store for fresh fruits and vegetables. Yet there are many culturally diverse peoples whose labors we rely on, which support our standard of living in the United States. Teachers with these emotions may not feel connections with people from other communities, especially those from low-income, culturally diverse communities. Defensiveness or unconnected feelings can leave a person inactive. Other teachers may also feel *helpless*. They do not think they can do anything to change things.

Along with helplessness, a person may also feel *guilty*. She may realize she had nothing to do with oppressive events of the past, yet may feel somehow responsible for past inequities. Her feelings of guilt may arise, in part, from hearing racist, gender-biased, or homophobic comments from your parents, grandparents, siblings, or significant others. She may have family members who are extremely racist, gender-biased, or who hold prejudicial beliefs about gays and lesbians. She may be held hostage by these feelings and rationalize that acts of discrimination are committed by ignorant people. Or she may be a person who bends over backwards to assist culturally diverse people, women, or gay individuals because of long-standing family prejudice. These feelings may lead to the fourth emotion, benevolence.

European Americans and other teachers may feel *benevolent*. These feelings can fuel a "savior" or "missionary" orientation. Sometimes a person may be "preaching" the importance of equity in a somewhat condescending manner. Though she may be well intentioned, she may not understand how her actions can also be oppressive if patronizing. One possible message is, "I can solve your problems. Though you cannot help yourself, I can help you." There is an undercurrent of superiority, which reinforces the separation between different communities. People may need more communication and dialog with others in order to come up with collaborative solutions.

As you become more aware of your emotions, you may feel a strong connection and *solidarity* with others from different communities. You begin to develop a commitment to all peoples and learn how to care for others. You begin to understand the human interconnectedness you have with those who you thought were "the others" or outsiders. As a member of the human family, you understand that what you do also affects others and you want to get to know others who may have different cultural and racial backgrounds from your own. The richness and gifts of diversity are exciting and expand your understandings of life.

Hopefully you will also feel empowered to be an *agent of change*. You may be a European American teacher who respects, accepts, and values each student and diverse communities. You are realistic about society and work against racism, sexism, homophobia, and classism in the classroom as part of your everyday life. You understand how your destiny is intertwined with all (U.S.) Americans. You may be actively working with culturally diverse peoples on community issues, whether they deal with homelessness, voter registration, or lack of health services. We can redirect our energies from negative emotions into empowerment and become proactive. For example, there are teachers who understand that some culturally diverse students from low-income communities may not have had the opportunity to develop extensive computer skills, so teachers have created after-school computer clubs. In these clubs, teachers help students work on individually chosen projects, which may involve using databases, creating complex software programs, and teaching students how to communicate with other students using electronic mail.

We all have various feelings and responses to differences. Since we live in a nation and world that is culturally diverse, it is important to examine how people develop racial identity. The next section of this chapter is devoted to the racial identification process for European American and culturally diverse people.

Racial Identity Formation for European Americans

What process do many European Americans go through in their awareness of their own racial identity? In the past three decades some individuals are more open about discussing issues of race. Within that context, many European Americans have become more aware that they are members of a racial group and sometimes referred to as White. Just as people from underrepresented groups deal with racial identity, European Americans also pass through different states of awareness and development about who they are. I like the definition of racial identity as given by Beverly Tatum, a psychologist at Mount Holyoke College. Tatum says that racial identity formation "refers to a process of defining for oneself the personal significance and social meaning of belonging to a particular racial group" (1997, 16). She (Tatum, 1992, 1997) has studied the development of racial identification and believes her students pass through stages of White racial identity as described by Janet Helms. These stages are contact, disintegration, reintegration, pseudo-independence, immersion/emersion, and autonomy (Helms, 1990). From my experiences with many European American teachers, it is helpful to know that White teachers go through a process of understanding who they are and must struggle with racial identity. Table 6.1 is an adaptation of the work of Helms and Tatum.

I believe there are five major stages European Americans may pass through in developing their racial identity. The following is an explanation of the stages given in Table 6.1:

1. **Acceptance of Status Quo.** In this stage, European Americans are unaware of societal racism. Individuals in this stage have thought little about culture and racism. Though people in this stage may intellectually understand that racism is a problem in society, they do not see institutional racism. They may consider racism to be individual acts of discrimination and not a system of legitimized practices. People in this stage also do not understand that as members of the majority, they benefit from White privilege (McIntosh 1992).

   European Americans may be scared of people of color because they have internalized social stereotypes. These images shape the way people see others, especially when individuals have little knowledge of nonmajority communities. When individuals from the majority come into contact with people of color and begin to see acts of racism, they may find themselves in the next stage.

TABLE 6.1

White Racial Identity Formation

Stages

1. Acceptance of Status Quo	Little knowledge of culture and racism, individual and institutional. Does not see cultural differences in students or other people. Accepts dominant culture as standard. Does not question learned stereotypes of others. "I'm just normal" (Tatum 1997, 95).
2. It's Not My Fault: Uncomfortable	Feels guilty and defensive. Avoids discussion of racism. Wants acceptance of peers. Sees some inconsistencies in society and a little of one's own racism.
3. Denial: I'm an Individual	Begins to look at inequalities in society. Angry and upset toward those who question racial inequities. Believes strongly in individual merit and White privilege reflects that merit. "I don't feel I have any advantage because I am White."
4. Clarification of Whiteness	Examines racial self-identity. Seeks information about others. Rejects White superiority. Seeks historical information. Begins to understand how White privilege is perpetuated in society. People feel ashamed for being White and not sure what to do (Tatum 1997).
5. Acceptance of Self and Group	Accepts membership in White collective. Realizes being White does not mean a person is racist. Accepts positive and negative aspects of own group. Studies White anti-racist role models.
6. White Anti-Racism: Change Agents	Sees role of European Americans in fighting racism. Forms alliances w/ people of color. Dedicated to changing society.

2. **It's Not My Fault: Uncomfortable.** In this stage, European Americans may feel guilty, ashamed, or angry because they become aware of racism and the underlying belief of White superiority in society (Helms 1990). Sometimes European Americans in this stage may blame victims for oppression (Tatum 1992; 1997). Others in this stage may try to convince their close friends and

family that racism is a powerful problem. For example, when someone tells a racist joke, persons in this stage will challenge the person who told the joke. However, those in this stage may return to accepting the status quo because they want to remain accepted by their majority peers. They may avoid discussion of racial issues or have little interaction with people of color. Guilt and defensiveness may manifest itself as feelings of anger and resentment toward people of color. A person in this stage may feel attacked and say, "It's not my fault that there's prejudice in the world. What do you expect me to do? I can't help being White."

3. **Denial: I Am An Individual** (Tatum 1997). In this stage, a person is struggling with being a member of the White collective. Though this person understands there is racism in society, she does not want to be identified with the racism and so rejects her membership in the community by saying, "I'm an individual. I am not like those other people. Judge me for myself and not the group." People feel uncomfortable with others judging them based on their group membership. They may feel extremely frustrated in this stage. Persons do not understand how, as members of the dominant culture, they have privileges nonWhite people do not have. There is still a strong value in individual merit and a belief that the system rewards individual merit equally.

4. **Clarification of Whiteness.** As European Americans explore their racial identity, they challenge themselves to delve into the question of what it means to be White. A person in this stage may distance herself from others in the majority who are extremely racist. The individual in this stage may have mixed feelings about the White collective, so she may seek information about her history and culture which can assist her in working through the myths and stereotypes about her group, which may include issues of superiority or missionary zeal (Tatum 1992; 1997). In addition, reading biographies of White Americans who have been instrumental in fighting racism provides role models for those who believe in activism.

   Others in this stage may initiate conversations with colleagues of color to find out more information about culturally diverse communities. They want to better understand how the system of privileges is supported and how culturally diverse peoples are systematically denied access to the opportunities in various aspects of society. People begin to understand that there is institutional racism and they have an ethical responsibility to work toward equity in society.

5. **Acceptance of Self.** In this stage, European Americans understand the importance of challenging racism and social oppression in everyday life. People accept themselves as members of the White collective and as interdependent with others. They see that feelings of guilt and anger do not change society, but their energy should be channeled into actions aimed at equality. There is a truer view of oneself in this stage. People see that being White does not mean someone is racist, but that racism is part of society and that Whites benefit from the way society has been set up. So it is imperative that European Americans are active against racism.

6. **White Antiracism: Change Agents.** In this stage, European Americans confront racism on both individual and institutional levels. They have a healthy understanding of themselves and their racial identity. People in this stage are committed to learning more about racism and to making alliances with people

from diverse communities to eradicate oppression; they may find out about Civil Rights activists like Viola Liuzzo, James Reeb, or Michael Schwerner (Tatum 1992; 1997). They know that White Americans have a moral obligation to examine their privileged status and must choose to act to rid our social system of inequities (McLaren 1997). Those in this stage seek new ways of thinking and solving our social problems.

In looking at this model of White racial identity development, the key is openness and an ethical commitment to care for others by getting to know yourself better, to understand your own personal shortcomings and strengths.

In order for teachers to change, they must understand that racism has impacted their lives. It is not something only for people of color to deal with and eradicate. Racism and other forms of social oppression are not easy to get rid of in our society. In the next section, I describe one of the most of difficult issues for teachers to understand, White privilege.

White Privilege

One of the most difficult concepts for European Americans to understand is that they are members of a group often referred to as White, White Americans, Caucasians, European American, and EuroAmerican. Similarly, I never realized I was part of a group known as Japanese American. I thought I was Val and that I was like everyone else. I found out when I went to school that other children saw me as someone who was different because I looked different. I was not an American or even Japanese American; I was that "Oriental" kid. I think it is a struggle for European Americans to understand that they are also members of a racial grouping. Though they may not identify with being European American or White, others may place them into those categories because race and ethnicity are important aspects in society.

I have found it difficult for many of my majority teachers to understand this social concept. As part of the majority they usually are not confronted with their racial membership. However, Peggy McIntosh (1992) believes that European Americans do not understand that it is a privilege that they see their lives as morally neutral, normative, average, and ideal; a life which others should adopt.

In McIntosh's article "Unpacking the Invisible Knapsack: White Privilege" (1992), she describes some of the privileges that she and her peers have as members of the European community. I will share a few with you:

"I can, if I wish, arrange to be in the company of people of my race most of the time."
"I can turn on the television or open to the front page of the paper and see people of my race widely represented."
"I can be sure that my children will be given curricular materials that testify to the existence of their race."
"Whether I use checks, credit cards, or cash, I can count on my skin color not to work against the appearance of financial reliability."
"I can speak in public to a powerful male group without putting my race on trial."
"I am never asked to speak for all the people of my racial group."
"I can criticize our government and talk about how much I fear its policies and behavior without being seen as a cultural outsider" (McIntosh 1992, 34).

To continue the discussion about White privilege, I asked teachers the question, "What does it mean to be White?" This was challenging for many teachers because they rarely must explain their group membership. Some felt defensive. However, after the several class sessions where this topic was discussed, many of the European American teachers began to realize that they had privileges that others did not. Yet, they do not feel privileged.

Here are a few of the comments the teachers shared:

Val: What does it mean to be White? How do Whites view racism?

Tammi (European American): I never thought about what it means to be White until today.

Dawn (European American): I never thought much about being White either. It just wasn't an issue I thought about. I didn't have to think about being White because I am part of the majority.

Sally (European American): I think White people should start looking at their ancestors. White is so vague. I don't know much about my family and maybe if we did we would be more understanding.

Bruce (African American): We are being so nice. Yet Whites have little information about African Americans. They gave us the shortest month [February] to celebrate Black history.

We aren't all the same. People say we are but we aren't. Why can't I feel good about myself. I've taken White history. How many classes in African American or Latino history have you taken?

Michael (European American): None.

Bruce: I go into a store and a cashier follows me around. My White roommates are beginning to see it when they come with me. They are shocked how I am treated.

Kathy (Japanese/European American): There's also a lot of racism between groups of color too.

Tammi: I didn't realize how deep-rooted racism is. I have taken for granted my privileges. I only think of racism in its extreme forms like the Ku Klux Klan. But many of us are "innocently" racist because we are ignorant of the racism within our institutions.

Joe (European American): White racism does exist and it is completely intertwined within our society. I think most of us in the White society do not want to jeopardize our "position" so we don't talk about racism.

Tim (European American): I agree. We don't want to discuss racism because we don't want to give up our lifestyle, privileges, and resources that we took from others. Basically I believe I must stop pointing fingers and look at myself first.

Joyce (European American): I know that we are racist, but I don't think it is right to overgeneralize about White racism. I don't think we stick together about issues of race. I have a Black brother-in-law and though it took a while for my family to accept him, we have. So people can move ahead.

Victoria (Vietnamese American): I don't see White people as a race, I sort of see past them. But I think they can contribute greatly to the discussion of racism.

Kristen (Mexican American): Whites don't openly talk about racism. Other races talk about it more openly. Whites are more likely to discuss cultural differences than racism or Whiteness.

Elizabeth (European American): I never realized that racism was institutionalized, not just individual. I think we tend to surround ourselves with Whites with similar views in order to legitimize our ideas. I don't think most people are conscious of their racism.

Joe: White people don't take racism personally because they don't think it will affect them. Therefore, people tend to be inactive when it comes to fighting racism.

The teachers carefully began to examine the issue of White racism. Though it was a challenging topic, I noticed when they broke up into small groups, there was even further discussion. I believe caring teachers will take on tough topics like this. They will not push them under the rug, but listen to other viewpoints. Many European American teachers find these discussions hard, yet they feel that they learn more about themselves and how others see them. The teachers develop a deeper understanding of how we are all part of a society that has built-in systems of privileges, which favor majority people. Sleeter has written that White racism is "the system of rules, procedures, and tacit beliefs that result in Whites collectively maintaining control over the wealth and power of the nation and the world. For at least 500 years, Europeans and their descendants have taken huge amounts of land, wealth, labor, and other resources from peoples of color around the world . . . We seem to have agreed tacitly to continue to reap the benefits of the past, and not to talk about it, except largely in ways that render present race relations legitimate" (1994, 6). Though this can be a tough topic for many people who are part of the majority and other teachers too, I believe it is important for us to talk cooperatively about institutional racism. If we do not, then we will never be able to make the changes needed to create truly equitable schools or society.

As part of small-group discussions, I asked teachers to draw their views of White privilege on large poster papers. Here is a sample of two of the images which the teachers have created over the years.

Why do you think the teachers created these images? What messages do you think the teachers are sending? They represent the difference in social and economic power.

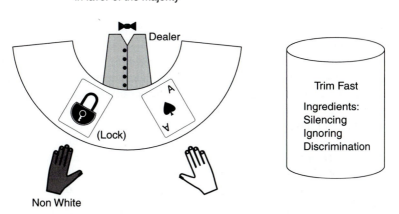

The deck is stacked
in favor of the majority

Dealer

(Lock)

Non White

. . . the race card always comes into play . . .

Trim Fast

Ingredients:
Silencing
Ignoring
Discrimination

❧ Racial Identity Formation in Culturally Diverse Young People

Just as White teachers go through a process of understanding their racial identity, your students of color go through a process of racial identity formation. Both children and teachers of color are not only members of groups that have less political, financial, personal, institutional, and social capital than majority ethnic communities (Gordon 1999), but also they must deal with the stigma of being physically different and easily identifiable. As you read through the next section, notice the similarities between the theoretical work of Helms and Tatum to Cross. William Cross (1991) has developed a typology that can be used to explain the confusing and difficult process that African American adolescents, in particular, pass through. Though this typology was developed for African Americans, it can also be applied to people from other racially and ethnically different individuals.

Cross (1991) identified five stages in his racial identity model: pre-encounter, encounter, immersion/emersion, internalization, and internalization/commitment. In many ways the process is similar to the one White Americans pass through in order to clarify their own identity.

1. **Pre-encounter.** Children learn about majority culture from the media, school, their friends, textbooks, and other ways. In this stage, African American children learn about the superiority of White Americans and learn that the standard for success is a European one. A child in this stage has not thought much about her own racial identity. At this point, a child learns a Eurocentric view of the world and takes in information from schools, media, and many other avenues without understanding the impact on her self-esteem or possible identity confusion.

2. **Encounter.** In this stage, the child has had contact with someone who either called her a name or excluded her from the group. This emphasizes the issue of race and the child will begin to question what happened and why the conflict arose. Cross believes that this can occur when the child is in middle school. As part of adolescence, a student may be questioning much about herself. Physical appearance becomes an increasingly important characteristic of a young person. Tatum (1997) found in her own research that African American students in this age group began asking questions about their ethnic and racial identity with parents and friends. She found dating became an extremely important issue at this stage of life and students became anxious about interracial dating, in particular. In addition, Tatum found African American males to be more aware of the negative role models they saw on the media, like African American men handcuffed or shown as violent.

    Unfortunately, Tatum (1997) discovered that some African American students developed an identity that confronted the White idea of success. Since Black students felt alienated from the majority society, they turned their backs on academic performance because they saw it as acceptance of European values and identity.

3. **Immersion/Emersion.** A young person in this stage explores and learns about her racial or ethnic community. Oftentimes the student may not only want to read about the history of her group, but also associate with others from the same racial community (Tatum 1997). The youngster enjoys learning about her group and becoming involved in ethnic or racially oriented community organizations. A high school student, who in the past had no interest in the Black Student Union, may now begin attending meetings at school and taking an active role in the activities. She may seek out a sense of safety and comfort that she finds in a same-race organization.

4. **Internalization.** In this stage, the young person becomes more secure with who she is and has self-identified her own feelings about racial membership. There is less anger toward Whites because the person feels comfortable with who she is (Tatum 1997). The student may now belong not only to the Black Student Union, but also to the Human Relations group on campus. She is active in both and works to develop coalitions between members of different communities.

5. **Internalization/Commitment.** In this stage, the student is secure in her identity as an African American person and has friends in both African American and other communities (Tatum 1997). The young person is committed to making life better in the African American community and works toward a more just society for all people.

This model shows the process a junior high/middle school student may begin. The journey can continue on to young adulthood or older. This developmental continuum can also describe the process an adult individual of color might pass through. As a child, the person may not have moved beyond the pre-encounter or encounter stage until she/he is an adult.

When Students from Ethnic Groups Challenge White Teachers

Just as you may find yourself with an array of feelings about ethnic and cultural groups, your students may also have developed strong perceptions of others based on cultural background. If you are European American, you may encounter children who first behave toward you as a member of the White collective. They may be hostile and not very trusting. Do not take this personally. They may have encountered many incidents of prejudice and group people into prejudged categories. Even if students have encountered only one European American teacher who is prejudiced, they had to sit through an entire year of discriminatory treatment no matter how covert. Students may see you not as an individual, but as a representative of a larger group. As in any human relationship, you may need to prove to children that you believe in them and that you are fair. Don't worry about being European American. Instead, take that energy and be fair, respectful, and caring and treat each child as an important person. Most children will respond to you in the same respectful manner. You can set the tone of respect or animosity, it is your choice. Students want to believe that you are pulling for each one of them.

Hopefully as you read through this book, you will realize that the issues of race, class, gender, and sexual orientation are part of society and cannot be avoided. You may even be called racist or gender-biased by a student. Will you know how to respond?

Linda Valli has written a helpful article about the dilemmas teachers find themselves in when dealing with the issues of race. She placed nine European American preservice teachers in high schools that had a majority of African American or other underrepresented students (Valli 1995). Several of the teachers were anxious and worried about teaching in an inner-city school because they had visions of violent students and out-of-control classrooms.

Initially, Valli found her teachers to be conscious of color. Race did matter to them. The teachers were worried and expected hostility from their students. They also felt that they stood out physically in the school because they were White. As time went by, the teachers did not ignore the issue of race. And race did not continue to become an obstacle to reaching students because teachers had a better understanding of their own feelings and the beliefs of their students.

It was not uncommon for students to accuse teachers of being racist. Teachers from majority and underrepresented groups have been challenged or tested. Students know that this can be a hot button, or threat, for all teachers. However, children also accuse their teachers because they are trying to better understand who they are and the parameters of race in society. Valli (1995) found when students accused the teachers in her program of racism, the teachers had to deal with color. They could no longer ignore it. Let's look at the experience of a teacher named Matt:

> "If I told him to sit down, he would stand up. Whatever I did, he totally did the opposite. And every comment was, 'Well, you're just pickin' on me because I'm Black.' Or 'You're doing this because I'm Black.' And I was like 'No, It's because you're talking.' By muttering things under his breath like 'He's just trying to make me White,' Kahlil gave Matt the impression that his reactions were part of a broader resistance to White and White-imposed education (Valli 1995, 123).

What would you have said to Kahlil? Matt was being tested and he could have lost the entire class based on what he said to this one student. Before reading on, think about how you would respond. If you became defensive, what would the students say?

I believe one of the most effective strategies is to use humor because it often defuses the situation. Defensiveness most likely will escalate the issue. If you are consistently fair using the same rules for everyone and then use humor, students will know that you heard them, but that in this class it is their effort and ability that counts, not their skin color. Matt could have replied with, "Come on, Kahlil. You know that I believe in equity. I remind all my students who talk when they aren't supposed to. You know you're not that special." If Matt could have spoken to Kahlil with humor, yet still indirectly said that he is not racist just because he's European American, Kahlil would most likely drop the issue. Valli found that those teachers who dealt with the issue of race immediately and did not let it slide by were much more successful in their teaching.

What did Valli's preservice teachers learn? They learned that race is a school issue. Though initially her European American teachers had not thought a great deal about race, they found that it was an integral part of U.S. society. The European American teachers also realized that their skin color was neither neutral nor privileged. They had a race, and the students forced them to address their racial membership. Valli wrote about what her teachers learned, "Their students were engaged in the act of constructing Whiteness, an act in which they were the objects. Roles were reversed. Skin color had functioned as an interpretive lens in their own interactions with students. Now that lens was focused on them. But they, like most Whites were unaccustomed to this gaze" (1995, 124). To the students at the school, White was a color and their teachers were members of this collective. The students in the school continued to remind teachers that racism is an active issue in society.

Cleary and Peacock (1998) have written about difficulties some European American teachers find as they work with Native American students. They describe a good-hearted woman teacher from the Midwest who began working in a reservation school. Unfortunately, she encountered prejudice and discrimination from her American Indian students and became angry, frustrated, and bitter.

Here are her comments:

"These people can get anything. They can get money for school just because they're Native American. And they can take advantage of so much. They could go to any school they wanted to, free ride. We give them everything we've got as teachers, and all they've got to do is take it. And they don't. I don't understand it. But they kind of take it all for granted, and they don't spend the money on what they should spend it on. They spend it on booze. Ninety percent of them do. They're wasting themselves. Then they complain that it's our fault. It's my fault because I'm a white woman. I have to work my buns off to make $15,000 working in [this] cruddy school. That's not enough to live on . . . I know that what happened to the Native Americans shouldn't happen to dogs. But in another sense, what conquered nation has been given so much? It's kind of a sick thing to say, but when the Romans invaded all over the Mediterranean, were the Jews given a reservation? No. When the Galls or the Jesuits or the Anglos or the Saxons invaded Britain, what happened to the Britons? They were turned into slaves, and they were not given nearly as much as Native Americans have been given . . . If you really want to live your culture, then let's go back and take the houses off and help you reinstate yourselves into teepees and wigwams" (Cleary and Peacock 1998, 73–74).

In order for the teacher to become effective with the Native American students, she needed to review her own prejudices, which were probably acting as obstacles to her ability to reach students. Her students most likely sensed that she had these feelings. Caring teachers must look at their own attitudes and question overgeneralizations. In that process, a person must ask herself, what is it that I feel I do not want to give up and why is my belief so difficult to give up?

If we were her colleagues, how could we open lines of communication with her? What messages would you want her to hear from you? What would you say to a person as angry and frustrated as this teacher? Can we move beyond our own fears and prejudices? The task of living our principles of equity and social justice is not an easy one. We will need to learn to deal with conflict, build lines of communication, and design ways of moving forward *together.* I believe this teacher, on one level, did go to teach in a reservation school because she wanted to make a difference. So how could we assist her in looking at what was happening from other viewpoints and unpack other layers of resentment and prejudice she held?

Summary

People from many groups have felt discrimination. The experience can be emotionally disturbing especially if one has to deal with it continually. Discrimination can have severe impact on the feelings of self-worth, identity of children and adults, and learning. This chapter included stories from many teachers who have experienced discrimination. They have not forgotten it, even though the event may have occurred decades in the past. There are many kinds of discrimination. Some occur because of individual bias, others occur because of social beliefs, and still many instances arise from institutional prejudice.

One of the most pervasive types of oppression is racism. The discussion in this chapter explained the process that African Americans and White Americans pass through in developing their racial identity. The research of Janet Helms and Beverly Tatum found that White students go through a process that can be described as the following: acceptance of status quo, feeling uncomfortable with discussion of race, denial of inequities in society, seeking clarification of own racial identity, acceptance of self and group, and becoming a change agent. A similar process was found for African Americans by William Cross. He found that African American students first learn about how society views the African American community. Then as children, when young people encounter racism, they may begin to question their racial identity. In the next stage, young people begin to explore aspects of the community. Following this stage, people begin to become more secure with who they are and work toward making society a more just place.

White privilege is one of the most difficult aspects of racism to understand. Peggy McIntosh gives many insights into how people benefit from being members of the majority community without understanding how their membership provides opportunities that others may not have. In fact, she believes European Americans do not understand that it is a privilege that they see their lives as morally neutral, normative, and the standard for others.

Prejudice and discrimination are powerful forces in society. They can impact the way teachers act and react to their students, and vice versa. It is important to understand the process that people go through in order to understand who they are in a racially conscious society like the United States.

Teacher Reflections

Answer the following questions in your journal. Reflect on how your understanding of prejudice and discrimination is deepening as you think about the experiences and dialogue you have with others.

1. When you were discriminated against, how did it feel? What emotions did you have? How did the discrimination impact you and your ideas?
2. List the ways that prejudice and discrimination can be hurtful to others. Can you list situations where students have felt the sting and pain of prejudice and discrimination? Can you see why prejudice can cause trouble in the classroom?
3. If you are European American, read through the chart on White racial identity and find the stage which best describes you. If you are a person from an ethnic minority group, use William Cross's discussion of racial identity and find which stage describes where you would place yourself. Go back to the chart as you read through this book. Have you changed or are you staying in the same place? Why or why not?

Positive and Fun Activity

I do not want to leave you with the feeling that there is nothing that we can do, so I would like to suggest that you make a large poster called One Hundred Ways to Stop Racism or One Hundred Ways to Stop Sexism or One Hundred Ways to Stop Homophobia. I adapted the idea from the National Association of Social Workers, who have a poster called "100 Ways You Can Stop Violence . . . " I have used many of their ideas in my example. Have your students help you create the poster. I find young people have exceptional imaginations and will extend the activity beyond my original vision. Add another 50 ways to complete a 100 ways list.

One Hundred Ways You Can Stop Racism, Sexism, Classism, and Homophobia

1. Smile at ten new people from other groups.
2. Make someone else laugh.
3. Learn about another's group history.
4. Say positive things about other people.
5. Write a positive letter to someone.
6. Object to an ethnic or gender-biased or homophobic joke.
7. Read children's books with positive role models of women and people of color to your students.
8. Appreciate differences.
9. Learn a new language.
10. Watch movies like *Sarafina, Picture Bride, Soul Food, Zoot Suit, Mi Familia, Secrets and Lies, Amistad,* or *Shall We Dance?*
11. Be fair with your students.
12. Teach children how to talk out a conflict.
13. Be respectful of your students and colleagues.
14. Invite students to lunch.
15. Teach children an integrated U.S. history.
16. Help children see African American history as U.S. history.
17. Help children see women's history as U.S. history.
18. Help children see Asian Pacific American history as U.S. history.
19. Help children see Native American history as U.S. history.
20. Help children see Latino history as U.S. history.
21. Invite guest speakers from different communities to the classroom.
22. Call parents every Friday congratulating their children for excellent work.
23. Put on a play about Angela Davis or Malcolm X, or César Chavez.
24. Invite a class from another school to lunch.
25. Invite parents to school for lunch.
26. Don't blame, find a solution.
27. Take students on a field trip to a photography exhibit on immigration.
28. Have books in your class library written by such authors as James Baldwin, Alice Walker, Marilyn Chin, Sandy Cisneros, Alan Lau, Frank Chin, Joy Harjo, Gloria Steinem, W.E.B. Dubois, Rita Dove, Garrett Hongo, Jimmy Santiago Baca, and Maya Angelou.
29. Use community newspapers to teach differing points of view.
30. Write to your congressional representatives about injustices you see.
31. Hold a learning fair for the children in your neighborhood or apartment building.
32. Invite new people to play ball with you at the park.
33. Promote peace.
34. Get others to help you make 1,000 origami cranes to symbolize peace and community.
35. Work for equal rights.

36. Don't let jokes about women go by. Don't let jokes about men go by.
37. Volunteer to work on a school climate committee.
38. Be positive.
39. Practice speaking and acting respectfully even if you don't feel it. It may rub off on you.
40. Look at an issue from the viewpoint of someone who is a member of another ethnic group.
41. Use words like "we" instead of "us" and "them."
42. Monitor what you watch on television.
43. Be a good model, don't use words like "you people" or "those people."
44. Listen to every child equally.
45. Don't let males dominate the classroom conversation.
46. Don't overgeneralize about men or women.
47. Be friendly.
48. Stop children from harassing others or name-calling.
49. Change is slow. Keep working to make life more just.
50. "Don't get discouraged. 'Hope is like a road in the country. There never was a road, but when many people walk the same path, a road comes into existence.' " National Association of Social Workers poster

To order the National Association of Social Workers poster on violence write to 750 First Street, NE, Washington, D.C. 20002.

Further Readings

McIntosh, Peggy. 1992. Unpacking the invisible knapsack: White privilege. *Creation Spirituality.* January/February: 33–35, 53.

This is an excellent article about privileges that European Americans hold, but are often unaware of. The article talks about the unearned power that members of the majority have in society. To McIntosh it is clear that racism is an institutional issue. When we are silent or deny the existence of the advantages given because of racial group membership, she believes the pattern of dominance continues and is reinforced.

After reading her article or the statements on page 141 of this book, write additional statements in your journal about the privileges that you see.

Stavley, L. 1989. *The Education of a WASP.* Madison: University of Wisconsin Press.

This is an excellent book to help you look at how society has different rules for different groups of people. Stavley found through her own experiences in the 1960s that even though, as a nation, we espouse the values of justice and fair play, in reality African Americans were being discriminated against in schools, on the job, and in the media. She realized that much of our views of other groups has been transmitted by television, movies, the newspapers, and magazines. Let me ask, "If you have had little contact with others from another group, how did you learn about who they are and what they believe in?" Most time it is through the media. Reading this book can give you a deeper understanding of how there is a system of rewards and punishments in society and that it is based upon factors like skin color, gender, social economic class, and sexual orientation.

Tatum, Beverly D. 1997. *Why Are All the Black Kids Sitting Together in the Cafeteria?* New York: Basic Books.

Beverly Tatum has written one of the easiest to read texts on racial identification formation. She carefully includes theoretical frameworks of Erik Erickson, Janet Helms, and William Cross. Much of the literature on racial identification is hard to understand, but Tatum has written a book that you will learn from and enjoy. As an African American professional, she shares her real-life experiences. The mother of two youngsters gives a special view of how she helps her own children deal with racism and racial identity.

References

Allport, Gordon W. 1954. *The nature of prejudice.* Reading, Mass.: Addison-Wesley.

Brislin, Richard. 1993. *Understanding culture's influence on behavior.* N.Y.: Harcourt Brace College Publishers.

Cross, Jr., William E. 1991. *Shades of black: Diversity in African-American identity.* Philadelphia, Pa.: Temple University Press.

Daniels, Roger, and Harry Kitano. 1970. *American racism: Exploration of the nature of prejudice.* Englewood Cliffs, N.J.: Prentice Hall, Inc.

Gordon, Edmund W. 1999. *Education and justice: A view from the back of the bus.* N.Y.: Teachers College Press.

Knowlton, Clark. 1972. The New Mexican land war. In Edward Simmen, ed., *Pain and promise: The Chicano today.* New York: New American Library.

Loewen, James. 1995. *Lies my teacher told me.* N.Y.: Simon and Schuster.

McIntosh, Peggy. 1992. Unpacking the invisible knapsack: White privilege. *Creation Spirituality.* January/February: 33–35, 53.

McLaren, Peter. 1997. Decentering Whiteness: In search of a revolutionary multiculturalism. *Multicultural Education, 5*(1): 4–11.

Nelson, Jack, and Valerie O. Pang. In press. Race and ethnicity in social studies education: How racism and prejudice are perpetuated in the field. In Wayne Ross, ed., *The social studies curriculum: Purposes, problems, and possibilities.* 2nd ed. Albany, N.Y.: SUNY Press.

Omi, Michael, and Howard Winant. 1994. 2nd ed. *Racial formation in the United States: From the 1960's to the 1990's.* New York: Routledge.

Paley, Vivian Gussin. 1979. *White teacher.* Cambridge, Mass.: Harvard University Press.

Pang, Valerie, and Jesus Nieto. 1995. *The emotional responses of European American teachers to issues of prejudice and discrimination.* Unpublished manuscript.

Ryan, William. 1976. *Blaming the victim,* rev. ed. N.Y.: Vintage Books.

Sleeter, Christine. 1994. White racism. *Multicultural Education, 1*(4): 5–8, 39.

Takaki, Ronald. 1993. *A different mirror : A history of multicultural America.* Boston: Little, Brown and Company.

Tatum, Beverly Daniel. 1992. Talking about race, learning about racism: The application of racial identity development theory. *Harvard Educational Review, 62*(1): 1–24.

Tatum, Beverly Daniel. 1992. African-American identity, academic achievement, and missing history. *Social Education, 56*(6): 331–334.

Tatum, Beverly Daniel. 1997. *Why are all the black kids sitting together in the cafeteria?* New York: Basic Books.

Valle, Ramon. 1997. *Ethnic diversity and multiculturalism: Crisis or challenge.* N.Y.: American Heritage Custom Publishing.

Valli, Linda. 1995. The dilemma of race: Learning to be color blind and color conscious. *Journal of Teacher Education, 46*(3): 120–129.

Zinn, Howard. 1980. *A people's history of the United States.* N.Y.: Harper and Row.

Zinn, Howard. 1990. *Declarations of independence.* New York: HarperCollins.

Chapter 7

Aren't Mary and Michael Too Young to Be Prejudiced?

How Children Learn Prejudice

I believe most of us learn prejudice about others while growing up. One of the articles that helped me to get a clearer picture on how children are taught values and beliefs without really consciously taking in the ideas was an interview with Robert Coles, the child psychiatrist. Coles has written more than fifty books on children and remarked that he found many children to be aware of racial differences as young as 2 or 3 years old. In interviews with first and second grade children, Coles also discovered children to be extremely aware of class differences. Though adults may believe children do not know much about social class, gender, and race, children have learned that these things should not be talked about because they are embarrassing matters (*Teaching Tolerance* 1992). Coles discovered children to be very savvy about how people are treated differentially because of race and class.

A teacher relayed a story about his young neighbor. He was out in the yard talking with a White mother and her child. The child was almost 3 years old. An African American child who lived several houses away asked to play with the younger child. The mother politely said, "She needs to take her nap now, so she won't be able to play." When the mother took her daughter inside to the porch, her tone changed dramatically. She said harshly, "I don't want you playing with any of those ugly children. Don't let me catch you with them." The young daughter's eyes opened wide as she carefully listened to her mother. The little girl didn't say anything. The teacher, who overheard the conversation, was shocked by the comments of his neighbor. He couldn't believe what he had heard. He knew that this young person could grow up thinking negatively about African Americans.

Another teacher from one of my classes gave a similar example. Her daughter had a close friend who was Japanese American. The Japanese American young woman was seeing a Latino. Her parents never said anything directly to oppose the young man; however, one summer her parents suggested that she go to cultural activities at the Buddhist church. The young woman asked, "Why do you want me to go with you?" Her father said, "I want you to learn about Buddhism and Japanese history. It will be a wonderful experience." He paused, then said, "You might find another boyfriend too, one who is more like you." Prejudice can be taught by people who we trust and care for; some may be members of our family.

Who Am I and Who Should I Be Like?

Children begin to make sense of the world by understanding themselves first. They know their name and who are members of their family. Later they begin to distinguish between those who are uncles, aunts, and cousins as being relatives, while neighbors and others are friends. Children also show fear of strangers at about six months of age (Allport 1954). These strangers may wear different colors or talk to children in an unfamiliar way. As children grow, they develop a sense of who they are while they are learning prejudicial attitudes from their environment.

As children come into contact with others, they learn about people and make generalizations about life. Allport (1954) believes that children adopt the prejudices of others and develop prejudices as part of life experiences. When children adopt prejudice, they accept and take in the attitudes and stereotypes of important people in their lives. Allport believes that children who grow up in a highly authoritarian and disciplined family are sensitive to the approval and disapproval of their parents. Oftentimes, they are taught that authority and power are key aspects of interpersonal relationships rather than trust and care. Allport believes children who are brought up in authoritarian families are more likely to be fearful or suspicious of others. And if children are criticized a great deal, they are going to develop a personality which is more critical of others (Sleeter and Grant 1987). On the other hand, children who grow up in families where love is unconditionally given are more likely to acquire higher levels of self-esteem and confidence. They are also more likely to accept others because their parents have accepted them.

Stages of Prejudice and Identity Development

Children learn who they are as they learn who they are not. Prejudice and identity formation are integrally linked. The prejudice children learn may be due to race, ethnicity, culture, class, gender, language, and other social categories (Byrnes 1988). As you read through this section, remember there are many layers of identity. Though this section deals primarily with racial identity, many children develop other ideas of who they are like ethnic identity, religious identity, national identity, and family identity. These are complex constructs, yet they are often developing simultaneously. Children are trying to figure out where they fit in with their families, as a person with particular physical characteristics, as a member of a family that has ties with an ancestral country other than the United States, and as a member of something called the United States.

Stage One: Curious of Others

As children mature, Allport has identified four stages of prejudice, and they are listed in Figure 7.1. In the first stage, children as young as 2 years old are curious about differences they see in others (Allport 1954). They may notice that someone's skin color, hair texture, or name is different from their own (Goodman 1964); the differences are not negative ones. At this time, children begin to sort out distinctive characteristics of people and place them into categories like race, language, gender, and physical abilities (Derman-Sparks, Higa, and Sparks 1980). Simultaneously children see that their differences have social categories. Have you ever heard a child ask their parent or sibling, "What am I?" One mother told the story about how her 4-year-old daughter, Helen, began developing a sense of self and how it involved a discussion of others.

> " 'You're an American, and so am I, and so's your father.' At nursery school the other day, she asked the teacher, 'What are you?' Mrs. X said, 'I'm an American,' and Helen drew herself up very proud and said, 'I'm an American too.' . . . And then a little while back Mary said she'd rather play with David than Helen. Mary said, 'He's white and you're colored.' But she wasn't takin' that. She came right back with, 'Oh no I'm not. I'm a tantalizin' brown!' " (Derman-Sparks et al. 1980, 7).

In this conversation, Mary, another 4-year-old, had already developed a belief about racial categories, skin colors, and national identity as an American (U.S. citizen). Yet Helen, with the help of her parents, had created her own racial identity and she was not hurt by what Mary said. Three- and four-year-olds are sorting out characteristics by saying things like "I'm no girl—I'm a boy," or "I got curly yellow hair." (Derman-Sparks et al. 1980, 8).

Young children learn to categorize people based on identifiable physical characteristics since our country has strong political and social orientations toward race. Young children, 3 to 5 years old, are interested in their physical differences and those of others. Skin color is usually one of the attributes children focus on. "A frequently reported question asked by White children about Black children: 'Will the color come off in the bathtub?' " (Derman-Sparks et al. 1980).

At this age children are not only attempting to identify who they are, but they are beginning to understand the concept of group. I believe that these young children are not "color-blind," but that many grow up in an environment that continually reinforces the

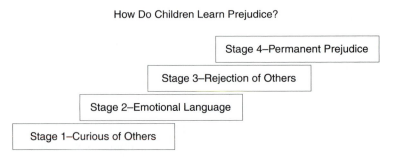

How Do Children Learn Prejudice?

Stage 4–Permanent Prejudice

Stage 3–Rejection of Others

Stage 2–Emotional Language

Stage 1–Curious of Others

Figure 7.1   *An Adaptation of Allport's Stages of Prejudice: How Do Children Learn Prejudice?*

belief that racial and other differences have positive and negative values attached to them. These beliefs come from their environment and experiences children have with adults and other children.

Like Goodman, Derman-Sparks and her colleagues found preschool and elementary grade students to be "color conscious" (Derman-Sparks et al. 1980). They discovered that young children were not color-blind, rather they were extremely aware of racial differences. The children asked questions like:

> Why are there Black people?
> Is Mexican my color?
> Why am I called Black if my skin is brown?
> If I'm Black and White, and Tim is Black and White, how come he is darker than me?
> Do Indians always run around wearing feathers?
> Why is my skin called yellow? It's not yellow, it's tan.
> (Derman-Sparks et al. 1980, 8).

Young children, especially preschoolers, are struggling with their own identity as they learn about social categories.

Children also learn about gender differences. Sometimes that knowledge is biased knowledge. Young children may come to school with definite perceptions about the roles of women and men. The comic above shows that Zoe and Hammie were surprised when their new doctor was a female. This is an example of how positive role models can generate powerful new learning in students.

Stage Two: Emotional Language

Though children do not always see differences as negative, how do children learn that differences have values attached to them? In the second stage, Allport believes children begin to notice that the words people use to describe others have strong emotional connotations attached to them. These words are sometimes used to hurt another and by the age of 4, many children have learned that the differences have values attached to them. Derman-Sparks and her colleagues (1980) found one of the most important developmental tasks young children of color must deal with is to build positive racial and ethnic identities. This can be difficult especially within the context of a White society, where labels and images from the media and from others may be negative.

Stereotypical images of people are found in many places. The media often reinforces biased views (Byrnes 1988). Asians are often portrayed as karate-fighting mobsters who are so devoted to their cause that they will even commit suicide because of fanatical loyalty. African Americans are usually the drug smugglers or dope addicts. Heroes are usually physically attractive and many villains still wear black. The image of beauty usually involves a thin, tall, blond, shapely woman. These beliefs are reinforced continually by children in the hundreds of hours they watch television every year.

During this stage of identity formation, children are also trying to understand how national identity as an American (in this context I am referring to a U.S. citizen, native or naturalized) and ethnic identity can be related. I believe it may take many years, even into adulthood before a person of color understands her/himself. Although the person is an American—whether American-born or naturalized citizen—if she/he has not been accepted by the majority culture, then the person may not feel like a full-fledged partner in the process. Prejudice can cause people to question themselves and it tears away at their self-esteem.

National and ethnic identity can be an extremely complicated aspects of some children's lives. In San Diego, there are many new immigrant families from all over the world whose children go to public school. Children have migrated from countries like Somalia, Korea, Russia, Iran, Mexico, and Vietnam. Many of these children must begin to build a sense of who they are within this new cultural and political context. I believe as the children grow up in their new home, the United States, they develop a complicated self-concept, which is a combination of new American values and behaviors mixed with home-country culture. Many times this adjustment is extremely difficult, especially when prejudice and discrimination are directed toward them because of differences due to language, accent, behaviors, clothing, and traditions.

Stage Three: Rejection of Others

In the third stage of prejudice, children begin to reject the people their parents, friends, and important role models also do not like. This occurs at about 7 to 11 years of age. They accept their parents' values without question. Allport wrote about a child who ran home and asked her mother, "What was the name of the child I was supposed to hate?" (Allport 1954, 292). Since the young child wanted to please her mother, she had a sense of labels that people used to call each other as being "bad" and wanted to make sure that she did what her mother wanted her to do. She wanted to dislike the people her mother did not like. During this stage, children may totally reject those in a group. They may not want to play with someone who is from another race, or they may choose children who are only from their group.

Children of color and majority children need the support of their parents and teachers when they deal with issues of prejudice and discrimination. Parents, teachers, and other adults can help children develop in positive ways through their modeling. Children of color, whose parents teach a strong sense of family and cultural pride, often are more able to deal with prejudice because they know their roots. For example, a child who has been called "Jap" at school probably will be hurt; however, if her parents have taught her to be proud and that her family has a long legacy of culture and commitment to civil rights, the child knows that her family is strong and has triumphed over prejudice in the past.

My husband and I knew our daughter and son would encounter racism in their lives and we tried to prepare them as best we could. When they were babies, we would say things like, "I love your beautiful black hair and skin," or "You have beautiful brown eyes." And as they grew old enough to go to school, we were careful to tell them that they should not allow other kids to call them names.

As any mother, I was concerned that they someday would have to deal with the name-calling and exclusion that racism can bring. Our daughter is somewhat quiet. She is not shy, but she is not an aggressive person and I worried about her ability to deal with bullies and name-callers. I thought she would ignore any name-calling. One day in the fifth grade, she came home somewhat upset. I asked her what happened. She said several children on the playground taunted her with the sing-song rhyme, "Ching Chong Chinaman." As she walked around with her friends at recess, my daughter turned around, looked directly at them, and said, "Cut it out." Even though she is a caring individual, she is also a strong person and would not allow others to tear her down. Fortunately, she had supportive friends and they also told the kids to stop their taunting. They quit. I told her I was proud of her because she had the courage to stand up for herself. She beamed. Children need feedback from their parents, teachers, and other adults to help them filter through the thousands of messages they receive every day about race, class, and gender.

Stage Four: Prejudice Becomes Permanent

By stage 4 prejudicial attitudes become more fixed when children become teenagers. During this part of their life, children have developed cultural categories dealing with characteristics like sexual orientation, race, ethnicity, class, and gender. In addition, young people do not usually reject everyone from a group. In addition, children in this stage are not as prone to overgeneralizations. Allport believes this is a stage of differentiation. Teens make exceptions for individuals. They may say, "I'm not prejudiced. My best friend is Black." Interestingly Allport reminds his readers that while children are learning prejudice, people are also talking about democracy and equality (1954, 295). So children learn about the complexities of prejudice within a society where equality is valued, and though underrepresented groups may have positive qualities, their negative ones justify censure.

I believe that children learn from infancy values of race, class, and gender. These values are part of their everyday lives. They learn who they are and who they should be like. They also learn who they should not like. They take on the values of the people they trust and who are their role models.

❧ An Experience as a First Grade Teacher

When I began teaching first grade, I didn't realize children's views of race affected their impressions of others. The following story describes the color-conscious values of a 6-year-old. He seemed to be between stage 2 and stage 3. He did not outright reject someone who was different, but he did seem to hold strong values about those differences.

During the first several days of first grade, I had small groups of four children and their parents visit school for an hour. This was done to help first graders make the adjustment to a full day of school. I noticed one child standing outside the classroom not wanting to enter (Pang 1988). I asked his mother what was wrong. She said, "My son, Rodney, doesn't want to come in." I began to worry. What was I going to do? Finally, I asked, "Is he scared?" "No," she said, "Rodney says he doesn't want to come in because he can't speak Chinese!" At first I couldn't understand the problem, because I am Japanese American not Chinese American. It did not occur to me that this 6-year-old had looked into the classroom and decided that since I looked Asian, I wasn't an American (U.S. citizen) and therefore couldn't speak English. He thought I could only speak Chinese. I was surprised by Rodney's matter-of-fact belief that I must be a foreigner since I did not look European American.

Many children like Rodney who enter school are aware of many messages society holds about group membership. Five- to eight-year-olds realize they are members of different social groups. They learn about the characteristics of their social, cultural, and racial groups developing identities with groups. Children develop categories about other children and may exclude them because of their skin color, accent, physical attributes, neighborhood, and language. Unfortunately, children at this age also can be acutely aware of racist, gender-biased, and classist attitudes of others and take on prejudicial attitudes of parents, friends, and neighborhoods. Name-calling is common at this age and children understand that these names are used to hurt others. At this age children struggle with gathering accurate information about others, but children of color also must struggle with racial self-identity in a society where the ideal models presented are to look like "Barbie and Ken." Teachers need to be aware of how to help reinforce each child's cultural identity.

An Anti-Bias Curriculum

An important component of multicultural education is reducing prejudice and discrimination in students. If you teach preschool or the primary grades, I suggest that you read the book, *Anti-Bias Curriculum: Tools for Empowering Young Children,* by Derman-Sparks and her colleagues (1989). It is an excellent resource because it may answer your questions about how to guide children away from prejudicial attitudes and discriminatory behavior. The book covers issues of race and gender and also has a chapter aimed at helping youngsters develop anti-bias attitudes toward children with learning and developmental differences. There is a continual thread throughout the book that children need to learn to accept each other in a safe and respectful environment. This setting must also provide children with new ways of interacting with each other. Just placing children together does not necessarily build bridges of communication among students.

Derman-Sparks and her colleagues have identified several important goals for learning about culture, which will help all children develop a positive sense of self while learning to foster healthy social interactions. I believe these goals can help you create a classroom that cultivates equity and cultural diversity. The following is an adaptation of their goals:

1. A teacher affirms and fosters children's knowledge and pride, not superiority, in their cultural identity.
2. A teacher fosters children's curiosity, enjoyment, and empathetic awareness of cultural differences and similarities.
3. A teacher expands children's concept of fairness and feeling of empathy for others.
4. A teacher helps children change uncomfortable and inappropriate responses to differences into respectful, and comfortable interactions.
5. A teacher helps children think critically about stereotyping.

1-26
©1996 Bill Keane, Inc.
Dist. by Cowles Synd., Inc.

"Why are kings higher than
queens? Aren't men and women
s'posed to be equal?"

6.   A teacher helps children develop the tools and self-confidence to stand up for
     themselves and others against prejudice and discriminatory behavior.

When students are encouraged to think and question, they often raise interesting questions on their own. In the comic above Dolly has come up with an important question.
The teacher could turn her question into a teachable moment about gender bias.

Dealing with Biases in Children

How can you help children become aware of racist, gender-biased, or classist behavior?
As a teacher, you can help children see that when their behavior excludes others, they
are discriminating against someone. Students are treating others in an uncaring way. For
example, when name-calling occurs, teachers should talk with their students right away.
It is important that children realize that racist, gender-biased, and classist terms are un-
acceptable. Like adults, children need to understand that when someone is called a name,
it threatens justice for all of us. Help children understand the "we" of a community. Even
though they may not be the perpetrator or victim of a particular situation, when the dignity of one person is threatened, our communal values of justice and equality are also
being questioned. Relating prejudice to children's notions of fairness helps young students realize they can eliminate prejudice. The following excerpt shows how a young
child can question his/her own perceptions.

> When D. was about seven he began dancing one day to a record of Navajo music we
> have. All of a sudden he stopped himself, looked at us and said, "You know, I don't
> know how they dance. I'm just making it up." Another day, he told us, after seeing a
> movie, "I know one way that movie was racist. It only had white people in it."
> (Derman-Sparks, et al. 1980, 7).

We can help children learn to respect each other's cultural ways and understand how
powerful messages about cultural differences are given in society all the time.

Helping Older Students Deal with Prejudice

Many students have told me how much it hurts when someone throws a racial slur at them. It is almost as if the hurt goes down to their souls. Their sense of self can be seriously damaged, especially in the adolescent years. For some very young children, the impact may not be as piercing on the self-esteem because they are not as oriented toward their peers and oftentimes they make up quickly after a conflict. However, with older students the role of prejudice may be much more disturbing and long lasting.

As students grow older, they may find that they must deal with more severe aspects of prejudice. The comments may be more cutting. The actions of peers may be more deliberate. When students feel like their "arms have been tied behind their back" due to an act of prejudice, then that feeling can lead to further feelings of helplessness. The prejudice may be even more destructive because students feel victimized. In addition, when prejudice is felt at this age, the experiences may tend to reinforce stereotypes they were forming about members of a particular group. For example, though Mary intellectually knows that it was only "three (name of an ethnic group) girls" who pushed and terrorized her in the bathroom, she may transfer this image to all young women in the group and not feel comfortable making friends or talking with other students in her classes from the same ethnic community as the perpetrators.

Encouraging students not to generalize is an important aspect of dealing with prejudice. As with the example of Mary, it would be helpful if her friends, teachers, parents, and others suggest that she remember other people she has worked with from the ethnic community who have been positive, encouraging, and collaborative. Looking at other role models in that community can help a young person understand that several individuals do not represent an entire community.

Teachers can employ long-term strategies that help young people deal more effectively with prejudice when it is directed at them.

1. Affirm the self-esteem of the students. When this is done consistently, students will have the self-confidence to respond to the event from a position of personal "centeredness" rather than one of defense.
2. Affirm the ethnic/cultural self-esteem of students. When students are knowledgeable about the strengths and weaknesses of their cultural orientations, they may develop a more rational identity. This ethnic identity is not built on feelings of superiority in comparison to other groups. This is especially important for students from underrepresented groups that have been historically oppressed.
3. Teach students about the diversity found in society. Knowing the history, culture, and beliefs of other ethnic communities can assist them in understanding another perspective and to see that prejudice may arise from historical viewpoints. For example, there are many nation-state conflicts that students bring to the United States from other countries. These conflicts may have risen from long-standing wars of the past.
4. Teach students the process of how people become prejudiced and racist, sexist, and homophobic. When students understand the process, they are more likely to stop themselves from developing biases.
5. Opposing messages are given out by society about prejudice. Students need to think about how society presents the value of equality and justice; however,

there are many institutional practices that give privilege to members of the dominant group.

There are also short-term strategies that can be taught to students when the name-calling or incident occurs and must be dealt with immediately.

1. Support students without "saving" them. Students must be encouraged to work through the event without teachers protecting them so much that they do not learn how to deal with opposition and conflict.
2. Suggest to students that they not "personalize" the comments. They do not know what motivated the perpetrators. There may be many reasons that stem from the perpetrator's own experiences and have little to do with the "victim."
3. Explain to students that "It's not about them. It's about the person who is prejudiced." Students may not realize that when someone discriminates, it says much about the perpetrator and not necessarily about the victim.
4. Help students understand that messages given by families may contradict student judgment or what is expected at school. Students must make their own decisions on how to deal with the situation. This can be difficult because some families recommend that their members fight back, while school officials may discourage this. Other students may want to fight back, but their parents tell them not to. However, in some settings, it is important to set boundaries of respect for oneself.
5. Build trusting relationships with people from many different cultural groups. This not only helps students create networks of support, but also gives them the opportunity to find others to help them to debrief the situation in a cross-cultural setting/discussion.
6. Students must not feel disempowered. One of the most destructive aspects of prejudice and discrimination is that it makes the victim feel powerless. It is important that students feel that they are acting—and acting in a way that they felt was most appropriate—even if it meant walking away. They must look at the event as learning something or demonstrating that they made a specific rational choice.

Curriculum That May Reinforce Stereotypes: Moving Away from Christmas around the World

Do you know of well-intentioned teachers who include a "Christmas around the World" theme for first graders? The children like coloring pictures of other children in traditional clothing and eating rice crackers, tacos, and anise cookies. They also may make colorful masks, paint beautiful eggs, and learn traditional dances; however, what do children really learn? Do you think these activities help to develop respect and a deep knowledge of others? Does it build a sense of fairness in children about others? Do these activities help children understand the values of others?

I know many teachers and students who really enjoy their activities that center around "Christmas around the World," yet I also realize many countries do not have a Christian worldview. In this way, countries in the Middle and Far East are not studied. This unit often centers upon European countries. The messages can be simplistic and reinforce stereotypes about those who seem foreign or strange. Many times the traditions and outward manifestations of culture are seen; however, the values which lie beneath them are not understood. Without understanding the values of a group, stereotypes can be created and reinforced. Let's look at an example of someone who comes to the United States.

What if a tourist from China, Mei Lee, arrived in Seattle, Washington, to visit the United States at the beginning of July. During her stay in Seattle, she often ate at Burger King and Wendy's. Since Mei Lee wanted to take souvenirs to her family, she went downtown shopping and bought tee shirts. In the evening, Mei Lee went to a musical called "Tommy." On her last day in the United States, Mei Lee went to a Fourth of July picnic and ate potato salad, barbecue chicken, and jello salad. Her friends invited her to a neighborhood tug of war and they laughed and laughed. At night she watched beautiful fireworks. The next day Mei Lee boarded the airplane and left for home. What did Mei Lee learn about what is important to us in the United States?

I think Mei Lee probably had a fun time and may have really enjoyed the food she ate, but I hope that she could return to learn more about our values as a community. For example, in Seattle there is a strong sense of social justice and numerous programs exist to house homeless and low-income families. King County has a federal job-training program in West Seattle, which places unemployed adults into positions where they can become self-sufficient. I hope that we try to help our students gain a balanced view of others. Unfortunately, much of what we cover about cultural groups deals with food, customs, and holidays. I have seen fifth grade teachers also use "Christmas around the World" as a theme. Oftentimes a teacher will focus upon the superficial elements of a cultural group; however, some teachers do delve into more substantial issues like gender roles, family relationships, and religious beliefs.

When young children do not have the experience of living in another country or neighborhood, quick units like "Christmas around the World, become a "travel brochure" study of others (Nakagawa 1996). There is little discussed about the values and beliefs of a people. Unfortunately, many teachers believe that "Christmas around the World" or a similar unit will help children better understand other groups. Many times this "travel brochure" to other cultures and countries reinforces stereotypes because culture is presented in isolated pieces. Heroes, holidays, and foods are emphasized rather than the values by which people live their lives. It is easier to focus upon the explicit culture of a group rather than the implicit culture.

Instead of traveling around the world eating and dancing, have your students learn about the communities that surround the school, city, or area. In this way, children have the chance to make connections with their peers in class. Children can share many aspects of their family cultures with each other. I know teachers who encourage students to bring in an important person from their family, a special toy, share several words from a home language other than English, and other precious gifts. When teachers ground discussion of culture to the lives of children, students are less likely to overgeneralize because they will see how culture is dynamic and ever-changing. Using relevant and personal cultural knowledge, children are encouraged to build connections with others. When they share things from home that are important to them, they will not only develop a stronger sense of self, but also help other children to understand other cultural ways and beliefs. There is the creation of a flexible and open atmosphere. We need to be attentive to and understand the values of people from other cultures. Cultural differences do not separate us, rather it is our *response* to differences that creates gaps between people.

Some teachers are able to incorporate the use of arts experiences, such as singing and dancing, into their curriculum. With proper sensitivity and attention to the cultural context, music and dancing can convey cultural beliefs, traditions, values, and customs in more effective ways than just telling students or having people read about these aspects of culture. The aesthetic quality of the artistic experiences can unify and connect people of various cultures. Teachers who have a deep respect for and understanding of a cultural community can provide these experiences for their students. For example, the teacher who taught her students the song, "De Colores," which can be found on page 220, wove the words of the piece with the history of civil rights and her personal experiences as a child with her mother.

Derman-Sparks and her colleagues (1989) suggest that an alternative to a December holidays unit can be a unit on the struggles of communities for freedom, justice, and peace. They suggest honoring community people who have worked hard for civil rights. The unit can be called "Community Heroes."

The work of these community heroes can be tied to the children's experience with fairness. Often I hear children tell their teachers, "But that's not fair." By using dolls or puppets who represent various people, children can learn about how individuals contributed to making our society more just. Bring in community people who can tell stories about how they changed unfair practices or instituted collaborative programs. This unit can be tied in with Martin Luther King, Jr.'s, birthday in January and/or a discussion of César Chavez.

❧ Using Anti-Racist Role Models: An Accurate Portrayal

Students in upper elementary school should be asked to examine social structures for institutional bias. A unit on community heroes should include information about how these heroes changed society. They not only worked to make life better for themselves, but they were committed to challenge social practices that were unfair to all people.

One of the most important pieces I ask teachers to read is called "The Myth of 'Rosa Parks the Tired': Teaching about Rosa Parks and the Montgomery Bus Boycott" by Herbert Kohl (1993). The article is powerful because Kohl explains how children can become change agents for civil rights and justice.

Kohl was in the audience of a fourth grade play about Rosa Parks and the Montgomery bus boycott. In the play Parks is portrayed as a tired person who would not move from a seat at the front of the bus to a seat in the back. Next, a mixed crowd of African American and European American students carried signs that said "Don't Ride the Buses," "We Shall Overcome," and "Blacks and Whites Together." A child playing Martin Luther King, Jr., then spoke to the crowd and told them that African Americans and European Americans boycotted riding buses in Montgomery because Rosa Parks had been arrested. Students gave the audience the message that it was through the cooperative efforts of Blacks and Whites that justice prevailed.

Unfortunately, Kohl found the children did not really understand the meaning of the Parks story and the boycott. First, the Montgomery bus boycott was organized and carried out by African Americans; European Americans were not involved in boycotting buses (Kohl 1993). Kohl felt it was crucial for students to know that the people who are oppressed have the power to confront their oppressors. This is a key point. Second, when

Rosa Parks is presented as a person who was too tired to move, children get the impression that she was just tired and stubborn that day. In reality, Parks was a long-time community activist who was committed to fighting segregation. Third, the boycott had been planned by E.D. Nixon and other African Americans in Montgomery. Martin Luther King, Jr., was first reluctant to join the others, but later he did become an important force in the boycott. And finally, the community was already organized to support a bus boycott. Rosa Parks knew what she was doing when she refused to move from her seat and her friends knew that she had the courage to be strong. As soon as Parks was arrested, the boycott began and lasted for 381 days.

The most important aspect of teaching about Rosa Parks and the Montgomery bus boycott is the issue of racism. Kohl found that children did not really understand what were the underlying reasons for the boycott. Yes, they did know that Black people could only sit in the back of the bus; however, they did not really tackle the social issue of racism. Teachers need to ask their students, "Why were African Americans not treated as equals? Why were there laws that wouldn't let African Americans use the same facilities as European Americans? Why did they have to sit in the back of the bus? Why couldn't they use the same toilets, swimming pools, and schools?" (See Chapter 10 for additional ideas in teaching a unit about the contributions of Rosa Parks.)

Children need to talk about how racism today and in the past hurts all of us. Children need to know that racism is part of our social structure. Another question children can think about is "Why do some groups live in this part of town and others live in that part of town?" Children need to understand that prejudice can be deep seated in society and that it is called racism. People are treated in a negative way not because of what they have done, but because there are preconceived notions of who they are based on their group membership, whether it is race, ethnicity, or skin color.

Older students, intermediate grades and higher, can examine other issues of oppression where institutional racism and sexism have impacted society. For example, historical issues such as: What impact did the Revolutionary War have on the Iroquois League? Why were Japanese Americans placed in internment camps? What were the goals of Manifest Destiny? How has the institution of slavery affected the African American community today? Why did the United States have a quota system of immigration? Why haven't we elected a woman president? Why hasn't the Equal Rights Amendment passed? These questions will help students examine how prejudice impacts society. These are complicated issues. I think that as teachers we must help children to develop the mindset of openness and action. In addition, it is crucial that children understand no one has to stand by and allow discrimination to repeat itself. We all have the responsibility to make sure equity is not only an ideal, but is a reality in society. Caring teachers are advocates for their children, and they are important role models who show their students that talking about oppression is not enough. We all must be active citizens trying to make our nation and world more caring, equitable, and free for all. In this way I hope children will learn that racism, sexism, classism, handicappism, and homophobia should not be accepted and that we must be active participants against those who treat others unfairly and without respect.

White Anti-Racist Role Models

When I ask teachers to name people who have been important in our fight against racism, they offer names like Martin Luther King, Jr., Harriet Tubman, and César Chavez. However, when I ask teachers to think about racism in a different way and ask the following questions, they seem to struggle with their answers.

Who Are Our White Anti-Racist Models?

There will be a long silence, then someone may suggest Abraham Lincoln. Then another person says, "Well, I am not sure if he is a good model." There will be more silence. Role models are extremely important in teaching people what can be possible in life. A role model exemplifies not only a set of beliefs, but a person who has acted upon those beliefs and made a difference in society. This is one of the most powerful ways to get teachers and students to explore the issue of racism.

When this question is posed, teachers and students must decide in their mind what is the criteria for an anti-racist, and that includes what kinds of actions that person would take. We often discuss the issue of racism in schools but not of anti-racists, especially those who are White.

Since many of our students are White, having White role models who stand out is extremely powerful. Otherwise, what I find is that students do not have a real vision of how a white person who is anti-racist would act in life. Students begin to realize that an anti-racist isn't just a person who does not like prejudice or someone who is against racism, but it is a person who takes action, and those actions take courage and great commitment. Their actions are usually directed at institutional practices of prejudice because they know that unless power relationships are changed, people from underrepresented groups will continually find themselves in oppressed positions.

It is also important for students from underrepresented groups to know about White folks who see their responsibility in eliminating racism and who act on their values. Students may then see the importance of creating cross-cultural coalitions that include Whites. Change will not occur if only people from ethnic "minority" communities fight racism. It will take members from all groups to make any substantial changes in institutions like schools, businesses, and government, because racism is so pervasive.

Who can you name as **White anti-racist** role models? Here are a few people you might want to consider:

Eleanor Roosevelt
Levi Coffin
Lillian Smith
Lloyd Garrison
John Brown
Lyndon Johnson
Henry David Thoreau
Harriet Beecher Stowe
Morris Dees

Some of these you may agree with and others you may not. What criteria would you use to decide if they were appropriate role models for students?

This is an important aspect of teaching about racism. Students must know that there are people who worked hard to get rid of prejudice and discrimination in society. It is critical that students, all students, understand that name-calling and discriminatory actions do not need to paralyze them, but that they can do something. Then students will feel less impacted by the oppression. Role models help them to understand that they can act positively against prejudice.

Leonard Covello

One day I found myself in a book store off of Harvard Square after an educational conference. I saw a title that caught my eye, *Teacher with a Heart*. It was a book about Leonard Covello, a principal and teacher for 45 years in New York City schools, by Vito Perrone. The book was the first in a series of books designed by one of my favorite educators, Herbert Kohl.

Since that wonderful find I have learned that Leonard Covello was a White educator who dedicated his life to children and to fight racism. Covello was a teacher and principal at Benjamin Franklin Community High School in East Harlem for 22 years (Perrone 1998). He devoted himself to the community of the school. Perrone describes Covello's philosophy as focusing on the students; he had a firm belief in their ability and future. He wrote that teachers like Covello who "are fully engaged with their work see possibilities, not liabilities. They lose the language of pathology, the language of stigmatization" (Perrone 1998, 25).

One of Covello's core beliefs was to see life from the perspective of his students and parents. For example, when he understood the problems of new immigrants, he could help them work through their struggles. Covello did not see his students as victims because the students did not see themselves as victims (Perrone 1998).

When Covello began his career, many of his students were Italian Americans or new Italian immigrants. He was able to use his own cultural knowledge to better understand the perspectives of his students. Since he spoke Italian, Leonard could communicate effectively with parents and students. He organized English classes and academic tutoring programs in the neighborhood East Harlem branch of the YMCA. One of the clubs he organized was the Young Men's Lincoln Club of Little Italy to assist young people in developing a positive bicultural identity, bridging home and society. Later Covello organized several Latino organizations for the community, too. He felt cultural studies was important to young people and could not understand why schools would not make it a central component to schooling (Perrone 1998). The curriculum of schools needed to be relevant to students, and to be relevant, schools had to facilitate students in solving social problems.

As the population of the community changed, Covello found more Puerto Rican immigrants and African American families moving to the neighborhood. He had a great compassion for the new families because, like the Italians, they faced similar struggles. He honored the cultures and languages of the community. For example, a Puerto Rican mother visited the school with her son. He spoke to her and her son in Spanish. He wrote, "The only language of education is the language which people can understand—no matter where it originates. To this simple Puerto Rican woman I have become more than the principal of an English-speaking high school. I am a human being who understands and is trying to help her. In the eyes of the boy I have given respect and status to his parent. The process of education has been translated into human terms" (Covello, quoted in Perrone 1998, 37, 38).

At Benjamin Franklin High School, Covello was extremely aware of the need for intercultural education. By 1938, intercultural issues were woven throughout the curriculum and in teacher discussions. In fact, one of the committees in the school was the Racial Committee, whose purpose was to direct the school in integrating culture through the curriculum and to sponsor forums revolving around issues of race (Perrone 1998). The school also sponsored several major conferences on race and ethnic relationships.

One of the major goals of Covello was to include issues from the community in an integrated school curriculum to develop in students skills and knowledge that they could use in addressing social problems. The English teachers had students read traditional writers like Shakespeare and Milton, but they also had young people study Upton Sinclair and Ida Tarbell, who discussed relevant social issues. The social studies teachers had students look at various aspects of the community. The art teachers led students in mapping the community. The students found in East Harlem 41 churches/missions, 22 political clubs, 9 labor organizations, 506 stores that sold candy, 26 junk stores, 378 restaurants, 74 dentists, 297 doctors, and 262 barber shops (Perrone 1998). The young people also discovered the area housed 28 liquor stores and 256 bars. Students were concerned because in comparison to the 284 bars and liquor stores, there were only 3 public halls, a couple of playgrounds for kids, and no neighborhood newspaper. From this project students chose various social issues to research and to develop plans of action. Students developed not only knowledge of the community, but also a sense of community responsibility, and they became active in neighborhood change.

One of the projects students from the high school chose to tackle was affordable housing and the threat of speculators purchasing land on the river that would drive up the price of apartments in the area (Perrone 1998). Students researched various configurations of city dwelling and they built a variety of models and had a public showing of their work. They were able to rally the community and gather signatures on petitions. The land on the river was saved for new low-income housing. This was an important community victory.

Since Covello wanted to learn as much as he could about his students, he went to Puerto Rico (Perrone 1998). He visited the extended families of many of his students back in New York City. In this way, he came to know the culture of his students through a comprehensive lived experience, meeting people, listening to the music, viewing the physical scenery, and learning about the roles of various people in the family.

Covello believed the high school was to be the center of the community. He welcomed parents and other members of the neighborhood into the school. Covello had a community advisory board made up of individuals from civic groups, religious organizations, businesses, and social services. Initially, many of the members argued against becoming involved in the school; however, Covello conveyed to them that they were responsible for the success of students along with teachers in the school. The school also became a center for afterschool community activities. For example, the high school housed adult education classes in English, preparing for citizenship, cultural studies, art, and dance (Perrone 1998). Covello was a teacher with a heart and a valuable role model for all of us.

Summary

This chapter describes how and why children learn prejudicial attitudes that later turn into discriminatory actions. Though people think that young children do not learn prejudice early in their lives, research by Allport, Helms, and Tatum demonstrates that children adopt and accept bias views of parents, friends, and other people who they see as important. In addition, children who grow up in loving families where criticism is minimal are more likely to grow up as confident adults and develop a healthy view of life.

Much of this chapter deals with self-identity. As young people grow up, they are trying to figure out who they are and where they fit in society. Young children want to feel accepted at school, with peers, and in their families. Their identity is integrated with group memberships such as race, ethnicity, culture, religion, and gender. This sense of identity is often tied to their physical characteristics. The United States is not a color-blind society. The physical characteristics of various groups have positive and negative meanings that society attaches to them. Children from communities of color must sort through those connotations.

As they come in contact with people, children note that certain words are used to describe differences in others. These words often have strong negative feelings attached to them. Older students may reject those who are different because of the negative messages they have learned from others. As teenagers, the prejudice becomes more permanent and their categories based on social characteristics such as race, class, sexual orientation, or gender are more firmly set.

Teachers should work daily at reducing prejudice and discrimination in students. This can be done first by providing an affirming classroom and then by teaching students how to interact with respect and compassion. This way students begin to build bonds of trust, and when conflicts like name-calling arise, the teacher has already set a foundation of working things through. Teachers can also present White anti-racist role models like Leonard Covello, an educator in New York City.

Stereotypes are overgeneralized images based on inflexible social categories and it is important for teachers to carefully review their curriculum for materials and lessons that may reinforce these images. Schools unfortunately, in their concern to present cultural information about people from underrepresented communities, have not clearly identified strong educational objectives. This can result in the "Christmas around the World" travelogue curriculum. Unfortunately, many teachers will focus on elements like food or dance without giving students the opportunity to learn about the underlying values of a group. This oftentimes reinforces the exotic or strange stereotypes of people who come from diverse communities.

An alternative may be to present community heroes who have helped to build our city of many people. This study can highlight those who have led the struggle for freedom, justice, and peace. Students can look at the lives of people like Leonard Covello and find important role models.

Teacher Reflections

Continue writing in your journal. These questions will help you reflect on the issues presented in the chapter.

1. Read the passage from Vivian Paley's book, *White Teacher,* on pages 45–46. (If you cannot find the book at the library, I have summarized the situation for you.) Write answers to these questions in your journal:

How important is race to this situation? Why do you think that?
Why would Barbara use a racial term?
Do you agree with Janet's decision and comments to Barbara and Ellen? Why or why not?
How would you have dealt with this situation?
How would Ellen feel? What impact does this situation have on both children?
What are possible alternative actions? What consequences or impacts does each have?

2. *White Teacher* (summary of pages 45–46):

Paley talks about a situation where a White child excludes a Black child. This happened when Paley had a student teacher named Janet. As an African American, Paley wondered how Janet would deal with this incident in particular, because it dealt with race.

When the students were getting ready to take a walk to a neighborhood pond, a White child named Barbara loudly proclaimed, "I don't want Ellen again. She always wants to be my partner. I want someone White" (Paley 1979, 45).

The student teacher was extremely calm and naturally said to the kindergarten African American child, "Ellen, Barbara feels like walking with someone who looks like her. Sometimes people get that feeling. Can I help you find another partner for this time?" (Paley 1979, 46). Ellen then found a different White child to be her partner and they went to the pond.

When Paley asked Janet why she handled the situation in the way she did, Janet carefully explained that she did not believe using guilt was a positive manner in resolving the issue even though it was hard to step away from the situation and not feel somewhat beaten upon.

Further Readings

Comer, James, and Alvin Poussaint. 1992. *Raising Black children.* New York: Penguin Books.

Comer and Poussaint are two psychiatrists who have written an excellent question-and-answer format text for teachers, parents, and community people. Their book begins with discussion of the development of infants and continues to answer questions about the teenage years. The authors provide excellent responses to difficult questions about racism, curriculum in the schools, sex education, and many other aspects of growing up. For example, the answers to these questions will assist both teachers and parents:

My son's teacher says he is hyperactive and should be put on drugs. Do Black children tend to be more hyperactive or is this a racial stereotype on the part of the school? What should I do? (p. 181)

If Black parents are really interested in education why aren't more of my students' parents involved in the school program? (p. 190)

Some of the children in my first-grade class call each other names when they are angry—"black nigger," "black pig," and so on. How should I handle this? (p. 212)

References

Allport, Gordon W. 1954. *The nature of prejudice.* Reading, Mass.: Addison-Wesley.

Byrnes, Deborah. 1988. Children and prejudice. *Social Education, 52*(4): 267–271.

Comer, James, and Alvin Poussaint. 1979. Foreward. In Paley's *White Teacher,* Cambridge, Mass.: Harvard University Press.

Derman-Sparks, L., C. Higa, and B. Sparks. 1980. Children, race and racism: How race awareness develops. *Interracial Bulletin for Children, 11* (3 and 4): 3–9.

Derman-Sparks, Louise, and the ABC Task Force. 1989. *Anti-bias curriculum: Tools for empowering young children.* Washington, D.C.: NAEYC.

Goodman, Mary Ellen. 1964. *Race awareness in young children,* New York: Collier Books.

Kohl, Herbert. 1993. The myth of "Rosa Parks the Tired": Teaching about Rosa Parks and the Montgomery bus boycott. *Multicultural Education, 1:* 6–10.

Nakagawa, Mako. 1992, July. Private interview.

Pang, Valerie Ooka. 1988. Ethnic prejudice: Still alive and hurtful. *Harvard Educational Review,* *58,* (3): 374–379.

Perrone, Vito. 1998. *Teacher with a heart: Reflections on Leonard Covello.* N.Y.: Teachers College Press.

Sleeter, Christine E. and Carl A. Grant. 1987. An analysis of multicultural education in the U.S.A. *Harvard Educational Review, 57:* 421–444.

Teaching Tolerance. 1992, Spring. Celebrate values (an interview with Robert Coles), *1*(1): 18–22.

Chapter 8

How Can I Look Beneath the Surface for Prejudice in Schools?

S chools are busy places. There is much going on that we often do not see or have time to reflect on. I hope this chapter will give you a chance to think about the inequities in schools. They are part of the systemic inequities that flourish in society. I thought that most schools were fairly democratic and just places; but as I think more clearly about what happens in schools, I am reminded that schools are products of our society, its successes and its weaknesses.

Are our schools fairly democratic? Don't you think that we provide a fairly equitable place for learning? Let's begin by looking beneath the surface.

❧ Five Levels of Prejudice

When I first began thinking about bias, I didn't realize how damaging prejudice and discrimination could be. Prejudicial attitudes and beliefs filter and shape the information we receive. I use Allport's (1954) five levels of prejudice to help teachers understand how prejudice escalates from casual remarks to exclusionary practices. The levels are antilocution, avoidance, discrimination, physical attack, and genocide. As you read through the levels of prejudice, see how one level becomes more damaging than the next.

Level One: Antilocution

Has anyone ever told you an ethnic joke in private? About the Irish? About the Polish? Or about African Americans? Maybe you laughed at a joke someone told about women, men, or Muslims? You were participating in antilocution. It is Allport's first stage of prejudice where negative things are said in the privacy of close friends. People use labels to describe others in gossip-like conversations. Oftentimes this type of conversation is a way people reinforce their own beliefs because others laugh or agree. It is also a way to say, "I am like you because I think like you. I don't like those people either." It supports the idea that "we" are different from "those people" and "our group" is better. This reinforces an "our group" orientation. Name-calling is part of this level. Antilocution can lead to the next level of prejudice, avoidance.

Level Two: Avoidance 기피

If a person avoids a specific group of people because of a social category and does not know the individuals, then the person is engaging in Allport's second level of prejudice. I have heard parents tell their children not to talk with "those kids bused in from the ghetto" because they are dangerous. Some parents can be heard telling their children, "Be careful of those kids because they will mess with your head." Individuals may choose not to talk with or get to know someone because they have been taught to avoid all people in "those" groups.

Level Three: Discrimination 차별

People may not always act on their prejudices, but when they treat someone unfairly or inequitably, then the individuals are discriminating. For example, though many of the laws dealing with redlining in housing, because of social biases or membership clauses in country clubs that discriminated against people of color, have been eliminated, exclusion of people still exists.

Several culturally diverse teachers have described in class how they would call for information on an advertisement for apartment vacancies. Often they are told to come immediately to see the apartments because there are vacancies. Yet when the students arrive within an hour, the apartments are mysteriously no longer available. One of my teachers was a light-skinned African American female who had a very dark-skinned husband. One year, the couple encountered so much discrimination that they finally developed the following strategy.

The wife would first look at the apartment by herself and she would place a deposit on the apartment. She would fill out most of the paperwork. Later, her husband would go with her to finish signing the lease. The couple found that since housing near the university was difficult to get and that many apartment managers did not want African Americans living in their complexes, the managers were visually screening renters. Since the wife had fair complexion, many apartment managers did not think she was African American.

Level Four: Physical Attack

You can probably guess what this level of prejudice is. When people's emotional feelings are strong, this can lead to aggressive behavior. There are organized groups like the Ku Klux Klan and Aryan Nation who actively lobby, write, and organize events that are aimed at people of color. People who have strong prejudices have bombed stores that belonged to Jews, Mexican Americans, Korean Americans, and many others. During the Persian Gulf War, a grocery store owned by an Iranian American family was looted and set on fire. There are Black gangs and Mexican American gangs who fight for territory. These are examples of how prejudice can escalate into violence.

Level Five: Genocide

The most extreme form of prejudice is genocide. The history of the United States is filled with many instances of lynchings of African Americans. If you are unaware of this part of U.S. history read John Hope Franklin's excellent book, *From Slavery to Freedom.* Slavery was an institution that was widely accepted in the colonies and later the states. Because of our country's dependence upon the labor of slaves, prejudice and extreme forms of discrimination against African Americans were an integral part of U.S. economics. Allport explains that when these attitudes were combined with poor law enforcement during those early days of this nation, lynchings occurred. Even when killers were apprehended, most were never prosecuted because a "social norm" of acceptance existed. Do you think that we have genocide today?

Genocide is a global problem. Recently we have seen the massacre of millions of people in many countries. For example, people have been killed in Kosovo, Indonesia, Tibet, and Rwanda. This is part of our contemporary history. This is not about the past. Students and teachers need to be aware of and review their values about issues like ethnic cleansing and genocide. These problems are part of our world community today. One way to help students understand the destructive nature of genocide is to bring the issue to their own lives.

Teachers and students may have some knowledge of the Holocaust where over 6 million Jews were killed in concentration camps during World War II. Do they realize another 6 million people, who included gays, lesbians, mentally ill, and Gypsies, were also killed during the same time under Hitler? The "our group" mentality became so pervasive that people who belonged to the "other group" were seen as less than human. Do people realize what it means in human terms that 6 million Jews died? It is easy to read things in a book and not

1·20·99 THE PHILADELPHIA INQUIRER, UNIVERSAL PRESS SYNDICATE.

really take in the human meaning of these actions. I use the following activity in class to help teachers more fully understand what these numbers mean in human life (Frelick 1985).

Approximately 6 million Jews were killed in concentration camps during World War II. I ask, "How many people were killed in a year?" A student will raise his hand and say, "One million people per year were killed." Then I ask, "How many people were killed every month?" Usually someone in the class has a calculator and tells us that 83,333.3 human beings were killed every month. Then I ask, "How many human beings were killed every day?" The larger figure is divided by 30 days in a month and this means about 2,777.78 people were killed every day. The class then finds out that 115.74 people were killed every hour and that almost two Jews were killed every minute for six years. I usually have about thirty students in each class section and I tell them, "In fifteen minutes from the time we entered the classroom door, all of us would be gone. Since there are approximately 28,000 college students at our university, it would take only ten days before everyone on our campus would be eliminated."

Though this begins to give a sense of reality to historical numbers that people often gloss over when reading history, I continue with a discussion about local communities. I ask the teachers to give me the names of cities in this area and their populations. In some areas of the United States, an entire state may not have a population as large as 6 million. The teachers add up the population of cities and towns where they live. This allows them to put these large numbers in context. In some communities, the discussion will show that no one would be left living in several states. This gives teachers an everyday example that they can use with their students in order to help them to conceptualize the depth of the genocide. In addition, students can look at present-day examples of genocide in other nations like Bosnia, El Salvador, and Cambodia. There are also several hundred thousand children in the United States who are homeless every night, with nowhere to sleep. Though this is not an example of organized aggression against a group, students need to understand that when we lack a connection to others, it is easy not to do anything when someone else is being hurt or oppressed. The next section discusses how the five levels of prejudice exist in schools.

✍ Hidden Prejudice in Schools

I do not believe most teachers consciously discriminate against children; however, oppression based on race, class, and gender can also be found in our social institutions like schools. In the past schools were segregated, with children of color going to one school while European American students attended another school. Though this is no longer the case, there are still many instances where schools that serve large numbers of students of color have less funds than other schools (Kozol 1991). Another example of how many students have been excluded from schooling deals with the issue of disabilities. Not until 1975, when schools were mandated by the Education for Handicapped Children legislation to provide students with physical and psychological disabilities with the "least restrictive" education, have the needs of students with disabilities begun to be addressed. Many children had been excluded from participating in schools and these are examples of societal biases.

The purpose of this chapter is to identify how prejudice and discrimination appear in schools. Schools are institutions of society and mirror social values. Many school practices are antithetical to equity and caring. For example, some schools begin sorting

children as early as kindergarten when they place children in classes by ability groupings. Many students of color are placed in lower-tracked groups and sometimes are unable to move into higher-ability groups throughout their education. Students of color are
often disciplined in disproportionately higher numbers than majority pupils and the curriculum may not include the life experiences of students from low-income or culturally
diverse communities and have little connection with their lives (Nieto 1990; Oakes
1985). These practices demonstrate how inequities are a structural part of schools.

Unconscious prejudice may surface and enter into the workplace. I have gathered
a list of various examples of how prejudice looks in schools. I believe that teachers rarely
have the opportunity to examine how prejudice impacts teaching and the school's environment. I don't believe teachers intentionally engage in these behaviors; but like many
behaviors, they become part of the way we act because no one has challenged us to really think about the effect our actions may have. Read each level of prejudice and ask
yourself the following questions:

Have you ever found yourself thinking or doing these things?
Do you think there is anything wrong with being this way?
How can you move away from being prejudiced?
Do you find some of this in your school?
Can you bring it up during a staff meeting?

☞ Examples of the Five Levels of Prejudice Found in Schools

Sometimes it is difficult for us to understand how theory is translated into practice.
Teachers have helped me gather examples of how the five levels of prejudice may look
in schools. Many times teachers are unaware of how lower levels of discrimination can
develop into more serious and pervasive actions. These examples are provided to help
you understand how easily we may fall into the trap of being discriminatory. These examples are not to be used to implicate anyone. I believe how we think has been shaped
by social biases. We must all work toward eliminating them from our minds. These are
only examples and should not be considered behaviors in which all teachers engage.

Level One: Antilocution

Teachers are usually talkative people. Unfortunately, this kind of talk, though often done
in private, may limit the way other teachers see children from diverse racial, ethnic, language, and socioethnic classes, and limit views of females. The following are a sample
of examples my teachers reported:

- Teachers talk about children in the teacher's lounge, by saying, "My Black
  students always . . ."
- Teachers name children by social class, with comments like, "Those kids from
  the projects are troublemakers. They'll never make it. I don't want to waste my
  time with them."
- A teacher tells a parent aide, "Those migrant kids are always moving from one
  school to another, so there is no sense doing much for them. They will soon be

gone. Besides, this is America and those kids should be speaking English, not Spanish. This isn't Mexico. I don't think it is our responsibility to teach them if they can't even speak English."

- A new child moves to the neighborhood. The coach calls up the student on the phone to let him know about the first football practice. During the conversation, the coach asks, "Are you Black?" The student replied and the coach said, "Oh, that's good."
- A sixth grade teacher describes his female students in the following ways: "beautiful," "playboy-centerfold material," and "developing rather nicely." This teacher also made comments to his class about the teaching assistant saying, "Isn't Miss Smith sexy?"

Level Two: Avoidance

At this level, prejudice is more intense and individuals begin to act on their prejudice. People do not just talk about their feelings, but they begin to discriminate against another person or children. The following are examples of avoidance in school:

- Teachers avoid discussing incidents when children call each other names that refer to race, class, gender, physical differences, and religion. Teachers may not know how to talk about these incidents, but avoiding open discussion when children know the teacher heard the name-calling suggests that the teacher does not object to the use of those terms. It is passive acceptance of the discrimination.
- Teachers may avoid calling upon culturally diverse students or females. There are numerous studies that show that teachers call on males more often than females and that this is an unconscious rather than a conscious form of discrimination.
- Teachers place students in group activities or in seating arrangements that segregate students by race, gender, or class.
- Teachers avoid going on home visits to students who are bused in from the "ghetto" or "inner city" but may visit students who live in suburban communities.
- Teachers avoid calling parents from inner-city communities because they feel that the parents do not care.

Level Three: Discrimination

In this level of prejudice, discrimination becomes more overt. These examples demonstrate how prejudice escalates in schools:

- Teachers may get frustrated understanding students whose English is not fluent and not call on them because it takes these students longer to explain their points of view.
- Teachers may give more individual attention or feedback to students who come from families with professional parents and who live in more affluent neighborhoods.
- Teachers may give more challenging work to students who are from majority middle- and upper-class families in comparison to students from African American and Latino lower-class communities.
- Teachers divide physical education into boys sports and girls sports within the same class. Boys engage in wrestling while girls learn to dance.

- Teachers may isolate children who wear baggy pants because they fear these students are members of gangs, yet their parents may like baggy pants because they can be handed down and fit several children of different sizes.
- Out of ten junior high students to interview a famous astronaut, seven males and only three females were included.
- A male high school student was called a "girl" by his peers and the teacher assumed that the student was gay.
- Several sixth grade girls ask their teacher if they could be included in the baseball game. The teacher says laughingly, "Girls can't play baseball. Go back to the kickball game."
- A fourth grade student moves to a small town. The teacher introduces the child by saying, "Michele, our new student, is from Hollywood where all the movie stars and rich people live." Students in class call her "a Hollywood snob" or "rich brat."
- Many more children of color are bused from their neighborhoods than majority children.
- A teacher gives an Asian American high school student a B when his grades totaled 92 percent, though White students with 88 percent were given an A. The student was told that since he was Asian, he was expected to score higher than other students to receive an A.
- In a preschool class, the teacher asks his young students to sit in a circle. A child finds a place and sits down. A boy screamed, "Nigger get out of my spot."
- A high school chemistry teacher says to a blond female student, "Wow, I'm impressed. I thought you were just one of those blond airheads."
- A teacher places students with no or limited English skills in special education classes instead of newcomer programs, sheltered English classes, bilingual education, or tutored situations.
- The curriculum systematically excludes the contribution of culturally diverse individuals/communities in the United States in most subject areas.
- The curriculum and instruction of most schools stem from a European American worldview. A few units and guest speakers about culturally diverse groups may be added, but are not integral to the curriculum.
- Two captains are appointed by the teacher for two teams in kickball. Tall and physically large boys are chosen first for team. Shorter boys are picked next.
- A Latina enrolls in a high school biology class. When the teacher reads the roll, she calls her name and asks, "Is Jorge Rodriguez your brother?" When the student says yes, the teacher says, "You'd better leave my class because I am going to fail you, because I hate your brother and I hate Mexicans." The student transferred from this class.

Level Four: Physical Attack

In this stage, prejudice leads to acts of violence or the heightened use of physical strength. The following are examples found in schools:

- A teacher is more physical in breaking up a fight between two African American students than two White students.
- A teacher loses her temper and pushes a Latino male and yells at him saying he needs to get himself under control.

Level Five: Genocide

Gordon Allport considers prejudice to be at its most extreme in this stage. Though I don't believe that teachers attempt to physically exterminate children, I do believe that if we do not question school practices that give some students less opportunities, we are contributing to this level of prejudice. Their opportunities in life may also be restrained or eliminated because the students were not encouraged to develop their capabilities. The following are examples teachers have found in their schools:

- Culturally diverse students often find themselves in lower academic and vocational tracks even though they aspire to a college education.
- Teachers assume students whose first language is other than English should develop their talents in math and science classes rather than creative writing, advanced history, and drama.
- Schools in some inner cities do not have the same financial resources necessary to properly equip a classroom and to hire enough teachers for smaller classes. (Read Jonathan Kozol's book, *Savage Inequalities.* Kozol documents that in the same area of a state, per pupil spending can range from $5,585 to $11,371.)
- Teachers expect all children to respond to the same learning modes and do not provide for diverse learning styles, ways of behaving, and worldviews.
- A Black high school baseball player is an important player in the school winning the state championship. Teachers let him slide by and coaches do not encourage him to study. With his grades, he has no chance for a collegiate athletic scholarship.
- Disproportionately more students of color and male students are suspended or expelled from school than other students.
- Classes for gifted and accelerated students have disproportionately more White students than any other group.
- High dropout rates of students of color jeopardize the economic, political, and educational health of communities.

Prejudice and discrimination usually go hand in hand. We all have attitudes about other groups, which may result in our excluding or treating others unequally. I believe that if teachers realized that these kinds of things were happening, they would take proactive steps to examine their own actions and the structures of schools in order to move away from biased and damaging practices. Prejudices easily can creep back into your garden like weeds. Prejudices can be hurdles to our being the best teacher we can be. These hurdles in our mind can be eliminated, but it requires effort and courage.

Examples of Racism and Sexism in a High School English Vocabulary Assignment

People have difficulty visualizing how racism and sexism can be a part of the curriculum. Districts have worked hard to select textbooks that are bias free. They have provided staff development for their teachers so they can include culture into their instructional day. As research has shown, teacher quality is the most important component of school achievement in students. When teachers do not understand how to examine their own biases, the curriculum the educators create can be outstanding and relevant, but it can also present prejudicial attitudes.

A teacher shared some examples of what Allport would describe as discrimination. He found the information in his son's homework. He was surprised to see that in 2000 these kinds of things were still part of the high school curriculum. The homework materials were developed by a high school teacher and she had been using these examples for several years. Not one student, parent, or colleague had ever suggested that she review them for bias.

Here is a sample of the materials that were shared with me. Ask yourself the following questions:

What messages are given in the materials?
Are these messages true?
What impact could these messages have on students?
Whose viewpoint do the materials support?

Vocabulary Lesson

Students were asked to memorize the definitions and companion sentences.

1. Abolish—to retard, to do away with
   One of Lincoln's goals as President was to abolish slavery.
2. Ambush—to lie in wait or hiding for an attack
   The Indians tried to ambush the settlers as they went by.
3. Impromptu—unplanned, done on the spur of the moment
   She was so happy that she did a little impromptu dance on the table top.
4. Rapture—ecstasy, thrills, keen delight, supreme joy
   She was filled with rapture when he kissed her.

The teacher has positional power in a school. When she presents information as if it is true, students tend to believe what she teaches. Although this was a sophomore English class, the messages were about different groups in society. The attitudes in these examples seemed to say that women, or at least some women, find dancing on table tops as acceptable and that women want the attention of men. In addition, I felt that the rapture example seemed to indicate that women are the receivers not the actors in a relationship, and that men are the people in charge of female-male relationships. What underlying views and hidden messages are the sentences in the English lesson communicating to young women and men?

I felt the examples about Indians and Lincoln, gave inaccurate information. The sentence about Indians (Native people) was extremely offensive. The teacher basically conveyed to students that Indians ambushed settlers and so indirectly reinforced the stereotypical view of Native people as warring, primitive, and cowardly people. The sentence about Lincoln is also problematic because many historians debate whether Lincoln wanted to abolish slavery.

Abraham Lincoln struggled with the issue of slavery continuously through his life (Bennett 1984; Loewen 1995). Loewen, a historian, explained that Lincoln's racism was like that of any average person. He wrote, "If textbooks recognized Lincoln's racism, students would learn that racism not only affects Ku Klux Klan extremists but has been 'normal' throughout our history. And as they watched Lincoln struggle with himself to apply America's democratic principles across the color line, students would see how ideas can develop and a person can grow" (Loewen 1995, 179). Lincoln began the desegregation of the White House by inviting Blacks to serve in the White House, which continued until Woodrow Wilson became President. However, Lincoln also had his staff explore the possibility of departing or "colonizing" African Americans to Africa or Latin

America (Loewen 1995). Loewen believes that Lincoln knew slavery was morally wrong and, within the context of the times, Lincoln's *Gettysburg Address* richly explained his views against slavery.

Other historians like Bennett (1984) questioned Lincoln's attitudes about slavery. Referencing the materials of Frederick Douglass, he presents the view that Lincoln did not provide strong leadership against the entrenched institution of slavery. After Lincoln had his advisors explore the possibility of sending African Americans to other countries in 1862, members of the Black community strongly protested. Lincoln's position was that there were differences between Black and White folks and both groups were suffering from a country that combined the two communities. Douglass was extremely unhappy with Lincoln's comments and said, "No, Mr. President, it is not the innocent horse that makes the horse thief, nor the traveler's purse that makes the highway robber, and it is not the presence of the Negro that causes this foul and unnatural war, but the cruel and brutal cupidity of those who wish to possess horses, money and Negroes by means of theft, robbery, and rebellion" (Bennett 1984, 193).

Another historian, Howard Zinn, presents a similar view. Zinn writes in his book that Lincoln did not believe in slavery, but "could not see slaves as equals, so a constant theme in his approach was to free the slaves and to send them back to Africa" (Zinn 1980, 183). Zinn also provides further information about slavery in Northern states. Though many teachers may believe that most citizens in the North opposed slavery during the 1850s, this is not generally true. In fact, a free African American in New York was not able to vote unless he owned at least $250 in property, though this was not a requirement for White voters (Zinn 1980). When the Emancipation Proclamation was put into effect, only slaves living in "areas still fighting against the Union" were freed (Zinn 1980, 187). Zinn presents a great deal of information about the United States after the Civil War in his chapter, "Slavery Without Submission, Emancipation Without Freedom."

The sentence the English teacher presented gave her viewpoint about Lincoln and his position about slavery. As the materials above discuss, there are varying views of Lincoln's attitudes about racism and his actions to eradicate it. Like much prejudice found in school, it is not necessarily vicious in nature, but it can have a far-reaching impact on students.

❧ How Prejudice Can Influence Teacher Confidence

This chapter has described how prejudice can be hidden in individual and school practices. Most teachers do not consciously exclude or hurt students; however, many educators from all communities do not really examine what they think or believe. My colleague, Velma Sablan, and I conducted a study on how confident teachers felt teaching African American students (1998). We used a questionnaire that was well designed and accepted in the field by Gibson and Dembo (1984). In this way we could examine more specifically how prejudicial attitudes may impact teacher attitudes.

The instrument we used looked at two different areas. The first area examined how teachers viewed their own personal teaching competence. Did they feel they were personally effective as a teacher? The second area examined if teachers in general are competent. Did they feel that teachers can influence the learning of their students? Having two dimensions in the questionnaire helped us study how teachers felt generally about teaching and then explored how an individual teacher felt about her or his ability to reach students. Past research demonstrated that teachers with low levels of efficacy were more distrustful of students, tried to exert strong "controls" over students, and did not use a variety of instructional strategies. In comparison, high-efficacy teachers developed warm relationships with students, gave more positive feedback to students, and held high expectations for all students (Pang and Sablan 1998).

Teachers were asked to respond to thirty questions indicating one of the following: strongly agree, agree, uncertain, disagree, and strongly disagree. The only difference we made in the original questionnaire was to add the term *African American.* Read through a sample of the statements:

1. If an African American student masters a new math concept quickly, this might be because I knew the necessary steps in teaching the concept.
2. The hours in my class have little influence on African American students compared to the influence of their home environment.
3. If an African American student in my class becomes disruptive and noisy, I feel assured that I know some techniques to redirect him or her quickly.
4. If African American parents would do more with their children, I could do more.

We were concerned with how teachers looked at personal and general teaching efficacy as related to African American students. We also hypothesized that pre-service and in-service teachers would show similar beliefs. Of the 100 pre- and 75 in-service teachers surveyed, 74 percent (129) were European American, 13 percent (24) were Latino, and the other 13 percent were made up of Asian Pacific Americans, African Americans, Native Americans, and several interracial individuals. Several of the questions we looked at were:

1. What perceptions do pre-service and in-service teachers have regarding their African American students and African American communities?
2. What levels of personal and general teaching efficacy do pre-service and in-service teachers hold as related to African American students?

The results were quite disturbing. We found racial attitudes did affect teacher efficacy beliefs of pre-service and in-service teachers in our sample. Pre-service teachers were more positive about their ability to reach African American children than in-service educators. They indicated more ability to assess, redirect, teach, and adjust to the needs of African American students. Sablan and I believe that in-service teachers had been influenced over a period of time by others who have not been able to address the needs of African American students. Then as problems arise, new teachers may use cultural conflict and lack of knowledge about African American students as scapegoats for academic failure.

One of the most troubling findings was that a large number of teachers, 65 percent, indicated that they did not believe even with good teaching strategies that they would be able to reach African American students. However, the subjects did believe that teachers are powerful forces in the lives of students.

Though the responses of teachers were mixed, our study seemed to show that generally teachers did not feel confident about their personal abilities to teach African American children and that school failure was not due to teacher failure. This can seriously impact the attitudes teachers not only bring to the school, but also to the classroom. Racial bias is sometimes difficult to detect; however, our study demonstrated that stereotypical views of Black families, low student interest, and lack of parental discipline are powerful perceptions and do impact teachers' belief systems.

Summary

Unfortunately, prejudice and discrimination are found throughout our schools. Bias can be found in the attitudes of students, teachers, parents, and administrators. It can also be found in our school policies, practices, curriculum, and many other components. Allport has provided a framework that we can use to examine how prejudice and discrimination seep into what we do no matter how unintentional. His five levels of prejudice, antilocution, avoidance, discrimination, physical attack, and genocide, demonstrate that it is a problem that all of us must struggle with and act to eliminate.

Schools must be places where students feel safe and accepted. Bias that is overtly shown through name-calling and other actions that are more obvious are easier to combat and question. However, the practices and behaviors of people that are more covert or hidden are the most difficult to get rid of. Many people will say that we are all the same, but in reality may favor some students over others in small ways like the tone of voice used.

The only way that prejudice and discrimination can be eradicated is if all people in the school, from the custodians to food workers to students to principals to teachers, work together to address and find ways to reduce these destructive attitudes and actions. A study by Pang and Sablan demonstrated that both pre- and in-service teachers held negative feelings about their ability to reach African American students. These beliefs seemed to arise from a cultural deficit point of view. The cultural deficit model assumes that students from underrepresented groups lack the ability or have inadequate parenting or both because they have not culturally assimilated into mainstream society. In other words, there is something wrong with the student's culture and/or family.

In comparison, Pang and Sablan (1998) encouraged teachers to move to a culturally relevant and caring model of teaching, where relationships are at the core of the learning process. In addition, teachers can integrate culture through a multipronged approach. Instructional strategies, curriculum, policies, materials, counseling strategies, the school calendar, and other areas in school must reflect the lives of students and be meaningful.

Teacher Reflections

How Can I Limit Prejudice and Discrimination?

What are ways that you as a teacher, colleague, parent, or community person work to eliminate social oppression in schools? Because schools are an institution of society, they harbor some of the same prejudices that individuals hold. In your journal, please answer questions 1 and 11.

To be caring advocates, I believe all of us must deal with the hidden hurdles that exist in our minds. There are many things that you can do as a person and as a teacher to try to get rid of, or at least limit, prejudice and discrimination. Here are some suggestions.

1. Ask yourself what stereotypes or prejudices you have toward others. Where did you get these biases? Do you catch yourself thinking about others in stereotypical ways?
2. In the classroom or in the school hall, stop name-calling as soon as you hear it. Don't allow it to continue. Your inaction can be interpreted as acceptance of the name-calling.
3. After an ethnic joke has been told, talk about how people feel when they are ridiculed by others. Ask students why people like to put down others. What do they gain by that kind of behavior?
4. Do you ever refer to "those children" or "those people" when talking about students and culturally diverse communities? This can be a clue to your considering members of cultural groups as "others" or being in the "out-group."

5. Discuss the issue of prejudice with your students. The following questions may help create important sharing and reflection in your students.
   - Has anyone ever said anything to you that hurt you?
   - How did you feel?
   - Have you ever said anything mean to someone else?
   - How do you think they felt?
   - Have you ever wished you would have said something to someone who shared an ethnic joke or made a racist, gender-biased, or classist comment? Now that you have had time to reflect, what could you have said?
   - What does it feel like to be treated as an outsider or foreigner?
6. Videotape yourself in the classroom. Are you fair in how you interact with each child? How much time do you spend with each child? Do you tend to spend more time with some children than others? Do you take more time to answer questions of some students?
7. Do you accept each child and her/his communities and characteristics without judgment? Do you celebrate the ethnic group, gender, or neighborhood of children whose identities are highly interconnected with the groups to help them keep a positive self-concept? A child of color's self-acceptance can be strongly reinforced in the classroom. In addition, this is crucial in a society where prejudice and discrimination can threaten a child's self-image.
8. Do you use cooperative learning and integrate groups with children who represent various social classes, gender, and racial groups? Provide students with a common goal in a group where they have equal status. Personal interactions can help to break down prejudice (Byrnes 1988, 269).
9. Role playing also is an important activity, which can help students better understand the worldview of others (Byrnes 1988, 269–271). Children can act out the incident when Rosa Parks stood up for equal rights and against discrimination.
10. For lesson ideas, call your local chapter of the Anti-Defamation of B'nai Brith. They have excellent materials that have been developed for use in the classroom.
11. Examples in this chapter show how prejudice and discrimination are part of the structure of schools. Looking at systemic changes in schools can help to promote equity and affirm diversity. I would like to share with you some of the questions Nieto has suggested teachers think about (Nieto 1990):
    - If your school and/or classroom is not de-tracked, what can you do to avoid the negative effects of tracking in your classroom? (p. 290)
    - Are there classrooms in your school (including special education, bilingual, and English as a Second Language) that are substantially separate from others? Develop a plan to work with some of the teachers in those classrooms. (p. 290)
    - Encourage parents and other community members to participate in committees in which disciplinary policies are discussed. (p. 295)
    - Find out how standardized tests are used and how other criteria may be better employed. (p. 291)

References

1992. Celebrate values: An interview with Robert Coles. *Teaching Tolerance, 1*(1): 18–22.

1996, January. The wage gap. *The National Times, 5:* 4.

Allport, G. 1954. *The nature of prejudice.* New York: Doubleday Anchor Books.

Bennett, Jr., Lerone. 1984. *Before the* Mayflower: *A history of Black America.* New York: Penguin Books.

Boyle, T. C. 1995. *The tortilla curtain.* New York: Viking Press.

Brown, Tom. 1992, May 8. Joel Barker: New thoughts on paradigms. *Industry Week,* 12–19.

Byrnes, Deborah. 1988. Children and prejudice. *Social Education, 52*(4): 267–271.

Delgado, R. 1995. *The Rodrigo chronicles.* New York: New York University Press.

Derman-Sparks, L., C. Higa, and B. Sparks. 1980. Children, race, and racism: How race awareness develops. *Interracial Bulletin for Children, 11*(3 and 4): 3–9.

Frelick, Bill. 1985. Teaching about genocide as a contemporary problem. *Social Education, 49:* 510–515.

Fulwood, III, S. 1995, October 15. Farrakhan calls men shunning march "fools". *The Los Angeles Times:* A-1, A-14.

Franklin, John Hope and Alfred A. Moss, Jr. 1988. *From slavery to freedom: A history of Negro Americans.* New York: Knopf.

Gibson, Sherry, and M. H. Dembo. 1984. Teacher efficacy: A construct validation. *Journal of Educational Psychology, 76* (4): 569–582.

Goodman, M. E. 1964. *Race awareness in young children.* New York: Collier Books.

Helms, Janet, ed. 1990. *Black and White racial identity: Theory, research and practice.* Westport, Conn.: Greenwood Press.

Kohl, Herbert. 1993. The myth of "Rosa Parks the Tired": Teaching about Rosa Parks and the Montgomery bus boycott. *Multicultural Education, 1:* 6–10.

Kozol, Jonathan. 1991. *Savage inequalities: Children in America's schools.* New York: Crown Publishers.

Loewen, James W. 1995. *The lies my teacher told me.* New York: Touchstone Books.

Nakawaga, Mako. 1992. Private discussions. July.

Nieto, Sonia. 1990. *Affirming diversity: The sociopolitical context of multicultural education.* New York: Longman.

Noddings, N. 1984. *Caring: A feminine approach to ethics and moral education.* Berkeley, Calif.: University of California Press.

Oakes, Jeannie. 1985. *Keeping track: How schools structure inequality.* New Haven, Conn.: Yale University Press.

Pang, V. O. 1988. Ethnic prejudice: Still alive and hurtful. *Harvard Educational Review, 58*(3): 374–379.

Pang, V. O. 1994. Asian Pacific American students: A diverse and complex population. In J. A. B. C. M. Banks, ed., *Handbook of research on multicultural education.* New York: Macmillan Publishing.

Pang, Valerie Ooka, and Velma A. Sablan. 1998. Teacher efficacy: How do teachers feel about their abilities to teach African American students? In Mary Dilworth, ed., *Being responsive to cultural differences how teachers learn.* Thousand Oaks, Calif.: Corwin Press.

Ryan, William. 1971. *Blaming the victim.* New York: Vintage Books.

Sleeter, Christine. 1994. White racism. *Multicultural Education: 1*(4): 5–8, 39.

Swim, J., Kathryn Ikin, Wayne Hall, and Barbara Hunter. 1995. Sexism and racism: Old-fashioned and modern prejudices. *Journal of Personality and Social Psychology, 68*(2): 199–214.

Tatum, Beverly Daniel. 1992. Talking about race, learning about racism: The application of racial identity development theory. *Harvard Educational Review, 62,* (1): 1–24.

Valli, Linda. 1995. The dilemma of race: Learning to be color blind and color conscious. *Journal of Teacher Education, 46,* (3): 120–129.

West, C. 1993. *Race matters.* Boston, Mass.: Beacon Press.

Zinn, Howard. 1980. *A people's history of the United States.* New York: Harper and Row.

Part Four

Creating a Caring and Culturally Meaningful Classroom

Chapter 9

What Is Culturally Relevant Teaching?

*A*n evening in one of my college classes, I introduced the term *culturally relevant teaching*. During the break, James, a teacher of color, came up to me and said with much emotion, "*Those* kids won't work. They are never ready for class. They don't even have a pencil and I teach an English class. All they want to be are boxers and they aren't interested in what I have to say. Nothing I use seems to get through. Now, why do you think anything about culture is going to make any difference? I don't believe you."

James looked at me with frustration in his eyes and raising his hands in the air in desperation. You could see he cared or he wouldn't have brought up the issue. But he conveyed his unhappiness about how he believed the Chicano students in his class weren't interested in school. And as a teacher he felt that he was failing his students. I suggested that he consider integrating culturally relevant teaching. Of course his first question was "What is culturally relevant teaching?" Let me share with you my views about this approach, and at the end of the chapter I will let you know what this teacher did. Previous chapters have discussed how culture is an integral aspect of life. This chapter will attempt to present how culture can provide important links from the everyday experiences and knowledge of students to school knowledge, concepts, and skills.

❧ Making Connections with the Learner's Cultural Background

Culturally relevant teaching points to the importance of making connections with the learner. For example: Does the learner understand the purpose of the learning? Does the learner understand where this knowledge will fit in his/her life? Why is this knowledge important? Teachers often have the same concerns with culturally relevant teaching. They don't see the relevance of culture in schools. One of the subjects we teach in schools is history. For example, we teach about the purpose of a democracy, important people who have shaped the policies of our country, and important events in our nation's

record. A seventh grader said, "Why do we have to learn about this stuff? It's boring and it's past. It doesn't mean anything to me."

The teacher knew that she couldn't ignore her statement, because she might lose this student and others who also thought the same but who weren't as bold to say something. So the teacher said, "Carol, where were you born? Did your family always live in Chicago?"

Carol then began to tell about how her family was originally from Arizona. Her grandfather was a member of the Pima nation near Phoenix. When he was a youngster his father wanted him to join the army so he would learn discipline. He didn't want to leave the reservation because his family and friends were there, but his father won. Carol's grandfather enlisted in the army. After his service, he found himself in Chicago. Her grandfather decided to go to the University of Chicago on the G.I. bill in the 1950s. He studied accounting and got a job as an accountant. This was how she began her family story.

Following Carol's sharing, the teacher then made the bridge to U.S. history. The teacher said, "Carol's family story is part of our national family story that is what we call history. Our national story tells about the people, like what their struggles were, what values they lived by, what issues they were concerned about, and what they did." Before this lesson, most students saw history as a list of boring events and not as part of a large story. The teacher was trying to make connections between a student's personal lifeline and our national chronology.

Let's review another example of why culture can act as a bridge. In Chapter 1 I shared the example of what health officials in Mexico did to address the issue of malnutrition. Since tortillas are a major staple in the diet of many people, they convinced companies to fortify tortillas with vitamins! Children gained weight and developed more physical and mental strength. If health officials had fortified bread, their work might not have been as successful because tortillas, not bread, are the most common food that people eat. The researchers looked at lives of people within comprehensive context and found an important connection. This must also be done in learning too. We, as teachers, can use cultural bridges that children already bring to school. The next section will describe culturally relevant teaching more specifically.

❧ *What Is the Sociocultural Context?*

When I began my journey in understanding culturally relevant teaching, it was easy to understand that there are role models from the community I could talk about in my class. There was also literature that I could have my teachers read, like Walter Dean Myers novel, *Young Landlords,* about a group of teenagers who take over the management of an apartment building in a large urban city. Cultural content is easier for me to illustrate, but how can I explain sociocultural context?

What really helped me was the opportunity to watch teachers from various ethnic groups teach. They have different styles and rhythms in their classrooms. Some teachers are traditional, some are casual, some are strict, some talk a lot, and there are some teachers you can hardly hear and their students are busily working.

How do you like to learn? Do you prefer working in a group where you can bounce off ideas with your peers or do you like the independence of working by yourself? As a child, were you hoping your parents knew how well you were doing in school or did you prefer that they didn't know what your grades were? Do you like to be verbally expressive and role play situations as part of the performance assessment or do you prefer to choose from multiple choice answers? Do you need to see the relevance of what you are learning? Do you prefer a lecture when you are learning how to do something or do you like watching someone demonstrate the new skill?

All of these questions give rise to different sets of social situations in learning. There are many students from ethnic communities who prefer to work in small groups rather than independently. I have seen many students from African American, Asian Pacific American, and Latino communities feel more supported by a sense of community. Yet, there are individuals from these communities who prefer working alone because they are task oriented, and when a group of learners get together the process takes longer and this can frustrate them. So even though there may be trends in a group, not everyone will behave or respond to those cues. These trends do not fit the many individual differences that can be found in any group.

To understand that there is a sociocultural context, teachers need to identify various elements. Susan Philips's book, *The Invisible Culture,* gives excellent examples of important components. Philips conducted an ethnographic study of the Warm Springs community in Oregon. She clearly describes how the cultural context of the classroom is the major component of the learning process. She talks about accepted and expected behaviors of people in the community.

As a result of her study, Philips found the Native American students were more reserved and less responsive in their verbal interactions with the teacher than students from the majority culture. Students often conveyed their feelings through gestures, facial movements, or expressions with their eyes. The students were also oriented toward their peers and not the teacher, so teachers who are not part of the community have difficulty understanding this style of interaction. The students were also more apt to look at their peers rather than the teacher when the teacher was speaking so it appeared as if they were not listening. If a teacher uses a fixed gaze as a management technique, it may be seen as extremely hostile. Young people preferred team games rather than games like Follow the Leader. Students were also more likely to take turns collaboratively. This is in contrast to mainstream students who try to take control of classroom conversations by calling out to get the attention of the teacher. Some young people rejected school because it represented mainstream society, a society that has oppressed Native peoples for many years. And they did not want to sell out to the oppressor.

These elements demonstrate how the learning context includes not only accepted behaviors, but also interactional patterns, value orientations, historical understandings, and nonverbal communication styles. Teachers may become frustrated with students who do not actively participate in class discussions or who do not seem to be attending to them while they are talking. Teachers are not the center of the learning in Warm Springs classrooms; the students as a community are the center.

What can teachers do to address the context issue? For example some Native American students may reject school because schooling may seem like an assimilationist tool teaching them to be more White. Historically, ethnic communities have come into conflict with and often feel the pressure to assimilate to majority culture. Hap Gilliland (1986), a Native American teacher, suggests that educators should be open to conversations about the conflicts Native American students may have with mainstream society. In addition, integrating social science lessons on events like the Trail of Tears, The Long Walk, Baker Massacre, Sand Creek, and Wounded Knee can create opportunities for communal discussions (Gilliland 1986) that include the study of controversial issues such as treaties, land management, and cultural assimilation. Teachers also can make comparisons with other events in history, like the Overthrow of Queen Liliuokalani, the Japanese American Internment, the Sleeping Lagoon Case, the Zoot Suit Riots, and March on Washington. Through the presentation of these events, teachers can bring in issues-centered discussions that focus on governmental policies and their impact on ethnic minority communities. To provide a balanced view of the struggles of people from underrepresented groups, it is also imperative for teachers to present information about how the communities empowered themselves to change society. The self-determination movement could be a theme that is incorporated into the curriculum. Instead of feeling like pawns, there have been many Native people who have gained control over medical, educational, and business programs as well as restoring tribal government to their communities (Olson and Wilson 1984). For example, Native people fought for the passage of the Indian Self-Determination and Education Assistance Act in 1975 (Olson and Wilson 1984). With this act, the power of tribal governments was strengthened and the law established the ability of tribal governments to set their own goals and priorities for social service funds and financial resources targeted for education. Teachers can assist Native American students in understanding that in order to make changes in a society, they must have the skills to do so. They must be able to read, write, and compute, and more importantly students must also understand the system they are a part of as members of this country (Delpit 1995). Using role models like Malcolm X, Helen Keller, Scott Momaday, and César Chavez, teachers can discuss the anger, frustration, and disillusionment of others, and present how these individuals developed political knowledge and skills that were needed to effectively change national policies and practices.

The cultural context is extremely important to the learning process. This includes not only the behaviors and ways of communicating that students bring to school, but it also refers to the value orientation of students. For example, in the institution we call schools, many educators, who may come from a range of ethnic communities, come with a mainstream orientation where they perceive schools to be places where teachers lead the class and hold authority because of their position. Much of the work is expected to be completed individually. Knowledge is seen as objective. Also the teacher is visually at the center of instruction and regulates classroom talk (Philips 1993). However, the cultural community context of students may come into conflict with the teachers' context. For example, as was discussed previously, some students from culturally diverse communities come to school with the concern that they do not want to do well because this would be considered "acting White." (Gilliland 1986; Delpit 1995; Fordham and Ogbu 1986). They would be giving in to an oppressive White society and accepting assimilation. This belief may result in behaviors that are seen as obstinate and uncooperative. As part of the cultural context of the classroom, teachers must consider and address the issue because context is as much a part of the learning process as instructional content. So even though lessons may contain cultural content from a student's home—as in the case of bringing in ethnic newspapers—in order to fully utilize culturally relevant teaching, teachers need a comprehensive understanding of student communities to appreciate the fuller meaning of issues reported in the newspapers.

Listening and observing students can provide teachers knowledge of interactional patterns, expectations, frustrations, and underlying values. This information can assist teachers in knowing how to motivate, affirm, present concepts and issues, and appropriately respond. In the case of students from a culture like the Warm Springs nation, the teacher would need to take a student-centered approach where there is more emphasis on communal activities. Otherwise young people might withdraw completely from what was going on in the classroom. Philips found that students completed group tasks but an identifiable leader was not chosen. Instead, they quickly divided responsibilities and the work was done. She found the cultural context to be a powerful component of the learning process because the expectations of Warm Springs students directly conflicted with mainstream practices.

Another Example of the Power of Cultural Context: A Yup'ik Classroom

One of the Native communities in Alaska is the Yup'ik. Jerry Lipska (1996) has researched how experienced Yup'ik teachers built their classroom activities on a culturally relevant pedagogy while affirming the students' ethnic identity. Overall, Lipska reported a rhythm and flow of learning in the classroom. He watched a lesson focusing on the beaver round-up festival, which signals the end of the winter. In the discussion about how to trap and skin beavers, the male students in this fifth grade classroom spoke in animated tones and quickly about how to stretch the beaver pelt. The teacher reinforced their responses with a short, "Right." He used the term *aqsatuyaaq* (young beaver) in his lesson. At first, the teacher gave directions how to make the beaver blanket using their art materials. Then he allowed the students to make their blankets on the floor or at their own desks. The teacher continued to make his own beaver blanket at his desk. Some students went up to the desk to watch the teacher. Students talked to each other as they worked. When several students came into the room from another activity, the teacher did not stop to tell them what to do. Rather, other students explained the activity to them. In this way the teacher was a collaborator in the classroom, not the center. The teacher asked those students surrounding his desk what they might write on the blanket when they were finished creating them. As he made his beaver blanket, the students also were engaged in making their own. The teacher and students held respect for each other.

To outside observers, the lesson seemed to lack substance; however, to the Yup'ik teacher it was a carefully built lesson that integrated the themes of survival, sustenance, respect, care, and patience. The teacher not only taught how a beaver is trapped, dried, pelt and stretched, he also instructed students in how they were expected to act during this process (Lipska 1996). Not only must students be skillful in how they trap a beaver, but they also must use care and patience because survival depends on their abilities. This lesson incorporated not only cultural values of the community regarding the end of the winter, celebrating the beaver, but also how the Yup'ik's survival depended on their knowledge of the land.

Responding to the cultural context in a classroom is challenging especially when there are twenty different cultures represented. I don't think it is possible to create one environment that is culturally congruent to all students all the time. However, it is possible for teachers to create an affirming environment that values the cultures students bring to school and to make adjustments as possible.

If you are interested in reading about other scholars who have specific programs or knowledge of what works for students from underrepresented groups, I recommend that you get to know the work of educators like Kathryn Au, Lisa Delpit, Donna Deyle, Joyce King, Bob Moses, Susan Philips, and Karen Swisher. I have included a list of further readings at the end of book that you might want to investigate. Each educator began their work focusing on a question or issue that interested them and then became educational detectives. They first identified the issue and then began to look at a variety of ways to address it. Their work can assist you in better understanding what to be sensitive to, and what to look for and expect in your classrooms.

ᐴ *Culturally Relevant Teaching: A Definition*

Culture is a broad concept. It encompasses everything that is created by people. In the classroom, I view the following as a working definition of culturally relevant teaching:

> Culturally relevant teaching is an approach to instruction that responds to the sociocultural context and seeks to integrate cultural content of the learner in shaping an effective learning environment. Cultural content includes aspects like experiences, knowledge, events, values, role models, perspectives, and issues that arise from the community. Cultural context refers to the behaviors, interactional patterns, and underlying expectations and values of students. Culturally literate teachers develop an insider perspective of a cultural community. They understand that cultural elements operate simultaneously and respond in congruence with their students. Culturally knowledgeable teachers are keen observers, understand the importance of context, and can read nonverbal communication cues like facial expressions or hand gestures of students.

Good teachers are aware of and integrate culturally relevant teaching because they understand how it makes them more effective. For example, researchers like Jackie Jordan Irvine (1990) and Janice Hale-Benson (1982) have studied African American students. They found many who came to school with behaviors that contrast with those expected in schools. So they advised teachers to observe their young people to determine if they come with a strong cultural orientation. If so, then teachers may provide students, who are expressive and higher in energy, with opportunities to make presentations as a vehicle for displaying their competence rather than always being required to perform on written examinations. Researchers like Park (1997) and Litton (1999) found that Filipino American, Korean American, Vietnamese American, and Chinese American students had a learning style preference for visual learning in comparison to their European American peers. With these populations, teachers may need to utilize more three-dimensional models, graphic organizers, photographs, concept mapping, charts, and writing on the board while teaching to convey their ideas. Since many Latinos and Asian American students are immigrants and they come to the United States with different cultural understandings, Cheng (1998) recommends that teachers provide students with opportunities to practice colloquial patterns and interactional behaviors using scripted role plays. In addition, Fung (1998) suggests teachers present interdisciplinary units on immigration. These units would integrate cultural content from all major subject areas like mathematics, science, history, and music. For example, educators may have students compare and contrast different types of musical instruments that were brought to the United States as part of the immigration process. Students could also be directed to study the multiple reasons for migration. All of these recommendations demonstrate the importance of adjusting teacher practices in the classroom to meet the needs of culturally diverse students.

Culturally relevant teaching can also refer to the process where students' cultures are used to affirm their identity and act as a lens from which to examine the way inequities have been and continue to be fostered in our nation (King 1994; Ladson-Billings 1994; Lipman 1998; Pang and Cheng 1998). It is most important that students understand how society gives out negative messages about people who differ whether it is due to aspects like ethnicity, culture, race, gender, social class, religion, or sexual orientation. Students must be able to "unpack" those messages and empower themselves. There are powerful links between power and culture. However, I believe that the first level of culturally relevant teaching centers on creating learning environments where students are academically successful and culturally affirmed. Within that context, teachers will be more effective in guiding their students to address the issues of politics and social justice.

Why do cultural elements work? Cultural elements can assist us in our teaching because they provide us ways to enhance the learning process. The next section discusses how teachers can use Vygotsky's theory of the zone of proximal development, which is a theory of how to increase the zone of learning in a person.

Zone of Proximal Development: Looking at Learning Holistically

Many teachers wonder, "How can theory help me in the classroom?" or "What does it have to do with what I do in the classroom?" Vygotsky was a researcher who developed a theory of learning. His theory of development does not look at an individual in isolation; rather, he believed that learning had to be viewed within a social context. Children develop through their social interactions with others (Tharp and Gallimore 1988). As part of his sociocultural framework for cognitive development, Vygotsky constructed the concept of the zone of proximal development. Vygotsky saw the role of a teacher as someone who could assist students in learning more than they could on their own (Tharp and Gallimore 1988). Can you think of teachers who did this by the questions they asked or the materials they gave you to read? The zone of proximal development is the extended range of a child's learning, from the actual developmental level to the level achieved through the guidance of an adult or collaboration with a more knowledgeable peer (Tharp and Gallimore 1988). Vygotsky was not referring to the teaching of specific, isolated skills or knowledge; he was opposed to drill-and-kill instruction (Moll 1990). Rather, he believed that teachers should provide a well-developed set of social interactions and meaningful content. As the child learns skills from interactions with the teacher or others in the first phase, he/she moves into the second phase of the zone of proximal development by guiding the use of the skills on her/his own. In the third phase, the child internalizes the skill or capability, and in the fourth phase, the student may have forgotten a skill and may ask the teacher for help and the process repeats itself: (1) performance is assisted by more capable others; (2) performance is assisted by self; (3) performance becomes internalized or "fossilized"; and (4) assistance is requested and the process begins again (Tharp and Gallimore 1988).

Utilizing Vygotsky's theory, Goodman and Goodman (1990) believed teachers should act as initiators. They shared an example about how a teacher, along with his eighth grade students, designed a unit on evolution. The teacher wanted students to better understand the issues of creationism and evolution and also to sharpen their reading comprehension and social studies skills in the process. As an initiator, the teacher assisted students by selecting materials for the unit, providing time for student discussions, and encouraging students to choose pieces of literature that would deepen their understandings of the issues. However, the teacher did not control the learning process. Students independently defined terms like evolution and creationism, and also picked a biography about Charles Darwin. The students used the filter of examining the role of science while reading the novel. This example demonstrated how both process and content were important aspects of the learning. Not only did students become more competent readers, they also built on what they already knew and investigated various aspects of the issues. Their understanding of the conflict and difference in value orientations between creationism and evolution became more rich while they learned reading and social studies skills, such as reading for meaning, reading for evidence, and grasping the difference between fact and opinion. Students learned specific skills, but within a large context. Their zone of proximal development was increased because the teacher assisted them in developing their thinking processes and challenged them to think beyond the acquisition of knowledge by encouraging students to examine complex issues. Learning was increased because the concepts and knowledge students gained arose from a meaningful context.

In this process, learning occurred on two planes. First, learning was a socially constructed phenomenon where students learned by interacting with the ideas and with other people. Second, students grew because they thought about and reflected upon those experiences. They developed a metacognitive understanding of their own thinking. Through this process, the skills become automatic or internalized. When people share with each other perspectives, information, ideas, and practices, the understandings and comprehension of students can be expanded. Children can learn on their own, but greater growth can be achieved when students are assisted by teachers or peers. The role of the teacher as an active participant in the learning process is to assist students in providing modeling, feedback, coaching, instructing, questioning, and cognitive structuring (Tharp and Gallimore 1988).

The zone of proximal development can be greatly increased when teachers have clear goals, provide assisted performance opportunities, and evaluate the progress of students with the aim of guiding them to become independent learners and problem solvers (Moll 1990). The learning is placed within a meaningful sociocultural context; interactions are key elements of the process. In contrast, much of the teaching found in schools lacks interaction and often relies heavily on rote learning. However, using this theory of cognitive development, teachers not only facilitate further cognitive growth in students, but interactions also guide students to develop skills that they regulate and utilize themselves. The next section discusses how Vygotsky's theory of cognitive development was utilized to develop a holistic orientation to teaching.

Funds of Knowledge: Teaching Within a Holistic Orientation

Teaching the whole person means to know the whole person and that means their cultural background too. The Funds of Knowledge project is founded on the belief that students come to school with a rich bank of information. Some teachers have misconceptions that students from blue collar families do not have information-wealthy lives. Researchers have found that children come to school with rich family networks and a vast knowledge of diverse kinds of information.

Luis Moll and his colleagues have demonstrated that a holistic orientation toward learning is more effective than teaching skills in isolation. When the curriculum and context of learning arises from the lives of students, not only are the knowledge and culture of students seen as valuable school resources, but also students can build on what they know. With his colleagues, James Greenberg and C. Valez-Ibanez, Moll studied the cultural knowledge of family relationships and social networks of thirty-five Mexican families in a working-class community of Tucson, Arizona (Moll and Greenberg 1990). Their average yearly family income was $14,500. The cultural riches of the family were called "funds of knowledge." What did the researchers mean by "funds of knowledge"? Every family and community holds information about relationships and activities in everyday life. For example, funds of knowledge include information about how families use their money, how families prepare nourishing meals, knowledge of ethnic traditions, and knowledge of how to solve household problems. Every family has a large "bank" of knowledge, which contains skills on how to survive. For example, Moll, Vélez-Ibáñez, and Greenberg (1988) discovered that families knew about different kinds of soils, veterinary medicine, ranch economy, carpentry, masonry, herbal medicines, and midwifery. They also had knowledge about society and could find out about school programs, enroll in local community college classes, and other community services.

So how have teachers used Moll's model of cultural learning in the classroom? The researchers worked with a sixth grade bilingual teacher who was in her fourth year of teaching. All her children were Mexican American and spoke Spanish. Her goal was to integrate more writing activities into her curriculum. The teacher decided to introduce a unit on construction because many of the parents had experience in building and this unit could become a bridge between home and school knowledge. The teacher was particularly sensitive to the parents because she felt they did not feel welcome at school. She wanted to do something to encourage the parents to become partners in the classroom; then they would become more involved in their children's learning.

This is the process through which she took her students:

1. The class brainstormed and suggested possible topics they could research at the library.
2. Students researched history of dwellings and how to build different kinds of structures. In fact, they used their mathematics skills to figure out how many bricks would be needed in one of the projects.
3. Students built a model of a building and wrote a short essay explaining their research and how they built their model. In fact, one of her students compared the analogy of building a house to the human body. He wrote, "Without steel rods, you couldn't maintain a house upright. It would fall to the ground like a puppet without strings to sustain it. A house without a frame would fall the same way. Nevertheless, the frame (*esqueleto*, skeleton) of a house is not constituted by bones like ours, but by reinforced steel" (Moll and Greenberg 1990, 338).
4. The teacher then invited parents, who held funds of knowledge, to school. Since their parents lacked formal schooling, the students were surprised that she would invite them as experts to share their knowledge.
5. About twenty parents (carpenters, masons, draftspersons, and others) shared their intellectual knowledge about construction to the learning process of the classroom. Students wrote detailed essays about the parent visits.
6. Students wanted to extend the unit on construction by creating a community of many buildings. They researched extensively on what made up a town. For example, they learned about how to obtain water and electricity. In addition, students had to look into the development of streets, services, parks, schools, and other public service agencies. Writing became a meaningful way to present their research.
7. At the end of the year, the teacher developed a career unit based upon the work and questions students raised during the construction unit. She guided their work with the question, "What do you see in your future?" (Moll and Greenberg 1990, 344). Students created posters showing different professions. They invited a variety of people, including university professors, to talk about their work and what steps they would need to take in order to get a job in that career.

The unit centered upon a fund of knowledge found within the children's families. The knowledge that community people shared with the students helped them to identify topics, increase their understanding of construction, and motivate the students to write about what they learned. They interviewed many members of their families, engaged in much library research, and were taught important writing skills in the process. Their skills in spelling, grammar, and conceptualization improved.

The sixth graders read and wrote in both English and Spanish. Their skills of expression and analysis increased because they engaged in a series of writing assignments around a culturally meaningful topic. The activities were not isolated or unrelated. The teacher also instituted peer-editing groups and taught students how to critique each other's work so that their recommendations would help a peer write more clearly. The students were engaging in the third phase of the zone of proximal development, internalization/fossilization. This approach encouraged a more holistic orientation to teaching, connecting the everyday life of students with the classroom. Skills were not taught in isolation; they were taught within a comprehensive community-based curriculum.

There have been other programs that have utilized the Funds of Knowledge approach (Moll, Amanti, Neff, and Gonzalez 1992). This project developed a holistic curriculum. In the first phase of the curriculum development, teachers became ethnographic researchers, interviewing family members and going to student homes gathering information about people's family histories, interests, careers, and other household experiences. They took field notes describing their observations. Teachers were especially interested in understanding how relationships among family members create various types of networks. These networks dealt with employment, child care, hobbies, and other aspects of life. As teachers learned more about family life of their students, they often developed stronger and reciprocal relationships with community members (Moll, Amanti, Neff, and Gonzalez 1992). In the second phase, teachers reflected upon and thought about how they could draw upon the lives of their children and relate them to academic subject areas. In the last phase, teachers developed a curriculum for use in the classroom and invited parents and community members to participate in class activities.

One of the examples that Norma Gonzalez (1995) described focused on ethnobotany. One parent interviewed was an expert in medicinal plants. The teacher developed a language arts unit around these plants. Students wrote about various regional plants and their health benefits. In another example, Amanti (1995) found during her home visits that several of the families of her students knew about horses and how to care for them. In many ranches in Mexico, horses have contributed to cattle ranching. She developed a unit on the evolution of horses, explored animal behavior, presented information on saddles, created horse math, and used literature and movies that focused on horses (Amanti 1995). The teacher even borrowed a video that an uncle of one of the students had filmed of his own horses. The students made true-to-size graphs of different breeds of horses and investigated their various characteristics. The students were experts on the topic and they had more control in the study of the unit because the curriculum reflected their local cultural knowledge. Some of the students also visited relatives in Mexico, and these family members owned ranches. Many of the children had natural and cultural ties with this topic. In addition, family members came into the classroom to discuss their work with horses.

The knowledge of students is affirmed and valued within this program. Relationships between students, teachers, and community people become strengthened and reciprocal. Ties of trust are built and maintained. Students are engaged in motivating instructional units that focus on higher-level thinking skills rather than recitation or drill because students are sources of information and have more control of their own learning.

The work of these researchers is extremely exciting because it guides teachers in developing anthropological and cross-cultural skills that assist them in creating motivating and effective learning contexts for students. In addition, this program centers upon building trusting and reciprocal relationships with parents. Though it is not possible to go to every student's home, it is possible to learn about a community through interacting with students and parents from the neighborhood.

One of the strengths of the Funds of Knowledge approach is that it addresses the issue of school power. Many of the leading multicultural educators focus a great deal of attention on what Lisa Delpit (1995) calls the culture of power. The culture of power refers to the beliefs, behaviors, standards, and expectations for success in U.S. society. Delpit believes children are asked, in both small and large ways, in schools to give up their culture. Sometimes children give up small things, like what they eat at lunch; sometimes the cultural elements are much larger, like speaking Cambodian or Spanish at school. Because the Funds of Knowledge teachers build instructional units that arise out of the living experience of their students and because they ask parents to become active instructional partners within the classroom, the program naturally addresses this hierarchical power issue. At the same time, stronger support networks of care develop between teachers and families.

Many multiculturalists believe the ultimate goal of schooling is to develop social action skills in students and teachers so they become active in changing society. I agree with these educators that social action is the ultimate goal of schooling; however, I disagree with their push toward changing society before addressing how to restructure our teaching so that students become academically successful. Another excellent program is the Algebra Project.

The Algebra Project: "If We Can, We Should Do It"

The Algebra Project is another example of how a culturally relevant curriculum can have profound results. Bob Moses, the founder of this program, is a civil rights activist and he believed all students should have equal access to education. When he found African American students were either failing algebra or not taking it, he became concerned because he knew they would not be able to get into college without algebra. Working with other parents, Moses developed a curriculum that used concrete student experiences in teaching mathematical skills. Like Funds of Knowledge, the Algebra Project was another holistic approach to learning. The math skills that students learned were part of a larger community project that was based on the values of equal access to schooling and the importance of preparing young people for college. Math was taught not only within the social context of students and their cultural knowledge like the subway, but it was part of a larger community movement. This project not only included culturally familiar knowledge, but also the social networks and motivation of the African American community. These are powerful social forces for students because they convey the message that math skills are not just isolated schools skills, but members of the African American community also expected them to acquire these skills and to be successful.

Bob Moses was concerned that African American students did not have the same access as other youth to higher-level math classes. He found that many seventh and eighth graders were not taking algebra. Instead, most African American students were funneled into lower-level math courses. Algebra was a gatekeeper course for many students from underrepresented groups who wanted to go into college (Silver 1997). Students had to pass algebra to be admitted into college. Though some districts have mandated that all students have access to algebra, this across-the-board change can have a negative impact on student success if students do not have proper preparation (Silver 1997). In addition, Moses wanted African American students to have the option of taking advanced math classes in junior and senior high school. Bob Moses, was already committed to equality. He and his colleagues developed the Transition Curriculum to teach concepts in the middle school that prepare students for high school algebra.

Then in seventh and eighth grade, students take algebra and this prepares them to take geometry and other higher-level courses in high school. This program is the Algebra Project (Moses, Kamii, Swap, and Howard 1989).

In order to reach African American students, Moses and his colleagues felt that it was critical for young people to see the relevancy of algebra (Moses et al. 1989). Two questions that he asked parents and students to think about were "What is algebra for?" and "Why do we want children to study it?" Through Moses's direction, parents and students realized that young people needed math skills not only to get into college, but also to become full members of society and develop their career dreams. Members of the community became more actively involved in schools and aware of the importance of math skills. Moses built a strong community of people who were interested in school reform. These parents continuously participate and monitor the progress of local sites of the Algebra Project and work with local school district teachers and administrators.

Algebra had to be more than separate and unrelated theories and formulas. Moses developed a transition curriculum using the experiences of students. For example, students knew how to use the subway. Their knowledge of the subway and the map of travel were used to guide them to raise questions about math concepts like the number line, positive and negative integers, and measuring distance.

In another activity, sixth graders made lemonade. This unit on lemonade concentrate centered upon the importance of ratio and how the concentration of the lemonade was related to proportions. Another example of an innovative unit that taught ratios used African drums. Students explored the concept of proportions and ratios in making the drums. This particular unit utilized a variety of learning activities from visual, aural, and kinesthetic learning.

The curriculum is built on a five-step process. The following list describes the steps:

1. Students participate in a physical experience.
2. Students draw a picture or model of the experience.
3. Students discuss and write about what happened in their own words.
4. Students discuss and write about the experience in formal language.
5. Students build and use symbols to express the experience.

Using the Algebra Project curriculum, teachers guide students from concrete and meaningful knowledge to abstract concepts and theories in mathematics. Moses found that many students he worked with did not understand how mathematical symbols and operational signs were put together to create an idea or thought. The abstract symbols had no real meaning to some students. This project used cultural knowledge from various subgroups. The African drum unit applied ethnic knowledge to math instruction, while the units on lemonade and the subway used local and personal cultural knowledge. In all cases, the shared lives of the children were taken into consideration and affirmed the student role in constructing knowledge and learning academic skills. The results of the program were impressive. The original group of students advanced to either the college preparatory mathematics series of courses or into Honor Algebra or Geometry (Moses, Kamii, Swap, and Howard 1989). Not only were the students proud of their accomplishments, but the parents and community also became more involved in schools. The next section describes a culturally oriented literacy program.

Organic Reading and Writing: Teacher

Culturally relevant teaching, student choice, and student life experiences are at the core of another educational program. It is another holistic-oriented approach where learning is seen within a community context. Skills are not taught in isolation. Children learn to read within the context of their desire to communicate to others. This program is described by Sylvia Ashton-Warner (1963) in her book *Teacher*. Though this is an old book, the method she uses has been utilized in various formats by many teachers over the years. Ashton-Warner described a method that she used to teach reading and writing in New Zealand which uses the vocabulary that the students suggest. Many of her students were from the Maori community. She began by having her students identify one-word sentences. These words had great emotional value to students; for example, "Mummy," "Daddy," "ghost," "kiss," "love," "touch," "truck," and "haka" (Maori war dance). Ashton-Warner described the best first words or key vocabulary as being the following:

> "First words must have an intense meaning.
> First words must be already part of the dynamic life.
> First books must be made of the stuff of the child himself,
> whatever and wherever the child" (Ashton-Warner 1963, 32).

Ashton-Warner found her students could understand the importance of words quickly because the words they picked had strong meanings to them. The strong emotions of key vocabulary urged students to write complex sentences and express themselves. The stories that students wrote described life in their society. Sometimes this had to do with violence or conflict in the family or community.

One of the examples a student wrote was:

> "When I went to sleep.
> I dreamt about the war.
> The Chinese never won.
> The Maoris won" (Ashton-Warner 1963, 97).

The books they wrote were full of the drama of living and not like "Dick and Jane," where everyday life was superficial and unreal to the students. Jane was never scared and Dick never fell and hurt himself (Ashton-Warner 1963). Reading and writing rose out of the lives of each student and what they were afraid of and happy about.

By using this method, a Maori child not only learned how to read and write, but also saw that reading and writing could mean something personal and often spontaneous to them (Ashton-Warner 1963). Writing was a way to communicate with others. Reading was also a source of great individual joy. This affirmed not only who students were, but also what they could do.

Summary: Three Holistic Educational Research Programs

Reflecting on the three holistic educational projects, Funds of Knowledge, the Algebra Project, and Organic Reading and Writing, can you list common elements? Write your comments in your journal.

These projects provide teachers with strategies and understandings that can enrich their teaching. The following are some of the shared characteristics of the three programs:

1. Teachers learned about their students. In each project, the educators became familiar with the culture and lives of their students within a comprehensive context. Their understanding of culture was not superficial or piece by piece.
2. The living experiences of students were integrated into the curriculum and acted as bridges to learning writing, mathematics, reading, and other academic skills and knowledge.
3. Communities of learners were developed where students became active and engaged partners and participants in the learning process.
4. Parents and other community people were invited to become partners with teachers and school personnel. Some parents acted as experts and taught along with teachers.
5. Trusting and reciprocal caring relationships were developed among students, teachers, parents, and community people, and they all became active members in the community of learners.
6. The teachers created learning activities that engaged students because the activities were meaningful, relevant, and hands on. The students understood the purpose of the units and made choices in their own learning.
7. Focus was on learning and student academic success. Students were not asked to give up their culture in school and in so doing become more culturally assimilated.

These programs are excellent ways to incorporate cross-cultural knowledge and skills within much of the district, state, and federal standards that teachers must follow.

Cultural Models: Movies in Our Minds

The previous section describes how numerous cultural elements are used together to create a holistic curriculum. The next discussion will describe a particular technique that teachers can use. I am always looking for better ways to explain concepts or ideas to students and believe cultural models have been overlooked in education. In fact, the Funds of Knowledge, Algebra Project, and Organic Reading and Writing programs use many cultural models throughout their curricula.

Cultural models are excellent tools that teachers can use from the lives of their students. Gee (1996), a sociolinguist, sees cultural models as videotapes or movies that are stored in our mind and represent what a person experiences in life or believes life should be. These cultural models contain a sequence or broad understanding of an aspect of life. Often cultural models include both context and content. These tools include aspects of life such as stories, sayings, patterns of behavior, procedures or policies, and conceptual understandings. In Chapter 2, I talked about choral reading. Remember when Miss Gray asked her first graders if they knew what the term "choral reading" meant? The students didn't know until she used the cultural model of a choir at church. In this way, Miss Gray utilized a series of understandings. First, students knew that the people sang together as one voice. Second, the students knew the people in a choir sang the same song. Third, the students knew that they were to follow her lead in order for everyone to read in coordination with each other. This was an example of a cultural model. It included a specific context, a group setting. In addition, there were particular behaviors associated with the example.

Remember the story about my friend's experiences at his grandmother's eightieth birthday party? The short movie in his mind not only included appropriate behavior and underlying values about family roles, but also the meaning of cultural symbols such as peaches and cranes. My friend's cultural model about his grandmother's birthday includes the importance of family role models like his aunt and how she had the authority to teach him what was appropriate to do in this social context. This was all part of the cultural model of the birthday party of a respected elder family member.

As I think about how cultural models can be used in the classroom, let me share with you something that happened in a first grade class. Most of the children were African American. I remember going over test-taking skills and the importance of reading each word carefully. As you know, there is a cultural model of test-taking that includes certain instructions about how to mark the correct answers. Also tests include vocabulary; some words are more familiar to some students than others. One of the vocabulary words on this particular test was the term *brush*. That seemed simple to me. The students were supposed to look at the picture on the left of a hair brush and then to circle the correctly spelled word on the right side of the box. Many of my students missed this item. I wasn't sure why. It didn't make sense to me.

One of the best readers in the class was Eugene. He was able to read on a second grade level, so I couldn't understand why he missed what I thought was an easy vocabulary word. Looking back at the situation, I remember that most everything in those days was on ditto paper so many of the pictures were somewhat smeared. And everything printed came out in the same bluish color.

I asked Eugene if he would help me. He smiled.

I showed him the dittoed paper. I pointed to the picture of the hair brush. He looked at it and his eyes went blank.

"Eugene, do you know what this is a picture of?" he shook his head no.

I was flabbergasted. Thinking that he was teasing. I looked at him again and asked in a puzzled voice, "You really don't know what this is?"

Eugene was beginning to look worried. His forehead wrinkled.

"I'm not sure."

I could see from his nonverbal reaction that he was not pulling my leg and so I said, "it's a hair brush."

Immediately Eugene said, "Oh that's right. But I don't use one. I use a pik in my hair."

Cultural models took on a clearer notion to me. I could better understand how people have different understandings and contexts, which they use to interpret their experiences. To Eugene it was obvious he used a pik to style his hair, while I used a brush. We have developed two different cultural models of taking care of our hair. This particular example showed me how home cultural knowledge can conflict with the cultural knowledge of schools.

The research of Moll, Greenberg, Moses, Gonzalez, Amanti, Gee, and Ashton-Warner demonstrates a great need for teachers to understand and use culture more effectively in our teaching. Children come to school with different ways of living and valuing. Teachers can use cultural models that can serve as bridges in the learning process from home to school. In this way, students can see the relevance of schooling and learn the culture of power at the same time. All students should be encouraged to reach beyond their home culture, whether it is from an underrepresented community or the majority (Gee 1996). Students then are given the opportunity to see how others interpret the world. This is a challenging goal especially for teachers unfamiliar with underrepresented ethnic, neighborhood, or family cultures. Yet educators should routinely provide students with opportunities that teach new perspectives and cultural models.

Teachers who value their students learn about and integrate cultural elements naturally into their teaching. This not only creates a more caring and comfortable environment, but also builds a more effective learning atmosphere. As Gee also wrote, "Just as many women have sought to replace our cultural models of gender roles with new ways of thinking, interacting, and speaking, so humans at their best are always open to rethinking, to imagining newer and better, more just and more beautiful words and worlds. That is why good teaching is ultimately a moral act" (Gee 1996, 89).

Key Beliefs About Culture and the Learning Process

Culturally relevant teaching is based upon key beliefs about the interconnections of learning and culture. Culturally relevant teaching stresses the importance of looking not only for cultural bridges, but also for cultural models of knowledge and the social context of the learning process. Students do not learn information in a vacuum. Students learn within a specific context. This context is a combination of many elements, such as the relationships and roles between individuals, the underlying assumptions and beliefs people hold, the meaning of nonverbal behaviors, and cultural models of information. Much of this information is embedded in what happens in the classroom. Teachers may not have time to think about how schools have specific cultural elements that all students are expected to know. Why is culture important in the learning process? The following presents six reasons why culture should be considered in the classroom:

1. Real-life experiences give relevancy to learning.
2. Using culture permits students to use their prior knowledge.
3. Using cultural models and analogies can serve as bridges to new concepts.
4. Children have learned at home through family and cultural practice and cultural context.
5. Culture provides the structure through which experiences are interpreted, patterns are seen, behavior is expected, and values and motivation are learned.
6. When children believe that teachers listen to them and value who they are and what they bring to school, trusting relationships are built and they form important educational, emotional, and motivational foundation for learning.

Curriculum Approaches to Culturally Relevant Teaching

Geneva Gay (1995) has written an excellent chapter reviewing the different conceptualizations and definitions of Multicultural Education. In that chapter she also discusses different types of knowledge that teachers use in their classrooms. Much of the knowledge that is taught in schools is traditional societal ideas and information based on a Western/European view of the world. Since the 1960s there has been a push for school reform and curriculum transformation. In this movement, the belief that knowledge is culturally and politically neutral has been challenged. Scholars have argued that much of the knowledge taught in schools has been chosen because it reinforces the way society is now structured (Gay 1995). Educators like Geneva Gay, Lisa Delpit, Luis Moll, Christine Sleeter, Carl Grant, and James Banks argue that the curriculum in many schools must be changed to reflect the pluralistic nature of our student population. In fact, these theorists also believe that our democratic values of justice, freedom, and diversity support a curriculum that does not arise from one cultural perspective. Though we have a common core of values, the curriculum must also represent our value in diversity. The infusion of culturally relevant teaching reflects one way in which schools can change from a monocultural curriculum toward a curriculum that includes diverse perspectives and worldviews.

One of the most prevalent ways that culture has been included in schools is through what James Banks coined as an additive approach to multicultural curriculum. In this way teachers present isolated pieces of information about groups, whether there is a holiday celebration about Martin Luther King, Jr., or the inclusion of a unit on indigenous peoples of New York. Unfortunately, because of the spotty, isolated, and surface presentation of information about people from underrepresented ethnic and cultural groups, students may not have a deep understanding of the cultural richness of the United States. Because the main focus of the school curriculum from kindergarten through twelfth grade is primarily Western and European, many students do not really understand the impact of other cultures on our society.

This hurts students from underrepresented groups because it does not affirm the belief that they are full participating members of society. In addition, the students may not learn about the important contributions individuals from their communities have made. Students from majority communities also are hampered from this misconception. They are not provided the opportunity to learn new ideas and ways of looking at life from other cultural communities. In addition, majority students may not perceive how society is structured to keep the status quo and how this impacts social relationships for everyone. This can lead to a lack of dialogue (Delpit 1995). Delpit suggests that to have serious communication between members of various communities, those in power must take more responsibility in opening dialogue. The discussions also should arise from open hearts and minds.

James Banks (1995) suggests that teachers consider integrating or restructuring their curriculum rather than making simple additions of holidays or foods. In order to build on Banks's recommendation, I recommend the following approaches:

1. Include themes or threads in your curriculum that focus on language, culture, power, and compassion.
2. Use a comparative orientation of study presenting diverse perspectives on the issue, theme, event, or concept.
3. Employ an issues-centered orientation.
4. Restructure existing units by using a culture/caring/social justice filter.
5. Teach by example.

Integrating units into the existing curriculum is easier for teachers to accomplish at first than restructuring a total curriculum. Instead of adding small pieces, use themes or the comparative approach to teaching. By adding a theme such as equity, interdependence, power, diversity, oppression, caring in a democratic society, multiculturalism, racial identity, bilingualism, gender roles, self-determination, Harlem Renaissance, Civil Rights Movement, or immigration, teachers can bring in knowledge from many groups. Let's take the Zoot Suit Riots for example. The instructor can encourage several students to bring in various Mexican American viewpoints from the time period, and other youths may find information about the perspectives of African Americans, White Americans, or Asian Americans who lived in Los Angeles during the 1940s. In this way, students not only learn the importance of using a comparative view as a skill, but also they engage in uncovering a comprehensive understanding of the case.

The Zoot Suit Riots could also be presented as an issue. Teachers can ask students to come up with open-ended questions to study. For example, students may suggest, "What role did race play in the Zoot Suit Riots? What impact did the riots have on Mexican American and police relationships?" In the next section, I will present a more comprehensive discussion of this approach.

Teachers have courses and units already developed; however, they may want to restructure them using a culture/caring/social justice filter. This filter may assist them in their own learning. For example, let's say Sally teaches a course in American (U.S.) government. She had, in the past, started with discussion of the Magna Carta and other documents from Europe. One of her students mentioned that he had read an article that talked about Benjamin Franklin's study of the Iroquois League of Nation's governmental structure. This organization was created to solve conflicts between groups and to promote peace (Olson and Wilson 1984). Each of the Indian nations elected delegates to a local council and then other delegates were chosen for the Grand Council of the League (Weatherford 1988). Sally discovered that the Iroquois Chief Canassatego proposed the federal model in 1744 (Weatherford 1988). After considerable research, Sally realized she needed to include knowledge not only about the Iroquois Confederation, but information about the diversity of political organizations found in the early days of this land (Olson and Wilson 1984). For Great Plains Indians like the Comanches and Cheyennes, there were representatives from small groups of hunters to a larger community council (Olson and Wilson 1984). In many Native American tribes, governing was egalitarian, and tribal heads of families made decisions. A few tribes in California did not have a central leader, whereas those in the Northeast had powerful chiefs. Sally restructured her class to include a comparative and cross-cultural view of governmental structures. In some ways, Sally is teaching by example. She told her students about her own growth and research and engaged them in a discussion of her findings.

The fifth approach to curriculum development, teaching by example, is one of the most powerful. When teachers treat students with respect, students are more likely to treat others in the same way. When teachers are fair to students, students will have daily examples of what their behavior and attitudes can be like. When teachers are open-minded and investigate topics that arise in class, students may learn how to critically examine and search for new information. When teachers are interested in learning about student cultures, they demonstrate their belief in cultural diversity. In the curriculum, teachers can model the importance of looking at issues from a culture/caring/social justice lens. For example, an educator can choose to present Helen Keller as a person to study during a unit on the socialist movement in the United States during the early twentieth century. In the discussion of her work, the teacher explains how he read *The Lies My Teacher Told Me* (Loewen 1995) and how this book sparked his research on Keller.

Though many people know that Keller had several physical disabilities, they do not know that she was committed to socialism (Loewen 1995). Keller fought for equality, especially economic equality. Keller discovered that many cases of blindness were found in low-income families because many had less access to health care or were involved in industrial accidents (Loewen 1995). History books do not provide a complete picture of Keller, and she would be disappointed to find that they focus on her early life and not on her political activism. The authors of these textbooks have filtered her life and in doing so have silenced her work. Teachers have limited resources and may not be able to develop the curriculum that centers upon the learner to the extent that the Funds of Knowledge project was able to create, but through their actions they can show respect, interest, and understanding of other ways of life.

Key Curriculum Elements in Culturally Relevant Teaching

It is important that teachers integrate culture into their curriculum in a planned way. Teachers can *link* several elements together in the same unit or lesson, which will provide a more holistic approach to cultural integration. When teachers do not have a plan of how to integrate both process and content into their lessons, student culture may be included in a disconnected way; like the image of throwing spaghetti at the wall, some of it will stick, but most of it will fall. Teachers might read a story about a famous person of color or serve tacos in the cafeteria, but there is no overall structured plan.

One of the best ways to integrate culture in a substantial way is to use an issues-centered approach. Students and teachers choose a public issue or problem and investigate significant questions surrounding them in order to make thoughtful decisions (Ochoa-Becker 1996). Students gather evidence, engage in reflective analysis, raise questions, and clarify their values before making a choice or decision. In this way, students have the opportunity to share comparative viewpoints and information and to examine various alternatives and their consequences. Students may investigate individual and societal issues such as free speech, school censorship, dress codes, admissions policies, immigration policies, academic tracking, and employment bias.

After teachers identify the key issues, problems, or themes, they can build their curriculum units by incorporating and naturally integrating the following seven major cultural elements:

1. personal experiences from children's/students' lives;
2. role models;
3. culturally grounded stories, songs, and photos (ways of expressing community values, beliefs);
4. language and linguistic expressions (analogies, metaphors, images, proverbs, sayings, symbols, dialect forms, and phrases from home languages);
5. multiple perspectives on the issue/theme/problem;,
6. formal subject content from traditional areas such as history, literature, art, and music; and
7. community issues.

Each of the components is valuable; however, because the knowledge and experiences that students bring to school are extremely important, I have placed them first on the list. Some elements can be identified readily, while others are more difficult and will take time to gather. It is best not to use one element in isolation but to use several together in order to provide a broader understanding of a community's cultural values and beliefs. Students do not learn well when given isolated information; they are more apt to retain knowledge when they recognize contexts, connections, and patterns. The goal of culturally relevant curriculum is to provide multiple ways to teach information and skills by using culture so that students understand the connection of the content to real life, see reasons for their study, and are successful academically. When culture is incorporated into the classroom in numerous ways, it becomes more of an integral aspect of the curriculum rather than an added or marginal component.

All of these elements are interconnected. For example, let's discuss a poem written by Langston Hughes that is often included in high school English classes. The poem was titled, "Harlem," but it is also often known as "Dream Deferred" (Hughes 1987: 268).

The poem begins with a powerful question, "What happens to a dream deferred?" Then Hughes goes on to describe numerous images of a raisin withdrawing in the heat of the sun or a raw sore that oozes over. In just over fifty words, he takes the reader through powerful images of frustration and desperation. Finally Hughes asks how a person whose dream has been extinguished would feel. He sees that individual not only slumping down from a heavy burden, but also feels the anger boiling over inside ready to explode.

This poem has many connections to the seven noted aspects of curriculum integration. First, Hughes raised the issues of racism and rage. Then he used a variety of images from his own life experiences. He described a dream that had been shattered. His use of strong images described a sore that smelled like rotten meat, but crusted over a deep scar. Hughes called our attention to issues of freedom, social justice, and community. He cared about others, so his writings emphasized the importance of standing up against prejudice and discrimination. He not only believed in justice but also held the moral commitment to speak out against oppression. In this short poem, Hughes used images like the heavy load and exploding, which evoke strong historical contexts and emotional understandings that are based on the experiences of African Americans.

Five elements of the curriculum integration model are included in this one poem. Hughes uses these numerous characteristics to reinforce and deepen the understanding of his cultural viewpoint. Teachers who integrate these many elements will strengthen their curriculum. In the next chapter, I will share an example of a play that extends the perspective found in Hughes's poem.

Summary

Culturally relevant teaching offers educators an effective way to develop, create, and utilize linkages from the lives of their students. Sometimes you can see the "ah ha" in students' eyes when they gain an insight from the example, story, picture, or comment that you utilize in your teaching. In this way, you as their teacher serve as a cultural mediator by providing important links. I believe this is an exciting aspect of teaching. When you learn about the lives and cultural background of your students, you can naturally bring in stories about what they know, value, and experience. Programs like Funds of Knowledge, the Algebra Project, and Organic Reading demonstrate how caring and committed educators have developed curriculum that incorporated more of culture than a holiday or food. These programs integrated the beliefs, dreams, values, and expertise of their students and parents. They brought the community into the classroom and the students became the center of the curriculum.

There are five approaches presented in this chapter. Teachers may use interdisciplinary themes, a comparative orientation, and an issues-centered approach. In addition, they may restructure their curriculum and teach by example. The approaches can include key curriculum elements such as the personal experiences of students, community role models, key events, culturally grounded stories/songs/photos, language, linguistic expressions, analogies, multiple perspectives, and traditional content of formal subject areas.

The knowledge that you gain from your students is unlimited. They will bring to the classroom a richness that reflects the diversity of our nation. The cultural models that you learn from your students will not only enhance your ability to reach students, but they will also strengthen your teaching. You will be able to bring to your teaching exciting new examples and cultural models, which make learning relevant and meaningful. In addition, it is fun to see students light up because you remember what they told you or shared with the class, and that you are able to link this information in the lesson. In this way, teaching not only affirms students, but also motivates and enhances their understanding of the skill or knowledge that you are teaching.

Culturally relevant teaching is like the fertilizer in the garden. It enriches learning. Students will benefit from the scaffolding that you naturally integrate throughout the curriculum. Not only will the knowledge that you convey to your students seem more relevant to their lives, they will also see themselves as valued members of the learning community.

Remember James, the teacher at the beginning of this chapter, who was very skeptical of culturally relevant teaching. On the last day of our college methods course he came up to me and said, "I didn't think it would work. I really didn't think it would."

James threw up his hands and then said, "But I was surprised. *These* big huge kids who were boxers began coming to class prepared. They brought pencils and notebooks. They were sitting in their seats. They were ready to listen."

Of course, I was anxious to find out what James was doing that was reaching his students, so I asked, "So, what did you do?"

"I designed an issues-centered unit based upon the questions, 'Was Pancho Villa a hero or was he a villain as portrayed by others?' I brought in passages about Pancho Villa. They researched his life and then wrote about different aspects" (Allen 1999).

"In addition," James said, "because I was teaching English skills, I was able to include various morphology skills. For example, I explained that -er can be added to a verb to indicate a person who does the action: box to boxer, play to player, and lead to leader. In Spanish, -er has a corresponding morphology, -dor. So, when using the following examples, the students were better able to make that code switch: *correr* becomes *corredor, ensenar* becomes *ensenador,* and *jugar* becomes *jugador.*"

James paused, "I can't believe the students actually come to school now ready to learn. The students are Chicano and, though I didn't believe you, I was desperate so I decided to try the culture thing. I guess culture can make a difference. I didn't believe you, but it worked for me." James smiled widely.

James is primarily bringing in content. However, by choosing topics that interest the students and that have roots in Mexican culture, the cultural context of the curriculum is also shifting. James plans on considering other cultural aspects, such as social interaction patterns, too. He sees how culturally relevant teaching can be used to reach his students.

Teacher Reflections

1. Integrating culture into the classroom curriculum is important. How can you learn about your students' living experiences? Do you have the opportunity to develop a ethnographic study as in the Funds of Knowledge or is it possible for you to use strategies from the Algebra Project to teach new skills? Develop a plan for you to learn about your students and their lives. Write what you learn and develop in your journal. Keep a log of your reflections. As time goes by, you will see that if you are persistent, you will become more efficient and natural in integrating the lives of students into the curriculum.

2. Using what you have learned about your students' lives, develop curriculum that incorporates cultural knowledge into your teaching. Use state and district standards and guidelines to assist you in identifying the skills and knowledge students need, but utilize other materials to teach those skills. Keep a culturally relevant teaching file and build upon it. You will find materials from many places. For example, if there is an article from the local ethnic or community newspaper about an issue that the students are discussing, cut it out and utilize it in your teaching.

3. To find more about teacher assisted performance, read Tharp and Gallimore's book, *Rousing Minds to Life*. The text provides many examples of how teachers learned to use culture and Vygotsky's theories in their teaching. The authors discuss in depth their work at the Kamehameha Elementary Education Program (KEEP) in Hawaii. By utilizing the knowledge of their students and the cultural patterns of student interactions, teachers became more responsive to young people. In this way, the focus of the learning moved from teacher-centered to student-centered and teachers built on the students' contributions. Teachers can learn how to observe and listen to their students more fully. Educators who are most responsive are able to draw in and involve their students so that they take more control of their own learning.

References

Allen, J. 1999. Pancho Villa: An issues-centered lesson plan. Unpublished manuscript.

Amanti, Cathy. 1995. Teachers doing research: Beyond classroom walls. *Practicing Anthropology, 17* (3): 7–9.

Ashton-Warner, Sylvia. 1963. *Teacher.* New York: Bantam Books.

Au, Kathryn H., and Alice J. Kawakami. 1994. Cultural congruence in instruction. In Etta R. Hollins, Joyce E. King, and Warren C. Hayman, eds., *Teaching diverse populations.* Albany, New York: SUNY Press.

Au, Kathryn H., and J. M. Mason. 1981. Social organizational factors in learning to read: The balance of rights hypothesis. *Reading Research Quarterly, 17* (1): 115–152.

Banks, James A. 1995. Multicultural education: Historical development, dimensions, and practice. In James A. Banks and Cherry A. McGee Banks, eds, *Handbook of research on multicultural education.* New York: Macmillan.

Cheng, Li-rong Lilly. 1998. Language assessment and instructional strategies for limited English
students. In Valerie Ooka Pang and Li-rong Lilly Cheng, eds., *Struggling to be heard: The
unmet needs of Asian Pacific American children.* Albany, New York: SUNY Press.

Cole, Michael. 1996. Cultural psychology: A once and future discipline. Cambridge, Mass.:
Belknap Press of Harvard University.

———. 1998. *Can cultural psychology help us think about diversity?* Presentation delivered at
the American Educational Research Association Meetings, San Diego, Calif., April 13–18.

Delpit, Lisa. 1995. *Other people's children.* New York: New Press.

Elliott, Stephen N., Thomas R. Kratochwill, Joan Littlefield Cook, and John R. Travers. 2000.
Educational psychology: Effective teaching, effective learning. Boston, Mass.: McGraw-Hill.

Fordham, Signithia, and John Ogbu. 1986. Black students' school success: Coping with the
'Burden of acting White'. *Urban Review, 18,* (3): 176–206.

Fung, Grace. 1998. Meeting the instructional needs of Chinese American and Asian English
language development and at-risk students. In Valerie Ooka Pang and Li-rong Lilly
Cheng, eds., *Struggling to be heard: The unmet needs of Asian Pacific American children.*
Albany, New York: SUNY Press.

Gay, Geneva. 1995. Curriculum theory and multicultural education. In James A. Banks and Cherry
McGee Banks, eds., *Handbook of Research on Multicultural Education.* N.Y.: Macmillan.

Gee, James. 1996. *Social linguistics and literacies.* Bristol, Pa.: Taylor and Francis.

Gilliland, Hap. 1986. Discipline and the Indian student. In Jon Reyhner, ed., *Teaching the Indian
child.* Billings, Mont.: Eastern Montana College.

Gonzalez, Norma. 1995. The funds of knowledge for teaching project. *Practicing Anthropology
17,* (3): 3–6.

Goodman, Yetta and Kenneth Goodman. 1990. Vygotsky in a whole-language perspective. In
Luis Moll, ed., *Vygotsky and education,* N.Y.: Cambridge University Press.

Hale-Benson, Janice E. 1982. *Black children their roots, culture, and learning styles.* Baltimore,
Md.: Johns Hopkins University Press.

Irvine, Jacqueline Jordan. 1990. *Black students and school failure.* New York: Greenwood Press.

Hughes, Langston. 1987. *Selected poems of Langston Hughes.* New York: Vintage Press.

King, Joyce E. 1994. The purpose of schooling for African American children: Including
cultural knowledge. In Etta R. Hollins, Joyce E. King, and Warren C. Hayman, eds.,
Teaching diverse populations. Albany, New York: SUNY Press.

Ladson-Billings, Gloria. 1994. *Dreamkeepers: Successful teachers of African American
children.* San Francisco, Calif.: Jossey-Bass.

Lipman, Pauline. 1998. *Race, class, and power in school restructuring.* Albany, N.Y.: SUNY
Press.

Lipska, Jerry. 1996. Toward a culturally based pedagogy: A case study of one Yup'ik Eskimo
teacher. In Etta Hollins, ed., *Transforming curriculum for a culturally diverse society.*
Mahwah, N.J.: Lawrence Erlbaum Association Inc.

Litton, Edmundo F. 1999. Learning in America: The Filipino-American sociocultural
perspective. In Clara Park and Marilyn Mei-Ying Chi, eds., *Asian-American education:
Prospects and challenges.* Westport, Conn.: Bergin & Garvey.

Loewen, James W. 1995. *The lies my teacher told me.* New York: Touchstone Books.

Moll, Luis. 1990. *Vygotsky and education: Instructional implications and applications of
sociohistorical psychology.* New York: Cambridge University Press.

Moll, Luis, Cathy Amanti, D. Neff, and Norma Gonzalez. 1992. Funds of knowledge: Using a
qualitative approach to connect homes and classrooms. *Theory into Practice, 31* (2):
132–141.

Moll, Luis and James Greenberg. 1990. Creating zones of possibilities: Combining social
contexts for instruction. In Luis Moll, ed., *Vygotsky and education.* New York: Cambridge
University Press.

Moll, Luis, Javier Tapia, and K. Whitemore. 1993. Living knowledge: The social distribution of cultural resources. In G. Salomon, ed., *Distributed cognitions.* Cambridge, Mass.: Cambridge University Press.

Moll, Luis, C. Vélez-Ibáñez, and James Greenberg. 1988. *Project implementation plan. Community knowledge and classroom practice: Combining resources for literacy instruction.* Tucson, Ariz.: College of Education and Bureau of Applied Research in Anthropology.

Moses, Robert P., M. Kamii, S. M. Swap, and J. Howard. 1989. The algebra project: Organizing in the spirit of Ella. *Harvard Educational Review, 59* (4): 423–443.

Myers, Walter Dean. 1989. *The young landlords.* N.Y.: Puffin books.

Noddings, Nel. 1992. *The challenge to care in schools: An alternative approach to education.* New York: Teachers College Press.

Ochoa-Becker, Anna. 1996. Building a rationale for Issues-Centered Education. In R. Evans and D. Saxe, eds., *Handbook on teaching social issues.* Washington, D.C.: National Council for the Social Studies.

Olson, James S., and Raymond Wilson, 1984. *Native Americans in the twentieth century.* Chicago, Ill.: University of Illinois Press.

Pang, Valerie Ooka, and Cheng, Li-rong Lilly. 1998. *Struggling to be heard: The unmet needs of Asian Pacific American children.* Albany, N.Y.: SUNY Press.

Park, Clara. 1997. Learning style preferences of Asian American (Chinese, Filipino, Korean and Vietnamese) students in secondary schools. *Equity and Excellence in Education, 30,* (2): 68–77.

Philips, Susan Urmston. 1993. *The invisible culture: Communication in classroom and community on the Warm Springs Indian Reservation* (reissued). Prospect Heights, Ill.: Waveland Press.

Silver, Edward A. 1997. "Algebra for All": A real-world problem for the mathematics education community to solve. *NCTM Xchange, 1*(2) 1–4.

Swisher, Karen and Donna Deyhle. 1992. *Adapting instruction to culture.* In Jon Reyhner, ed., Teaching American Indian students. Norman, Okla.: University of Oklahoma Press.

Tharp, Ronald G., and Ronald Gallimore. 1988. *Rousing minds to life: Teaching, learning, and schooling in social context.* Cambridge, Mass.: Cambridge University Press.

Weatherford, Jack. 1988. *Indian givers.* New York: Ballantine Books.

Chapter 10

How Can I Make the Curriculum Culturally Meaningful?

How can you integrate cultural curriculum elements into your teaching? This chapter presents ways teachers have incorporated various components of culture into their curriculum. These elements can help make learning more relevant and meaningful. In addition, the curriculum becomes a vehicle for affirming the cultural heritage of many underrepresented students while teaching the cultural contributions and values of nonmajority communities to majority youth.

The following sections describe how the curriculum can be enriched through the use of the seven cultural curriculum elements described in Chapter 9. The seven components are as follows: personal experiences of students; role models; culturally grounded stories, songs, and photos; language and linguistic expressions; multiple perspectives; traditional content; and community issues. Though I believe it is best to take an issues-centered approach, it is not always possible to do so. In cases where teachers would like to incorporate diverse concepts, ideas, information or perspectives, I suggest using a combination of several elements. One or two elements by themselves provide only a limited view. Think about reading a book. When you read only one page or a chapter summary of the book, you get a limited perspective of the subject of the story or book. Try to utilize as many as possible of the seven cultural elements described in this chapter because together they provide a more comprehensive context of a cultural community. As you read through the examples, think about how you can build upon these ideas in your own classroom.

❧ Personal Experiences of Students

Infusing the experiences of students is a great way to motivate people to listen and to build curriculum bridges. As I shared in Chapter 9, one of the best examples of integrating the knowledge of students into the curriculum is demonstrated in the Funds of Knowledge

project. This can include children's hobbies, talents, roles at home, favorite books, chores, and information they learn from their families. I have found the strategy of integrating experiences and comments of students to be very effective at all levels. In my college classes, the more I know about students the easier it is for me naturally to tie in concepts and principles I am trying to teach. For example, when Tammy talked about her father working with many individuals in an employment office, I asked her to comment on the need for bilingual employees. Tammy then told the class how being fluent in Spanish or Vietnamese is an asset in many stores because when customers come in and need assistance, the clerk can make them feel at ease and answer their questions.

In another example, a third grade teacher naturally incorporated the comments and experiences of one of her youngsters. A student mentioned that she had just gone on a vacation. The teacher then responded, "That is wonderful that you went to Paris, France. What was it like?"

The little girl looked at the teacher and smiled. She said, "It was lots of fun. My mom drove us there to visit my aunt."

The teacher appeared to be a little perplexed. She then said, "Did you go to Paris in France?"

The little girl said in an unsure and quiet voice, "Yes, I went to Peris."

"Is it in California?" asked the teacher.

"Yes, it is," she said proudly.

Then the teacher finally realized that the little girl meant Peris, California.

The teacher reminded the students about homonyms, "Remember how some words sound the same but are spelled differently?"

She pulled down a map of California and showed the children where Peris, California, was located. The teacher then pulled down a world map and pointed to Paris, France.

The teacher naturally built on the comments of her student. She did not embarrass the student because of the misunderstanding that they had. In a caring way, the teacher carefully taught an impromptu lesson about homonyms and geography. It was one of those important teachable moments.

✎ Role Models

Role models are an important aspect of life. Many of us have role models who serve as inspirations for how we can strive to live our life. These models often show us how they have struggled against great obstacles while fighting for social justice or equality in society. They also provide insights into understanding of others and oneself. An excellent activity that I have seen used in middle and high school is the BioBoard (Biography Board). This is an instructional approach developed by Ron Torretto, a social studies and arts teacher at Grossmont High School in San Diego (Torretto 1999).

Ron Torretto has used the BioBoard in music, biology, art, language arts, and social studies because it is an adaptable interdisciplinary project. In history, students may choose to study someone like Chief Joseph or research an issue like the exclusion of Chinese immigrants due to the Geary Act of 1882. Art students may profile a particular musician like Mozart or present a genre of music such as jazz or the blues. In biology, students have studied important scientists like Francis Crick, who identified the structure of DNA. They would not only provide a biography of Crick, but also include a diagram explaining DNA. Mr. Torretto encourages students to develop BioBoards about people who are important to them. The student's job is to describe clearly the importance of this role model to whoever reads the board.

Students share their BioBoards with each other. Mr. Torretto has each one laminated and another student develops ten questions based on the information provided on the board. Later, other students are asked to choose a board and check its number. Then they go to the file and pick out a sheet with the student-created questions and answer them. The students can find all the answers on the BioBoard. In this way, students are involved in teaching each other. There are two examples of student work in the following text.

BioBoard #1

I remember a high school student who was happy to be given a brand new textbook. He paged through the book and saw many glossy color photographs. But as he studied it more closely, he looked up at me and said, "Where am I in this book? I am Filipino and there doesn't seem to be anything about me in the book. Filipinos are the largest Asian group in the country. Where am I? I am an American too."

Perhaps you, as the teacher, did not know what to say to the student. Maybe you didn't know much about the Filipino American experience. Maybe you didn't know that Filipinos were the first Asian immigrants to settle permanently in the continental United States in 1763. You did not want to ignore the student's comment, but what should you do?

Giving students choices empowers them to think and create. Let's say you are a history teacher. Each of your students has been asked to develop a BioBoard describing the contributions of an important role model. You approach the student who felt he couldn't find himself in his textbooks and suggest several possible role models like Carlos Bulosan, one of the first Filipino American novelists, and the artist formerly known as Prince, the rockstar. If those suggestions do not seem to spark any interest you might ask, "Do you know who Pedro Flores was?"

If the student couldn't answer, you might tell him the following:

Originally from the Philippines, Pedro Flores brought a new top-like toy to the United States (Cordova 1998). Flores migrated to the United States in 1920 and first began working in a hotel. He saw that people were fascinated with the actions of his yo-yo. Flores had good business sense, and so he decided to build a company and trademark his toy with the name of the Flores Yo-Yo (Klutz 1998). Flores was an early entrepreneur and built a toy business in Los Angeles. He was doing well selling yo-yos when Don Duncan became interested in his company. Don Duncan bought the Flores Yo-Yo Company for $25,000 from Pedro Flores in 1927 (Klutz 1998) and, as they say, the rest is history. Even after Pedro Flores sold his business, he continued to demonstrate yo-yos all over the United States. Today, yo-yos are a part of our popular culture and they have seen a revival in recent years. In fact, there are many contests around the world to see who can do the best tricks.

Yo-yos are said to have been around for thousands of years. Some people believe they were invented in China. In addition, there is evidence that children in Greece played with yo-yos made out of wood and clay. In the Philippines the yo-yo was used as a weapon. A yo-yo with sharp points on it was attached to a long rope and thrown at enemies to hurt them. The long rope made it possible to retrieve the weapon after throwing it.

The word *yo-yo* comes from Tagalog, a language from the Philippines. It means "come back." Who would have thought the average U.S. American would know a Filipino term?

The yo-yo was first taken into space by the space shuttle *Discovery* in 1985. David Griggs, an astronaut, conducted several experiments on gravity with the yo-yo in space (Klutz 1998). He found that because there is no gravity in space the yo-yo would not stop and spin at the end of the string. When done on the earth, this trick is called sleeping. The yo-yo didn't take much to come right back up because there is no gravity in space to keep things down.

Pedro Flores probably didn't realize that some teachers would use yo-yos to teach physical science principles. Yo-yos can be used to discuss concepts such as gravity, gyroscopes, centripetal acceleration, momentum, inertia, and rotational energy.

BioBoard #2

Here I will present another idea for a BioBoard. My daughter created a BioBoard when she was in high school. Her teacher, Mr. Torretto, asked each student to choose someone who they wanted to research and who meant something to them. My daughter had many ideas. She talked with me several times about who she might choose. Finally, I asked her who she chose. She said, with a twinkle in her eye, "Mom, you'll just have to wait and see."

Of course, I was very curious. We had talked about many famous U.S. Americans like Eleanor Roosevelt, Martin Luther King, Jr., and Albert Einstein. When she finished making her project, she brought it over for me to see. My daughter had chosen Sadako Sasaki. I didn't know who this was, but I remembered reading a children's book called *A Thousand Cranes*.

My daughter wanted to find out about the young girl who dedicated her short life to world peace. She had remembered the children's book and wanted to find out more about the real Sadako. In fact, the children's book didn't give Sadako's last name, but my daughter discovered her name was Sadako Sasaki.

Sadako dedicated her life to peace. She is known by some people as the Anne Frank of Hiroshima. Sadako wanted to be remembered as a peace maker.

When Sadako was only 2 years old, the United States dropped the first atom bomb on Hiroshima, where she was living. Because her home was so close to where the center of the bomb exploded, she was hurt by the radiation that fell.

Her mother, her brother, and she got in a neighbor's boat and tried to get away from the explosion. Unfortunately, there were many radioactive particles left in the air after the atom bomb exploded, which were falling from the sky onto everyone outside.

Sadako grew up like many other children in Japan. She studied, was healthy, and played with her friends. In fact, Sadako was called "monkey" because she was an agile and fast runner. About ten years after being showered by the radioactive rain, one day she developed a lump in her throat. Her parents thought she had a sore throat. She found out later that she had the atom bomb disease, leukemia, and was very sick.

Sadako was in the hospital for many months and hoped to get back to normal life. In fact, she started a project of making a thousand cranes, because cranes represented long life in Japanese culture. Some people believe that making a thousand cranes will bring a person good luck. Unfortunately, Sadako did not get better and she later died of leukemia.

In Hiroshima, there is the Children's Monument that is dedicated to peace and to the memory of children like Sadako. It is also named the Statue of Sadako.

Several of the questions that my daughter addressed were as follows:

Who was Sadako?
What happened to Sadako?
What did Sadako do to champion world peace?
What impact did Sadako have on world peace?

A larger question that this BioBoard includes is:
Why did the United States drop two atomic bombs on the civilian population in Japan?
My daughter let me share her BioBoard with you. This is what it looks like.

Figure 10.1   *BioBoard*

Her project focuses on Sadako's role in promoting peace. The BioBoard includes a short biography and picture of Sadako, a drawing of the sculpture of Sadako in the Peace Park in Hiroshima, and a timeline of her life in the context of other world events.

✎ Culturally Grounded Stories and Songs

Culturally grounded stories may come in the form of myths, legends, and folktales. These stories are often handed down from generation to generation. They are not necessarily what the general society calls formal literature. An example might be a story that a grandmother told her family about her leaving Mexico to work in the United States, or it might also be a story of the origin of a community like the Haida, a Native community from the Pacific Northwest.

I hesitate to suggest using a legend, myth, or folktale because although these represent important cultural stories, teachers may use them out of context. Teachers may not understand the underlying values that the story is trying to convey and so the deep cultural meanings are lost. Students may remember the storyline, but not much about the belief system of a community.

When I was a young teacher, a member of the Yakima nation from the state of Washington, told a group of educators that people from the majority may refer to American Indian stories as legends or myths and this was a misconception. I distinctly remember the consultant telling us that what others may refer to as legends or myths are actually stories of today because they suggest how people should conduct their lives. The stories are not of old. They are about present-day life. She was expressing her cultural viewpoint. She helped me understand how culturally grounded stories are important in people's lives today and why presenting multiple perspectives is vital in education.

Let me share with you a recent story that has become part of a community's cultural legacy. One holiday season a brick was thrown in the window of a Jewish home that had a menorah in the window. Several other Jewish homes were also vandalized. The members of this small rural town were very upset. They wanted the vandals to stop; however, they didn't know who was at fault. After much sharing in the community, they came up with a unique solution. The members of the town decided that they would all put a menorah in their window, then the vandals wouldn't single out any particular family. This strategy worked. The destruction stopped. But it stopped because everyone worked together. The town's story is used across the United States today to help students understand that it takes moral courage from everyone in the community to stop discrimination.

Teachers and parents often read children's books to their young people. There are many excellent ones like Jamake Highwater's *Moonsong Lullaby,* Sherry Garland's *The Lotus Seed,* Lucille Clifton's *Everett Anderson's 1 2 3,* Allen Say's *Grandfather's Journey,* Francisco Jiménez's *The Circuit,* Faith Ringgold's *Dinner at Aunt Connie's House,* Gary Soto's *Baseball in April,* Gary Paulsen's *Nightjohn,* Patricia Polacco's *Pink and Say,* and Walter Dean Myers's *The Dragon Takes a Wife.* These books depict various aspects of the lives of culturally diverse families in the past and present. However, I am concerned when teachers read picture books depicting a favorite folktale to young children who have no background in the culture presented in the book. For example, if teachers use the original version of the *Five Chinese Brothers* by Claire Bishop, students may learn stereotypical images of the Chinese. This book was published in 1938 and the drawings of the Chinese brothers are extremely stereotypical. I am disturbed by the depiction of the Chinese brothers with large teeth, small or no eyes, and everyone looking almost exactly alike. This book does not represent Chinese Americans or Chinese from China. It is an outsider viewpoint of another group's beliefs, their physical appearance, and story. The important message that the brothers cared for each other and that they each have a unique talent is lost in the negative depiction of the brothers and the others in the book.

Teachers must carefully review the materials they choose to use in the classroom. It is not possible to learn about Multicultural Education one day and then jump in the next day and present "cultural" information. Like many aspects of teaching, choosing materials that are sensitive to and reflect a general perspective of the group is a skill, which requires much knowledge. Cultural information and views have specific contexts, historical backgrounds, and a long tradition of values.

Songs also can reflect the deep values of a cultural community. Civil rights is one of the major contributions that African Americans have given all of us. The commitment of many African Americans can be seen in poetry, stories, folktales, musical styles, and songs. If a teacher is presenting a unit on the 1960s and the contributions of the Civil Rights Movement, she could teach the following song to her students. Some students may already know it; others will have the opportunity to learn a new song. It may even peak the interest of those who have little chance to sing.

A song that has strong civil rights messages is "Lift Ev'ry Voice and Sing" by two teachers who were also brothers, James Weldon Johnson and J. Rosamond Johnson. The song is about fighting for freedom without losing hope. Many African Americans are extremely spiritual and believe in God; this belief is strongly reflected in the piece. This song is often called the Black National Anthem (Johnson 1993). It represents an anthem that African Americans sing about participating fully in society. Here are the lyrics to the song:

Lift ev'ry voice and sing
Till earth and heaven ring,
Ring with the harmonies of Liberty;
Let our rejoicing rise
High as the listening skies,
Let it resound loud as the rolling sea.
Sing a song full of the faith that the dark past has taught us,
Sing a song full of the hope that the present has brought us,
Facing the rising sun of our new day begun
Let us march on till victory is won.
Stony the road we trod,
Bitter the chastening rod,
Felt in the days when hope unborn had died;
Yet with a steady beat,
Have not our weary feet
Come to the place for which our fathers sighed?
We have come over a way that with tears has been watered,

We have come, treading our path through the blood of the slaughtered,
Out from the gloomy past,
Till now we stand at last
Where the white gleam of our bright star is cast.
God of our weary years,
God of our silent tears,
Thou who has brought us thus far on the way:
Thou who has by Thy might
Led us into the light,
Keep us forever in the path, we pray.
Lest our feet stray from the places, Our God, where we met Thee,
Lest, our hearts drunk with the wine of the world, we forget Thee;
Shadowed beneath Thy hand,
May we forever stand.
True to our GOD,
True to our native land.

This song not only provides a cultural story of the values of many African Americans, it also gives another perspective on the oppression African Americans have encountered and still face today. The song is direct in talking about the slaughtering of people, and yet how people rose above the terrible oppression with great faith in God.

Any discussion of issues within U.S. history should include multiple perspectives. In doing so, teachers present a more comprehensive view of our nation and students will gain deeper understanding of our ongoing struggles. The following comic strip explains how African American churches imparted cultural history, viewpoints, and values into the community. Though the person in the comic does not see the song as an anthem, some members of the African American community refer to it as an anthem.

Since a comparative viewpoint provides students with a more comprehensive view of an event, issue, or concept, I also suggest that in teaching the African American National Anthem, you consider using the lesson given in Carl Grant and Christine Sleeter's book, *Turning on Learning,* called "Our National Anthems." They have included an excellent lesson on how students can be guided to look at the issue of national anthems and review different ones (Grant and Sleeter 1998, 217–221). They suggest the following national anthems: "The Star-Spangled Banner," "*Himno Nacional*" (Mexican national anthem), "Lift Ev'ry Voice and Sing" (Black National Anthem), and "Bread and Roses" (women's anthem).

‏ℳ Language and Cultural Expressions

In some ways language provides teachers the most important vehicle for culturally relevant teaching. Much of culture is transmitted through language. There are many teachers who can translate terms, phrases, and ideas into another language. This is a natural aspect of communication. Bilingual education specialists like Eugene Garcia and Lilly Wong Fillmore emphasize the need for children to learn literacy skills in their home language so that those skills and vocabulary will be learned more easily and quickly in English.

Language includes cultural expressions such as metaphors, similes, analogies, images, proverbs, sayings, symbols, and phrases that can be easily included in a teacher's lesson. As I discussed in Chapter 2, these types of cultural expressions bring along not only important cultural images, but also connotations and values. It is important that teachers listen to the phrases and terms children use with each other and those that parents use with their children. For example, one of my African American students often said to me, "Have a blessed day." I was warmed by her kindness and felt a special closeness to her because she shared an important family and cultural saying of good wishes. I later thanked her and wished her "a blessed day" too. Teachers can incorporate affirming cultural phrases into their teaching if they understand the meaning and context in which these expressions can be appropriately used.

My mother used to tell us "*gambare*" which means to grin and bear it. If my teacher had said something like that when I hit my knee I would understand that I am to be tough and hold my head up because I am a strong person. She would not be referring to my physical strength, but to my character. So much is understood in that one word. In this way, my teacher would also be affirming who I was as a Japanese American and know that the word communicated much to me.

There are many examples of cultural phrases and expressions in the Spanish song, "De Colores." The song is about spring and includes a linguistic interpretation of the sound of the rooster, hen, and baby chicks. For example, the hen says, "cara, cara, cara." The rooster says, "quiri quiri quiri quiri quiri." The chick says, "pio, pio, pio, pi." Students can compare the sounds of the animals in various languages found in the classroom.

"De Colores" is a fun song and reminds many people of their childhood. My friend told me that her mother used to sing this song to her when she was a toddler. Then she began to sing it to me and I could hear the happiness in her voice. The song reflected the warmth my friend felt when she and her mother sang the song together, which ties in with the theme of caring and family. "De Colores" is often sung at Latino community affairs because it signifies the importance of unity. Like the many colors of the flowers, we as different people make up a beautiful rainbow. We make up a wonderful family, the human family.

De Colores

Spanish Translation by Cynthia D. Park

De colores
De colores se visten los campos en la primavera
De colores
De colores son los pajarillos que vienen de afuera

De colores
De colores es el arco iris que vemos lucir

Y por eso los grandes amores
De muchos colores
Me gustan a mi,
Y por eso los grandes amores
De muchos colores
Me gustan a mi

Canta el gallo
Canta el gallo con el quiri quiri quiri quiri quiri
La gallina
La gallina con el cara cara cara cara cara
Los pollitos
Los pollitos con el pío pío pío pío pi

Y por eso los grandes amores
De muchos colores
Me gustan a mi
Y por eso los grandes amores
De muchos colores
Me gustan a mi.

All the Colors

English Translation by Cynthia D. Park
All the colors
In springtime the countryside dresses itself in all the colors of the rainbow
All the colors
The birds which return each spring from faraway are marked by all the colors
All the colors
All the colors make up the rainbow which we see shining (across the blue sky)
For these reasons it pleases me that the greatest loves (of the world) are made up of
    all the colors of the rainbow.
Sings the rooster
Sings the rooster with his kiri kiri kiri kiri kiri
(Also) the hen
The hen with her cara cara cara cara cara
And the baby chicks
And the baby chicks with their pío pío pío pío pi
For these reasons it pleases me (greatly) that the greatest loves (of the world) are
    made up of all the colors (of the rainbow).

Another example of the use of language is having students translate traditional literature, like Shakespeare's *Julius Caesar,* into everyday English and place the story in modern terms using their own experiences to frame the plot (Lipman 1998). The students feel more ownership in the learning process and have a deeper understanding of how language takes on many forms. In her research on restructured schools, Lipman (1998) also discovered that when teachers make changes in the curriculum so that it has more meaning to students, there is a lighter climate in the school. One of the teachers she studied said, "You can feel a cheerfulness. It's almost like a song" (Lipman 1998, 256).

Another excellent example of the power of language is the connotations of words. For example when teachers cover various topics in social studies or English, they may want to consider the differences in the way students may respond to terms like slavery and the Holocaust. These terms can represent complex issues with strong implied meanings. A Jewish student whose family members had personal experiences with the Holocaust may have a powerful emotional response to the word and discussions of the issue. The student may also have a more comprehensive understanding of the topic. This can also be said for the issue of slavery. There are members of families who have handed down stories about how the institution of slavery had a devastating impact on their family lives. These descriptions also contain values and beliefs about the issue and shape the way some students view the topic today. Teachers can tap into the rich resources of their students in understanding how phrases, terms, and stories of family members have molded their viewpoints on various aspects of history and understandings of social issues. Teachers may ask students what emotions words evoke. For instance, to some students, the word, slavery, may be almost a neutral term, a term from a textbook, however to another student, the word may evoke strong personal feelings. Students can discuss how the connotations surrounding words may arise from the shared experiences and history of a community.

❧ Multiple Perspectives

One of the most critical ways to facilitate learning is by presenting multiple perspectives on an issue, event, concept, or idea. Multiple perspectives offer students more than one way to understand what is being taught, which is especially important when there is a complex issue to consider.

We live in a world of diversity and it is important for people to hear various viewpoints in resolving issues, whether they are based on city or country, employee or employer, student or teacher, older person or younger, Buddhist or Muslim, mathematician or biologist, or the many other things that we traditionally consider in Multicultural Education. Of course this doesn't mean that we always agree with each other, but as my father used to say, "Life is not supposed to be simple." In a high school conference I attended, students saw diversity in a broad way. They identified themselves as members of various social groupings, such as a jock, Christian, heavy metal, Latin dancer, lesbian, vegan, gay, Jewish, athlete, surfer, born in East Los Angeles, and short. Sharing multiple perspectives encourages dialogue and the possibility of finding common ground. Most important aspects of life need dialogue. When people examine diverse viewpoints, they come to a deeper understanding of their own positions and a respect for those who have opposing views (Nelson, Palonsky, and Carlson 2000).

Let's take the issue of immigration for example. My class watched the movie called *El Norte,* "The North." The movie was about the journey of a sister and brother from Guatemala who sought safety and work in the United States. The two came to the United States without their parents because their father had been murdered by the military and their mother had been taken away and the children did not know where she was. The movie provided information about the struggles of immigrants from Guatemala. Before the teachers viewed the movie, they held many misconceptions. For example, most of the teachers thought that since Mexicans and Guatemalans looked similar, they were from the same place.

After viewing the movie, the students shared the following misconceptions:

a. "I didn't realize there was so much turmoil going on in Central America."
b. "I did not know there was prejudice against the Guatemalans from Mexicans."
c. "I didn't realize that when people come here that they leave behind important aspects of their lives like family, respect, and cultural connections."
d. "I didn't know that people are escaping persecution."

In comparison, the teachers also watched *Becoming American.* This film showed a Hmong refugee family from Laos. The family first lived in a camp in Thailand and finally, after living there for several years, were allowed into the United States. They could not bring everyone in their family and they cried because their extended family couldn't come with them.

Some teachers in the class made the following comments:

a. "I didn't realize the United States used the Hmong as fighters for us."
b. "There is such a rift now between the parents and kids because the kids assimilate much easier than their parents."
c. "I didn't realize how much people give up to come here. Even though they were tortured and killed, the people love their country so much they really don't want to leave it. Leaving must be so difficult."

The teachers examined the similarities and differences of the experiences of each family. Both families missed their countries. Both families had to learn English and found it hard to find jobs. In each situation they were refugees fleeing from persecution. The Guatemalans fled from a country with an oppressive government. The Hmong family fled because they had been allies with the United States during the Vietnam War, and with the Communists in power, the Hmong were seen as the enemy. However, since the Asian family came from a preliterate tradition, they had little knowledge of written communication or schooling. In contrast, the brother and sister from Central America had gone to school and learned English quickly. The process of assimilation for the Guatemalan family seemed to go more rapidly.

The two films gave two perspectives on the issues of immigration and persecution. Both families shared common problems and struggles, but they also displayed different ways of dealing with those struggles. By presenting two different views, the teachers were able to look at the issues in more depth.

❧ *Formal or Traditional Subject Content*

This section describes the traditional subject content already found in schools. The curriculum in schools already includes subjects like history, literature, philosophy, psychology, government, sociology, music, dramatic arts, and visual arts. Is it possible to integrate culture into the traditional content being taught?

The following describes how some teachers have rethought their curriculum roots in social studies. Most history textbooks primarily focus on the growth of the thirteen colonies; history is seen as a movement from the East to the West of the United States.

Many books include mention of Ellis Island in New York, where immigrants were housed before they were allowed in the United States. However, some groups have a different orientation to this history. Angel Island in the San Francisco Bay marks the beginning of the history of many Asian immigrants, because they were held there for many days and months before allowed into the United States. The experience of many Chinese American families begins on the West Coast and moves eastward. A more complete view of U.S. history can be taught when multiple perspectives are presented.

Some educators have made a conscious effort to utilize history texts that provide a comprehensive view of our history. For example, much of our history does entail a movement from the south. States such as California, New Mexico, Arizona, and Texas have roots in Mexican history. The history of many families does not entail a move from east to west, but rather from south to north. My family immigrated to the United States almost a hundred years ago from Japan. My grandfather settled in Hawaii and became a citizen there, and my own father moved to Seattle, Washington. My family history moves from the Hawaiian Islands to the mainland. My neighbor's family is originally from St. Thomas in the Caribbean Islands. He was raised in New York City and now lives in California. Though the East Coast may be the beginning of our formal governmental institutions, citizens have taken many routes of settlement because we are a nation of many peoples.

In fact, indigenous people are the original inhabitants of what we now know as the United States. The Native Americans from the Pacific Northwest do not view history in the same perspective as is presented in our students' textbooks. Many communities believe that their people have arisen from the land and animals that first inhabited the area. These viewpoints should be included because they represent the beliefs of the earliest people. Our traditional subject areas, like history, can include comparative perspectives to demonstrate the diverse nature of our nation.

History, as a formal content area, has begun to accept the contributions of various scholars who present different understandings of diverse groups. The works of researchers like John Hope Franklin, Ronald Takaki, Wilbur Jacobs, and Lee Francis have enriched our knowledge of U.S. history. There are still teachers who see history of underrepresented groups as ethnic history, but many other educators understand that the events, contributions, and people of ethnic groups are integral to U.S. history and therefore pertain to all of us. The teachers are careful to integrate the history of these groups naturally into the curriculum because it is U.S. history.

Literature is another area where cultural content can be easily integrated into the curriculum. In recent years, the curriculum may include literature by writers like Lawson Inada, Sandra Cisneros, John Okada, Toni Morrison, Gary Soto, Alan Lau, Scott Momaday, Garrett Hongo, James Baldwin, Joy Harjo, and Richard Rodriguez. The inclusion of the work of these gifted artists provides another window into the diversity of our nation by providing different points of reference. These authors may not write about well-known cities like Boston or New York City, but rather a small town in central California called Marysville. These authors also present different values. They may challenge blind patriotism. They may utilize different heroes and images. Their heroes might question the status quo. Their written language may arise from a home language other than English and may not adhere to mainstream conventions of grammar and form, but these writers represent U.S. America too.

❧ Community Issues-Centered Curriculum

Integrating community issues into the curriculum can vitalize learning. These issues are part of who students are, what they see as important, and what students stand for as members of communities. The communities may represent a nation-state like the United States or various subgroups that are defined by ethnicity, sexual orientation, hobbies, region, religion, or political interests. Since I believe in encouraging students to think and to critically analyze complex social issues, the most effective approach to higher-order thinking and the integration of subject-matter content is an issues-centered one (Nelson 1996). Jack Nelson provides insights into why this approach benefits all areas in schooling: "Throughout human existence and across cultures and regions, issues have been at the core of the human quest for knowledge. Issues provide motivation, challenge ideas, inform scholars and students, and set criteria for judging progress in civilization. They represent the cauldron within which myth, theory, fact, value, and perspectives mix with multiple realities" (Nelson 1996, 22). Nelson also reminds us that solutions are usually not simple, easy, or quick.

One of the most difficult set of skills that teachers can pass on to their students deals with decision making. It is critical for teachers to provide students with opportunities to explore, clarify, deepen their understanding, and develop ways to make society a more compassionate and just community. There are many ways to accomplish this goal. Issues-centered teaching provides one excellent way to offer comprehensive and motivating study. A real-life example of a person's impact on a social issue is illustrated by the story of Rosa Parks.

Let me share with you the conversation of a group of student teachers and how they came to study the life of Rosa Parks. (Though Rosa Parks is a national hero, the students in your classroom may pick a local hero. To adults and children in this school, she is a national hero with strong local ties.)

Example 1: Teaching About Social Protest: Rosa Parks

A group of student teachers were asked what issue they wanted to develop for an issues-centered assignment. The student teachers first brain stormed. Someone suggested pollution. Another person suggested homelessness. Another student teacher brought forth the idea of Rosa Parks and social protest. There was a chain reaction from the last suggestion. Here is a little of that conversation:

Lucy suggested, "We are going to be teaching at the Rosa Parks Elementary School. I think we should know something about her. That's a great idea."

"I only have a little understanding of what she did. I think it is important that we teach our students who she is. It will give all of us more of a sense of identity and purpose," Bob said enthusiastically.

"Hey, that's a wonderful idea because she visited the school last year and the kids were very excited to meet her," Laura remarked. "She is a great role model of social justice and has so much courage."

After their discussion, the student teachers decided that they would develop a unit, initially for their own understanding. The focal unit question was What should we teach the students about Rosa Parks? The subquestions that they came up with were as follows:

Who is Rosa Parks and why is she important in U.S. History?
What did she do, and why does it exemplify an important social issue?

Rosa Parks: "I sat down for justice."

What is social protest?
What was the Montgomery Bus Boycott; what if it had not happened?
What is the NAACP and why is it important?
Why were Jim Crow Laws enacted and who was responsible?
Why was there segregation in society?
What values did people have in order for segregation to exist?
What role did Rosa Parks play in the Civil Rights Movement?
Should Rosa Parks have defied the law? Why or why not?
Why did she refuse to get up from her seat?
What does she mean to the children at Rosa Parks Elementary School?
Why should we teach students about Rosa Parks and her role in the Civil Rights
        Movement?
Should students today continue to fight for equality and social justice? Why?

Since there were 30 student teachers, they divided themselves into six groups and decided what information and questions each group would address in order for them to gather a comprehensive understanding of the life of Rosa Parks and civil rights issues. Here is a list of the group assignments:

Groups 1, 2, and 3:   Develop a web page that answers the following questions:
        Group 1:   What was Rosa Parks's life like before the bus boycott?
        Group 2:   Why was Rosa Parks arrested? What was the Montgomery Bus
                Boycott?
        Group 3:   What did Rosa Parks do after she was arrested? What impact did
                she have on the national civil rights movement?
Group 4:   Create a teacher newspaper called "Civil Rights For Children Newsletter."

Group 5:   Produce a video called "The Bus Ride: What Happened on December 5, 1955."
Group 6:   Simulate a talk show: Interviewing Rosa Parks, the bus driver, police officer, and passenger.

The student teachers also developed lessons covering important historical information about segregation and the civil rights movement, presented information on the
National Association for the Advancement of Colored People, and reviewed the change
of U.S. policies from segregation toward integration and equality. In addition, the unit
included the following vocabulary words and their definitions: segregation, integration,
racism, oppression, stereotypes, prejudice, discrimination, civil rights, Jim Crow Laws,
equality, boycott, and NAACP.

This information gave the group of student teachers background into the courage, actions, and beliefs of Rosa Parks, as well as the social and historical setting in which she
acted. She became much more than a distant image, but a real person who had great courage.

In their own study, the student teachers discovered that Ms. Parks demonstrated
how one person can make an important stand against racism. As part of an organized
movement against segregation, Rosa Parks was a highly respected member of the community. She was the secretary of the National Association for the Advancement of Colored People (NAACP) in Montgomery, Alabama. She kept track of instances when
African Americans were discriminated against. There had been several other arrests of
African Americans who refused to move from their seats on the bus, but the leadership
of the community was looking for a person who was well known and respected.

On December 1, 1955, Rosa Parks boarded the bus, paid the fare, and sat down
(Parks 1992). She sat in the section labeled "colored." However, when the front of the
bus was filled, the bus driver told her that she must give up her seat to a White man who
had just got on the bus. Rosa Parks refused to move and the bus driver had her arrested.
The police fingerprinted Rosa Parks and put her in jail.

Since many of the riders on the bus were African American, leaders in the African
American community believed a boycott of the buses would be a successful way to
protest inequality. The following message was written all over the city:

"Don't ride the bus to work, school, or any place on Monday, December 5, 1955."

This was the beginning of the Montgomery Bus Boycott. Leaders like E.D. Nixon had
already planned for a boycott, but were waiting for the right situation.

Rosa Parks had the respect of the community and was a woman of great courage.
The leadership decided it was the time to mobilize the boycott. In protest of the arrest of
Rosa Parks and segregation on buses, African Americans and others did not ride the bus
for 381 days (Parks 1992). Martin Luther King, Jr., helped to lead the protest. On November 13, 1956, the Supreme Court outlawed segregation on Montgomery buses. However, most African Americans still would not ride the buses until the Supreme Court order became an official document and was sent to Montgomery.

How did the community deal with having no public transportation? People car-
pooled, took taxis, and walked all over the city during the long boycott. The taxis
charged the same fare as buses. In addition, Rosa Parks worked with the Montgomery
Improvement Association where the community bought cars and used them to take people to their jobs. As a dispatcher, Parks sent these cars out to various individuals
who called in. There were White people who also helped by giving rides to African
Americans. Many people, Black and White, were threatened during the boycott.

The most critical question that the teachers had to debate was Why was there segregation? This question led to an intense discussion about racism. Racism is a difficult issue to address in schools. Many teachers feel uncomfortable talking about it and are unsure as to what to say about it. However, students need the opportunity to think through and discuss racism because it has been and still is a critical problem in our nation and world. It is easier to glide over this as the core issue and talk about social inequalities.

One of the activities in the unit was a decision-making lesson in which the students teachers had to answer the question, Should Rosa Parks have defied the law? This was an important activity because each teacher was asked to take a stand. The decision was a difficult one because the teachers believed that we should obey the laws, but they struggled with what they should do if they believed the law was wrong. Social protest is an important perennial issue for us as citizens. We are members of a democratic republic and have laws that we must follow, but sometimes we may disagree with those laws. It is important for students to consider what their responsibilities are to challenge unjust laws and actions of society.

The student teachers gained a clearer and more comprehensive understanding of the role Rosa Parks played and continues to play in making the United States a more just society. In addition, the student teachers researched other aspects of the civil rights movement. For example, several teachers examined the work of Thurgood Marshall and the *Brown vs. Topeka Board of Education* Supreme Court decision ending segregation in schools.

When the student teachers taught a unit on Rosa Parks, they were able to introduce the activities using a video of Rosa Parks when she visited the school. The students and master teachers who had the opportunity to meet Rosa Parks excitedly talked about meeting her and hearing her speak. It was a great way to excite the students and affirm their identity as a school community. History came alive for students. The students saw that history is not only about the past, but also about today.

In their discussions, students saw Rosa Parks as a caring person who is also a critical civil rights leader. Students took stands regarding the issue of when or how citizens, along with an organized group, can defy a law that they believe is unjust. In addition, student teachers and their children contributed to the school website after studying about Rosa Parks and her courageous actions. They also created a large photo mural of civil rights leaders, both national and local.* This unit was an opportunity for students to see that Rosa Parks was part of a larger movement to make a difference in society. It took the courage of many people, primarily African American, to make our nation address its values of freedom, democracy, and equality.

Example 2: Teaching About Malcolm X: Literacy and Humanity

I have already stressed the importance of enhancing the curriculum by integrating content that interests students. A familiar figure for many students from underrepresented groups is Malcolm X. I asked a friend of mine, Michael, why he chooses to incorporate the life of Malcolm X in his curriculum and classroom.

---

*Many thanks to Joshua Anthony, Lucy Torres, Leslie Fisher, Heather Hawkins, Elizabeth Sparks, Dawn Silhavy, Roseanne Hodges, Bob Ford, Sandy Smith, Rob Gibbs, Dennis Panganiban, Patrice Duggan, Vikki Viarmontes, Linda Villareal, Donna Miller, Sara Camm, Jennifer Bytheway, Suzanne Ellet, Lisa Castro, Annie Bretado, Melissa Ontingco, Laura Mansell, Julia Mulvey, Serena Mulvey, Shauna Howard, and Julie Walsh for sharing their issues-centered units on Rosa Parks.

"I have a picture of Malcolm X and Martin Luther King, Jr., on my wall. Malcolm X and Martin are in a picture together and they are pointing at the temple of their minds and what I use that as is they're pointing to their minds as thinkers. No matter what went on in their life personally, they stood for their beliefs . . . and were willing to die for them. And I gear more towards Malcolm because of his experience with losing his parents and being street-wise and then converting into religion, then rising to become international and not just national . . . I use Malcolm's life as a parable."

Michael continued to explain what students can learn from the life of Malcolm X.

"He is a hero to many African American males, especially those who are struggling in life. Malcolm is also a role model with Mexican American males . . . because what they've been through, what their ancestors have been through . . . "

When asked to talk about what issues of life Malcolm brings to students, Michael said,

"We have to realize we're all human. We make mistakes. We have to reach down. And this is what Malcolm X did. He reached down to people [African Americans and others who have been marginalized by society]. Martin did this too. But Martin had the degree that Caucasians respected. Malcolm got his from in jail when it was nighttime, he was up reading the dictionary, learning the words of the slave master and those same words he used them against them and used them to protect himself when they tried to attack him . . . He studied so much that it caused him to have to wear glasses because he strained his eyes reading so much at night.

Malcolm knew that truth is knowledge and those without knowledge are the ones who are left behind or they're left with the left overs . . . I tell my students that they're a slave to the system if they don't have the knowledge in order to combat ignorance."

Michael shared his insider viewpoint and beliefs about Malcolm X. Michael gave me a richer understanding of Malcolm X's life and how as an African American male he was moved by Malcolm X's work and dedication to the community. Malcolm X is my friend's role model and his life represents the struggle that he and his family go through every day. He gathers strength and a clearer understanding of his own role as a teacher from reflecting upon Malcolm X's life, because Malcolm cared passionately about people, especially those who society had abandoned.

Just after I interviewed Michael, another colleague recommended Theresa Perry's book, *Teaching Malcolm X*. Perry has edited an excellent text where various authors present critical ways to examine and utilize the life and values of Malcolm X in a classroom that is based on democratic reflective thinking and dedicated to a compassionate and just society. I encourage you to read this book because she clearly explains the following important beliefs of Malcolm X:

> Reading and writing affirms one's humanity (Perry 1996, 9).
> Reading and writing is an act of resistance (Perry 1996, 9).
> Reading and writing is a political and communal act (Perry 1996, 9).
> Literacy is freedom (Perry 1996, 18).

Malcolm X: The Interconnections of Literacy and Civil Rights

As I began to study the life of Malcolm X, I was struck with his passionate love of reading and learning. He became a voracious reader. As a child, he had been an excellent student and well liked by his peers. He was someone who also believed in the equal rights and freedom of every citizen and was willing to speak out and ultimately died for his beliefs. In studying Malcolm X, students understand not only the work of an individual, but also how he exemplified and challenged members of the community to become active in their own learning and in the restructuring of a better society.

Since students must be able to interpret, analyze, synthesize, and evaluate information, they must be taught how to examine complicated issues and problems. Many teachers are unsure how issues-centered curriculum differs from a thematic approach. Table 10.1 demonstrates the difference between a theme and issues approach to curriculum. Students gain a broader understanding of Malcolm X's contributions and roles in our lives today by using an issued-centered orientation. In addition, students can learn of the social context of the time. In one of my classes, several teachers, Suzanne Negoro, John Allen, and Lisa Hernandez, raised the following questions while developing a unit on Malcolm X:

1. How might your personal values bias your teaching of Malcolm X? How can you best present the material in a fair and responsible way?
2. What are the ways to teach both the strengths and weaknesses of Malcolm X's life?
3. How can you teach about racism and systems of privilege in a way that will not alienate students who come from privileged status groups?
4. What values does Malcolm X represent of the African American community?

They used these questions to guide them as they developed the unit.

TABLE 10.1

Comparing a Theme Approach to an Issues-Centered Approach
Using the Life of Malcolm X

Theme Topics on the Life of Malcolm X	Focal Questions of an Issues-Centered Curriculum on Malcolm X
Malcolm X	Why was civil rights important to Malcolm X? What role did Malcolm X play in the Civil Rights Movement and U.S. history? Why did Malcolm X believe racism had to be addressed before Black Americans could achieve civil rights in the United States? What if Malcolm X had not lived?
Civil rights	How does Malcolm X exemplify some of the key issues of the Civil Rights Movement? What impact does literacy have on civil rights participation? Why is literacy important to civil rights?
Freedom	Why did Malcolm X believe education was freedom? How can reading and writing impact community and political roles? What role does education play in a democratic nation?
Malcolm X: His life and work	Why are many people unaware of the work and life of Malcolm X? Should students study his life? Why or why not?
Literacy and self-affirmation	Why did Malcolm X believe literacy was a key aspect of what it means to be human? How can literacy be used to affirm a person's humanity?

My preferred model of inquiry and decision making in issues-centered education comes from the work of Byron Massialas and C. Benjamin Cox (1966), Shirley Engle and Anna Ochoa (1988), and Oliver and Shaver (1966). The following adaptation of their models guides students through the identification, research, decision making, and action of an issue. It provides one possible way that the life and work of Malcolm X might be taught in an issues-centered classroom. The questions posed are suggestions only and your students will create much more insightful ones. The more involved students become in shaping the study of an issue, the more effective the unit/lesson will be.

TABLE 10.2

An Issues-Centered Approach to Malcolm X

Orientation	Teacher brings in a poster of Malcolm X.
In this phase, students begin to think and learn about Malcolm X.	Teacher poses questions (examples): **Focal Question:** • Should teachers cover the life of Malcolm X? Why or why not? **Subquestions:** • What were the social issues that Malcolm X passionately addressed in his life? Are those issues still prevalent today? • Why did Malcolm X believe that education was freedom? • Do you think Malcolm X's actions hindered or advanced the progress of civil rights? Why? What role did Malcolm X play in the Civil Rights Movement? • What impact does his race have on how people perceive Malcolm X? Teacher has students read the *Autobiography of Malcolm X* (high school/adult level) by Alex Haley or *By Any Means Necessary: Malcolm X* (middle school level) by Walter Dean Myers. Students begin to explore and clarify aspects of Malcolm X's life. They have posed the following questions: • Who was Malcolm X? • What do you know about his life? • What were his goals? Were any of them like yours? • Why are there many misconceptions about him? • Who killed him and why? • What does the X stand for and why doesn't he have a last name? • Was he racist?

(Continued)

TABLE 10.2 (CONT.)

Identification	Students collaboratively make a timeline of Malcolm X's

Identification

In this phase, students identify key issues that are important to study and research. They also identify facts and concepts and define terms.

Students collaboratively make a timeline of Malcolm X's life. They may also find other materials to read about Malcolm X. In addition, the class lists key issues that would provide important new understandings and knowledge.

Students may also write statements about what they learned discussing Malcolm X.

- Through literacy people could more effectively fight social oppression.
- Freedom of the mind was more important than freedom of the body.
- People must work for and be committed to community and the struggle for equality.
- Malcolm Little fought for the rights of all people, especially the people like African Americans, who had not been treated equally.

Evidence and Multiple Perspectives

In this phase, students seek evidence and describe multiple views and perspectives of the issue.

Students identify different perspectives about Malcolm X. Some people think he was an important leader in the civil rights movement. Others believe he was a hoodlum and was destructive because he defied the law. They can organize the information they have found. Students can identify various communities and individuals and how they differ in their views of Malcolm X.

Students examine competing values and clarify their own beliefs.

Students review original questions from the orientation phase to see if they have gathered sufficient information to answer those questions.

Values and Beliefs

In this phase, students identify their own values and beliefs in relation to the person, event, or issue being studied.

Students identify their own values.

Students identify the values of others.

For example:

- "I thought Malcolm X believed in violence. I can see that he didn't want violence. He believed in community, but also wanted to challenge the system. I agree, but I don't have the courage he had."
- "Malcolm X was too angry and couldn't see part of his anger. Though I felt bad about what happened to him, I think he shouldn't have been as aggressive. That ties in so much with the stereotypes about African American men."
- "I never thought that education gave me freedom in my mind. I thought it was just something I had to do."

TABLE 10.2

- "Malcolm X was about reading and doing. He was awesome. He is my role model now. I think I will try to do better in school because I can be somebody."
- "I believe teachers are afraid to talk about him because they don't know what might happen. Maybe kids will get too aggressive."
- "Malcolm knew it took courage to speak out. People should stand up to change things not sit back and just complain about how things are not fair."

Solutions/Perspectives and Their Consequences In this phase, students deal with values and ethical conflicts and differences. Students look at various perspectives or ideas about resolving a problem. In addition, they identify consequences for each one.	Teacher again asks: Should we teach about Malcolm X in schools today? Why or why not? What if Malcolm X had not lived or he had not become nationally and internationally known? How would the Civil Rights Movement have been different? Students share their views about the impact of Malcolm X on today's youth and society. Teacher asks about consequences of each student position/decision. Possible student discussions: <ul><li>"If we don't talk about Malcolm X we may be losing an important person in our civil rights history. He challenges people to do something about unfairness in society."</li><li>"If we talk about him, people might get mad at each other. He brings up stuff from the past. What happened to Blacks in the past is over. It is only adding salt to the wound."</li><li>"If we don't talk about him, then we are discounting the contribution of a person from the Black community. There is already so much rage about being left out of society or not being treated fairly."</li></ul>
Take a Stand and Justify a Decision In this phase, students provide their argument about why they have decided on their position.	Students replies: <ul><li>"I still believe teachers do not want to teach about Malcolm X because they don't want to talk about racism."</li><li>"Teachers don't really understand Malcolm X. They think he was about violence, but he was really about education because he thought education gave people freedom, freedom of the mind, and that is what was most important."</li><li>"Malcolm X was too violent. He broke laws. Is that right? We must all follow the law or else there would be chaos. He might have gone about getting equality in other ways, more like Martin Luther King, Jr., using nonviolence."</li><li>"Malcolm X stood for all people no matter what their race. He stood for equality and justice. That goes above any one color."</li></ul>

(Continued)

TABLE 10.2 (CONT.)

Action	
In this phase, students develop a plan for action.	• Students may write a letter to the history department in the school asking that more time be spent on the life of Malcolm X.
	• Students may give the book to their friends to read and discuss it with them.
	• Students may decide on volunteering in an after-school program helping younger students with their homework because they see how important education, and literacy in particular, is to kids.

Creating an Integrated Unit on Various Civil Rights Leaders

The previous section presented two units on civil rights leaders, Rosa Parks and Malcolm X. Instead of having separate units, you may want to combine the study of the two individuals as well as adding other role models. I recommend teachers find out more about other important leaders like César Chavez, Mitsue Endo, Black Elk, Minoru Yasui, Eleanor Roosevelt, Gordon Hirabayashi, Lillian Smith, Philip Vera Cruz, and John Brown. As community leaders, they dedicated their lives to social justice. They addressed issues of racism and civil rights. Key questions students might investigate while studying the lives of these important U.S. figures are:

What is justice?
Is the United States a just society? Explain your position.
Are there issues that we as U.S. Americans must address in order to make society
    more just? If so, what issues must we tackle? Whose responsibility is it to take
    on those changes?

In this way, students could examine perennial issues and how these individuals impacted the way society conceived of, acted on, and responded to social justice concerns. Students will develop a more comprehensive understanding of the historical context of each person's life and how his/her actions contributed to a long legacy of civil rights in our country.

An Issues-Centered Unit in Mathematics: Carrying On the Tradition of Malcolm X and Carter Woodson

Teachers often ask me how they can integrate civil rights issues into their math instruction. Bill Tate (1995) has written an excellent article explaining how he collaborated with a teacher, Sandra Mason, who incorporated a social issue into her math class. She taught middle school math in a school that was primarily African American. Mason believed that the goal of schooling is to prepare students to solve the issues that arise in their lives (Tate 1995). Mason had a three-phase teaching approach that integrated math with decision making, student experiences, and participation in a democracy.

The students began the unit by naming issues they believed were hurting their community. In this way, students had the opportunity to express their opinions about a variety of issues and to look at these issues from the viewpoints of others. Students suggested issues like drugs, the AIDS epidemic, sickle-cell anemia, and building the city for the future (Tate 1995). In the first part of the process, they focused upon one problem that the class would address as a community. The students decided to examine the proliferation of liquor stores in the neighborhood and problems that alcohol brought to the community. In the second phase, students researched the issue and decided on strategies to address the problem of too many liquor stores. In the third phase of the activity, students were actively involved in doing something about the liquor stores and the selling of alcohol too close to the school.

The students developed an action plan. They read through the local laws and regulations. In their research students found there were financial benefits for liquor stores to be open for business in the neighborhood. As part of their mathematics, they developed a new incentive plan using percentages, decimals, and fractions (Tate 1995). Next, the young people gathered information about local city codes and measured the distance from the liquor stores to their school.

Next, the students talked with a newspaper editor, who wrote an editorial about the liquor store issue. Students developed short presentations in which they used mathematics to discuss the issue and carefully describe their arguments. This led to a meeting with congressional representatives in the state capital. The members of the class also developed a plan to move the liquor stores and presented their proposal to the city council. Their plan included a tax savings benefit for those liquor stores who moved away from the school. Through the brave actions of the students and their teachers the police gave over two hundred citations to various liquor stores and two of the stores were even pushed to close. In addition, the city council passed a resolution that stated liquor could not be drunk within six hundred yards of the school.

Sandra Mason's educational beliefs grew out of a civil rights orientation and the work of Carter Woodson. She believed it was critical for schools to address the realities of the lives of African American students. She felt it was even more important for students to learn mathematics skills and concepts because many African American young people have not been successful in math. Tate summarized the accomplishments of the teacher: "Mason's pedagogical strategies represent efforts to 'center' her students in the process of acquiring knowledge for social change. Her success represents the power of returning to the root of African American tradition" (Tate 1995, 172).

Using an Issues-Centered Approach to Teaching Science: Research Findings

What have researchers found about using an issues-centered, relevant, integrated approach to teaching? I have shared with you various studies focusing on language arts skills development, social studies, and mathematics. Jeffrey Weld (1999) looked at the research in teaching science. He found that teachers using the Science/Technology/Society (STS) approach had improved academic achievement. STS is an approach that integrates contemporary issues facing students and society. Students problem solve. For example, students in a high school ecology class may list topics they would like to research. Let's say they decided to investigate the level of pollutants in a neighborhood creek. Students choose various roles. One person may go to the library to find out background information about the creek, such as its history and any news stories about it.

Another student would interview local ecologists who might have studied the creek and the wildlife. Others may develop a multimedia presentation at the conclusion of the unit so all the information can be shared with the entire class (Weld 1999).

The STS approach has been extremely successful (Weld 1999). Young women find science is fun and they perform as well as their male peers. In addition, the attitude of most students is significantly more positive. In one research study, Weld reports that girls and boys had similar success on the Iowa Tests of Basic Skills after being part of STS science classes. Results with students of color are also impressive. These students were more positive about science after STS classes and they made more gains on the Iowa Tests of Basic Skills in comparison to underrepresented students in traditional class-rooms. The context in which information is presented has a powerful role in the motiva-tion, interest, and performance of students.

✎ Caring and Justice:
Integrating the Two Values in the Curriculum

In this chapter, culture and curriculum were brought together to talk about culturally rel-evant teaching. Caring and justice are two values that continually appear throughout the chapter. Educators must focus on teaching students how to care for each other and them-selves within a society that values freedom and justice. Teaching how to care must be part of the common curriculum of schools.

Nel Noddings provides suggestions for a curriculum of care in her book, *The Chal-lenge to Care in Schools*. Noddings recommends that students be encouraged to think about themes of caring. Here is a sampling of questions that she suggests:

Overarching question: How can we prepare students to build a better society?
Subquestions:

What can we do to ease racial tensions?
How can women and men learn about caregiving?
Why do we have insider and outsider groupings?
What can we do about unequal relationships?

Noddings goes into depth about caring from a variety of viewpoints such as an individ-ual, within a friendship, and at a distance from those we do not know. The book is an ex-cellent way to begin to think about the ethic of caring. She stresses the importance of continuous dialogue with others in order to address and solve our social problems. She also notes that students need the opportunity to understand themselves and the groups of which they are members. Noddings also emphasizes caring for ideas. Students should be engaged in creating and thinking.

As a teacher educator, I believe we must guide our students toward intellectual growth. We must also mentor our students to learn how to communicate with people who have many different values. Students must be able to talk with people from many dif-ferent communities who represent various cultural and linguistic styles and values. I see that people from various communities understand the concept of caring in different terms. For example, a fourth generation Japanese American young woman told me she thought it was important to tell people what she felt even if it wasn't what the other per-son wanted to hear. In the same conversation, an Asian Indian woman, who was born in

India, disagreed with the first woman saying that she thought a caring person would understand the cultural laws of the panAsian community and know that it wasn't appropriate to be that brash or outspoken because it could be interpreted as being too critical. Since they had reciprocal trust, they were willing to continue talking in an attempt to find some common ground. This was not easy, but they were finally successful.

Here are a variety of questions for you to consider, which all have to do with the ethics of caring:

What is caring to me?
Why do people care for each other and for ideas?
How are caring and community interrelated?
What are the characteristics of a caring community?
What role do the values of caring play in my personal and professional life as a
    teacher?
What does caring mean in other cultures?
How do different cultures operationalize caring?
What common ground can I find with those who seem to be from unfamiliar
    communities?
What linkages can I make with parents, students, and other teachers?
What do I do now to teach them how to be more caring?
How can I make the classroom more democratic and caring?

The answers to these questions will vary depending on your own personal relationships, membership in various community groups, and values. I encourage you to reflect upon each question and find ways to ask your own students about them. I feel that our job as teachers is not only to encourage intellectual growth, but also human growth. This is an extremely challenging task, but we can do it. As Noddings writes, "The primary aim of every teacher must be to promote the growth of students as competent, caring, loving, and lovable people" (Noddings 1992, 154).

Summary

In this chapter I suggested ways to integrate cultural content into the curriculum. Using curriculum as a vehicle is often the most comfortable way for many teachers to integrate culture into their classroom. Using an issues-centered approach, teachers can guide their students to examine complex social problems. This approach focuses on higher-order thinking and decision-making skills. When that is not possible, teachers can use the following seven components to integrate cultural content into their curriculum: students' personal experiences, role models, culturally grounded stories, songs, and photos, language and linguistic expressions, multiple perspectives, formal subject content, and community issues.

In collaboration with cultural content is the sociocultural context of learning. As I have discussed in previous chapters, there is a cultural rhythm in many classrooms where teachers understand the culture of their students. However, as I mentioned previously, when teachers have children from twenty different cultures in their classroom, it is not possible to holistically respond to each culture because that requires insider knowledge. Yet, teachers can provide other ways to integrate the home and cultural knowledge of students, which affirms who they are and provides a cognitive bridge to new information and skills. This is an exciting challenge and requires teachers to spend much time observing and listening carefully to their students. Your students are often the most important cultural resources in a school.

Have fun being creative. When you get to know your students, they often act as cultural mediators for other students. In this way, you will learn much from them. Teaching is always a two-way street. You present information to students and they respond and present new ideas to you!

Teacher Reflections

1. Role models are an important aspect of teaching and living. Identify several of your own personal role models and why you chose them. Now let me ask you to list White people who are civil rights activitists or antiracists. Many teachers talk about reducing prejudice and discrimination, and yet they offer few antiracist role models who are White. This has been the most difficult question that I have asked teachers in class. They cannot come up with many names of White people who have worked hard to eliminate racism. When I ask for African American civil rights role models, immediately they say Martin Luther King, Jr., or Harriet Tubman or Jesse Jackson. Can you list White civil rights role models that you know in your journal? Teachers have mentioned Branch Rickey, the manager for the Brooklyn Dodgers who first hired Jackie Robinson. There is also Morris Dees who founded the Southern Poverty Law Center. John Brown was another role model, but someone few people know. He was an important abolitionist. There is also Eleanor Roosevelt. If you can't think of any white antiracist role models, maybe that would be a good research project for you to consider.
2. Teaching students how to care for themselves and others is an important educational goal. If schools are to be centers of caring as Noddings has suggested, what units or issues could you integrate into the curriculum? As she has recommended, the units may deal with personal health, health costs, the study of religions, relationship building, and moral development. Which issues would you present, knowing the needs of your students? Make and list and begin thinking of how you might develop those issues.

Further Readings

Au, Katherine. 1992. Constructing the theme of a story. *Language Arts, 69:*106–111.

Cajete, Gregory. 1993. *Look to the mountain: An ecology of indigenous education.* Skyland, N.C.: Kivaki Press.

Cleary, Linda Miller, and Thomas D. Peacock. 1997. *Collected wisdom: American Indian education.* Boston, Mass.: Allyn and Bacon.

Nelson, Jack L., Stuart B. Palonsky, and Kenneth Carlson. 2000. *Critical issues in education.* Boston, Mass.: McGraw-Hill.

Pang, Valerie Ooka, and Li-rong Lilly Cheng. 1998. *Struggling to be heard: The unmet needs of Asian Pacific American children.* Albany, N.Y.: SUNY Press.

Philips, Susan. 1972. *The invisible culture: Communication in classroom and community on the Warms Spring Reservation.* New York: Longman.

Ramirez, Manuel, and A. Castaneda. 1974. *Cultural democracy, bicognitive development, and education.* New York: Academic Press.

Swisher, Karen Gayton. 1994. American Indian learning styles survey: An assessment of teachers' knowledge. *Journal of Educational Issues of Language Minority Students, 13:* 59–77.

References

Amanti, Cathy. 1995. Teachers doing research: Beyond classroom walls. *Practicing Anthropology, 17*(3): 7–9.

Bishop, Claire Huchet. 1938. *The five Chinese brothers.* New York: Coward-McCann.

Clifton, Lucille. 1977. *Everett Anderson's 1 2 3.* New York: Holt, Rinehart and Winston.

Cole, Michael. 1996. Cultural psychology: A once and future discipline. Cambridge, Mass.: Belknap Press of Harvard University.

———. 1998. Can cultural psychology help us think about diversity? Presentation delivered at the American Educational Research Association Meetings, San Diego, Calif., April 13–18.

Cordova, Fred. 1998. The legacy: Creating a knowledge base on Filipino Americans. In Valerie Ooka Pang and Li-rong Lilly Cheng, eds., *Struggling to be heard: The unmet needs of Asian Pacific American children.* Albany, N.Y.: SUNY Press.

Delpit, Lisa. 1995. *Other people's children.* New York: New Press.

Engle, Shirley and Anna Ochoa. 1988. *Education for democratic citizenship: Decision-making in the Social Studies.* New York: Teachers College Press.

Garland, Sherry. 1993. *The lotus seed.* San Diego: Harcourt Brace Jovanovich.

Gee, James. 1996. *Social linguistics and literacies.* Bristol, Pa.: Taylor and Francis.

Gonzalez, Norma. 1995. The funds of knowledge for teaching project. *Practicing Anthropology, 17*(3): 3–6.

Grant, Carl, and Christine Sleeter. 1998. *Turning on learning.* 2nd ed. Columbus, Ohio: Merrill.

Highwater, Jamake. 1981. *Moonsong lullaby.* New York: Lothrop, Lee and Shephard.

Jiménez, Francisco. 1997. *The circuit: Stories from the life of a migrant child.* Albuquerque, N. Mex.: University of New Mexico Press.

Johnson, James Weldon. 1993. *Lift ev'ry voice and sing.* New York: Walker and Company.

Klutz. 1998. *The Klutz yo-yo book.* Palo Alto, Calif.: Klutz.

Lipman, Pauline. 1998. Race, class and power in school restructuring. Albany, N.Y.: SUNY Press.

Massialas, Byron G., and C. Benjamin Cox. 1966. *Inquiry in social studies.* New York: McGraw-Hill Books, Inc.

Moll, Luis, Cathy Amanti, D. Neff, and Norma Gonzalez. 1992. Funds of knowledge: Using a qualitative approach to connect homes and classrooms. *Theory into Practice, 31* (2): 132–141.

Moll, Luis, Javier Tapia, and K. Whitemore. 1993. Living knowledge: The social distribution of cultural resources. In G. Salomon, ed., *Distributed cognitions.* Cambridge, Mass.: Cambridge University Press.

Moses, Robert P., M. Kamii, S. M. Swap, and J. Howard. 1989. The algebra project: Organizing in the spirit of Ella. *Harvard Educational Review, 59* (4): 423–443.

Myers, Walter Dean. 1995. *The dragon takes a wife.* New York: Scholastic.

Nelson, Jack. 1996. The historical imperative for issues-centered education. In Ronald W. Evans and David Saxe, eds. *Handbook on teaching social issues.* Washington, D.C.: National Council for the Social Studies.

Nelson, Jack, Stuart Palonsky, and Kenneth Carlson. 2000. *Critical issues in education: Dialogues and dialectics.* Boston, Mass.: McGraw-Hill.

Noddings, Nel. 1992. *The challenge to care in schools: An alternative approach to education.* New York: Teachers College Columbia University.

Oliver, Donald W. and James P. Shaver. 1966. *Teaching public issues in the high school.* Logan, Utah: Utah State University Press.

Parks, Rosa. 1992. *Rosa Parks, my story.* With Jim Haskins. New York: Dial.

Paulsen, Gary. 1993. *Nightjohn.* New York: Delacorte Press.

Perry, Theresa. 1996. *Teaching Malcolm X*. New York: Routledge.

Polacco, Patricia. 1994. *Pink and say*. New York: Philomel Books.

Ringgold, Faith. 1993. *Dinner at Aunt Connie's house*. New York: Hyperion Books for Children.

Say, Allen. 1993. *Grandfather's journey*. New York: Houghton Mifflin.

Soto, Gary. 1990. *Baseball in April and other stories*. San Diego: Harcourt Brace Jovanovich.

Tate, William F. 1995. Returning to the root: A culturally relevant approach to mathematics pedagogy. *Theory into Practice: Multicultural Education, 34* (3): 166–173.

Torretto, Ronald. 1999. Private interview, March 25, 1999.

Weld, Jeffrey. 1999. Achieving equitable science education. *Phi Delta Kappan, 80* (10): 756–758.

Chapter 11

How Can I Remain Reflective in My Teaching?

$\mathcal{T}$his is the last chapter, but it is not the final word. I hope this chapter gives you much more to think about as you continue on your journey of teaching. This is not the stopping point; the goal of this chapter is to present suggestions and questions that can help you continue your process of reflection. I present two models; one can assist you in assessing how meaningful your teaching is to students and the other summarizes the six areas of reflection that I have covered in this text.

Caring-Centered Multicultural Education calls for *teaching that is meaningful and affirming* to students. When teachers care for their students they reflect on what they say and do and how it impacts their students. Teachers continually think about the following key questions:

Are my students learning?
What am I doing to create a caring and affirming learning community?
How am I integrating the cultural context of students in my classroom every day?
In what areas can I improve my skills and knowledge? Who can I ask to help me?
Am I a good role model for social justice and caring? How do I act toward students?

In the classroom, students must understand the connections to and relevance of what we do every day. Though everything we teach in schools cannot be fun, a teacher who cares listens to students and makes relevant connections between school skills and the real world.

For example, when I was 9 years old, I told my fourth grade teacher that I got an allowance of 25 cents the first of every month. I would be so excited around the end of each month. I would look forward to the quarter my dad gave me; I could hardly wait. I did not like learning my times tables because I thought it was extremely boring, so my teacher told me how many candy bars I could buy using multiplication. I learned my times tables more quickly. If I saved two months' allowance, my teacher reminded me that I would have 50 cents. The small corner market, George's, would sell candy bars at 5 cents a piece each or six candy bars for 25 cents. So if I could save up two months' allowance, I could buy twelve candy bars. If I could save three months' allowance, I could get eighteen candy bars and eat them all AT ONCE. What a wonderful vision. Not only did my teacher create a motivating context for learning the times tables, but she also conveyed her belief that she knew I could learn them if I would just apply my brain!

Get to know your students so that you might be able to come up with a context in their lives and relate the information you are teaching to their living experiences.

❧ Setting Goals and Knowing Where You Are Going

It is important that teachers set clear goals that will assist them in reaching each student. I encourage you to think about your classroom and school's goals and write them in your journal. One of the books that I have found most helpful in giving an overview of how to develop goals and ways educators can implement them was written by General John Stanford with Robin Simons. It is called *Victory in Our Schools*. Stanford was a much loved superintendent for the Seattle Public Schools in the 1990s. Initially, few people believed that a retired general would be able to turn a school district around, because he wasn't a former teacher. Many skeptics did not realize that General Stanford had a positive vision of what a community could do for its children, and he had the skills to lead them. He was able to energize the city behind his vision. His vision became the city's vision. The children and students believed in him as well. Here is the oath that he wrote and shared with the city on the first day of school when students, parents, and teachers gathered at a large stadium:

Oath on Behalf of Children

- I, John Stanford, do solemnly affirm that I will love, cherish, and protect every child entrusted to my care.
- I affirm that I will endeavor to prepare all students to meet the highest standards of achievement, conduct, and citizenship possible, knowing that this will help to maintain the health of our city both now and in the future.
- I affirm that I will work cooperatively with parents and members of the community to produce a world-class, student-focused learning system for our precious children and students." (Stanford, September 1997).

Stanford focused on creating clear goals and a plan to reach those goals based on his philosophy shared in the oath (Stanford and Simons 1999, 16). He stressed the importance of every element of the plan to directly support a goal. The goals must also be measurable so we can tell if we have reached them. Each person who is involved in the process must be accountable for the success of the plan. In our schools, our goals must have time tables and people identified as responsible for them. A collaborative task force for the district identified the following five goals for Seattle schools:

1. Increase academic achievement.
2. Recruit, develop, and retain an effective diverse workforce.
3. Create and maintain a healthy, safe, and secure learning environment.
4. Seek stable and sufficient funding for schools.
5. Increase the ability of the district to respond to and meet the needs of diverse students and parents and to attract and retain more students.

From these broad goals, teachers in each school developed school plans with detailed strategies that put into place new practices. For example, the staff at one of the elementary schools, Sanislo, set the goal of increasing parent involvement because they felt that would fit into their goal of increasing academic achievement. The school faculty created and put into place many activities for parents. Parents were asked to require their children to read twenty minutes every night and then children were to bring in signed sheets from their parents. The school followed up with a "Reading Thermometer" so everyone could see they were contributing to the school goal of 50,000 nights of reading. In addition, teachers developed weekly homework packets and included letters to parents describing how they could help their children in completing their work. They established a family reading night once a year when families bring sleeping bags and stay overnight at the school. Everyone brings books to read and it is fun to see parents and children spread on blankets and tumbling mats in their pajamas. Another innovative activity is the family fitness night. Families come to school and they join in many different physical activities, like jump roping, roller blading, or juggling. To increase literacy, books on tape are also available in the school library for parents or students to check out with cassette tape recorders.

Superintendent Stanford was an excellent leader not only because of his skills in setting goals and developing plans, but also because he had a deep commitment to children, which came from his soul. He was a bright light in a dark storm, showing people that not only did they need technical skills, but they also had to believe in the children, believe that they could make a difference. Stanford was a role model of both leadership and love; one did not come without the other. One of his sayings was, "Loving and leading means creating victories every day."

When Stanford talked about love in the schools, he also meant that teachers and principals needed to be cared for too. In order for teachers to be successful they must also be loved. Stanford gave an example of a caring principal in his book (Stanford and Simons 1999). He talked about the leadership of Eric Benson at Nathan Hale High School. Benson showed his love of his staff through the many little things he did every day. He fought for the resources they requested. Benson found resources to provide his faculty with the planning time they needed. In addition, he often celebrated and congratulated his teachers. For example, he remembered their birthdays and put notes of thanks in their mail boxes. He honored their success whether it was with specific students, earning advanced degrees, or engaging in volunteer work. Benson had yearly teacher appreciation dinners and thanked teachers with dinner certificates, hotel getaways, and other gifts from local businesses. Within this context, teachers and students grew in environments that were meaningful and that honored them.

❧ Meaningful Teaching

What is meaningful teaching? It is teaching that oftentimes comes out of and incorporates the lived experiences of students. Meaningful teaching is relevant, interesting, and purposeful to *all students*. When we respect and are committed to our students, we want to listen and know about them. This shows how we care. Looking at life from other perspectives enriches our knowledge of the world, especially in a classroom where children may speak ten different languages and come from many communities. This challenge is a difficult but exciting aspect of being a teacher, creating a community of learners who come from diverse backgrounds.

An excellent way of designing relevant programs for students is to ask them their opinions about the needs of the community and use that information in creating relevant curriculum. In Philadelphia, the University of Pennsylvania organized the West Philadelphia Improvement Corps (WPIC) after interviewing several teachers and approximately one hundred students about what could be done to improve their schools and neighborhoods. From their responses, WPIC designed and implemented a plan that included landscaping, removal of graffiti, and other neighborhood beautification projects (Nothdurft 1989). WPIC was a coalition of the University of Pennsylvania, local corporations, community agencies, and schools, and the project rose out of the beliefs of the students; therefore, the young people could see how school and the real world were linked. They also saw their efforts did make a difference! Through this program, students learned geometry and carpentry by being involved in rehabilitating row houses, learned biological principles by running a greenhouse, and learned economic principles in being responsible for a school store. Dropout rates decreased and the academic achievement of students increased. Several of the WPIC schools have become community centers with outside funding. This program demonstrated that connecting learning in schools to real life is a key element.

Another aspect of relevancy in the classroom deals with culture. Evangelina Bustamante-Jones (1998) believes that teachers must act as cultural mediators. Teachers should explain to children and help them understand the differences in values and social contexts. In this way, teachers can honor both the world of the child and the majority society. As cultural mediators, teachers can affirm both the home and school cultures. Teachers must have the ability to take school information and skills and make connections to the lives of their children.

In order to be cultural mediators teachers must have time to reflect upon the five areas found in Table 11.1. These areas highlight key aspects that contribute to meaningful teaching practices: collegial discussions, personal reflection of values and beliefs, meaningful content knowledge development, meaningful practice, and purposeful accountability. Teachers must reflect on all components of the meaningful teaching model. Together, the five components work collaboratively and integrally as if to create a large tapestry. If any area is missing, a hole in the fabric will appear. Each component contains a series of recommendations, but they are not separate lists. The suggestions represent attitudes, knowledge, and skills teachers need to consider when creating a caring, culturally affirming, and effective classroom. Table 11.1 explains each of the five areas.

Collegial Discussions

One of the most exciting aspects of teaching is to find others who are willing to share and learn together in a safe, nonthreatening environment of encouragement. Changes in schools can occur when teachers have open lines of communication with each other. Collegial discussions serve as a support system, but they also help teachers to grow and develop their teaching gifts and understanding of the school system. Many times teachers are so busy trying to survive on their own, having a support group of others helps to breathe life into the profession. Discussions may focus on the following questions:

TABLE 11.1

Meaningful Teaching

Collegial Discussions	Personal Reflection of Values and Beliefs	Meaningful Content Knowledge Development	Meaningful Practice	Purposeful Accountability
• Create/ clarify mission, integrating values of caring, justice, culture, and effective teaching. • Discuss institutional issues of equity, such as tracking, discipline policies, and monocultural curriculum. Design ways to address them. • Discuss impact of culture (language, cultural conflict, cultural relevancy). • Discuss prejudicial attitudes (such as racism, sexism, classism, homophobia) found in the students and teachers. Find ways to eliminate them.	• Review one's personal biases. • Look at one's own competing values. • Reflect on personal behavior. • Reflect on contrasting viewpoints. • Review teaching goals. • Review one's expectations of students. • Reflect on one's understanding of race, class, ethnic, and gender issues and how they impact one's teaching. • Reflect on growth as a teacher.	• Learn about the history of underrepresented groups. • Learn about the history of women. • Review current immigration issues and immigration history. • Learn about language acquisition processes, bilingual education, and multicultural education. • Reflect on how the economic status of various groups impacts their social status. • Learn about the cultures of students in the class. • Strengthen your knowledge of liberal arts and science, math, and technology. • Learn about caring in various cultural contexts. • Find out what issues are impacting students' lives.	• Tie instruction to the student's world. • Use relevant content. • Build caring relationships with students. • Use cultural experiences, such as cultural analogies, stories, history, literature, and shared life experiences. • Use purposeful decision-making and problem-solving activities. • Model the concepts one teaches. • Assist students in finding common ground with each other through cooperative group work and dialogue. • Create an issues-centered curriculum based on students' lives.	• Seek evidence demonstrating student learning for all groups of students. • Seek evidence that changes are being implemented to create a caring and equitable school. • Keep a journal of progress of students, strategies that work and do not work, and insights. • Review the articulation of skills and knowledge one teaches. • Listen carefully to your students—they often provide important feedback. • Build a professional portfolio focusing on teaching effectiveness.

What is our mission?

What kind of classroom am I trying to create?

What do caring and social justice mean on the classroom level?

What works best with children?

How can I best understand institutional barriers that may be biased?

How can I change those institutional barriers?

What can I do with my colleagues to change those institutional barriers?

What richness do my students and their parents bring to the classroom?

Let me give you an example of how powerful dialogue can be. In a high school, several students went to speak to an English teacher. This teacher was one of the informal leaders in the school, but the students did not know that. They saw him as a caring and listening adult at the school.

Here is a sample of their conversation:

Cindy: "Mr. Johnson, we wanted to talk with you about something that bothers us here. We knew you would listen. We don't know if there is anything we can do."

   She begins to look down at the floor. Her friend interjects.

Araceli: "Mr. Johnson, some of the kids aren't eating lunch. They won't get in *those* lines." Her voice is emphatic and frustrated.

Cindy: "Yes, it's humiliating. It isn't right."

Mr. Johnson: "Can you explain why kids aren't eating? What lines are you talking about?"

Cindy: "We feel ashamed of getting free lunch. Didn't you know there are separate lunch lines for kids on free or reduced lunch?"

Mr. Johnson shook his head no.

Araceli: "Mr. Johnson, we aren't the only students not eating. There are so many kids who just won't get in those lines. They feel the other kids are looking at them. We are in high school. This is different from elementary school. Don't the teachers care about how we feel?!!!!"

Cindy: "I graduate this year and I am counting the days. I can't wait to get out of here because the school doesn't care about us."

The lunch bell rang. It was time to return to classes.

Mr. Johnson: "I didn't know this was happening. I usually eat lunch in the teachers' room so I don't see what the students are doing at lunch. Let me look into this. I don't want you to miss your lunch. Thanks for letting me know. I will let you know if something can be done. In the meantime, let's work out something so you two will eat your lunch."

The students hurried to class. Mr. Johnson was left in his portable watching his fifth period students come into class. His face was serious. Mr. Johnson was extremely troubled after talking with Cindy and Araceli.

Since Mr. Johnson was the head of the English department of the high school, he felt it was best to raise the issue first with teachers on his team. He wondered if other teachers were aware of this problem.

When he shared the lunch line issue with members of his team, he found that few teachers knew this was happening. They looked at Mr. Johnson with blank stares.

Mrs. Wong said, "I didn't know this was happening to students. Why wasn't something done right away?"

Mr. Rodriguez agreed. "I don't think most teachers know about it."

After some discussion, they asked a small group of teachers and students, led by Mr. Johnson, to see the principal. A coalition of teachers and students working together became an empowered group. This coalition not only helped teachers become more sensitive to the needs of their students, but it taught students how to develop their own "voice" and become active in social change.

The principal was aware of the problem and knew that there were students who were not eating their lunch. He said, "We just don't know what to do. This has been a continual problem over the years. In the beginning we had few students who qualified for the reduced or free lunch, but now there are many more. So to accommodate them, we put in two lines only for free and reduced lunch students. It is a cafeteria management issue."

After some discussion, the principal agreed to bring up the issue at the monthly school faculty meeting.

Few teachers knew of the practice.

Mr. Johnson became very frustrated. He felt the school had numerous oppressive practices and this was one of them. The issue of social class had become an important one because the high school, though located in an upper-middle-class neighborhood, also bordered a lower-income community. This practice showed the school was insensitive to class issues.

Apparently, separate lunch lines was a district practice because the cafeteria division had mandated it. After numerous meetings with district administrators, high school administrators, and teachers, the small group of faculty and students led by Mr. Johnson finally convinced district administrators to provide students with individual lunch numbers. Students told clerks their number when paying for lunches. Though this was not a perfect solution, it did eliminate separate lines for free/reduced lunch participants and other students. For the school of 2,000 high school students, this was a major change.

Many teachers at this school did not know about the issue, but since some were open to students, their students shared their frustrations. Schools are extremely hierarchical systems. Cindy and Araceli learned to take a stand about an issue that was important to them. The students realized that their high school was not as democratic as they had thought, and they had to challenge the school structure.

Teachers at this high school needed time to reflect on school practices and what some of those practices said to students. Change was slow, but a compromise was made. When committed teachers and students continue to bring up important issues as shown in this situation, it is possible to make structural changes.

Some students at this school did not feel that they mattered. How welcomed do you think the hungry students felt? Some teachers felt that the students had made a choice not to eat and that was their own problem; however, other teachers felt that the school was also responsible for this problem, which impacted the learning process of some of the students they were desperately trying to reach. The food issue also became an opportunity to put into practice the citizenship skills the students were learning in history. It also reminded teachers and students that together they were more powerful to make changes, than working separately or ignoring problems.

The following comic explains how everyone wants to be treated with respect. In the lunchroom issue, some students felt they had been forgotten. They were upset about missing lunch, but the students were most upset about not being treated with dignity.

High school students may have adult-size bodies, but like many younger students, they continue to need nurturing, care, and guidance. Lack of food and understanding impacted the learning of some of the students at this high school. The lunch line was much more than just one issue; it was symptomatic of the isolation and frustration some students felt because of class differences. Because the school did not address class issues, there were students who did not have a sense of belonging to the school community.

Personal Reflection of Values and Beliefs

The second area for reflection is values and beliefs. This book is primarily aimed at personal change. All of us must examine our views, beliefs, and values about race, ethnicity, class, gender, religion, sexual orientation, neighborhood, physical appearance, and many other social aspects of life. Most of us operate from a complex belief system and many of our values are not clearly understood until we are challenged to look at them or when we have taken the time to clarify them. One's behavior often indicates one's values, and others may comment on what they see in us. Though we might not agree with what others see in us, we can begin to examine our behaviors and values with the goal of becoming more effective and caring teachers.

As the lunchroom example demonstrated, we must also examine how schools as institutions, through their practices and policies, teach and support certain values. For example, the issue of the lunch line indicated that the management needs of the district cafeteria personnel at that high school were more important than the feelings of the students. The students knew this. The school was part of a large bureaucratic system and making changes in that system was difficult. However, as teachers responsible for the education of every student, we must work tirelessly to make those institutional and personal changes.

We are part of a community. We do not have all the answers and never will, but if we work with students and parents, we can examine what we think, believe, and do. For example, teachers have found that they may ask male students more often than female students to take on leadership positions. Reflect on your unconscious and conscious beliefs. Reading pieces by educators like Herbert Kohl have challenged me to reflect on my own personal behaviors and how my actions may reinforce institutional values that are clearly wrong. Kohl (1982) gave an eye-opening story in his book, *Basic Skills,* about Christine, a bright high school student, who was labeled as "handicapped" by her teacher in fourth grade. One day, five dollars was stolen from a student in her class. The teacher demanded to search every student's desk or pocketbook. Christine resisted, saying that if the teacher searched her purse, she would search the teacher's. Christine knew she did not have five dollars and it was more likely that the teacher had five dollars. Christine said that whoever had the money would be the thief. She was sent to the psychologist and reassigned to a special education class. Not only was the labeling of Christine as "handicapped" disturbing, but also the teacher's actions toward her were unloving and undemocratic (Kohl 1982). Searching every student's desk and purse was not a way to build a sense of trust or community. However, Kohl believes that both students and teachers suffer from school systems that are demoralizing and depressing. Christine showed she believed in herself by standing up, and later in her schooling she became president of her high school.

Meaningful Content Knowledge Development

Lee Shulman, a former professor at Stanford University, has specifically focused upon the importance of the teacher's knowledge. This knowledge can be of teaching methods, but he also means knowledge of core subject areas. Teachers need a strong liberal arts, math, science, and technological background. In many universities, elementary teachers earn a degree in liberal studies in order to develop a strong comprehensive content background. Some teachers also seek out historical and cultural knowledge, because the United States is a nation of many peoples and educators must be able to present knowledge of our diverse communities.

Teachers must have a comprehensive understanding of U.S. history, and the contributions of both majority and underrepresented communities. For example, teachers must have knowledge not only of the original thirteen colonies and their beginnings, but also of Native American nations who aided the colonists and who were the original inhabitants of the area. I was going to use the term "settlers," but this would not be accurate because many Native American peoples believe they are ancestors of the earth and arose from the land. Few Native Americans see themselves as "settlers," which has a connotation of people moving into an area and making changes. Many Native peoples came from and lived in balance with their natural environments.

The following story shows how a high school U.S. history teacher took a dry passage in the student history book and made it more meaningful. She was covering the Articles of Confederation in her class discussions. Most students had little knowledge that the Articles of Confederation were the first Constitution of the United States (Bailey and Kennedy 1994). The teacher told the students that they were connected to the 1780s. It didn't seem possible to the high school students. What would they have in common with "those old folks" who had white hair and died many years ago? She explained that one of the first laws that the new Congress of the Confederation passed was the Land Ordinance of 1785 (Bailey and Kennedy 1994, 167). The students were still skeptical.

The teacher said, "How do you think schools are paid for? Do you pay for your education?"

One student answered, "We pay taxes. And the school gets its money from our taxes."

"Yes," said the teacher, her eyes smiling. She still had a historical secret to share with them.

"But in those days remember the second Continental Congress did not have the power to collect taxes from states. What could they do to support public education?"

"Students would have to pay for their own education," said a young woman in the middle of the second row.

"Then it would be a private school and not a public school," interjected a young man with a diamond earring in his left ear.

The teacher said, "Let me ask again, who would pay for your education? It costs lots of money to build a school and to pay teachers. What should be done?"

She paused and then continued, "To ensure that public education would really take hold in new areas of the union, the Congress passed the Land Ordinance of 1785. In this law, every sixteenth section of each township sold in the Old Northwest would go to fund schools. A township was a piece of land six miles by six miles. It was divided into 36 pieces of land and sold. Money from the other 35 parcels of land would be used to pay the large debt from the Revolutionary War. Over two hundred years ago, the founders of our nation believed in education and they set aside the funds for schools."

"The second Continental Congress made a critical decision for you! They believed in you and education."

Some of the students smiled, while others just looked surprised. The teacher was wise enough to engage them in thinking about their own schooling and history. She used a bridge from their lives to their textbook in order for students to make history more meaningful.

In addition to knowledge of subject areas like math, science, and social sciences, as part of meaningful content, teachers would benefit from knowing and understanding the culture and languages of their students (Echevarria and Graves 1998). Culture and languages are not easy to learn, but the knowledge will pay off in their ability to reach students.

Some teachers may have a classroom where there are many different home languages. If teachers know how language is acquired, they can better find ways to teach English learners. For example, a teacher relayed to me how he was frustrated with a Vietnamese American high school freshman, Alexandra, in his English class. He was interested in culturally relevant teaching and had students write about their lives, a method that worked well with many students. Alexandra was smart and she did try to write, but her English grammar was poor. Both the teacher and the student were getting more and more frustrated. The teacher attended a workshop on Vietnamese culture and language that his district offered. He didn't want to go, but felt pressured by the school.

During the workshop, he realized that Alexandra was making consistent errors. She did not know how to code switch. Vietnamese is a tonal language and tenses are communicated through changes in tones and pitches, not through word form, which explains how the same verb form could be used to convey the present, past, or future (Tran 1998). In addition, the teacher learned the Vietnamese language has no articles like "the" or "a," so that is why Alexandra often omitted them in her writing. Another aspect of the language that he could see in her writing was that she did not add an "s" to show a plural form of a word. However, the teacher discovered that in Vietnamese, markers are used with nouns to show plurals, but the noun is not changed (Tran 1998). Because of what he learned, the teacher was able to systematically analyze Alexandra's grammar mistakes. The teacher became a cultural and language mediator and helped her understand grammatical and syntax differences between Vietnamese and English.

Alexandra is now a teacher in a middle school. She teaches English. It was the guidance of her English teacher that made a big difference in her life. Now she is a bridge for her students whose first language is not English.

Though many people seem to believe culture divides people, culture actually can be used by a wise teacher in finding common ground between various students. It is through our understanding of each other and ourselves that we can grow, learn, and discover our common humanity. Culture can be used to connect us rather than separate us.

Meaningful Practice

Most children like to learn, but sometimes they may not seem too interested in school. This attitude may come about when students do not believe the teacher is interested in them or if they do not understand the purpose of the activity. Students may also rebel or act bored when they see little purpose to the information. Oftentimes teachers methodically write the daily learning objectives on the board, but these can become muddled by lack of connection to the real world of children. Caring teachers are extremely sensitive to being relevant. Meaningful practice encourages teachers to find ways to connect content with what students know and how it will impact their lives.

Lisa Delpit (1995) gives the example of how Martha Deminentieff, a Native Alaskan teacher of Athabaskan students, gives a meaningful context to her writing assignments. She explains that there is a difference between writing in "Our Heritage Language" of her students and writing in "Standard English." She carefully describes the nuances and ways English is used in their heritage, more informal, language. The teacher explains to them that it is almost like being at a picnic enjoying oneself. Then she takes the same message written in Formal English and compares the two styles. She explains to students that academic writing is like eating at a formal dinner. Demientieff has her students dress up in formal attire and set up tables with tablecloths, china, and silverware. In this way the students understand that academic writing uses Formal English. At this meal the students speak formally. The students follow the meal with writing that is academic. The students are involved in a series of writing activities that provides important contexts for writing. Demientieff teaches standard linguistic forms within powerful cultural contexts (Delpit 1995).

Now let's take the issue of the lunch line that was discussed in the previous section and develop meaningful practice like Martha Demientieff did. Teachers could have asked their students to write letters to the principal of the high school and superintendent of the district expressing their views. In this way students not only would learn how to write business letters, they would also practice using their Formal English skills and sharpen their skills of writing a strong persuasive argument.

Both of the examples demonstrate the power of meaningful practice.

Purposeful Accountability

Teachers must continue to look at their effectiveness. Standards can help us focus upon and identify important knowledge and skills that we need to teach. They represent a general core curriculum and often do not address local and personal knowledge students may have. Standards are primarily knowledge and skills educators believe students need in order to participate in the general society.

If we want to close the achievement gap between underrepresented children and majority students, we must be able to assess accurately the competence of our students. I think standards are important, however I feel much of the movement toward them represents what students will need from a majority view of knowledge. Teachers must also understand that standards can be used to culturally assimilate our students without their making that choice. Teachers must find a balance between accountability as measured by standardized tests and support of the cultural identity and background students bring to school. Much of what we teach is Western oriented so we as teachers must understand how schools can be tools of assimilation.

Don't misunderstand me. I do believe all students need to learn how to use the computer, read, write, and compute. They need a basic body of knowledge in order to survive in society. However, I also believe students need skills to seek multiple perspectives on an issue, respect and listen to other people's views, and place themselves in the "shoes" of someone else to gain a more comprehensive understanding of the world. Teachers face the challenge of having a balanced classroom that respects the culture of students while they also learn the skills and knowledge of the general society. Much of what we teach, how we teach, and what we reinforce is rooted in the majority culture. Yes, students will need to know what is expected of them in order to make it in society, but it is possible to weave into the curriculum cultural aspects of students. As the work of Luis Moll has shown, it is possible to teach the writing and communication skills students need by using the cultural and personal experiences of youth as the vehicle for learning.

In addition, I would like to share a caution about scripted teacher's guides. Today much of the curriculum is carefully prescribed and sometimes the teacher has few opportunities to bring in local or cultural knowledge into a lesson. However, good teachers are continually bringing in examples from the lives of their students. They are careful observers of their children and they utilize the living knowledge of youth in their curriculum. Tharp and Gallimore's work (1988) reminds us that if the lesson is so scripted by a teacher's guide, when children bring up new ways of thinking about the topic being covered, the teacher may not feel she can respond to the child's comments or build upon them because they are not part of the lesson as presented in the guide. Relying on a teacher's guide limits the teacher's ability to be responsive and—in the context of this book—culturally responsive to their students.

Many of us know that standardized and mandated testing will not fix our schools. The Spring 1999 issue of the journal *Rethinking Schools* is devoted to testing. In the issue, Bob Peterson and Monty Neill (1999) carefully suggest alternatives to standardized testing. These alternatives move away from the belief that one correct answer is what schooling is about. Instead, they suggest using student portfolios, cautiously implementing multiple performance exams, exhibiting more student work, organizing parent-teacher conferences, and employing trained school quality review teams. A combination of these strategies is probably the most effective.

Teachers must be accountable and to do this they must develop means of assessing the learning of their students. The following section describes some aspects of authentic assessment.

Authentic Assessment

Linda Darling-Hammond, Jacqueline Ancess, and Beverly Falk (1995) studied schools that used "authentic" assessment. What do they mean by authentic? In this type of assessment students are engaged in real-life activities (Darling-Hammond, Ancess, and

Falk 1995). They pointed out that assessment is a process that does not end with a product like a student exhibition, rather those products are catalysts for further reflection and discussion among teachers, students, and parents. They write,

"It is the action around assessment—the discussions, meetings, revisions, arguments, and opportunities to continually create new directions for teaching, learning, curriculum, and assessment—that ultimately have consequence. The 'things' of assessment are essentially useful as dynamic supports for reflection and action, rather than as static products with value in and of themselves" (Darling-Hammond, Ancess, and Falk 1995, 18).

The purpose of assessment is for students and teachers to collaboratively work with each other to learn and build critical thinking skills. In this way, students have the opportunity to engage in real-life and meaningful activities that also affirm cultural diversity.

Excellent teachers have always given substantial and meaningful feedback to their students, and they have a "finger on the pulse" of the classroom. They know which students are doing well and which students are having difficulty. They know when it is appropriate to intercede and make suggestions to students or when it is best to encourage them to struggle with the material with limited guidance in order to teach important problem-solving and decision-making skills.

Teachers often keep journals or logs of their own impressions, shortcomings, successes, and funny stories that happen in class. These journals are valuable tools for self-reflection and collaborative discussions.

Meaningful teaching focuses the classroom on the lives of students. Students share wise perceptions. Write them down in your journal and think about them later if you don't have time to respond to students immediately. Many times young people are insightful and can provide important reasons why an activity or assignment is not successful.

Meaningful teaching must be supported by a framework that emphasizes community, culture, and social justice. The next section describes six dimensions that are needed in order to implement Caring-Centered Multicultural Education.

Caring-Centered Multicultural Education: Six Dimensions for Implementation

This book has focused on presenting six dimensions of Caring-Centered Multicultural Education. As part of the process of growth, teachers should consider each one carefully. They represent four intimately tied areas of schooling: philosophical orientation, professional development, curriculum and instruction, and school policies and structure. Because professional development and philosophy are major keys to teacher belief and practice, much discussion centered on the framework. This framework arises from the ethic of caring, education for democracy founded on social justice, and the socio-cultural context of learning. Culture is also an integral aspect of learning, and the book emphasized culturally relevant teaching. However, the inclusion of critical professional development and subsequent curriculum changes will not occur if we do not look at our school policies and structure. The philosophical orientation for a caring, socially just, and collaborative community must be incorporated in the way our school system is designed and policies are set. In this way the six dimensions represent different components of schools. They are as follows:

Dimension 1: Understand the ethic of caring.
Dimension 2: Review and eliminate prejudice and discrimination.
Dimension 3: Understand the impact of culture.
Dimension 4: Utilize culturally relevant teaching.
Dimension 5: Blend and integrate caring and social justice into teaching and the school.
Dimension 6: Design and implement classroom and school change.

These six dimensions are parts of a large whole; they fit together like a puzzle. When one segment is missing, the puzzle is not complete. First, it is critical for educators to hold a moral commitment to care and create trusting relationships with their students. This dimension is foundational. Then, building upon the ethic of caring, teachers must actively work to eliminate prejudice and discrimination. Oppressive attitudes and actions will undermine the building of a compassionate and just community. The third and fourth dimensions emphasize the impact of cultures and the cultural context on the learning process. It is imperative that teachers know how to design and implement culturally relevant teaching. The fifth dimension focuses on the blending and integration of caring and social justice. Both must be present in order to foster relationships that are compassionate and just. These five components integrate caring, social justice and culture into teaching. Finally, the sixth dimension centers around the importance of implementing structural changes in schools so that they become centers of care that affirm culture, and they become communities where social justice and democratic practices are found throughout the curriculum, school practices, and policies. Figure 11.1 provides a visual of the integration of the six dimensions of Caring-Centered Multicultural Education.

The process of change takes time, and Table 11.2 summarizes the areas in the framework. What beliefs would you add to those listed? Write them in your journal as you read through the table.

Let's review the six dimensions.

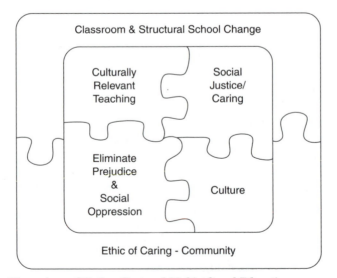

Figure 11.1 *Dimensions of Caring-Centered Multicultural Education*

TABLE 11.2

Caring-Centered Multicultural Education:
Six Dimensions for Implementation

	Phase 1: Understand the Ethic of Caring	Phase 2: Review and Eliminate Prejudice and Discrimination, Individual and Institutional	Phase 3: Understand the Impact of Cultures	Phase 4: Utilize Culturally Relevant Teaching	Phase 5: Blend and Integrate Caring and Social Justice into Teaching and the School Culture	Phase 6: Design and Implement Classroom and Structural School Change
Selected Beliefs	The goal of schooling is a happy, fulfilled person who is a critical thinker and works to make society a caring and socially just community.	Prejudice and discrimination work against the building of a caring and just society.	Children are complex beings who live, think, learn, speak, write, share, and identify with a complex combination of linguistic and cultural communities.	Students become independent learners by actively engaging in hands-on, meaningful, and cooperative learning that is relevant to their lives. Teachers build on what students know, what they are interested in, and what they can do.	Caring forms the foundation for a just society; caring and social justice are intimately connected.	Teachers examine practices and policies using the lenses of caring, social justice, democracy, and culture.
	An ethical commitment to care serves as the foundation for teaching and trusting relationships.	Educators, students, and parents examine all aspects of schooling for biases that act as barriers to equal educational access and success.	Learning is shaped by sociocultural interactions and contexts.	Teachers are cultural mediators who believe in a holistic orientation where cognitive development is linked to social, emotional, and ethical development.	Caring teachers work in collaboration with students and parents to create the most effective, meaningful, and successful educational environment.	Students join their teachers in designing and implementing mechanisms and practices for democratic and caring classrooms and schools.

(Continued)

TABLE 11.2 (CONT.)

Caring relationships are built on trust, respect, and reciprocal responsibility.	The United States and most other countries are color/class/gender-conscious and not color/class/gender-blind societies.	Children are taught about caring within a cultural context, which varies from group to group and also differs because of family interpretations.	Teachers believe learning occurs within and through social interactions and within the individual student.	Students, parents, and teachers develop a caring theme/curriculum within the context of a democratic, culturally diverse, and just society to be integrated throughout all subject areas.	Students and teachers develop caring projects that may result in programs like peacemakers, peer mediators, or peer tutors.
Learning should be a life-giving process of joy and self-fulfillment.	There are various types of prejudice: personal, institutional, cultural, and social. All must be addressed and eliminated.	Teachers prepare students to function in the general society and cultural communities while affirming their bicultural/multicultural and linguistic identities.	Educators teach the basic skills and critical thinking skills that will enable children to address and solve social issues; students become contributing and responsible people.	Students create avenues where they can raise and discuss issues in a compassionate forum; students will take actions to address these issues.	Community members and parents participate in caring school projects like career day (taking students to work), reading to students, tutoring, and other activities.

Dimension One: Understand the Ethic of Caring

Like the basis for this book, the ethic of caring is an important foundation for teachers to use in shaping and creating their classroom. Caring is more than hugs. Caring really means a lot of hard work. For example, caring means being supportive toward each student even when an individual is obstinate or difficult. It means addressing the individual needs of students while simultaneously keeping your fingers on the pulse of the entire classroom family. As the teacher, you work with students and parents to create a compassionate and collaborative learning family. This support network encourages learning, but also a sense of personal and group efficacy (Kohl 1982).

Strong and trusting relationships form the elements for personal growth, development, and change. James S. House, a professor of sociology at the University of Michigan, talked about his research and why he feels trusting and supportive relationships are so important in people's lives.

"There is a sense, whether you take it from religion or psychology, that people have a need for meaning, coherence, understanding of the world. People need a sense that their life, their existence, has some purpose . . . that sense of meaning and purpose is defined . . . most strongly, by the relationships they have with other people—with spouses; with other family, parents, children; with friends, with people they associate with at work or in voluntary organizations" (Ornish 1998, 240).

When the lives of young people are integrated with school, the environment can be a place of meaning, respect, and trust. Unfortunately, school also can be a place of isolation where learning is abstract and not related to life (Kohl 1982; Goodman and Goodman 1990). A caring-centered teacher understands the importance of developing a community where students feel a sense of belonging and acceptance. Within this context, the teacher sees education as being alive. She inspires students. Students learn not only their basic skills like reading, writing, math, and technology; they also learn critical thinking skills, value clarification strategies, and collaboration. The classroom becomes a place of intellectual stimulation and challenges, where students are taught how to wrestle with social issues such as responsibilities versus rights of citizenship, individualism versus community, minority versus majority needs, and protection of civil rights through the integrated lens of caring, compassion, and justice. Focusing on the whole person is important, but with caring-centered multicultural education there also comes a holistic view of growth (Moll 1990) that includes not only cognitive gain, but also social, emotional, and ethical development.

Dimension Two: Review and Eliminate Prejudice and Discrimination

Prejudice and discrimination hurt. They hurt both the victim and perpetrator because they create a wall between people, which makes it difficult to create trusting relationships and to work toward building strong communities where the needs of individuals and the whole group are addressed. In addition, prejudice and discrimination can result in the loss of thousands of students who drop out of school. We all lose when their potential and abilities are lost.

This book addresses what individual, district, and building-level educators can do to make their schools more meaningful and therefore more academically successful; but I want to point out how we as a collective, a society, contribute to an almost impossible situation in our schools by ignoring issues of unemployment, housing, and living conditions. The largest ten districts in the United States are made up of students from underrepresented groups. These students may be from low-income families or members of African American, Asian Pacific American, or Latino communities. Jean Anyon's book, *Ghetto Schooling,* clearly demonstrates that unless underlying issues of racial isolation and poverty are effectively addressed, restructuring schools or bringing in new teaching methods will have minimal impact (Anyon 1997). The members of inner-city families must have improvements in their living conditions and access to educational and political opportunities; otherwise, the anger and frustrations of their day-to-day struggles will limit what teachers can do. Anyon believes that our personal biases have impacted our willingness to act. People do not understand their connection to others in the community. For example, she cites the continual cutting of taxes for schools and points to the cost of society's inability to keep high school students in school; every year we are losing $50 billion in lifetime earnings from dropouts (Anyon 1997, 182).

As members of a caring community, it is critical that all of us, students, teachers, administrators, parents, and community people, examine ourselves and our institutions for bias. This is a difficult process, but it must be accomplished in order to address the inequities that can be found in schools. For example, "Why do schools in the same state have chemistry labs where specialized experiments can be conducted, while schools five minutes away have no lab at all?" Jonathan Kozol (1991) not only asked these questions, but courageously found answers to them. Kozol discovered that schools in Camden, a depressed city of New Jersey where most of the students were Latino and Black, had only about $4,000 a year to spend on each pupil while the neighboring high-income community of Princeton spent over $8,000 per student. Kozol often found that the poorest schools represented segregated situations. Unfortunately, through his national study of schools, Kozol discovered that many students from underrepresented groups did not have the same opportunities to learn as others. The schools often lacked safe and comfortable physical spaces, complete copies of textbooks, adequate science equipment, working computers, and well-paid teachers.

Discrimination is often unconscious, but whether conscious or unconscious, it hurts all parties. In some states there have been attempts to fund schools equally. Schools built in higher-income neighborhoods do not benefit from higher property taxes of the area in comparison to schools built in lower-income areas. In this way, students who attend schools in inner cities will have the same resources as those who live in more prestigious areas. However, there are other ways that schools can raise money. For example, parent and booster clubs can raise large sums of money that pay for various services such as teacher assistants, technology instruction, physical education programs, and other programs (Smith 1999). So schools in wealthier neighborhoods can provide benefits that schools in low-income communities cannot (Smith 1999). Stu-

TABLE 11.3

Uneven Distribution
Private Contributions to Schools

School	Community	Budget	Per Student
Van Nuys Medical Magnet	Van Nuys	$ 56, 855	$244
Westwood Elementary	Westwood	$163,443	$235
Coeur d'Alene Elementary	Venice	$ 59, 598	$222
Pacific Palisades Elementary	Pacific Palisades	$100,007	$215
Serrania Elementary	Woodland Hills	$120,750	$194
Community School	Pico-Robertson	$ 63,991	$178
Wonderland Elementary	Hollywood Hills	$ 42,451	$175
Wilmington Park Elementary	Wilmington	$198,343	$172
Canyon Elementary	Pacific Palisades	$ 54,790	$170
Grant Communication Science Magnet	Van Nuys	$ 59,000	$156
Multnomah Environmental Science Magnet	Los Angeles	$ 18,359	$150

Adapted from Lynn Meersman's chart in Doug Smith's article, "Funding and Fairness Clash in Public Schools," *Los Angeles Times,* Tuesday, February 16, 1999, A17.

dents can benefit from this increase of money into a school, but the issue of equality of funding and services arises.

The *Los Angeles Times* conducted an analysis of almost $7 million that was donated to the Los Angeles Unified School District. The district has a $200 per student maximum rule that schools can raise to supplement their budget. However, the analysis demonstrated that some schools have raised more money than is allowed. These schools can be found in more affluent areas of the district (Smith 1999). The district also has rules regarding how the funds can be spent. Additional funding can be used to support teaching aides, but not to fund a teacher. Schools have gone to raising money because California ranks as one of the lowest of all fifty states in per pupil funding. This has led to problems like large classes, lack of physical education instruction, and inadequate personnel needed for attendance tracking.

The issue of raising outside money for schools does not directly deal with prejudice but it does raise the concern of equality of programs and discrimination that can occur because of the disparity among schools. The *Los Angeles Times* reports that many donations are not recorded so the difference in school funding cannot be fully known (Smith 1999). Table 11.3 is a partial chart from the *Los Angeles Times* that indicates how the funding varies among schools. There were 26 schools that recorded funds more than $100 per student and 22 were from more affluent neighborhoods in the Westside of Los Angeles or the San Fernando Valley (Smith 1999, A17).

Discrimination can occur on many different levels. We must be aware of the ways our institutions can reinforce or support social oppression so we can work to prevent it. Schools, in their need to bring effective education to students, can integrate practices that are unequal. When a school can raise more than $200 per student, it can provide additional services that poorer schools will not be able to offer. Most people think about outward signs of prejudice like name-calling, but more complicated issues like this one also impact our students and our ability to provide equal educational opportunities to all.

We must also look at our personal biases. Teachers and students may treat each other in ways that are hurtful and discriminatory. They can choose to communicate or relate to each other in a way that conveys trust or fear. Teachers and students can choose to become tools of change rather than tools of hurt.

Teachers can use a variety of important strategies that will increase the students' awareness and skills in dealing with prejudice and discrimination. The following strategies can assist teachers in addressing this issue:

1. Students establish clear expectations for classroom behavior and discuss values of community, respect, dignity, and honor.
2. Teachers can provide positive anti-racist role models from various ethnic groups.
3. Students are encouraged to review and clarify their values and behaviors.
4. Students reflect upon their own actions and how they impact others.
5. Students are encouraged to place themselves in the shoes of another.

In order to address the pervasive nature of social oppression, students must examine not only their own personal biases, but also the injustices found in our institutions and organizations.

Dimension Three: Understand the Impact of Culture

Culture is a critical aspect of how children and adults identify themselves, interpret the world, and value. For many teachers, culture is hard to identify because they are born into a family culture and it surrounds them. Like the air we breathe, culture is there but almost invisible because it is so ingrained in the way we think and act. Culture is a natural aspect of one's life.

Teachers may not realize that they are operating from a particular cultural orientation even when they come into contact with or conflict with students, parents, or others who have different cultural backgrounds, values, or behaviors. Teachers have specific expectations, behaviors, and ways of doing things. They may always write things on the board. They may expect quiet all the time. They may allow students to walk around the room. There are rules and expectations continually operating in schools and they differ from room to room.

Asa Hilliard is an educator who has given great insight into how culture impacts learning. He has contributed much to my understanding. In one of my favorite excerpts from Hilliard's writings, he identifies major teacher competencies and attitudes that he believes are essential in an effective teacher of diverse students. Think about his insights and how they may impact your teaching.

"Teaching is always a cross-cultural encounter" (Hilliard 1974, 44). Each student brings to the classroom a different cultural context, and the teacher brings her own cultural dynamics also.

"The personality, values, and social background of the teacher are critical cultural inputs" (Hilliard 1974, 45). You are a cultural being and your very personal ways have profound impact on students.

"All teaching is culture bound" (Hilliard 1974, 44). Everything we do, everything we say, everything we present: These are all aspects of our personal culture. When children do not see themselves in schools, they do not feel valued or honored.

"The classroom is not a benign context but a potent matrix" (Hilliard 1974, 44). The teacher affirms or rejects students in the way she labels, rewards, controls time and space, selects, presents, requests, and an infinite number of actions that occur in class.

One way to understand how we come from different cultural orientations is to watch a movie that is told from a different cultural perspective. For example, I suggest viewing the following:

Shall We Dance?—This is a film from Japan that shows the Japanese nonverbal communication styles of several protagonists. In addition, it presents some values dealing with female/male relationships, work ethic, and family roles. Though much is missing in the subtitles, see it with someone who speaks Japanese and ask for a fuller explanation of the characters and values they represent.

Smoke Signals—This is a film about two young men from the Coeur d'Alene community in Idaho. The two men exemplify the differences and similarities of Native Americans from this part of the Northwest. One character represents the views of "the warrior" while the other protagonist seems to signify "the storyteller." The cultural conflict between the majority and the Coeur d'Alene community values is easily seen in this movie. The humor is delightful.

Mi Familia—This film provides insights into a Mexican American family who deals with the problems of life. The movie displays the warmth of the characters and the struggles they work through not only as family members, but as members of an underrepresented group that must deal continually with cultural assimilation. It shows a rich tapestry of family life.

Malcolm X—This film is based on the autobiography of Malcolm Little and was produced and directed by Spike Lee. It presents to the viewer the type of continual oppression that African Americans have had to deal with in society as individuals and as members of a physically identifiable group. *Malcolm X* provides the audience with a deeper understanding of the cultural values, religious roots, and belief in freedom of many African Americans.

Dimension Four: Utilize Culturally Relevant Teaching

Much of what is taught and how it is taught arises from mainstream culture. For example, why is more Mark Twain or Robert Frost read than Langston Hughes in many junior and high school English classes? Many times these choices are cultural rather than academic. The choice and construction of knowledge and skills is, in great part, a reflection of cultural values. Much of what is taught in schools comes from a Western tradition. However, I found in my own teaching that many students from underrepresented groups identified with and had stronger personal connections to the life of Malcolm X rather than John F. Kennedy. Both figures are important to U.S. history. Though each role model made critical contributions to the civil rights movement, students from many communities preferred reading about Malcolm X. Many students of color that I know identify with and feel a sense of community with Malcolm X. They have an understanding of the struggles that he suffered as a person of color. He is an important role model who came from a community like theirs and taught himself not only the importance of intellectual development, but also how to fight racism. By including people like Malcolm X, teachers can expand the curriculum to include cultural and community knowledge that is more meaningful to students and their life experiences.

Culturally relevant teaching represents not only meaningful content, but also refers to a holistic way of teaching. Teachers know that their students learn within a sociocultural context. Goodman and Goodman (1990) recommend that teachers watch and talk with their students and find out what they are interested in, what they know, and what they can do. The goal of a teacher is to guide students into being independent learners. They also believe the values and beliefs students bring from their lives play an important role in how they interpret and understand school materials. Goodman and Goodman (1990) believe teachers must be mediators in the learning process. They are not to control the learning context, but they are to assist students in their learning. They shared a lesson where Black fourth grade students were reading Langston Hughes's poem, "Mother to Son" (Goodman and Goodman 1990, 237). The students were leading the class discussion of the poem. The teacher was not sure what Hughes meant in the poem by the term, "crystal stair." The teacher explained that she thought it meant that the mother was trying to raise herself out of difficult conditions, because Langston Hughes often wrote about social oppression. Students shared another viewpoint. They believed that the image referred to the mother climbing up the struggles of life, the "crystal stair," to heaven.

In this context, the teacher made a choice of the poem and so acted as an initiator for the lesson. However, learning was reciprocal between students and teacher; they learned from each other. The teacher was a mediator in the learning. The poem she chose had definite connections to the lives of her students, and she encouraged and respected their viewpoints. In this way, the teacher included a selection in their learning that had cultural linkages and the focus was on comprehension.

The use of culturally relevant teaching is particularly important for students who are learning English. If the lesson incorporates content that builds on the students' unique linguistic and cultural backgrounds, the students are more likely to see connections to new material or skills being taught. The more examples and paraphrasing that the teacher uses in their teaching, the more likely the student will learn the knowledge or skills being conveyed. Cultural examples can be used not only as important scaffolding for learning, but also reinforces the identity and home background of students. When abstract concepts are being taught, educators should use additional photographs, stories, nonverbal gestures, graphs, video pieces, posters, and books to communicate complex ideas. Writing new vocabulary words or key phrases on the board also provides an additional mode of teaching besides verbal communication. Teachers should also be more willing to wait for students to respond and encourage them to ask questions to clarify or to demonstrate their new understandings. This is extremely critical for students who feel uncomfortable in publicly exhibiting their English skills.

With society's overemphasis on standards and national textbooks, teachers must look for ways to bring into the curriculum the lived experiences of various cultural groups to make learning real and authentic. Teachers often feel they must follow the curriculum as set up in their teacher's guides; however, when the materials have little in common with students, meaningful learning may not occur. I have seen teachers so intent on following the scripted guides of textbooks that they do not feel they have time to incorporate additional cultural examples into their lessons. Students may flounder because they do not have a clear understanding of the content or context of traditional materials.

Dimension Five: Blend and Integrate Caring and Social Justice into Teaching and the School

Caring and social justice are intimately connected in a culturally pluralistic and democratic society like the United States. Caring can enhance our understanding of justice because the ethic of caring emphasizes trust and respect of others. The word *caring* was chosen rather than care, because caring is a word of action and not only a value orientation. When we care for others, we act. This is how caring and social action are inseparably linked. We care for others, we treat others with fairness and respect, and we continually act with care and fairness in our everyday and professional lives to build a strong community. Caring is at the core of social justice and community. Within a school context, teachers must be especially aware of the need to integrate culture in order to make schooling more meaningful and relevant to children who are not successful. Caring and social justice values point to the great importance of equal educational opportunity and achievement outcomes for all students.

Providing equity is not easy to accomplish. In one of my graduate classes, Stefan, a chemistry teacher in a school that is primarily African American, shared his frustrations with having an average of 35 students per period and trying to care for each one of them. He has almost 200 students a day attending his classes and it takes much emotional and physical energy to even say "hi" to each student as they come into the room.

One of the issues he continually wrestles with is homework. Many of the students work or take care of siblings after school. He knows that students also goof off. In order to develop strong study skills in his students, he must continually remind, prod, and demand that they do their homework. He cares deeply for his students, but his frustration increases when he realizes that he has only so much time. There is not enough time to call the parents of 15 to 20 students every day to follow up on their homework. It took several years for him to understand that caring means he must not only proactively care for students, but also teach students and parents how to create a more supportive environment that encourages study and homework skills. He, as the teacher, cannot do it all alone. Students and parents must be responsible for their own actions too. He understands that he can be the catalyst in creating a caring community that focuses on academic excellence.

ONE OF THE
WORST DISEASES
IS TO BE
NOBODY to NOBODY

MOTHER TERESA

Dimension Six: Design and Implement Classroom and School Change

Throughout the six dimensions, teachers must look not only at how they can change their classrooms, but also they must examine how schools can be restructured in order to implement a commitment to caring and social justice. Are there practices, policies, or beliefs that act as obstacles because of unconscious prejudice or ignorance of other cultural values? Some of the obstacles to structural change may occur because of lack of communication between members of various communities.

I believe that we need total school reform. For example, all schools should not be larger than about 300 students and a class should not have any more than 20 students. I believe individuals and groups of teachers can make needed structural and pedagogical changes in schools. One way to enrich their classroom curriculum is by naturally infusing culture into them as the Algebra Project did in Cambridge, Massachusetts, and Funds of Knowledge accomplished in Tucson, Arizona. You, as an individual teacher, may not be able to change everything about a school that is not working, yet you can improve what you are doing to reach students more effectively. One of your long-term professional goals may be to work with the teachers, administrators, and parents in your school to plan for and institute total school reform.

Sometimes it is easier to make structural changes in your own classroom, rather than tackling total school reform. For example, Paul Skilton Sylvester (1994), a third grade teacher in the large district of Philadelphia, changed the social structures in his room rather than simply replicating current practices. Sylvester and his students created a classroom economy that they named "Sweet Cakes Town." He wanted to teach students real-world skills and to demonstrate that they could control their own life. Sylvester (1994) believed in a critical pedagogy approach that emphasized students learning knowledge and skills within the context of self-empowerment, decision making, and continual questioning.

Sylvester was a caring teacher whose commitment toward his students manifested itself in creating a learning context that exposed social and economic inequalities and assisted students in developing skills that would serve them to overcome discrimination in society. Sweet Cakes Town was a real neighborhood. Students created the money for the neighborhood and the teacher paid them for being "good students," which included social behavior and academic performance. Each day students rated their performance of being a good student using the class guidelines for jobs they had accomplished. They added up their pay for the week on Fridays. From the funds they received, students were then able to take on roles in the neighborhood such as bankers, small business owners, clerks, and beauticians. They not only used basic skills like multiplication and division in order to calculate their profit and losses, students also developed much deeper understandings of the obstacles in society such as lack of jobs, need for higher-level skills, and lack of public transportation (Sylvester 1994). Later, students realized they needed governmental officers like the mayor in order to run the city, and so each citizen had to pay taxes. Sweet Cakes Town connected the learning of basic skills with real-life purposes. In addition, students saw why their participation was needed in order for social changes to occur.

Change can also come about on a community level. Some schools today invite their local neighborhoods to become their partners, knowing that it does "take a village to raise a child." For example, the Chula Vista School District in California built a school next to a senior center and retirement home. Some seniors in California are opposed to their taxes going to schools; however, the district took a proactive stand. They invited representatives from the local senior citizen organizations to help create the direction and goals of the schools. The partnership has become a wonderful success. Elder Americans take an active role in volunteering and providing needed tutoring to children of all grade levels. Some of the volunteers often use their second language of Spanish and act as a nurturing liaison to many of the children whose home language is not English. They demonstrate their care for youngsters in the neighborhood. In addition, the children are learning what it means to be part of a caring neighborhood community. The children write letters to their senior friends, visit them, and often give holiday musical concerts and plays.

At a nearby high school, a dance was sponsored by the Associated Student Body. After they hired the band, ordered the food, and planned the decorations, the ASB decided to charge each couple $10 to attend. Unfortunately, there were many students who could not afford the charge. Resentment among students began to fester. The principal was concerned about this issue of equal access to school functions, but did not know what to do. The faculty was apathetic, because most of the teachers did not think it was an important issue.

A group of students cared about their community and wrote a letter to the school newspaper suggesting that one first period class be devoted to discussing this issue and developing possible suggestions. Initially, the faculty felt forced by students to allow this discussion; however, by engaging faculty in this process, they took some ownership of the equal-access issue. Student facilitators, trained by school counselors, were used in some classrooms where faculty felt incapable of leading a discussion of the topic. The issue was not resolved immediately, but it was also discussed in various club meetings, such as the Human Relations and the Community Service clubs. In addition, the ASB made the issue one of its priorities for the year. They made a policy limiting the price of general school dances.

Change does occur. It often is a struggle, but when students, parents, and teachers work with each other to make a more just and caring environment, structural changes can occur.

Summary

Learning and teaching can be empowering processes. For continuous growth, I believe each of us must be continually involved in reevaluation of our teaching and our students' learning. To do this, I suggest that teachers carefully monitor the progress of their students, looking for patterns of success and failure. Are there students who are always failing? Are you able to integrate culture in one part of the curriculum more effectively than others? Whose parents have you developed partnerships with in the class? There is a teacher who shared with her peers that she wanted a way to invite parents to come to an informal and fun event at school. The teacher developed a newsletter, but there were many parents who did not read English well. She was able to have some newsletters translated into Spanish and Lao; however, she thought the best way to reach parents was to talk to them in person. So she created a monthly "lunch bunch celebration." The teacher now invites parents of various students to come to school for pizza. Approximately six young students and their parents share lunch and the teacher talks about the accomplishments of the students at the celebration. Everyone has the opportunity to invite their parents. This has been a big success in the school. Teachers are looking for ways in which they can build a sense of caring with their students and parents. This example affirms the importance of home life and the coordination of parents with teachers.

The six dimensions of Caring-Centered Multicultural Education provide important suggestions regarding what teachers must know in order to create an affirming, caring, and culturally relevant learning environment. The six dimensions represent an integration of different aspects of education: philosophy, pedagogy, school policies, and professional development.

1. Understand the ethic of caring.
2. Review and eliminate prejudice and discrimination.
3. Understand the impact of culture.
4. Utilize culturally relevant teaching.
5. Blend and integrate caring and social justice into teaching and the school.
6. Design and implement classroom and school change.

Each of the dimensions is important in creating a community of learners that is based on social justice and compassion. In addition, it is important for educators to examine their teaching to see that it is meaningful. Teachers can make their teaching more relevant and connected to the lives of their students by talking with each other and examining personal biases. Teachers can learn how to reach culturally diverse students by increasing their knowledge of the literature and history of various groups.

These areas may be labeled as Chicano literature or Lakota literature, for example, but they are also part of American (U.S.) literature. Practice must also be expanded to include models, styles, and strategies that not only build upon a caring orientation, but that also provide cultural contexts that may be more familiar to students than those presently used in schools. Finally, teachers must continually consider their effectiveness. In considering accountability, educators must keep the goal of academic achievement at the top of their list.

The suggestions shared in this chapter are designed to assist you in thinking carefully about how to make schools a place of life and joy. *Caring is exciting and hard work.*

Teacher Reflections

Read through the questions in Table 11.4. Use them as guides. Create your own questions too. Try to answer one question a day from each of the sections and write about specific actions that you might take to address the issue posed.

Make a list of changes that you can implement in your classroom, today and in the future. Come up with ideas for each of the six dimensions of Caring-Centered Multicultural Education.

References

Anyon, Jean. 1997. *Ghetto schooling: A political economy of urban educational reform.* New York: Teachers College Press.

Bailey, Thomas A., and David M. Kennedy. 1994. *The American pageant.* Lexington, Mass.: D.C. Heath.

Bustamante-Jones, E. 1998. *Mexican American teachers as cultural mediators: Literacy and literacy contexts through bicultural strengths.* Claremont, Calif.: Claremont Graduate University and San Diego State University.

Darling-Hammond, Linda, Jacqueline Ancess, and Beverly Falk. 1995. *Authentic assessment in action: Studies of schools and students at work.* New York: Teachers College Press.

Echevarria, Jana, and Anne Graves. 1998. *Sheltered content instruction: Teaching English language learners with diverse abilities.* Boston, Mass.: Allyn and Bacon.

Goodman, Yetta M., and Kenneth S. Goodman. 1990. Vygotsky in a whole-language perspective. In Luis C. Moll, ed., *Vygotsky and education.* New York: Cambridge University Press.

Heller, Carol, and Joseph Jawkins. 1994. Teaching tolerance: Notes from the front line. *Teachers College Record, 95*(3): 337–368.

Hilliard, Asa. 1974. Restructuring teacher education for multicultural imperatives. In William A. Hunter, ed., *Multicultural education through competency-based teacher education.* Washington, D.C.: American Association of Colleges for Teacher Education.

Irvine, Jacqueline Jordan. 1990. *Black students and school failure.* New York: Greenwood Press.

Kohl, Herbert. 1982. *Basic skills.* Boston, Mass.: Little, Brown and Company.

Kozol, Jonathan. 1991. *Savage inequalities.* New York: Crown Publishers.

Moll, Luis. 1990. *Vygotsky and education: Instructional implications and applications of sociohistorical psychology.* NY: Cambridge University Press.

Nothdurft, William E. 1989). *Schoolworks: Reinventing public schools to create the workforce of the future: Innovations in education and job training from Sweden, West Germany, France, Great Britain, and Philadelphia.* Washington, D.C.: Brookings Institution.

TABLE 11.4

Questions for Teacher Reflection:
Using the Six Dimensions of Caring-Centered Multicultural Education

	Phase 1: Understand the Ethic of Caring	Phase 2: Review and Eliminate Prejudice and Discrimination	Phase 3: Understand the Importance of Culture	Phase 4: Learn and Utilize Culturally Relevant Teaching	Phase 5: Blend and Integrate Caring and Social Justice into Teaching and the School	Phase 6: Design and Implement Classroom and Structural School Change
Questions for Reflection	• What is caring? • Why do people care for each other? Ideas? • How are caring and community interrelated? • What is a caring community? • What role do the values of caring play in my personal life and as a teacher?	• What is prejudice? What is discrimination? • How is social oppression defined in terms of race, ethnicity, gender, sexual orientation, and handicapping conditions? • Why do people discriminate against others? • How are the values of caring and social justice related to issues of discrimination and prejudice?	• What is culture? How do I define culture? • What impact does culture have in my life, in my students' lives, and in other people's lives? • Why is culture important in how people live, learn, and identify themselves? • What do children learn as members of various cultural communities? • What is the difference between culture, ethnicity, and race?	• What impact does culture have on the learning process? • How does culture shape the values, beliefs, expectations, and actions of a person? • What is culturally relevant teaching and how does it relate to content and strategies?	• What are the connections between caring and social justice? What does caring mean in a democracy? • How can caring, social justice, democracy, and cultural relevancy be integrated into the curriculum and instruction? • How can caring enhance our understanding of justice? How are caring and social action integrally linked?	• What changes need to be made in the classroom and school to implement a moral commitment to caring and to social justice? • How can the classroom become a more caring and democratic place? • What principles should guide change?

TABLE 11.4

- How do different cultures operationalize caring?
- What linkages can I make with parents, students, and other teachers?
- How can I model caring?
- How can I make the classroom more democratic and caring?

- How can dialogue within a caring framework be used to discuss sensitive issues of prejudice and discrimination?
- Are there groups of students who are continually at the margins in relation to academic performance, social activities, status in school?
- How much power do students have in making changes in the school?
- Whose goals are being served in the school?
- How much cross-cultural discussion is being conducted with the goals of stronger communication, development of collaborative projects, or structural change?
- What other actions can teachers and students take to get rid of social oppression?

- How can understanding my own cultural groups more clearly help me to understand the culture of others?
- How are various cultures similar? different? Do children from different cultures develop in the same or diverse ways?

- Why is culturally relevant teaching important?
- How does a culturally relevant educator think and act differently from other teachers?
- How can I integrate culturally relevant teaching into my classroom?
- What role can students have in creating a culturally relevant and academically successful classroom?

- How does student maturation impact their understanding of caring and social justice?
- What are the issues of caring and social justice that children are concerned about in their own lives?
- How can those issues be addressed in the school curriculum?
- What knowledge and skills will students need in order to become more caring change agents?
- What projects can be instituted in the classroom where children actively work toward making society a more just and democratic community?

- What kind of classroom or school do we want?
- What changes can be made to ensure a caring and equitable education for all students?
- How can issues of caring and social justice become a thread in the curriculum, school policies, and all aspects of schooling?
- How can teachers empower and work collaboratively with students and parents in making a more caring and just community?

Ornish, Dean. 1998. *Love and survival.* New York: HarperCollins Publishers.

Peterson, Bob, and Monty Neill. 1999. Alternatives to standardized tests. *Rethinking Schools, 13*(3): 1, 4–5, 28.

Rodriguez, James L., Rafael M. Diaz, David Duran, and Linda Espinosa. 1995. The impact of bilingual preschool education on the language development of Spanish-speaking children. *Early Childhood Research Quarterly, 10:* 475–490.

1999. Why the testing craze won't fix our schools. *Rethinking Schools, 13*(3): 1–2.

Scribner, Sylvia. 1984. Studying working intelligence. Barbara Rogoff and Jean Lave, eds., *Everyday cognition: Its development in social context.* Cambridge, Mass.: Harvard University Press.

Smith, Doug. 1999. Funding and fairness class in public schools. *The Los Angeles Times,* Tuesday, February 16, pp. A1, A17.

Stanford, John, and Robin Simons. 1999. *Victory in our schools.* New York: Bantam Books.

Sylvester, Paul Skilton. 1994. Elementary school curricula and urban transformation. *Harvard Educational Review, 64*(3): 309–331.

Tharp, Roland and Ronald Gallimore. 1988. *Rousing minds to life: Teaching, learning, and schooling in social context.* New York: Cambridge University Press.

Tran, MyLuong. 1998. Behind the smiles: The true heart of Southeast Asian children. In Valerie Ooka Pang and Lilly Li-Rong Cheng, eds., *Struggling to be heard: The unmet needs of Asian Pacific American children.* Albany, New York: SUNY Press.

Epilogue

Dear Reader,

I saw a program on Fred Rogers, the creator of *Mister Roger's Neighborhood.* I was moved by what he said. Mister Rogers was talking about children, but I believe what he said refers to people of all ages. Mister Rogers believes that every child wants to be valued. He tries to send across as much love as he can to his young viewers. Later that day, I also received an e-mail message about the comments of Leon Botstein, president of Bard College. On *CBS News Sunday Morning* on April 11, 1999, this is what he said:

"[U.S.] American institutions of higher education don't need managerial skills, they need leadership that comes of a love of learning and a love of the subject and the love of the act of scholarship-teaching."

He shares important thoughts about education in general, and I want to add, "We need educators who care for others and their communities too."

Like Mr. Rogers said, I believe we all want to be valued. I wrote this book in hope that I might provide some new understandings about children, cultural differences, and institutional structures. My goal was to suggest ways to increase joy, excitement, growth, compassion, and collaboration in the classroom.

In my own life, the field of Multicultural Education has brought new people, new knowledge, new skills, and wisdom into my development as a person and as a teacher. This field has led to many new insights about education and life; however, my journey is far from over. I have much more to think about, learn, and implement in my own teaching.

As I thought about the teachers who have inspired me, I realized that they were teachers who cared. They quietly listened to me without interrupting and sometimes disagreed with me. They encouraged me to clarify my ideas and generously shared their insights with me. They brought new people and their work into my life. They let me bear my disappointments. They taught me how to forgive myself and others and helped me struggle through difficult times. They celebrated all students. And they taught me how to care.

The purpose of this book was to share with you how the underlying values of caring can support the building of an effective school. When we care, we realize we have responsibilities. We want to know more about our students. This includes knowing about their cultures because they are important aspects of our students' identities. When we care, we have the courage and strength to review our own biases and how our actions may contribute to the continuation of institutional oppression in schools. We address inequities. Although these are difficult tasks, our caring for others sustains us.

The characteristics of a successful student and a successful teacher are similar. They are people who believe in themselves and who work with others to create trusting and compassionate relationships. Please read through the following chart:

Characteristics of a Successful Student and Successful Teacher in a Caring-Centered Multicultural School

Successful Student	Successful Teacher
• Believes in self and teacher	Believes in each child/student and self
• Self-directed learner	Self-directed learner
• Happy, fulfilled person	Happy, fulfilled person
• Caring toward others and self	Caring toward others and self
• Empowered, contributes to the community	Empowered, contributes to the community
• Cooperative, community oriented; makes connections with peers and others	Cooperative, community oriented; makes connections with parents, students, colleagues, and others
• Supportive of classmates, friends, family, and teacher	Supportive of colleagues, students, parents, family, and others
• Open minded, flexible	Open minded, flexible
• Knows when to keep on task and when to provide assistance to classmates	Knows when to step in to assist students and when to step back and encourage students to direct their own learning
• Affirms the worth of self and classmates (includes culture, gender, language, social class, religion, etc.)	Affirms each child's/student's worth (includes culture, gender, language, social class, religion, etc.)
• Listens without criticism; accepts others' ideas; gives helpful feedback	Listens without criticism; accepts others' ideas; gives constructive suggestions
• Reflects on own learning	Reflects on own teaching and learning
• Is comfortable and can function within a variety of cultural contexts (culture, race, language, religion, etc.)	Is comfortable and can function within a variety of cultural contexts (culture, race, language, religion, etc.)
• Has high expectations for self and teacher	Has high expectations for self and all students
• Enjoys and is enthusiastic about learning	Uses a variety of instructional approaches to teach information and skills, monitor student progress, and provide feedback
Understands and works toward identified learning objectives	Has clear learning objectives and conveys them to students
Sees connection between school learning and real life	Conveys connection and meaning between school knowledge and skills and lives of students
Shares cultural background with others	Integrates the cultural background of children naturally into all aspects of the classroom, from bulletin boards to teaching basic skills
Develops a "voice" and speaks out on public issues; works to make society and the community a more just and compassionate place	Encourages students to develop their own value orientation and "voice"; supports students in learning to make their own decisions and to become active in directing their own education; speaks out on public issues and works to make society a more just and compassionate place
Desires to be part of and works toward a strong collaborative community in the classroom and school	Has goal of creating a learning community in the classroom and school that is collaborative and affirming for all participants—students, parents, community people, and administrators
Disciplined and successful learner	Disciplined and successful learner

The author wishes to thank Maria Marshall for her input to this chart.

DRESSED
FOR
SUCCESS

The profiles of successful students and teachers are quite similar. Are you surprised? What would you add to the profiles that I may have forgotten? What did I include that you may not have considered?

We live in chaotic and quickly moving times. Communal caring is what needs to remain constant. Caring-Centered Multicultural Education is founded upon the belief that we are all equal and worthy people. As teachers and students, whether one is 6 or 86 years old, we can encourage each other and build a caring community. The successful teacher and successful student mirror each other.

Every student who comes to your classroom believes in you and your ability to teach them. Even a student who says skeptical things to you is hoping that you will see her/his abilities and help her/him to develop and learn. As educators, we know that teaching is more than just conveying information; we must come to know the whole person. We can understand our students' dreams and hopes, guide them through their weaknesses, and enhance their strengths. When students care for others, they contribute to the creation of a community and build stronger human bonds with others. In the process, their own self-worth increases. Some of our students will find a cure for cancer. Some of our students will become great teachers and teach other students how to be peacemakers, Some of our students will provide important services to others as plumbers, librarians, and mail carriers. We have one of the most exciting and important careers that impacts all avenues of society.

Caring-Centered Multicultural Education is founded upon the belief that schooling should be an exciting and joyous part of life. Learning is really about being alive (Sark 1992). Life and learning cannot be separated.

Caring and sharing are keys to effective teaching. Remember the first grader named Eugene who used a pick instead of a brush to fix his hair? Eugene could have said to me about my lack of knowledge, "Mrs. Pang, why don't you know about a pik? What's wrong with you?" Instead, he patiently explained to me what a pik was. He did not think less of me; rather, he respected and cared for me enough to share his knowledge without criticism. That is one of the main insights I hope this book brings to you.

Children bring a wealth of knowledge to school. Children's knowledge of the world and the knowledge of schools are sometimes different. Neither is better than the other—their knowledge base is just different. In order to survive in this society, students will need general societal knowledge and skills to get a job and earn a living. However, students can live a bicultural or multicultural life where they are able to code switch according to the cultural context in which they find themselves. I have learned so much from students like Eugene. They have enriched my life and helped me become a more effective teacher.

When you are surrounded by people who say it isn't possible to reach all students, find others you can talk to who know teaching isn't always easy, but who are committed to making a difference. Build up your professional libraries. Read the work of dedicated educators like Geneva Gay, Jackie Jordan Irvine, Vivian Gussin Paley, Herbert Kohl, Alfie Kohn, Frank Smith, William Ayers, Robert Rueda, Nel Noddings, James Banks, Jack Nelson, Lilly Cheng, Christine Bennett, Patricia Larke, Gregory Cajete, Luis Moll, Lisa Delpit, Christine Sleeter, Carl Grant, Joyce King, Pauline Lipman, Jessica Gordon Nembhard, A. Lin Goodwin, and Jean Anyon. They say, "Yes, all children have great potential and yes, all teachers can be effective" and they provide ideas on how to reach even the most distant and disenfranchised students.

When we are really teaching and working effectively with students, we are also sharing life with others. When students are learning, they are living the fullness of life. Their minds and sense of selves are growing. Learning is meaningful to them. I know students who can't wait to get to school because it is a place of success and belonging. I believe that this occurs most frequently within the context of trusting, respectful, and caring relationships. Students and teachers form a family, a community of learners who care about each other, care for themselves, and care for ideas. However, caring teaching is not always easy. General John Stanford wrote:

"Loving and leading doesn't mean going easy on people no matter what they do; it means coaching people to do their best, it means pushing them farther than they want to go, it means letting them know when you think they can do more. Love and leading can mean giving tough love. We often assume, when people disappoint us, that they can do no better. But that's rarely true . . . Often, their problem is really our problem; the person isn't performing because we weren't clear in our directions . . . America, our children are waiting and we must not disappoint them. Let's all love them and lead them" (Stanford 1999, 206, 213).

Enjoy all the precious moments that your students share with you. Learning can be very joyous and exciting. Schools can become places of care (Noddings 1992). Learning is not only about ideas, it is about community and building a trusting and just place to live.

I hope that you never forget: *You* and your *students* are precious gifts of life. As Robert Fulghum has written, "no matter how old you are—when you go out into the world, it is best to hold hands and stick together."*

Take care,
Val

---

*Fulghum, Robert. 1988. *All I Really Need to Know I Learned in Kindergarten.* New York: Ivy Books, p. 6.
Noddings, Nel. 1992. *The Challenge to Care: An Alternative Approach to Education.* New York: Teachers College Press.
Sark. (1992). *Inspiration Sandwich.* Berkeley, Calif.: Celestial Arts.
Stanford, John, and Robin Simons. 1999. *Victory in Our Schools.* New York: Bantam Books, pp. 206–213.

Sing out loud.
Be silly.
Giggle.
Use caring words.
Listen to their dreams.
Smile widely.
Tell them great stories of kind deeds.
Smile with your heart.
Jump rope.
Laugh lots.
Dream of happy kids.
Build trust.
Cherish culture.
Foster curiosity.
Ask questions.
Encourage them to think and question.
Praise, praise, and praise some more.
Laugh, laugh, and laugh some more.
Celebrate each learner.

© 1998 Valerie Ooka Pang

Teacher Resources

Teacher Resources: Children's Literature, Reference Materials, and Videos

Part 1: Annotated Bibliography of Children's Literature for a Culturally Diverse and Caring Society

I recommend that you read the books prior to using them in the classroom. Each group of students reacts differently to books. Some of the books may have strong language or other aspects that you may need to explain to your students before they can understand the story. Reviewing them in advance ensures that the books are appropriate for your students and relate to your instructional objectives.

This list represents only a limited selection of new and old favorites.

Picture Books

Abells, Chana Byers. 1983. *The children we remember.* New York: Greenwillow Books. A powerful book of actual photographs telling the story of the Holocaust. Though the book has only about 170 words, much is conveyed. There is great sadness and hope presented in the text. The book is not for young children. It should not be presented without background information being shared first. (Grades 4–12, Jewish community, Holocaust, genocide, anti-Semitism)

Bradby, Marie. 1995. *More than anything else.* New York: Orchard Books. Booker wants to learn how to read more than anything else. He finds someone who can share the secret of reading with him. (K–3, literacy, Booker T. Washington, courage)

Bunting, Eve. 1988. *How many days to America.* New York: Clarion Books. A story of a family who leaves their home to find freedom in the United States. Their journey was difficult but they find freedom on Thanksgiving. (K–3, immigration, refugees, political asylum, hope)

Bunting, Eve. 1989. *The Wednesday surprise.* New York: Clarion. Anna has a secret. She is teaching someone she loves how to read. Who is it? Why will her father be surprised? Excellent story about the importance of literacy and the abilities of a young girl. (K–3, families, literacy, grandparents)

Bunting, Eve. 1994. *A day's work.* New York: Clarion. This is another wonderfully written picture book by the award-winning author. When Francisco goes with his *abuelo* (grandfather) to find work, he learns more than how to garden. Francisco learns the importance of telling the truth. (K–5, Latino families, honesty, truth)

Bunting, Eve. 1995. *Smoky night.* San Diego, Calif.: Harcourt Brace & Company. A story about how a community came together during a night of rioting to find a neighbor's cat. (Grades 3–6, cross-cultural understanding, compassion, community building)

Bunting, Eve. 1998. *So far from the sea.* New York: Clarion Books. This story is about Laura, a 7-year-old, who goes with her family to visit her grandfather's grave at the Manzanar Internment Camp in California. (Grades 3–6, Japanese Americans, family, Japanese American Internment)

Cannon, Janell. 1993. *Stellaluna.* San Diego, Calif.: Harcourt Brace & Company. Stellaluna, a fruit bat, loses her mother when an owl attacks them. Stellaluna is too young to fly and lands head first into a nest with three baby birds. She learns how to eat and fly like a bird. But one day Stellaluna finds her mother. She also learns how to eat and fly like a bat.

Stellaluna shares her new knowledge with her bird friends. They all find out that they are similar and different. However, what was most important was that they were friends. (K–3, friendship, cross-cultural differences)

Cha, Dia. 1996. *Dia's story cloth*. New York: Lee and Low Books. This book uses a story cloth to tell the story of a Hmong family who must leave their homes in Laos because of the civil strife there. The family later comes to the United States. Pictures of story cloths are used in the book. (Grades 1–5, Hmong families, refugee, civil strife, Southeast Asia, courage)

Clifton, Lucille. 1983. *Everett Anderson's goodbye*. New York: Holt. Everett Anderson's father dies and he goes through the five stages of grief: denial, anger, bargaining, depression, and acceptance. It is a beautiful story of a child who struggles with losing a parent. (K–3, death, love, the loss of a loved one)

Coerr, Eleanor. 1993. *Sadako*. New York: G. P. Putnam's Sons. Beautifully written story about Sadako Sasaki who contracted leukemia from the fallout of the atom bomb that was dropped on Hiroshima during World War II. Sadako becomes a symbol of peace and through her creation of a thousand origami cranes becomes an inspiration for many children and adults across the world. (K–5, peace)

Coles, Robert. 1995. *The story of Ruby Bridges*. New York: Scholastic Books. An important book for every person who believes in equality and social justice. This is a true story of Ruby Bridges, a first grader, who integrated an all White elementary school in Louisiana. A remarkable book about a special young person. (K–5, civil rights, African American families, forgiveness, inner strength)

de Paola, Tomie. 1989. *The art lesson*. New York: G. P. Putnam's Sons. A young boy delivers an important message to his teachers about individuality and art. (K–3, individuality, negotiation, nonconformity, following one's bliss)

Dorros, Arthur. 1991. *Abuela*. New York: Dutton Children's Books. The story is about a granddaughter who goes on a bus with her grandmother and explores the sights of New York City. Story also integrates some Spanish. (K–3, family, imagination, travel, Latinos)

Durrell, Ann, and Marilyn Sachs, eds. 1990. *The big book of peace*. New York: Dutton Children's Books. A wonderful collection of stories and illustrations about peace from exceptional children's authors like Steven Kellogg, Yoshiko Uchida, Maurice Sendak, and Diane and Leo Dillon. (Grades 3–8, peace, community building, respect, compassion)

Garland, Sherry. 1993. *The lotus seed*. San Diego, Calif.: Harcourt Brace & Company. One of the best picture books for young people about Asian Pacific Americans. This book tells the story of a grandmother from Vietnam who had to leave because of the Vietnam War. What does she take with her on the treacherous journey to the United States? The grandmother takes in her heart the image of the young emperor and the values that carried her through the struggles of life. Exceptional illustrations. (K–5, Vietnamese American families, inner courage, cultural values)

Hamanaka, Sheila. 1990. *The journey: Japanese Americans, racism, and renewal*. New York: Orchard Books. An exceptional book about the Japanese American historical experience. Hamanaka created a huge five-panel mural to tell this important story. (Grades 4–8, Japanese American historical experience, racism, courage, cultural conflict, social justice)

Hamanaka, Sheila. 1995. *On the wings of peace: In memory of Hiroshima and Nagasaki*. New York: Houghton Mifflin Company. Another excellent selection of poetry, stories, and illustrations to present information about the atomic destruction of Hiroshima and Nagasaki during World War II. The book celebrates peace and encourages all of us to become actively involved in eliminating prejudice, discrimination, and destruction. (Grades 5–12, peace, prejudice, war, discrimination, respect, community building)

Hazen, Barbara Shook. 1989. *The knight who was afraid of the dark*. New York: Dial Books for Young Readers. A humorous book about a knight named Sir Fred. This knight was terribly afraid of the dark. His love, Lady Wendylyn, was not afraid of the dark, but she was scared of bugs. The book is a funny take off of the Dark Ages. It can be used to discuss gender role bias. Though some teachers find the stereotypes of romance and bugs to be present, most educators utilize it as a springboard for discussion. (Grades 3–5, gender roles, fears)

Isadora, Rachel. 1976. *Max.* New York: Collier Books. Max is a youngster who loves baseball and ballet. He can do many things and likes himself too. (K–3, positive self-concept, gender bias)

Knight, Margy Burns. 1993. *Who belongs here? An American story.* Gardiner, Maine: Tilbury House. Nary, a young boy from Cambodia, knows of the horror of Pol Pot and civil strife in his home country. His family leaves Cambodia for a refugee camp in Thailand. Later they move to the United States where they find not only an abundance of food and freedom, but also prejudice. The book also presents definitions of words like refugee, information regarding the immigration of various groups, discussion of Pol Pot, and features knowledge about the leadership of Dolores Huerta and the United Farm Workers.

Miller, William. 1997. *Richard Wright and the library card.* New York: Lee & Low Books. The story tells the time in Richard Wright's life when he uses the library. Though there was much prejudice against African Americans, Richard found a way to check out books. The books became a way for him to learn about how many others, Black and White, were like him and longed for freedom. (Grades K–3, literacy, prejudice, racism, learning, friendship)

Munsch, Robert. 1980. *The paper bag princess.* Toronto, Canada: Annick Press Ltd. Princess Elizabeth learns how to rely on her own intelligence and courage to outwit a fierce dragon. (Grades 3–5, courage, wit, gender bias)

Palatini, Margie. 1995. *Piggie pie!* New York: Clarion Books. This is a fun read-aloud story for grades preschool through third grade. The story is about Gritch the Witch who is looking for her dinner. In this funny book, Gritch the Witch looks far and wide to find eight plump piggies for her piggie pie. The pigs use teamwork to stump the grouchy and hungry witch. (K–3, teamwork, humor)

Polacco, Patricia. 1991. *Applemando's dreams.* New York: Philomel Books. This is an inspiring story about young people who have colorful and alive dreams, until several adults in their hometown throw water on their dreams. However, find out how the youngsters used their dreams to find their way when they became lost. (Grades 3–5, courage, dreams, community, caring, belief in oneself)

Polacco, Patricia. 1992. *Chicken Sunday.* New York: Philomel Books. Grandma longs for a new hat, but without money, Stewart, Winston, and Patricia didn't know what they could do to buy it for her. Three youngsters learn that by doing something for others, their actions can snowball into more wonderful friendships. (K–5, teamwork, compassion, community building, caring for others)

Polacco, Patricia. 1998. *Thank you, Mr. Falker.* New York: Philomel Books. Trish feels stupid because she can't read. She works hard at learning how to read, but it doesn't seem to matter because the page just looks like a bunch of squiggles. Other kids laughed at her. She began to believe she was stupid, until Mr. Falker, her teacher, found a way to help her unlock the door to her reading disability. (Grades 3–6, caring, learning disabilities, teacher belief, self-efficacy, courage, autobiographical story)

Prelutsky, Jack. 1991. *For laughing out loud: Poems to tickle your funnybone.* New York: Alfred A. Knopf. A fun book of poems about animals, food, people and rattlesnake stew. Read the poems to your students. You will lighten up their day. (Grades 3–6, family, humor, community building, fun)

Rathman, Peggy. 1995. *Officer Buckle and Gloria.* New York: G. P. Putnam's Sons. Officer Buckle gives speeches all over Napville about safety. However, when Gloria, the police dog, becomes a partner, his speeches come alive. Kids really listen because they like Gloria's funny expressions. Officer Buckle and Gloria find out that they are an important team. (K–3, teamwork, humor)

Ringgold, Faith. 1991. *Tar beach.* New York: Crown Publishers. Cassie and her family spend many wonderful nights on the roof of their apartment building. Cassie teaches her brother how to fly over the various landmarks in the city. She tells him about her dreams and how she hopes for a more just world. Ringgold weaves in the African American historical value of flying. (K–3, family, caring, and social justice)

Ringgold, Faith. 1992. *Aunt Harriet's underground railroad in the sky.* New York: Crown Publishers. Harriet Tubman, one of the most famous conductors on the underground railroad, takes Cassie on a journey along the underground railroad to find her brother. (Grades 2–5, underground railroad, courage, racism, slavery, Harriet Tubman)

Ringgold, Faith. 1993. *Dinner at Aunt Connie's house.* New York: Hyperion Books for Children. Aunt Connie invites Melody to dinner and she learns about twelve accomplished African American women. (Grades 1–5, African American heroes, community, family)

Ringgold, Faith. 1995. *My dream of Martin Luther King.* New York: Crown Publishers. A picture book biography of the work and dream of Martin Luther King, Jr. The illustrations are extremely powerful and display King's passion for social justice. (Grades 2–5, Martin Luther King, Jr., civil rights, courage, social justice, racism)

Rosa-Casanova, Sylvia. 1997. *Mama Provi and the pot of rice.* New York: Atheneum. Mama Provi is the kind of grandmother many people would love to have. She makes delicious *arroz con pollo,* chicken with rice. As Mama Provi climbs the seven floors to her granddaughter's apartment, she shares her *arroz con pollo* with the neighbors and they share their yummy food with her too. (K–3, Puerto Rican community, family, sharing, grandmothers, caring, kindness)

Ross, Dave. 1980. *A book of hugs.* New York: Thomas Y. Crowell. A fun book about hugs. Read the book and find out how many kinds of hugs there are in the world. For example, there are fish hugs, piggyback hugs, knee hugs, and sandwich hugs. (K–2, caring, family, friends)

Say, Allen. 1993. *Grandfather's journey.* New York: Houghton Mifflin. A Japanese American young person describes his grandfather's journey to the United States. His grandfather loved both countries, his home land of Japan and his new home in the United States.

Spinelli, Eileen. 1991. *Somebody loves you, Mr. Hatch.* New York: Simon and Schuster. Mr. Hatch goes to work every day, eats a cheese and mustard sandwich every day, and pretty much keeps to himself. One day he receives a mysterious Valentine. It is a box full of chocolates from a secret admirer. When Mr. Hatch finds out that the box was given to him by mistake, he feels very sad. However, his neighbors rally around him and he finds out that others do love him. (K–5, caring, community)

Tsuchiya, Yukio. 1988. *Faithful elephants: A true story of animals, people and war.* New York: Houghton Mifflin Company. A moving story about the elephants at the Ueno Zoo during World War II. The text helps students understand the tragedy that war brings animals and people. Though this is a picture book, it is not for young children. (Grades 5–12, war, fear, sadness of war, peace, sensitivity to animals)

Uchida, Yoshiko. 1993. *The bracelet.* New York: Philomel Books. Emi is a 7-year-old who lived in San Francisco. Though Emi and her family were U.S. citizens, during World War II they were taken from their home and moved to internment camps because they were of Japanese ancestry. Emi received a bracelet from her friend Laurie. The bracelet symbolized friendship and their mutual love for each other. (Grades 3–6, war, fear, Japanese American internment, courage, caring, frienship)

Williams, Vera B. 1982. *A chair for my mother.* New York: Greenwillow Books. A young girl, her mother, and grandmother save for a wonderful new stuffed chair after a fire destroys everything in their apartment. (K–3, caring, family, saving)

Novels

Anzaladúa, Gloria. 1987. *Borderlands/La frontera: The new mestiza.* San Francisco, Calif.: Aunt Lute Book Company. Powerful text of prose and poetry about the life of Anzaladúa who grew up on the Mexico/Texas border. She focuses on her bilingual, bicultural experiences and the conflicts she faced as a person who straddled both communities. (Adult readers, self and ethnic identity, oppression, biculturalism, courage, family)

Elison, Ralph. 1947. *The invisible man.* New York: Random House, Inc. One of the most powerful books written about the experiences of an African American male who is confronted with the racism of society. The novel is full of important symbolism about the impact of materialism, sex, and racism on the development of African Americans. (High school–adult, African American communities, cultural assimilation, racism, materialism, social oppression, social justice)

Fox, Paula. 1991. *Monkey Island.* New York: Doubleday Dell Books for Young Readers. Clay Garrity, an 11-year-old, finds himself homeless in New York City. Where has his mother gone? What will he do? The weather is bitter cold. The story is about a young boy living on the streets and the two men who share their wooden crate in the park with him. (Grades 5–8, homelessness, family, personal growth, foster care, social services)

Myers, Walter Dean. 1988. *Fallen angels.* New York: Scholastic Inc. Richie Perry, a young man from Harlem, enlists in the army. He goes to Southeast Asia and has a difficult year during the Vietnam War. (High school–adult, Vietnam War, violence, personal growth, adult language)

Myers, Walter Dean. 1993. *Malcolm X: By any means necessary.* New York: Scholastic Inc. This is a biography of Malcolm Little who later took the name Malcolm X. An important story for many students to read. Shows the phases that Malcolm goes through in his life and how he transforms himself into an international leader for social justice. (Grades 6–10, Malcolm X, literacy, courage, leadership, social justice)

Paulsen, Gary. 1993. *Nightjohn.* New York: Delacorte Books. This novel describes the violence and inhumanity slaves were subjected to through the voice of a young girl named Sarny. The youngster learns how to read from John, another slave, who is persecuted for his knowledge. To John, reading and living were the same. (Grades 6–12, slavery, literacy, courage)

Okada, John. 1981. *No-no boy.* Seattle, Wash.: University of Washington Press. Story of a Japanese American who was released from prison because he would not sign a loyalty oath. The book also describes the inner conflicts of Japanese Americans in the cultural assimilation process. (High school–adults, Japanese American internment, loyalty oath, cultural conflicts, cultural assimilation, family issues, community conflicts)

Ryan, Pam Muñoz. 1998. *Riding freedom.* New York: Scholastic. Who is One-eyed Charley? Well, he's the best stagecoach driver in New England. This novel of historical fiction is about how Charlotte Parkhurst becomes Charley, gifted horse trainer. Charlotte was an orphan who later moved to California and became the first woman to vote in Santa Cruz County. (Grades 3–5, woman role model, California history, New England history, community, courage)

Soto, Gary. 1990. *Baseball in April and other stories.* San Diego, Calif.: Harcourt Brace & Company. This is a collection of eleven short stories about growing up in Fresno, California. The stories are about the fears and dreams of young people. (Grades 4–6, Latino youth, family, growing up)

Spinelli, Jerry. 1990. *Maniac Magee.* New York: HarperCollins. Jeffrey Magee became an orphan at 3 years old when his mother and father were in a trolley accident. Magee was left to live with his feuding aunt and uncle. Later Magee found himself without any home.

Humor is woven throughout the story about Magee's life and his activities as a hero. A book with heart. (Grades 3–6, homelessness, racism, caring, family)

Uchida, Yoshiko. 1985. *Journey to Topaz: A story of the Japanese American evacuation.* This novel is about the life of Yuki Sakane from Oakland who is taken with her family to the desert when 120,000 Japanese Americans were uprooted from their homes during World War II. Yuki first was taken to Tanforan Racetrack and then to Topaz, a concentration camp in northern California. (Grades 4–8, Japanese Americans, racism, internment, courage)

Young, Russell. 2000. *Dragonsong: A fable for the new millennium.* Auburn, Calif.: Shen's Books. A wonderful modern folktale about a dragon from China who travels the world and receives gifts from dragons of other cultures. Illustrations are especially beautiful. (Grades 1–4, dragons, China, England, Mexico, Central Africa, courage, hope)

Materials for Older Readers

Freedman, Russell. 1994. *Kids at work: Lewis Hine and the crusade against child labor.* New York: Scholastic. Excellent resource material for older students that describes the dedication of Lewis Hine, a school teacher in New York City, who worked to get child labor laws passed. As a photographer, Hine told a powerful story of the abuse of children who worked in factories, canneries, fields, and coal mines. (Grades 5–12, child labor, child labor laws, labor reform)

Part 2: Teacher Resources

Albom, Mitch. 1997. *Tuesdays with Morrie.* New York: Doubleday. One of the most insightful books about the wisdom that a teacher imparted to a student. Mitch Albom goes back to visit his sociology professor, Morrie Schwartz, and learns not only about death, but about love and life. Morrie shares with Mitch his philosophy about teaching and living. Morrie says that the most important values in life are love, compassion, responsibility, and community.

Asian American Resource Workshop. 1991. *The Asian American comic book.* Boston, Mass.: Asian American Resource Workshop. This is a comic book for use with high school students centering on the following issues: the impact of the internment on a Japanese American family, students dealing with cross-generational and cross-cultural conflicts, a refugee young person encountering racism and cultural differences, and the strength of a woman working to address labor problems in a factory.

Beyer, Barry K. 1987. *Practical strategies for the teaching of thinking.* Boston, Mass.: Allyn and Bacon. Excellent book for teachers providing various models and activities to teach higher-order thinking. Well organized text with strategies that can be used in many different subject areas.

Bigelow, William, and Norman Diamond. 1988. *The power in our hands: A curriculum on the history of work and workers in the United States.* New York: Monthly Review Press. Excellent collection of sixteen lessons that present valuable information about the history of workers in the United States. The activities are engaging and encourage students to look at their own values and make important decisions regarding labor issues.

Caduto, Michael J., and Joseph Bruchac. 1989. *Keepers of the earth: Native American stories and environment activities for children.* Golden, Colo.: Fulcrum Publishers. Excellent educational resource for elementary grade teachers about various Native American nations. The stories present information and activities about Native American values regarding the environment, focusing on themes like creation, fire, the seasons, plants, and animals.

Crawford, Susan Hoy. 1996. *Beyond dolls and guns: 101 ways to help children avoid gender bias.* Portsmouth, N.H.: Heinemann. A good reference for teachers on ways to fight and avoid gender bias. The author provides 101 ideas for educators to think about and to utilize in their teaching. She also includes various resources in the book, including a list of job titles that can be changed. For example, Crawford suggests we move from titles like chairman to chairperson or convener, and weatherman to forecaster or meteorologist.

Fadiman, Anne. 1997. *The spirit catches you and you fall down.* New York: The Noonday Press. This is an important book for anyone who would like to understand how cultural differences can have a devastating impact on the care of children. The clash of cultural values and language differences created serious problems for a Hmong family in Fresno. An excellent resource for educators who may not understand how culture can create serious conflicts among people who in reality have the same goals of living a happy and healthy life.

Fedullo, Mick. 1992. *Light of the feather: Pathways through contemporary Indian America.* New York: William Morrow. Mick Fedullo is a White teacher who learns about the struggles and triumphs of Indian communities. Fedullo is able to move beyond the cultural divide and learns about the richness of the Crow and Pima communities.

Levine, David, Robert Lowe, Bob Peterson, and Rita Tenorio. 1995. *Rethinking schools: An agenda for change.* New York: The New Press. Excellent text with a variety of readings from educators like Henry Louis Gates, Jr., Louise Derman-Sparks, Bill Bigelow, Linda Christensen, and Lisa Delpit. The articles challenge teachers to consider carefully the underlying messages that present practices in schools convey about equity issues, whether they deal with class, race, or other aspects of society. Important reading for all teachers.

Loomans, Diane, and Karen Kolberg. 1993. *The laughing classroom: Everyone's guide to teaching with humor and play.* Tiburon, Calif.: H. J. Kramer, Inc. A fun book that presents excellent ideas in how to teach with laughter and humor.

Perry, Theresa. 1996. *Teaching Malcolm X.* New York: Routledge. An outstanding collection of readings for teachers by teachers that explain how they have presented the life and ideas of Malcolm Little. The chapters share information from educators from the elementary grades to college level. The perceptions and insights are extremely valuable for anyone who is considering developing and teaching a unit on Malcolm X.

Shaver, James P., and William Strong. 1982. *Facing value decisions: Rationale-building for teachers.* New York: Teachers College Press. Excellent book that describes how teachers can utilize an issues-centered approach to teaching. The authors provide various lessons for teachers that cover values like democracy, human dignity, pluralism, conflict, cohesion, the Chicano Maverick, and civil disobedience. One of the most important aspects of teaching is to assist students in developing skills so they can effectively deal with conflicts, issues, and decision making.

Part 3: Videos for Teachers and Students

ABC News. Annenberg Foundation/CPB. 1994. *Calculating change.* New York: National Urban League, Inc. Video for teachers to look at how parents and educators have created successful programs in science and math education. Discussion of Bob Moses' *The Algebra Project.* (Distributed through the Annenberg/CPB Math and Science Collection, P.O. Box 2345, S. Burlington, VT, 05407-2345)

Family Communications. 1995. *The different and the same video series.* Pittsburgh, Pa.: Family Communications. Series of videos to use with grades K–2 about prejudice and discrimination. There is also a teachers manual and training video. This comes from the producers of *Mr. Rogers' Neighborhood.* (Distributed by GPM, P.O. Box 80669, Lincoln, NE, 68501-0669)

Filipino American National Historical Society. 1994. *Filipino Americans: Discovering their past for the future.* Seattle, Wash.: Filipino National Historical Society. Presents the history of Filipino Americans from 1587 to the early 1990s. Excellent resource. (Distributed by Wehman Video, 2366 Eastlake Avenue East, Suite 312, Seattle, WA, 98102)

Kroopnick, Stephen, and Stu Schreiberg. 1998. *Underground railroad.* New York: The History Channel. Excellent video about the history of the underground railroad. The film highlights the courage and actions of people like Frederick Douglass, Harriet Tubman, and William Lloyd Garrison. (Distributed by New Video Group, 126 Fifth Avenue, New York, NY, 10011)

McCray, Judith. 1995. *Mississippi, America.* Carbondale, Ill.: WSIU Carbondale and the Department of Radio-Television at Southern Illinois University at Carbondale. Excellent documentary chronicling the struggle for the right to vote in Mississippi during the summer of 1964. The work of many civil rights activists resulted in the passage of the Voting Rights Act of 1965. (Distributed by Warner Home Video, 4000 Warner Boulevard, Burbank, Calif., 91522)

Credits

Text and Line Art

Front Matter
Pro1.1: DENNIS THE MENACE® used by permission of Hank Ketcham and © by North America Syndicate, p. xxi

Chapter 1
TA 1.1: Reprinted with special permission of King Features Syndicate. p. 14.

Chapter 2
TA 2.1, TA 2.2: Reprinted with special permission of King Features Syndicate. p. 32.

Chapter 3
TA 3.1: © Lynn Johnston Productions Inc./Dist. by United Feature Syndicate, Inc., p. 52;
TA 3.2: FRANK & ERNEST reprinted by permission of Newspaper Enterprise Association, Inc., p. 63; **TA 3.3:** CALVIN AND HOBBES © 1990 Watterson. Reprinted with permission of UNIVERSAL PRESS SYNDICATE. All rights reserved. p. 81.

Chapter 4
TA4.2: Reprinted with special permission of King Features Syndicate. p. 90; **TA 4.3:** Dickenson © 1998 Copley News Service. Reprinted with permission of Copley News Service. p. 97.

Chapter 5
TA 5.1, TA 5.2, TA 5.3: JUMP START reprinted by permission of United Feature Syndicate, Inc. p. 114; **TA 5.4:** Reprinted with special permission of King Features Syndicate. p. 119.

Chapter 7
TA7.1, TA 7.2: Reprinted with special permission of King Features Syndicate. p. 159.

Chapter 8
TA 8.1: AUTH © 1999 The Philadelphia Inquirer. Reprinted with permission of UNIVERSAL PRESS SYNDICATE. All rights reserved. p. 173.

Chapter 10
TA 10.1: JUMP START reprinted by permission of United Feature Syndicate, Inc. p. 219.

Chapter 11
TA 11.1: © Lynn Johnston Productions Inc./Dist. by United Feature Syndicate, Inc. p. 248;
TA 11.2: Britt © 1997 Copley News Service. Reprinted with permission of Copley News Service. p. 264.

Epilogue
TA EP 1.2: Reprinted with special permission of King Features Syndicate. p. 275.

Index

DATE DUE

GRAD JAN 30 '03		
OHIOLINK		
OHIOLINK		
OHIOLINK		
OHIOLINK		
OHIOLINK		
OHIOLINK		
OHIOLINK		
Jan.4,03		
FAC JUN 30 '05		
JAN 30 '08		